THE WORKING CLASS IN AMERICAN HISTORY

Editorial Advisors

David Brody
Alice Kessler-Harris
David Montgomery
Sean Wilentz

A list of books in the series appears at the end of this book.

"Negro and White, Unite and Fight!"

"Negro and White, Unite and Fight!"

*A Social History of
Industrial Unionism in
Meatpacking, 1930–90*

ROGER HOROWITZ

UNIVERSITY OF ILLINOIS PRESS

Urbana and Chicago

Publication of this book was supported by a grant
from the Illinois Labor History Society.

UPWA logo courtesy of the State Historial
Society of Wisconsin, WHi (X3) 50895.

Manufactured in the United States of America

1   2   3   4   5   C   P   5   4   3   2   1

This book is printed on acid-free paper.

Library of Congress Cataloging-in-Publication Data
Horowitz, Roger.
"Negro and white, unite and fight!" : a social history of
industrial unionism in meatpacking, 1930–90 / Roger Horowitz.
p.   cm. — (The working class in American history)
Includes bibliographical references (p.) and index.
ISBN 0-252-02320-x (cloth : acid-free paper). —
ISBN 0-252-06621-9 (pbk. : acid-free paper)
1. United Packinghouse Workers of America—History.
2. Trade-unions—Packing-house workers—United States—History.
I. Title. II. Series.
HD6515.P152U554   1997
331.88'1649'00973—dc20   96-35703
CIP

To Hedda Garza: friend, teacher, comrade

Contents

Acknowledgments

This project started innocently in 1983 when fellow Wisconsin graduate student Rick Halpern suggested that the recently processed papers of the United Packinghouse Workers of America (UPWA) might contain good material for a seminar paper. Since that initial inspiration, my research has been influenced by the opinions, energy, and contributions of many people. But the greatest impact was made by the present and former packinghouse workers I met during the UPWA Oral History Project of the mid-1980s. I felt these men and women looking over my shoulder as I wrote this book, sometimes agreeing, sometimes suggesting more accurate formulations, and quite often arguing among themselves about what happened and who turned out to be right. Indeed, Ralph Helstein, Herb March, and Lewie Anderson supplied critiques of drafts of some of these chapters, and I have discussed many of my ideas with Les Orear.

Through their eyes, thoughts, and memories I saw the great tragedy of the collapse of union strength in meatpacking that serendipitously coincided with the oral history project. And in many conversations I found that the pivot linking the unionism of the past with the present was the 1985–86 strike by Local P-9 in Austin, Minnesota. When Rick and I traveled there to conduct interviews with founders of the Austin union (the first successful meatpacking union in the 1930s), we did so in a hall filled with strikers and their families. I was profoundly affected by not only that experience but also by the many discussions with retired UPWA members about the P-9 strike that took place after the formal interview. The present and the past were not separated for these unionists; it was all of one cloth, the seemingly endless struggle by working people in America to live respectably and have, as one put it, "some of the better things in life." It is this hope, so modest yet also so grand, to which I have tried to remain true in this book.

A number of institutions provided financial support for this project. The National Endowment for the Humanities funded the UPWA Oral History Project through a grant to the State Historical Society of Wisconsin and also awarded me a travel-to-collections grant. Support also was provided by the Henry J. Kaiser Foundation, the University of Wisconsin, the American Historical Association, the Charlotte Newcombe Fellowship of the Woodrow Wilson Foundation, and the University of Delaware. My present employer, the Hagley Museum and Library, has generously encouraged my research and writing.

The construction of the story took place in an academic setting and during the difficult search for a permanent position. Several professors at the University of Wisconsin initially shaped this project intellectually. Herbert Hill was an early inspiration and supporter of the work, as was J. Rogers Hollingsworth and Tom McCormick. Later on, David Zonderman, Joel Rogers, and Linda Gordon lent their talents to improving my arguments. An extremely talented cohort of graduate students also made an impact as comrades and friends: Kathy Brown, Bob Buchanan, Michelle Couturier, Bruce Fehn, Colin Gordon, Nancy MacLean, Ted Pearson, Leslie Reagan, and Paul Taillon. James R. Barrett influenced the project from its genesis to completion. Extended written comments by David Brody and David Montgomery have greatly improved the final result. I also benefited from discussions with Marvin Bergman, Dennis Deslippe, Cathy Matson, Arwen Mohun, Charlie Post, Bill Pratt, Peter Rachleff, Sheldon Stromquist, and Bill Warren and the support of my editors at the University of Illinois Press: Richard L. Wentworth, Karen Hewitt, and Mary Giles.

Research in printed and manuscript collections depended on the support and assistance of numerous librarians and archivists. I owe a deep debt to former colleagues at the State Historical Society of Wisconsin, especially Jim Cavanaugh, Michael Gordon, Harry Miller, and Donna Sereda. Archie Motley at the Chicago Historical Society graciously guided me to relevant collections, as did Scott Sorenson of the Sioux City Museum, Barbara Gorman in the Kansas City Museum, Mary Bennett at the State Historical Society of Iowa, Warner Phlug at the Archives of Labor and Urban Affairs, Dave Boutros at the Western Historical Manuscript Collection (Kansas City), and Jerry Hess at the National Archives. Dave Langenberg at the University of

Delaware Library, along with Marge McNinch and Lynne Joshi at the Hagley Museum and Library, were essential to the final stages of the project, as was Heather Latham, a truly magnificent research assistant.

I also owe a debt to individuals and institutions outside academia who supported and encouraged me and argued with me. The socialist journal *Against the Current* published several early articles drawn from this research in the mid-1980s. I learned a great deal from contact with individuals associated with *Labor Notes*, especially Kim Moody and Jane Slaughter. In Madison, Jim Cavanaugh played a dual role, first as director of UPWA Oral History Project and later as president of the Madison-based South Central Federation of Labor (AFL-CIO). Janice Herritz, a militant Oscar Mayer worker, always listened to me—and always kept me honest. Officials of the United Food and Commercial Workers (UFCW) aided this research by supporting the UPWA Oral History Project.

To an unusual extent, my research on packinghouse workers has been a collaborative effort with Rick Halpern. Many of my ideas developed out of cooperative work with Rick, either exchanging information from archival research, analyzing a jointly conducted oral interview, or wresting over a coauthored essay. Rick's meticulous comments on my dissertation had a profound impact on the form in which that research now appears. His consistently thoughtful comments, indefatigable energy, precise scholarship, and magnificent meals never failed to inspire me.

My parents, David and Louise Horowitz, provided indispensable financial and emotional support, and their intelligent comments on their son's writing found their way into the final product in ways that might surprise them. I am particularly thankful to my mother, a former university professor, for her advice on the UPWA Oral History Project grant proposal and other fellowship applications. My sister Marilyn, a fine writer herself, provided some critical pushes when I got stuck.

I had just begun this project when I met Marie Laberge, and she has never expressed doubt that I would see it through. Marie's contributions are woven into the text through her patience, comments on each chapter, and example as a historian of the American women's movement. Our shared project, Jason Daniel Horowitz, has contributed in his own way by getting me to play with him—and to remember the important things in life. To their tender encouragement in many difficult moments, I am eternally grateful.

Abbreviations

CCRR	Chicago Commission on Race Relations
CFL	Chicago Federation of Labor
CFU	Croatian Fraternal Union
CIO	Congress of Industrial Organizations
ESL	Employees Security League
GAW	Guaranteed Annual Wage
HUAC	House Committee on Un-American Activities
IAM	International Association of Machinists
IBP	Iowa Beef Processors
IEB	International Executive Board
IUAW	Independent Union of All Workers
IUE	International Union of Electrical, Radio and Machine Workers
IWW	Industrial Workers of the World
LIU	local industrial union
MPC	Meat Packing Commission
NAACP	National Association for the Advancement of Colored People
NAM	National Association of Manufacturers
NBPW	National Brotherhood of Packinghouse Workers
NDMB	National Defense Mediation Board
NIRA	National Industrial Recovery Act
NLRB	National Labor Relations Board
NWLB	National War Labor Board

PHWIU   Packing House Workers Industrial Union
PWOC   Packinghouse Workers Organizing Committee
RCIU   Retail Clerks International Union
SCLC   Southern Christian Leadership Conference
SWOC   Steel Workers Organizing Committee
UAW   United Automobile Workers
UFCW   United Food and Commercial Workers
UMWA   United Mine Workers of America
UPWA   United Packinghouse Workers of America
USWA   United Steel Workers of America
YCL   Young Communist League

"Negro and White, Unite and Fight!"

"Only If You Stay Together": Class, Unionism, and America's Packinghouse Workers

Stay here! Whatever happens
Do not break ranks!
Only if you stay together
can you help each other!

—Bertolt Brecht,
Saint Joan of the Stockyards

For labor militants and political activists of the 1930s, the unionization of America's mass production workers under the banner of the Congress of Industrial Organizations (CIO) was a dream come true. Industrial unionism was "Labor's Giant Step" to Art Preis, a leftist and a participant in the 1934 Toledo Auto-Lite strike. To him, the formation of the CIO was "the most significant event in modern American history." Preis and his comrades anticipated that industrial unionism would elevate workers' living standards and serve as a way station toward a class-consciousness movement that could remake American society.[1]

Unfortunately, disillusionment with the practices of organized labor after World War II and the precipitous decline of unions since 1980 have discouraged many who once believed that class could serve as a unifying force for movements for social change. All too often, CIO-affiliated organizations inhibited rank-and-file militancy, compelled loyalty to the Democratic Party, and entrenched patterns of racial and sexual discrimination. With occasional exceptions, hierarchical union structures and centralized labor relations supplanted the shop-floor organizations of the 1930s. Unions proved their value to companies by enforcing managerial prerogatives and contractual norms in return for steadily increasing wages and fringe benefits. Vibrant debates over union strategy were replaced by one-party rule of the union apparatus and the evisceration of local union autonomy. In many cases, unions devolved into apparatuses akin to insurance companies, providing medical coverage and other benefits, rather than dynamic labor organizations devoted to altering power relations between employer and employee.

This work seeks a balance between Preis's belief in the potential of a labor movement to make positive social change and the sober assessments of actual union practices. What continues to make class special as a basis for collective action is its objective dimension: The shared economic relationship of dependence on wages can induce cooperation among people who otherwise are very different. Put coarsely, common class interests have the potential to bring working people together who have little else in common and in fact may not like each other at all. Notions of personal identity and interests shaped by ethnicity, race, and gender can be mediated by organizations that respect those differences but try to establish a foundation for collective activity around objectives that will benefit all parties. Jimmy Porter, a black packinghouse worker, effectively used farming as a metaphor for this dynamic. "If you stay on your side of the fence and respect mine, we can coexist," he reflected. "If you want to borrow my axe and I borrow your shovel, we don't have to dig into each other, but we can dig enough space to grow." Even as profound differences remained among workers in the same organization, the cooperation engendered through shared experiences at work could give each the "space to grow."[2]

Porter's earthy imagery also indicates the limits to cooperation based on shared class interests. Identities informed by race, gender, ethnicity, and religion are not in any way eliminated by awareness of common class interests; deep social divisions can remain among workers who may cooperate in a union but live on different sides of the "fences" in American society. Because class-based organizations mediate among different fractions of the working class as well as between employers and employees, particular groups constituted along ethnic, racial, and/or gender lines can use a union in a manner that operates to the disadvantage of other workers. Whether, and to what extent, class-based organizations are imbricated with racism and sexism remains a contingent process that historians must investigate.

The case of industrial unionism in meatpacking provides a generally positive measure of what can be secured by male and female workers from different races and ethnic groups who cooperate inside a class-based labor organization. To an extent that was unusual in the industrial unions that remained in the CIO after 1950, the United Packinghouse Workers of America (UPWA) retained the insurgent spirit of the 1930s' workers' movement in the changed circumstances of postwar America. The union remained, by and large, democratic and accepted considerable internal political diversity throughout its existence. UPWA locals generally retained considerable influence over the work process through extensive shop-floor steward organizations and maintained horizontal connections with locals in other plants of the same national firms. Female and minority members were able to organize and voice their concerns within the UPWA and to receive a favorable hearing because of the union's sustained commitment to social justice. In particular, the UPWA's anti-discrimination activity on behalf of its black members far outstripped those of other CIO organizations after World War II and contributed materially to the development of the civil rights movement.

The UPWA's example had clear boundaries. Structurally, the political economy of postwar America imposed firm limits on a union with only a hundred thousand members. With considerable reluctance, the international union conformed—at least formally—to the limits on union behavior mandated by the Taft-Hartley Act, confined political action after 1950 to support for the Democratic Party, and secured fringe benefits through collective bargaining rather than expansion of federal entitlement programs. In addition to the influence of structural factors, the manner in which race and gender shaped class formation among packinghouse workers limited the extent to which the UPWA acted against racial and sexual discrimination. Black workers received extraordinary support for their initiatives against racism but were unable to use the union apparatus to force white-dominated local unions to engage in comparable efforts. Women workers found they received equal treatment as union members but wrestled with a dominant "masculinist" assumption that women worked only for unusual reasons and that the normative union member was a man. Union democracy, in this sense, provided an opportunity for women and blacks to use the union as a vehicle for collective action at the same time it constrained their initiatives.[3]

Accounting for the strengths and limitations of the UPWA mandates attention to the structural elements that encouraged the formation of a particular brand of unionism and the agency of packinghouse workers, who brought to fruition the potential for alliances along class lines. Three general factors are particularly important: the endemic conflict over work between labor and management in meatpacking, the inter-racial composition of the workforce, and the capacity of the union's founders to reproduce, in the 1940s and 1950s, a new generation of union militants. These features enabled the organization to negotiate the tightened strictures on labor organizations after World War II in a profoundly different manner than the dominant industrial unions.[4]

The meatpacking industry's structure, managerial strategies, and production methods set the parameters for labor-management struggle and encouraged a rank-and-file-oriented packinghouse unionism. A mature industry dominated by four firms, meatpacking in many ways pioneered American mass-production methods. Producing a perishable commodity at very low profit margins, management incessantly struggled to keep labor costs at a minimum and exercise a maximum degree of control over the pace of work. Aside from brief periods of union organization, these "authority relations" corresponded to the brutal drive system described by Sumner Slichter and Sanford Jacoby. The intensely subdivided work process, dispersed into dozens of physically separate rooms, encouraged local unions to adopt a decentralized departmental structure so as to reach into all areas of a packinghouse. Smoldering resentment among workers over unremitting production pressures induced organizers to use workplace grievances to win support for unionism. Concentration of ownership mandated that unions win workers' support in the key packing centers located in the midwestern grain belt and subdue the dominant firms in the industry through national collective bargaining agreements.[5]

The racial composition of the workforce provided a critical stimulus to the particular evolution of the UPWA. The presence of black workers in key departments such as the killing floors, along with their opposition to strikes in 1904 and 1921 and 1922, made their support a precondition for union formation in the 1930s. During the New Deal, consistent union support for black workers' grievances, including mobilization of white workers in support of aggrieved blacks, secured their allegiance to the UPWA. The black presence in turn imparted a broader social vision to industrial unionism in meatpacking. The early symbol of Chicago packinghouse organizers, black and white hands clasped in a handshake, was a message to both white and black workers of the union's opposition to racism. In the 1950s the UPWA accelerated its anti-discrimination program by dismantling racial segregation in many packinghouses, rendering importance assistance to local civil rights struggles, and significantly aiding the early efforts of Martin Luther King, Jr.

Although many white packinghouse workers no doubt retained racist ideas, the UPWA countered group identification based on racial superiority by promoting and demonstrating the material benefits of collective action based on class interests. Concerted inter-racial activity on the job and in confrontations with packing companies provided an alternative frame of reference for whites to evaluate black workers outside of the generally racist assumptions of American society and their usually all-white neighborhoods. Indeed, the UPWA's shop steward system and bargaining strength rested on support by workers of one race for those of another in conflicts with meatpacking firms. Reflecting the essential component of direct, personal interaction, the progressive impact of the race issue depended on the proportion of black workers in a particular plant and the presence or absence of articulate union leaders who sought to accentuate the positive dynamic interplay of race and class.

The structure of the industry and the composition of the workforce made these developments possible, but it took the conscious agency of a distinct "militant minority" of packinghouse workers to create and shape the UPWA. There were men and women who, in David Montgomery's formulation, "endeavoured to weld their workmates and neighbors into a self-aware and purposeful working class."[6] The vitality of these union stalwarts in the 1930s, and the reproduction of this cadre in the 1940s and 1950s, balanced the structural pressures emanating from the American state and the meatpacking industry and allowed the UPWA to maximize the potential of industrial unionism in mid-twentieth-century America.

Similar to union pioneers in other industries, the initial "militant minority" of the 1930s drew on prior experiences in leftist and labor organizations to present their strategic perspective to co-workers. There were three discernible groups: white ethnics rooted in their particular communities and influential in neighborhood-based networks; Communists, Socialists, Trotskyists, and Wobblies who creatively applied their sophisticated political analysis to the formidable obstacles obstructing union formation; and black workers who judged that their race had more to gain through cooperation with white workers than an alliance with the packing companies. To counter managerial authority and establish links with other workers, the militant minority developed an inclusive union apparatus to facilitate rank-and-file involvement and developed departmental organizations to represent workers in disputes with supervisors. In this manner the rank-and-file unionism of the UPWA, especially its use of an extensive shop steward system, provided a concrete linkage between the outlook and activities of the union's cadre and the larger rank and file.

The expansion of the union's militant minority during and after World War II through the accretion of new groups of workers sustained the militant traditions of the organizing era in the more hostile climate of postwar America. For packinghouse workers who entered the industry after 1940, widespread shop-floor bargaining and major strikes in 1946 and 1948 provided a shared experience of struggle with union militants shaped during the 1930s. Retention of the shop steward system greatly facilitated transmission of the UPWA's code of inter-racial, rank-and-file unionism to these new union members. The growth of institutions of union democracy, especially the "chains" of local unions in the plants of the same national firms and

periodic conferences on racial and sexual discrimination, solidified regional and national networks of local union activists. The steadily growing number of black workers, especially World War II veterans, were able to use the
principles of inter-racial unionism and the firm tradition of black leadership
in the organization to expand the UPWA's anti-discrimination activities dramatically. Increased militancy against racial discrimination in turn encouraged black and white women to assert their gender interests within the organization. Finally, leftists' aggressive support of the UPWA's social
unionism, and their sheer skill as union activists, preserved their influence
among the membership and averted any broad-based effort to purge the
union of Communists.

The UPWA's core militants were class-conscious in the sense that their
advocacy of industrial unionism constituted, in Perry Anderson's terms, "a
conscious programme aimed at creating or remodelling whole social structures." Although only a few sought to end private ownership of industry and
establish a socialist society, they shared a general commitment to reshape
economic and political relationships to the advantage of the working class.
The outlook of a majority of UPWA members, however, is more accurately
captured by Anthony Giddens's notion of "conflict consciousness": "Where
a perception of class unity is linked to a recognition of opposition of interest with another class or classes." Although these workers were dependable
union members in confrontations with management, they did not share the
militant minority's belief in the need to refashion American society. A third,
minority group of packinghouse workers were conscious of having distinct
class interests but did not conclude that their objectives were necessarily
antithetical from those of the packing companies. The first and second groups
constituted the UPWA's reliable base, whereas the third was made up of
weak union members and might cross a picket line, oppose anti-discrimination policies, or simply not participate in their local at all.[7]

Gender had a contradictory effect on the UPWA. The presence of wom-
en in every packinghouse at roughly 20 percent of the workforce impelled
the UPWA to address discrimination against women and support equal pay
for equal work. The concentration of women in distinct departments (because of a strict sexual division of labor) facilitated the development of wom-
en's leadership and a discernible women's movement in the UPWA, especially during the 1950s when black women became much more active.
Although the UPWA encouraged women's activity, women remained subordinate to the men in the organization and were unable to secure support
for measures that would alter gender relations in the packinghouses and the
union. In particular, the union accepted the sexual division of labor as "nat-

ural" and "axiomatic" and even encoded it into a rigid system of explicitly sex-typed jobs and separate male-female seniority lists.[8] When declining female employment in the late 1950s and early 1960s disrupted stable patterns of job distribution, substantial gender conflicts erupted in local unions as female shop-floor leaders pressed the union, and eventually took legal action, to end the sexual division of labor. In contrast to the UPWA's systemic opposition to racism, its activity on women's issues did not lead to a critique of mid-twentieth-century gender stereotypes or the boundaries between men and women's work within packing plants.

The UPWA's achievement must be assessed within the framework of America's postwar political economy and system of labor relations. Despite external influences largely beyond their control, packinghouse unionists retained considerable space within which to carve out their power in the plant and determine the system of labor relations with meatpacking companies. Leftists were more than simply a militant group on trade union issues; their radical analysis of racism and capitalism, although advanced by only a small minority, reached large numbers of packinghouse workers and influenced union programs and activities. At times besieged by government investigations, the packing companies, and hostile CIO leaders, the UPWA nonetheless improved the living standards and working conditions of its members and contributed to struggles against racial and sexual discrimination.

The example of the UPWA contradicts many assumptions in the literature on twentieth-century industrial unionism and poses some provocative issues for further investigation. Fundamentally, the UPWA's experience challenges the antinomies that scholars routinely draw between the union movement before and after the war. Although there are many variations in these interpretations, two overarching chronologies usually are brought into play. The first, usually advanced by critics of the union movement such as Jeremy Brecher and Staughton Lynd, is a declension narrative that contrasts the militant struggles of the 1930s with a bureaucratized postwar labor movement.[9] The second, generally presented by those more sympathetic to the labor movement such as Melvyn Dubofsky and David Brody, is an ascension narrative that portrays the episodic and limited (although certainly heroic) militancy of the 1930s as a prelude to the more successful state-regulated unionism of postwar America.[10] Although scholars differ over the timing of the transformative moment for the industrial union movement (ranging from the formation of the CIO in the 1930s to the 1950 UAW-General Motors contract), the dichotomy between the two periods remains a common organizing feature of American labor history.

The experiences of packinghouse workers do not fit neatly into either of these narratives, even though elements can be mobilized selectively to buttress either interpretive strategy.[11] The extent of rank-and-file militancy in meatpacking during the 1930s indicates a profound working-class upsurge in that decade. This militancy also contained a willingness by workers to reach an accommodation with their firms, however, so long as working conditions improved and living standards increased. After World War II, the failure of meatpacking firms to satisfy these objectives willingly injected a constant irritant into shop-floor relations and contract negotiations and stimulated repeated rank-and-file struggles. Moreover, commitment by the UPWA to social unionism and shop-floor bargaining in postwar America emerged from, and indeed exceeded, union practices before the war.

As the last point suggests, packinghouse workers also do not fit into the competing narratives because of the importance of blacks, and racial issues, to this sector of the working class. The presence of blacks in significant numbers and in key occupations posed the question of racial equality from the first days of unionism in meatpacking and in a manner far more profound than in most other sectors of the American economy. This lent a sharp edge to the union's efforts to secure a respectable life for its members, because ending discrimination on the basis of race was necessarily an integral component. The participation and influence of black workers reflected not only demographic dynamics but also the manner in which the union's ideology facilitated appropriation of its structures for blacks' racial and economic advancement. And unlike the story implied in the declension and ascension narratives, union commitment and activity on this issue vastly increased after World War II.

For their part, white workers could not avoid these issues inside the UPWA; either they went along with the union's arguments or they withdrew from participation. For the majority of whites who remained with the union (and whites always made up more than half the UPWA's membership), the prominence of the race issue mediated conservative cultural pressures and provided a constant spur toward a critique of postwar American society. Moreover, black union activism was a measurable asset to the efforts of white UPWA members to increase their standard of living and exercise control over their workplace. Union opposition to racial inequality thus influenced whites as well as blacks and shaped the character of the entire organization, not simply its stance on racial issues. The tremendous impact of race on the character of unionism in the meatpacking industry indicates how poorly we appreciate the way race has shaped white-dominated labor organizations in the twentieth century.

This book charts the evolution of industrial unionism in meatpacking from the nascent local unions of the 1930s to the collapse of union power in the late 1980s. It concentrates, although not exclusively, on four meatpacking centers central to the UPWA and the industry: Chicago, Kansas City, Sioux City, and Austin, Minnesota. Comparing local unions in these four areas over several decades illuminates the critical factors influencing union formation and the evolution of industrial unionism in meatpacking.

In the organizing era, these four centers were crucial arenas in the struggle for union formation despite their profound differences. Employees of the small Hormel packing company in the isolated, all-white town of Austin, Minnesota, established the first stable packinghouse union in 1933. In the diverse industrial city of Chicago, a coalition of Communists, white ethnics, blacks, and former union members first established during the early 1930s played a pivotal role persuading the CIO to enter meatpacking in 1937. In Kansas City, a small group of Socialists provided the cohesion for a union core of Croatians, blacks, and former mine workers who were able to spring into activity once the auto workers' sit-down strike subdued General Motors. In the important Sioux City stockyards, a predominantly white workforce led by Russian packinghouse workers supported unionism only after a CIO organizer arrived in the summer of 1937. These four areas were important pillars of the CIO-affiliated Packinghouse Workers Organizing Committee (PWOC) established in the fall of 1937.

Within the UPWA of the 1940s and 1950s these areas became the bulwarks of four administrative districts that included 75 percent of the organization's national membership and covered the heartland of the meatpacking industry. As the first successful local union, Austin was an influential supporter of the central UPWA leadership. Yet the local's isolation from packinghouse workers laboring in the large national firms gave it only an episodic role in the postwar union. Chicago became the stronghold of leftist influence and a critical source of support for the dominant center-left majority in the international union. It also was the showcase for union initiatives against racial discrimination. Reflecting the wariness of many local unions to any loss of autonomy to the central union bureaucracy, Kansas City remained a dissident center for most of the period. Sioux City typified the Iowa-based centrist forces that powerfully influenced the UPWA, but its predominantly white workforce mitigated against aggressive social unionism in the 1950s. The UPWA's policies were shaped by the tug and pull among the different currents represented by these local unions.

Chapter 1 establishes the context for relations between labor and capital in meatpacking by detailing the industry's structure, work process, and segmented labor force. The five subsequent chapters in Part 1 focus on the process of union formation in the 1930s and early 1940s that culminated in the creation of UPWA. Chapters 2 through 5 explore, respectively, the development of unions in Austin (Minnesota), Chicago, Kansas City, and Sioux City. Chapter 6 details the successful struggle of local unions to establish the UPWA in 1943 as a self-governing CIO affiliate.

The three chapters in Part 2 detail the development of the UPWA from the 1940s to the early 1960s. Chapter 7 addresses the consolidation of industrial unionism in meatpacking during World War II, the growth of rank-and-file power in the UPWA through unsanctioned wartime job actions, and the critical election of Ralph Helstein to the union's presidency in 1946. Chapter 8 focuses on the UPWA's capacity to survive the cold war against labor and the left in the late 1940s and rebuild after a bruising national strike in 1948. Chapter 9 examines the postwar UPWA's practice of shop-floor bargaining, its expanded programs to fight racial and sexual discrimination, and the clear limits on the union's practice of social unionism. All of the chapters in Part 2 explore the reasons for, and implications of, the UPWA's retention of union democracy and rejection of anticommunism.

Part 3 delineates the causes and consequences of declining union power in the meatpacking industry after 1960. Chapter 10 considers the changes in production methods, industrial structure, and workforce composition that undermined industrial unionism. When union power collapsed during the 1980s, the result was a precipitous drop in packinghouse workers' earnings and a dramatic increase in the intensity of work. Meatpacking in the late twentieth century manifests striking similarities to the industry a hundred years ago; only a resurgence of union strength can once again bring packinghouse workers out of the "jungle."

Throughout this study, the opinions and words of packinghouse workers interweave the narrative and inform its analysis. Interviews with more than a hundred former UPWA members provided an otherwise inaccessible vantage point on events and transformed the nominal objects of the study into living subjects of their own story. As a retrospective primary source, oral history cannot stand on its own; great care has been taken to verify information conveyed in interviews by consulting other witnesses and sources. When its message is appropriately heeded, however, oral history adds unmatched depth and richness to historical accounts. The memories of the participants in these events forcefully remind us of the dramatic social consequences and intense personal meaning of collective efforts to advance the living standards of the working class of people in America.

1

Purveyors to a Nation: Capital and Labor in the Meatpacking Industry

The stench is vomit-making as never before. The fat and plucks, the bladders and kidneys and bungs and guts, gone soft and spongy in the heat, perversely resist being trimmed, separated, deslimed; demand closer concentration than ever, more speed. A helpless, hysterical laughter starts up. Indeed, they are in hell; indeed they are the damned. *Steamed boiled broiled fried cooked. Geared, meshed.*

In the hog room, 108 degrees. Kerchiefs, bound around their foreheads to keep the sweat from running down into eyes and blinding, become saturated; each works in a rain of stinging sweat. Almost the steam from the vats seems cloud-cool, pure, by contrast. Marsalek falls. A heart attack. (Is carried away, docked, charged for the company ambulance.) Other hearts pound near to bursting. Relentless, the conveyor paces on.

Slow it, we got to slow it.

—Tillie Olsen, *Yonnondio: From the Thirties*

The primal character of meatpacking has fascinated as much as it has revolted our culture. In *The Jungle,* Upton Sinclair astutely recorded the mixed feelings of visitors intrigued by the marvelously sophisticated, yet curiously medieval, method of putting bacon on the table. Watching workers methodically slaughter ten hogs a minute "was too much for some of the visitors— the men would look at each other, laughing nervously, the women would stand with hands clenched, and the blood rushing to their faces, and tears starting in their eyes." Visitors were at first mesmerized by the modernism of the packinghouse, "pork-making by machinery, pork making by applied mathematics." Yet they left abashed, shaken by the brutal and curiously archaic killing process, "like some horrible crime committed in a dungeon, all unseen and unheeded, buried out of sight and out of memory."[1]

Troubled observers of the making of meat overlooked, all too often, those who made the meat. The "horrible crimes" experienced by packinghouse workers generally received far less attention than what they produced. A 1943 government study showed that the rate of disabling injuries (causing absence from work) in meatpacking was almost double the average for manufacturing, and minor injuries occurred at a rate of ninety for every serious one. Three plants employing 8,500 workers reported 30,499 injuries in 1940—an annual average of three per worker. On the killing floors, 20 percent of workers experienced at least one disabling injury; several had more than two dozen minor and major accidents in one year. In one case, "a bone shattered when an employee struck it with a cleaver." A splinter impaled an eye and cost the worker his vision. In the pork trim area, an employee "was operating a skinning machine while wearing gloves. His glove caught in the machine. One finger amputated." In a sausage-making operation, "while feeding meat into a grinder an employee got his hand caught in the feed. It was necessary to amputate his arm at the elbow." The pity for the poor pig and concern for the quality of meat rarely included an equivalent concern for the men and women who made the bacon.[2]

The modern, twentieth-century meatpacking industry was the creation of large national corporations that methodically reorganized the method of producing and distributing meat and attracted hundreds of thousands of migrants from agricultural regions in Europe and the Americas to work in stockyard districts. The workers, in turn, forged communities based around family ties, shared racial and ethnic heritage, and periodically tried to create labor organizations designed to alter the terms under which they toiled. When they finally succeeded in the 1930s and 1940s, the structure of the industry influenced the development of unions in several ways. First, the large national firms of Armour, Cudahy, Swift, and Wilson—collectively known as the Big Four—were the industry's pace-setters in production methods, wages, working conditions, and the "tone" of industrial relations. A labor organization could not significantly improve the standard of living of the nation's packinghouse workers without organizing the Big Four. Second, the concentration of the packing industry in the Midwest, where the large firms operated plants employing an average of a thousand workers in a handful of cities and states, mandated the targets of organizing activity and fostered coordination among workers in different locales.[3] Third, the structure and integrated production process of the Big Four's packinghouses encouraged a shop-floor organizing strategy. A decentralized union structure was the only way to reach workers spread through buildings honeycombed with dozens of physically separate departments. The killing floors, positioned at the start of the "disassembly" operation and the source of product for the entire plant, emerged as the focal point in the struggle for control between companies and the unions. Finally, low profit margins in the industry encouraged harsh "authority relations" and tight control over labor costs, inadvertently providing the source of many grievances encouraging unionization.

The Meatpacking Oligopoly

When restive packinghouse workers began to organize in the early 1930s, the Big Four firms (along with Morris, acquired by Armour in 1923) controlled the heartland of meat production, a swathe reaching from St. Paul in the North to Fort Worth in the South, stretching as far west as Denver and as far east as Chicago. Rail spurs extending into the countryside transported live animals from farms to central stockyards in large urban hubs, where buyers from adjacent packinghouses made their purchases for the day. Direct rail connections to the East sped the processed meat to consumers in major population concentrations. In 1916, Armour, Cudahy, Morris, Swift, and Wilson killed 94.4 percent of the cattle processed in the twelve cities (all in the Midwest except for New York) that produced 81 percent of the nation's beef. These five firms also controlled 81 percent of the hog slaughter in those centers. The structure of meatpacking changed little between World War I and the New Deal; the Big Four firms accounted for 78 percent of the total value of meat products sold in 1937.[4]

The expansion of the Big Four's midwestern plants rested on their ability to expand the productivity of labor significantly in order to take advantage of an extensive distribution and sales network. Before 1860 local firms provided most meat in the United States because there was neither the refrigeration nor transport capacity to allow for the perishable product to be shipped long distances. Refrigeration, both of the packinghouses and railroad cars, allowed firms employing economies of scale to displace local concerns.[5] Swift and Company was the first meatpacking firm to use refrigerated railroad cars to convey meat processed in midwestern plants to eastern population centers. Armour and other companies quickly followed Swift's lead, and firms that did not follow the same business strategy were either acquired by the large companies or restricted to local trade. Backward integration, in the form of ownership of central stockyards, assured the large midwestern plants of a reliable supply of livestock.[6]

Swift and Armour complemented their rail network by opening hundreds of branch houses and operating railroad car routes to dispense meat to local butchers. These outlets accounted for more than 55 percent of their sales in 1916. With large companies owning 90 percent of the nation's branch houses and car routes and penetrating into at least twenty-five thousand cities and towns, the Federal Trade Commission concluded in 1919 that independent firms found it "practically impossible" to "ship fresh meat out of the locality in which it is produced."[7]

In the 1920s the growth of the highway network allowed several new firms located away from major urban areas to grow, including dynamic businesses such as George A. Hormel & Company in Austin, Minnesota. The growth of national retail food chains also helped the independent packers because they could ship their product to a central warehouse for distribution rather than rely on their own network. These trends slightly reduced the Big Four's dominance during the 1920s and 1930s but would alter the dynamics of the industry only after World War II. On the eve of the depression, the dominant firms' control over the national production and distribution of meat products remained secure (Table 1).[8]

The extensive distribution network encouraged packing firms to branch out into other products to make more efficient use of the substantial capital already invested in the sales end of the business. Meat by-products such as leather, lard, fertilizer, and oleomargarine were natural additions to a meat-packer's sales portfolio because they used parts of the animal that otherwise would be discarded. By 1916 the Big Four firms controlled 84.7 percent of the nation's lard production, 75 percent of hides produced by interstate slaughterers, and 42 percent of the annual sales of oleomargarine. It was a short additional step for the national firms to market poultry and milk products, along with items such as cottonseed oil, soft drinks, cereal, coffee, and vegetables, to make its branch houses and car routes a source for more and more of a retailer's needs. Sales of eggs by the major packing firms reached 24.5 million in 1918, 33 percent of the national market.[9]

Table 1. Big Four Control over Interstate Commerce of Slaughtered Animals[a]

Year	Cattle	Calves	Sheep	Hogs	Total
1908	74.9	63.0	71.6	53.2	59.7
1916	82.2	76.6	86.4	61.2	68.0
1919	78.5	77.3	86.8	61.8	69.3
1924	73.2	72.9	83.2	52.7	60.6
1929	69.5	70.9	85.8	47.9	58.7
1935	67.1	71.0	85.3	51.9	66.2

a. Figures include Morris and Company before 1923.

Sources: Temporary National Economic Committee, *Large-Scale Organization in the Food Industry,* Monograph 35, 76th Cong., 3d sess. (Washington, 1940), 16; Federal Trade Commission, *Report of the Federal Trade Commission on the Meat-Packing Industry* (Washington, 1919), part 1, 33, 106, 129.

Vertical integration in the 1890s allowed a few packing firms to dominate the meat industry; expansion of their product lines after 1900 began to transform these companies into the purveyors of the nation's food. Deep suspicion toward the meat industry, and disclosure of many questionable business practices, foreclosed that possibility, however. A senate investigation in the late 1880s disclosed that major packing firms had met regularly at the Swift offices to fix prices and compel retailers to patronize only their firms. The 1890 Vest Report based on this investigation greatly contributed to the passage of the Sherman Anti-Trust Act a few months later, which outlawed these practices. The packers quickly devised other methods to coordinate their activities. Between 1893 and 1902 company officials met "informally" every Tuesday in the offices of accountant Henry Veeder to allocate sales territory and set wholesale meat prices. Members of this "Veeder" pool enforced conformity with their decisions by blacklisting local butchers who purchased supplies from independent companies.[10]

A federal investigation and court injunctions ended the Veeder pool in 1903, but the large firms easily surmounted the new legal obstacles.[11] First, they formed the National Packing Company, a firm that incorporated the holdings of all the major meatpackers except Cudahy. Its board of directors, including J. Ogden Armour, Gustavus Swift, and other leading packing executives, continued to meet in Henry Veeder's office at 2 P.M. on Tuesdays. Under the threat of a civil suit the packers dissolved National in 1912 but maintained their efforts to control the nation's meat distribution. The 1919 Federal Trade Commission (FTC) investigation showed that through informal contacts the five dominant firms continued to allocate market share, coordinate standard wholesale meat prices, and cooperate in a variety of shady selling practices to drive out competitors.[12]

The FTC investigation resulted in two important measures: a 1920 consent decree signed by the large firms and the 1921 Packers and Stockyards Act, which sharply defined the future configurations of the industry. The packing companies retained their distribution networks at the cost of abandoning all non-meat product lines and surrendering control of the stockyards to independent companies. The 1921 act also prohibited price-setting or apportionment of sales territory and theoretically gave the secretary of agriculture the power to regulate the industry. Despite the FTC's hope that federal intervention would "provide facilities for the competitive marketing of food," the 1920 and 1921 measures failed to increase competition within the industry because the distributional barriers to entry remained unchanged.[13]

Although there were no challenges to the Big Four's control over meatpacking, overcapacity and low profit margins plagued the industry during the 1920s (Tables 2 and 3). With clear limits on their opportunity to increase income through other product lines, leading packers yearned for the heady days when they could meet civilly for an afternoon and determine the market share and profit level of each firm. When the 1933 National Industrial Recovery Act promised to ease antitrust restrictions, the Big Four proposed a code which, according to the meat industry's main journal, "would have permitted allocation of livestock among packers based on their previous purchases; would have allowed the elimination of overshipments of product to consumer markets, and would have made it possible to restrain the competition of firms that ignored cost in pricing." Objections from small packers, and the residual "suspicion" of the Big Four's intentions, blocked their rather obvious effort to resurrect the pooling agreements of the late nineteenth and early twentieth centuries. The National Recovery Administration never issued a marketing code governing the meatpacking industry.[14]

Table 2. Average Slaughter, All Animals, 1926–37

Year	Percent 1929 Slaughter of 3,331,000 Tons
1926–30	99.6
1931	94.3
1932	91.5
1933–37	99.2

Source: Derived from Temporary National Economic Committee, *Large-Scale Organization in the Food Industry,* Monograph 35, 76th Cong., 3d sess. (Washington, 1940), 118.

Table 3. Company Profits in Meatpacking, 1927–36

Year	Earnings as Percent of Sales[a]
1927–30	1.83
1931	-0.14 (loss)
1932	0.23
1933–36	2.61

a. U.S. Bureau of Corporations, *Report on the Beef Industry* (Washington, 1905), 258–69, reported that the profit in meatpacking averaged 1.9 percent of total sales in 1904, similar to the figures for the 1920s and 1930s.

Source: Derived from Temporary National Economic Committee, *Large-Scale Organization in the Food Industry,* Monograph 35, 76th Cong., 3d sess. (Washington, 1940), 100.

The aspirations and growth of capital in the meatpacking industry is only half of the story. Commensurate with the rise of the large midwestern firms was a complete reorganization of the work process and the entry of thousands of unskilled workers into packinghouses. From just 8,000 packinghouse workers in 1870, the number of wage-earners in the booming slaughterhouses reached 70,000 by the turn of the century and 125,000 in 1925. The profits and growth of the Big Four rested on the arduous labor of men and women in America's pioneering mass-production industry.[15]

The Work of Slaughtering and Meatpacking

"The first step forward in assembly came when we began taking the work to the men instead of the men to the work," Henry Ford recalled of his pace-setting efforts to automate car production. "The idea came in a general way from the overhead trolley that the Chicago packers use in dressing beef." Ford's inspiration came from one of the first industries to combine a labor-intensive fragmented division of labor with a continuous-flow production process.[16]

While Frederick Winslow Taylor would have admired the care with which companies separated tasks and limited each worker to only a few movements, scientific management pioneers probably blanched at the obstacles to mechanizing meat production. The irregular size of animals and the peculiar angle of many butchering tasks made the introduction of machinery exceedingly difficult. "Skill has become specialized to fit the anatomy," John R. Commons observed in 1904. A study of five packinghouses in the early 1930s determined that machine operators or helpers made up only 20 percent of the workforce. Among the rest, skilled workers wielded knives and cleavers to make precise cuts in the animal carcass, and unskilled laborers hauled, carried, stuffed, or performed other operations with their hands, unaided by mechanical devices. The small number of skilled workers remained important at critical stages in the slaughtering and processing of livestock, but they did not set their own pace, as had nineteenth-century butchers.[17]

Henry Ford's "trolley," the continuous overhead chain that carried the freshly slaughtered animal down a "disassembly" line, was a revolutionary innovation in the early twentieth century because it gave management considerable control over the pace of the slaughtering operations. "If you worked in the killing floors, man it was murder because you had to keep up with the chain," recalled Omaha butcher Nels Peterson. Ability to regulate the slaughtering tempo in turn determined the rapidity with which the product flowed to other areas of the plant. Gravity provided the other major aid to the distribution of the product. Animals unwittingly saved their executioners trouble and money by climbing runways to the top floor of the packinghouse, between four and eight stories off the ground. After killing-floor workers dismembered the livestock, chutes using the product's own weight brought the meat to successively lower levels in the plant. While the offal and cutting departments were a floor or two below the killing beds, the processing, pickling, and by-product areas might be underground. Mechanized conveyer belts and small wheeled vehicles became commonplace in the 1930s; however, distributing the product downward remained the basic organizing principle governing the location of a packinghouse's many departments before World War II.[18]

Everything in a packinghouse depended on the supply of meat being funneled through the killing floors at the top of the building. Although the level of production might differ from plant to plant, the basic work process varied very little. In one Chicago packinghouse in the early twentieth century, a gang of 230 employees performing 78 distinct tasks killed 105 cattle an hour. Eighty percent of these workers earned between 15 and 23 cents an hour, and only 8 percent earned the highest rates of 40 to 50 cents. Stockhandlers first drove the cattle up the long runway and penned each animal into a narrow stall. With a single deft blow from a heavy sledgehammer, a knocker (paid 24 cents) rendered it unconscious, exercising great care to "not kill the steer because death would stop the heart action and thus prevent the rapid draining of blood."[19] A shackler received 18½ cents for the dangerous task of attaching the chain to the stunned animal's foot. The continuous chain, connected to the overhead "trolley," suspended the animal upside down in the air by one leg. A sticker earning 32½ cents then killed the steer with a single stroke of a short, curved knife that severed both an artery and vein to speed the drainage of blood. Immediately adjacent to the sticker, a worker paid the same rate beheaded the animal with a precise cut through the joint connecting the backbone and skull.

The carcass now was ready for the delicate hide removal operation. Laborers earning 20 cents or less lowered the animal onto the skinning bed and positioned it for the most highly skilled employees in the department. Between the hide and the flesh are two layers of tissue, known as the fell, and the skinner must cut between those layers to avoid nicking the hide—significantly lowering its value—or leaving a damaging bruise (termed a "black eye") in the meat. "Leg-breakers," "foot-skinners," and other butchers earning between 20 and 25 cents skinned the legs and opened the belly before the floorsman, receiving the top rate of 50 cents, used a long knife to skin the animal's stomach and sides. A backer, paid 45 cents, and rumper, earn-

ing 40 cents, largely completed the skinning process but left the hide hanging on the carcass until several laborers manually returned the animal to the
overhead chain. The "hide-dropper" and several other butchers earning 32
cents finished the job. Once inspectors examined the hide and recorded any
imperfections, several brawny workers dropped the heavy hides through a
chute to a salt-filled curing cellar in the basement of the plant.

Denuded of its outer skin, the carcass was "dressed" by a series of butchers who each performed a distinct cut, aided by laborers who had their own
particular tasks. Gut-snatchers, gutters, and other workers earning around
25 cents slit open the belly and removed the heart, lungs, liver, and intestines—known as the viscera or "pluck"—and dropped them down a chute
to the beef offal or gut-shanty department located underneath the killing
floor. Splitters (paid the same as floorsmen) using heavy cleavers severed the
carcass into two halves by splitting the backbone down the middle. One poor
stroke by these workers could ruin many of the consumer cuts. Butchers
removed the tail and sweetbread glands while laborers washed the eviscer-
ated carcass. Once approved by government inspectors, the two halves of
the carcass were shrouded by unskilled workers in salt-water-soaked mus-
lin and placed in a cooler to curtail spoilage.[20]

"This is all done by hand," recalled beef butcher Louie Tickal. "Back-
breaking is what it was." As the killing floors provided the raw material for
the entire plant, management and the inexorably moving chain pushed the
butchers to work with a furious intensity.[21] "Five minutes up there was like
five hundred dollars," recalled an Armour plant superintendent. Even at the
height of union strength in 1904, stickers, headers, and splitters in the beef
kill each handled 25 animals an hour, while workers with less complex jobs
repeated their tasks every minute. A poorly placed step on the floor, slick
with blood and other fluids that oozed from the dead cattle, could send a
worker reeling and leave him with an injured back, or a knife wound if he
collided with another butcher. Small cuts and bruises were part of the job,
as well as respiratory illnesses from the hot and steamy conditions and back
injuries from constant stooping and carrying. A warm department even
during the winter, in the summer killing-floor workers often labored in temperatures well over 100 degrees.[22]

The performance of skilled work under onerous conditions in the packinghouse's most important department gave killing-floor workers their pivotal role in the 1930s organizing drives. "You couldn't just take a person off
the street and put him in the killing floor," recalled Walter Bailey. On both
the beef and hog kill, skilled butchers were prized employees who the companies tried to retain against entreaties from other firms in the same city.

Some became "boomer butchers," skilled itinerant workers who only labored during the fall and winter rush and quit in the spring to move to another town. "I never had any trouble," recalled Jack Sechrest, a hog butcher who moved freely from plant to plant. "Even in the depression I was able to get a job." Efforts by management to control the slaughtering operation reflected the importance of the killing-floor pace to the entire plant's productivity, but the same pressure encouraged workers to look for "some kind of relief from the pressure, from the foot that's on their head."[23]

While the carcass chilled at below-zero temperatures in the coolers, workers in the beef and hog offal rooms immediately underneath the killing floors trimmed, separated, and routed to other departments the various components of the animal that could not be used in consumer cuts. Laboring under poor conditions for relatively low pay, predominantly female workers trimmed the meat off animal heads, cut out the tongues, and removed and cleaned the internal organs and intestines. The casings area, sometimes separated into different rooms for processing beef, pork, and sheep intestines, usually was next to the offal department. Workers separated the intestines into bungs, middles, and rounds, stripped fat off the outside, and washed out the feces by pulling the intestine over a water pipe. Women performed the cleaning and subsequent salting operations, but men inspected the casings before shipping them to the coolers or the sausage manufacturing area. Both the offal and the casings departments were at the same temperature as the killing floors, but the ever-present water added humidity to the oppressive heat, noise, and odors. Tillie Olsen, who lived in the Chicago stockyards during the 1930s, observed that women learned to breath exclusively through their mouths "to endure the excrement reek of offal." Arthritis was the most common affliction among the women who stood in water and worked rapidly with knives and other tools over the small pieces of the animal. Women who packed intestines routinely developed sores from constant exposure to salt. "It was terrible," recalled Virginia Houston. "THAT was a dirty job!"[24]

Once it was suitably chilled (a process usually taking twenty-four hours), laborers moved the animal carcass into the cutting and trimming departments. Usually the cattle halves were separated into hind and fore quarters before shipment to butcher shops, with hefty beef luggers using their shoulders to move the two-hundred-pound cuts from the cooler to railroad cars for shipment. Hog carcasses generally received more processing. Laborers (earning less than 20 cents an hour in 1904) pushed the pig carcasses, split into halves, out of the cooler on a chain to several ham sawyers, paid 27 cents, who dropped the dead hogs onto a series of moving conveyer belts. Choppers wielding a cleaver and paid 37 cents separated the carcass into its ham (rear leg), side (central portion), and shoulder (front leg). Boners, usually the elite in the department, skillfully removed the skin and small bones from the meat and sent the ham down another chute to the curing cellars, where it would pickle in a brine solution. A loin puller, paid 27½ cents, used a curved knife to separate the loin from the ribs before a series of other butchers trimmed and shaped those pieces. In the early twentieth century, a forty-person cutting department could handle five hundred hogs an hour. There was little technical innovation over the next three decades except for the use of power saws in place of cleavers for the larger cutting operations. The skilled butcher and his sharp blade—aided by several dozen less skilled workers—still were critical to the department's productivity.[25]

Unlike the overheated areas at the top of the packinghouse, the cutting and trimming departments in the middle of the plant were cold, dingy, and damp. "If you worked in the kills, it was hotter than the devil, and if you worked in the coolers or the chutes, it was colder than the devil," recalled a St. Paul employee. To keep the meat fresh, temperatures rarely exceeded 40 degrees. The chilled meat numbed hands, and workers used buckets of hot water to heat their knives to cut the pieces more easily. In this "ice hell," women kept warm by wrapping newspaper and gunny sacks around their legs and donning heavy sweaters under their work frocks. Water condensed on the walls—forming icicles when temperature dropped below freezing—and combined with the fat trimmed from the meat to coat the floors with a permanent slippery layer that caused many workers to slip and fall. In the pork trim, overhead chutes dropped meat onto the work tables, occasionally showering the unsuspecting workers with chunks of pork and causing knife injuries to workers startled in the middle of a cutting operation.[26]

Parts of the animal that could not be used for consumer cuts ended up in the various by-product departments. Blood drained from slaughtered animals was collected for use in fertilizer and animal food. The cattle hides slid down a chute to the hide cellar, a "stinking place." Workers shook out the hides (which usually weighed more than a hundred pounds), covered them with salt, and let them cure in huge piles for several months. Women stuffed scraps of meat from the head, internal organs, and cutting-room floors into intestine casings to make sausage. Animal brains went to the freezer, later to be sold whole or added to the sausage material. Scraps of beef and sheep fat were refined into oleomargarine, while pork fat cooked in high-pressure vats became lard. A pharmaceutical department refined glands extracted at various points in the production process for use in medicinal products. Skulls, other bones, inedible internal organs, spoiled meat, and any other miscellaneous scraps ended in the rendering department or tank house, where workers cooked and melted them down for use as glue or fertilizer. The rendering house and the hide cellar were well known as the most unpleasant jobs in a packinghouse. "You could wash four times," recalled Chris Wicke, "and you get home and your wife and children would say, 'Didn't you wash, dad?'"[27]

Incentive pay particularly affected the cutting and processing departments. While workers in the killing-floor and curing areas generally received hourly wages, men and women in the sausage, canning, cut, trim, boning, and bacon departments relied on incentive pay for a significant portion of their earnings. In the 1920s various "task and bonus" systems largely replaced the older piece-work pay methods. Typically, these schemes combined standard production quotas paid on an hourly basis with a bonus linked to the number of pieces that exceeded minimum requirements. Swift adopted the elaborate Bedaux System, which employed complex computations to accord bonus pay to speedy workers. While increasing earnings well above base pay, the various "slave-driving systems" also encouraged overwork and vicious competition among workers laboring on the same table. For example, women in the pork trim who were paid according to the amount of lean meat in a given chunk frequently squabbled over pieces of meat. "One [would] reach over here for a big piece of meat that had a lot of lean in it," recalled Philip Weightman, "another one would walk over and start fighting with the hook to get it." In the 1930s unions would struggle to recruit women who worked under incentive systems.[28]

The harsh nature of packinghouse work was compounded by irregular employment and labor market segmentation. Constantly shifting production needs, reflecting the patterns of livestock availability and consumer preference, encouraged firms to keep labor costs at a minimum through frequent hiring and layoffs. Total employment peaked during the hog rush that lasted from November to March, rapidly declined in the late spring, and stabilized through the summer until once again rising in the fall. Layoffs disproportionately affected new employees, who had been hired when production expanded. In the late 1920s more than 50 percent of the new female employees in three cities received layoffs within a month after they were hired; within six months 95 percent had been idled at least once. To retain more experienced workers, especially the skilled butchers, firms either reduced hours or shifted the workers into other departments rather than lay them off entirely (Table 4). The result, in Rick Halpern's phrase, was a "horizontally layered pyramid." At the bottom, a constantly shifting mass of temporary, unskilled laborers secured jobs for a few weeks or

Table 4. Weekly Hours, Cattle Butchers, in One Large
Chicago Packinghouse, 1905–6

Month	Weekly Hours	Month	Weekly Hours
July 1905	38	January 1906	38.6
August	35.4	February	34.5
September	45.5	March	34
October	50	April	32.25
November	46.75	May	38
December	35.2		

Source: Derived from C. W. Thompson, "Labor in the Packing Industry," *Journal of Political Economy* 15 (Feb. 1906): 91–92.

months at a time while successive gradations of semiskilled and skilled
workers relied on relations with supervisors to climb a firm's internal labor market and to avoid unemployment.[29]

The men and women who filled the places in meatpacking's employment
pyramid found their choices starkly limited by strong gender, racial, and
ethnic patterns of workplace segmentation. In the late 1920s women made
up approximately 20 percent of the meatpacking workforce and worked in
distinctly gendered occupations. Among the six thousand women in thirty-
four plants surveyed by the Women's Bureau in the late 1920s, 84 percent
worked in six predominantly female areas, all linked to the growing processing end of the business. Fifteen percent labored in the offal and casings departments "where," as Tillie Olsen wrote, "men will not work." One-half of
the black women in the industry worked in these two departments, with the
remainder toiling in harsh and poorly-paid "nigger jobs" on the killing floor
and in the rendering areas. Whites dominated the other female departments:
30 percent of all women worked in sausage manufacturing, 16.7 percent in
sliced bacon, 14.6 percent in the pork trim area, and 7.8 percent in canning.
In sliced bacon, a particularly desirable and clean department, firms routinely employed young, native-born white women dressed in immaculate work
clothing to impress visitors to this "show" area. Foreign-born and second-
generation ethnic women, on the other hand, tended to be concentrated in
the sausage and pork-trim areas.[30]

There was an equally defined racial and ethnic division of labor for men,
although it varied slightly in accordance with the mix of a particular workforce. By the early 1930s first and second-generation east European ethnics
held many of the central production jobs in the killing and cutting departments, while older immigrant stock (usually Irish and German) and Protestant workers dominated the highly paid mechanical trades, power house,
and other nonproduction line tasks. Whenever black men labored in a pack-

inghouse in the 1920s and 1930s, company practices and racial traditions confined them to a distinct array of jobs on the killing floors, in the hide cellars, and in the rendering operations. On the beef kill, blacks generally did not perform the better-paying skinning and splitting jobs and remained concentrated in the shackling, heading, and secondary butchering tasks as well as common labor. Worse conditions prevailed in the hog kill. Blacks rarely held knife jobs and performed labor-intensive tasks such as shackling hogs and staffing the particularly unpleasant scalding tub and resin bath that removed the pig's hair. Although racial antagonism marked shop-floor relations in the 1920s, the integrated character of the killing floors would boomerang on the packers and serve as the foundation for the UPWA's inter-racial unionism.[31]

The Problem of Labor Control

Company profits depended on control of the work process, because national distribution hinged on high-volume slaughtering, which in turn mandated the rapid movement of the product from farm to dinner table. Meatpacking firms were quite wealthy, financing their expansion through earnings rather than debt; their enormous income rested on high sales at a low profit rate, however. This made maintaining control over work, and reducing outlays for labor, of "critical importance in management psychology."[32]

Control over production, until the CIO era, rested on what Sumner Slichter termed the "drive" system: to obtain efficiency "by putting pressure on them [workers] to turn out a large output. The dominating note of the drive policy is to inspire the worker with awe and fear of the management, and having developed fear among them, to take advantage of it." In meatpacking, the drive system depended on the ability of front-line supervisors to generate high levels of production. Despite the growth of personnel departments after 1910 and the adoption of welfare capitalism measures in the 1920s, the "foremen's empire" remained secure so long as front-line supervisors maintained high levels of production in their departments. The segmented labor market graphically reinforced the foremen's power: job-seekers routinely crowded around company employment offices in the early-morning hours, hoping for a job or at least temporary respite from unemployment. Regardless of a firm's stated employment practices, workers knew that their foremen had the power to make work tolerable or pure hell or to send them off to join the mass at the factory gate.[33]

Throughout the 1920s and 1930s, foremen determined employment levels in their departments, controlled layoffs, and could influence hiring decisions by recommending individuals to the personnel office. "He'd go tell the hiring boss and he'd hire you," recalled Sioux City union founder Mary Edwards. "Every time you got laid off, if you was a good worker, they would call you, let you know they were going to hire and for you to come back." Under a "fair" foremen, a work gang could develop policies that protected each member, such as rolling layoffs at moments of low production so that each employee would share time off. A harsh supervisor, though, who relied on pressure and intimidation to keep production at a high pace, could make a worker's life miserable by favoring the "good workers" over perceived troublemakers or slackers. The widespread incentive, Bedaux and piece-work payment schemes also facilitated the drive system by encouraging employees to work as hard and as fast as possible for their pay.[34]

Workers, seeking relief "from the foot that's on their head," used moments of union strength in the early twentieth century to assert control over the pace and conditions of production. Between 1900 and 1904 and 1917 and 1921 the AFL-affiliated Amalgamated Meat Cutters and Butcher Workmen recruited tens of thousands of packinghouse workers. In addition to securing wage increases and regular hours, workers fought for control of the shop floor. Unofficial "house committees" that flourished from 1900 to 1904 reduced work loads and chain speeds, enforced seniority in layoffs and recall, and successfully pressured management to maintain employment levels during slack periods. Periodic departmental job actions erupted when workers used the union's shop-floor structures to contest management's control over the work process. John R. Commons observed at the time that "the first act of the union was not directed towards wages or hours, but towards a reduction of output." A dozen years later, during the tight labor market conditions of World War I, workers once again asserted their influence over pay levels and working conditions. Aided by the rulings of Judge Samuel B. Alschuler, the federal mediator of the meatpacking industry, the workers secured wage increases, the eight-hour day, and overtime pay and forced companies to once again negotiate with informal shop committees over numerous work-place issues.[35]

The corporate desire to control production and lower labor costs through wage cuts and increased production standards in turn provoked the corporate assaults on packinghouse unions in 1904 and 1921. "The domination of the packing plants by the union gradually had become unbearable," the companies complained in 1903. "Discipline grew lax and the men did not attend to their work as they should have." Moments of high unemployment provided an opportune moment for the packers to rid themselves of the unwanted union presence. In 1904 the companies provoked a strike by balking at the union's demand for a minimum wage; in a struggle lasting several months, they eliminated the Amalgamated Meat Cutters locals and the especially annoying house committees. Following the end of government-imposed mediation in 1921, the packers again forced the Amalgamated into a losing strike by reducing wages with the "approval" of newly formed employee representation councils. Pay cuts, faster chain speeds, heavier job loads, and the collapse of the union's shop-floor presence followed each defeat.[36]

Welfare capitalism, and the employee representation plans prevalent in the 1920s and 1930s, only modified the drive system for the upper tiers of the occupational pyramid. By alleviating some of the grievances that led to union growth during World War I, firms hoped to generate company loyalty among skilled and semiskilled employees. Vacations, partial protection against layoffs, a pension plan in the case of Swift, social programs, recreation, and other measures sought to reduce turnover and reinforce company allegiance. Programs typically required workers to be employed continuously, with no longer than a sixty-day break in order to qualify for these benefits. Unskilled laborers rarely achieved such security. After periodic layoffs they would once again seek reemployment through personal relations with a foremen or by joining the perennial crowd of unemployed at the factory gates. Employee representation plans, although providing some avenues for resolution of grievances, remained firmly under the control of management and did not interfere with the organization and pace of production. The threat of unemployment and the unrestricted retention of managerial control over the shop floor remained the backbone of company labor relations during the 1920s.[37]

The structure of the industry and the organization of production established the playing field upon which union advocates operated in the 1930s. The CIO-era organizing battles were fought out in packinghouse districts of the major agro-industrial centers of the Midwest, among them Chicago, Kansas City, and Sioux City. Efforts to link unionists in different plants of the same company proceeded from the bottom up, as packinghouse workers sought to counter their firm's capacity to deal with a local dispute by shifting production elsewhere. Disruption of the work process made supervisors listen to and workers respect the union, especially when the killing-floor workers made their concerns felt. All parties recognized that the decisive struggle was with the Big Four companies because victory in a small firm such as Hormel would always remain precarious until the industry pacesetters recognized the union. Hence the struggle for a master agreement, providing similar conditions for all the local unions in the plants of the same national concern, was an immediate objective for the local unions in meat-packing during the 1930s. Once unions secured their initial objectives and showed packers that they could not be removed from the plants, the struggle over control assumed the character of guerrilla warfare, its rules and theaters of struggle always shifting but remaining at the forefront of labor-management relations throughout the union era.

The conflict over control would frame union organizing efforts of the 1930s. In their rhetoric and practice, union pioneers who started organizing independently of each other during the 1930s universally appealed to the aspirations of packinghouse workers for equal and fair treatment at work. The importance of control, moreover, encouraged an inclusive unionism that sought to bridge the substantial divisions of race, sex, and ethnicity as the only way to secure a strong union organization. Favoring one group over another "was just one of those things that the company was using to make money off of both of us," a black Fort Worth union founder recalled point-ing out to white workers. "You done the same work, you produce the same amount of work, and the product that you produce is just as good as any-body else's, but the color of your skin and the color of my skin is causing them to use this kind of thing, and they was making money off it. Not only were you suffering, but I was suffering. Now, I was probably suffering more, but you're suffering too, because we probably both could get more." The notion that "we had to work together, not as individuals, but collectively, and that was the only way to get the job done," would be echoed repeatedly in the 1930s and 1940s as workers tried to fundamentally alter the conditions under which they labored.[38]

PART 1

"CIO, Let's Go!": The Origins of Industrial Unionism in Meatpacking

The workers were waiting for CIO, pounding on its doors long before CIO was ready for them. I heard the pounding as soon as I started work with CIO late in 1935—in delegations, on the phone, in the mail, in the news. It came from within the AFL, and from all the unorganized industries. . . . All said, "CIO, let's go!"

—Len De Caux

The origins of industrial unionism in meatpacking are captured effectively by Len De Caux's recollection. Beginning in the early 1930s, scattered nuclei of union activists seized on the immiseration of packinghouse workers (Table 5) and the political opening of the New Deal to organize their fellow workers. Stymied by the conservatism of AFL organizations and the weak support to labor rendered by Section 7(a) of the National Industrial Recovery Act, union pioneers descended on the newly formed Committee, and then Congress, of Industrial Organizations in 1936 and 1937. The formation of the Packinghouse Workers Organizing Committee in 1937 formalized the alliance between the CIO and rank-and-file union militants and established the foundations for industrial unionism in meatpacking.

The relationship between rank-and-file initiatives, CIO assistance, and government involvement in labor relations varied in each locale. Packinghouse workers in the Austin, Minnesota, plant of Hormel and Company provided the most successful initiative of the early 1930s. This was due to the talented leftist leadership of the nascent union, the vulnerability of their one-plant company to a strike, and the favorable attitude of the Minnesota's ruling Farmer-Labor Party (FLP). Chicago union advocates also made significant inroads in the early 1930s because of an alliance among leftists, white ethnics, black militants, and veterans of the meatpacking unions of 1917 to 1921. In Kansas City, a similar coalition established the basis for union organization before 1937. In both these cities, however, unionism attracted

Table 5. Employment and Earnings in Meatpacking, 1929–33

Year	Number of Plants	Number of Wage-Earners	Total Wages	Average Annual Wage
1929	1,277	122,505	$165,867,420	$1,353
1931	1,209	106,707	134,529,752	1,260
1933	1,073	113,911	112,001,652	991

Source: Derived from "Volume No. A, Code of Fair Competition for the Meat Packing Industry" [not adopted], UPWA Papers, box 492, folder 11.

broad rank-and-file support only after the CIO entered the scene. Although moderate material assistance played a role, the CIO's record of success in the auto and steel industries was a far more significant spur to union organizers in meatpacking. The CIO's contribution was especially important in Sioux City, where the absence of a coherent proto-union core meant that there was little union activity before the CIO dispatched a former United Mine Workers official to organize packinghouse workers.

As the union drives advanced, rank-and-file initiatives proceeded in close relationship with efforts to secure legal support for union activity. Organizers used the provisions of the Wagner Act to legitimize their efforts and secure concrete protection for pro-union workers. Although specific decisions of the National Labor Relations Board (NLRB) generally (although not always) helped the union, the elaborate hearings before the rulings were themselves a significant boost. Workers found to their delight that the government was willing to place management's heretofore unchallenged actions under public scrutiny. In Sioux City, for example, packing firms spent much of 1938 under investigation. Hearings concerning Armour lasted for two months in the spring, testimony regarding unfair labor practices by Cudahy consumed the summer months, and an inquiry into the causes of a strike at Swift lasted from October to December. Similarly, winning an NLRB certification election became not simply a victory in itself but also an enormous boost to the union's main objective—securing a collective bargaining agreement. Herbert March, a Chicago union pioneer, eloquently captured this dynamic. "You'd win an election, and the guys, instead of being afraid of employers, and having to bow down to them, they felt, we're equals, we're somebody, and by god, the bosses better listen to us instead of us just listening to them."[1] State sanction of union activity was as important ideologically as it was substantively to the union pioneers in meatpacking.

The role of blacks in the construction of local unions, especially in Chicago and Kansas City, would have a profound long-term affect on the UPWA's willingness to challenge traditional American racial norms. Where black workers were a significant minority, the formative local unions were built from the beginning with a commitment to racial equality. "We initiated the union, and developed the union, and carried it through as a union of black and white workers from the inception," recalled Herb March. "It was an integral part of the union's thinking from the word go." The inclusion of black workers also generally created a better environment for women to be treated as equals, although there was not an equivalent effort to challenge traditional gender roles in American society. In areas of lower black membership and participation, such as in Sioux City and Austin, local unions correspondingly did far less to challenge either racial or sexual discrimination. The persistence of social unionism in the UPWA after 1945 was a direct result of the presence of black workers, both because of their direct influence and the principles and practices they imparted to the formative unions.[2]

Local organizing drives, regardless of particular features, all emerged from the heartfelt grievances of packinghouse workers against mistreatment at work and their lack of power in American society. Each little humiliation on the job or slight on the street added to their simmering aspiration for a better way of life. At Chicago's Armour plant, "You felt like you were a slave," recalled union founder Sophie Kosciowlowski. "I wanted to feel like I was a human being, that I had some dignity." In Austin, a white Catholic recalled that "the morning when I put on the union button, I felt like a man when I walked through the gate; before I felt like a dog." William Raspberry, a black Kansas City packinghouse worker, expressed similar sentiments. Being in a union "gave me dignity. I felt like a human being, I felt like a person." Although the evolution of unionism in meatpacking was shaped significantly by structures only minimally under workers' control, it was nonetheless the shared anger and aspirations of black and white men and women that gave life to the organizing drives of the 1930s.[3]

Inexorably, the momentum for unionism at the local level led to efforts to create a democratic international organization. It was at this point that the development of unionism in meatpacking began to veer away from the pattern in industries such as steel. In the early 1940s shop-floor union cadres waged a bruising three-year struggle against CIO leaders determined to impose a highly centralized central bureaucracy on packinghouse workers. The fruit of this struggle would be an organization exceedingly well poised to preserve the insurgent spirit of the 1930s in the changed economic and political environment of World War II and the postwar era.

2

"We Worked for Everything We Got": The Origins of Packinghouse Unionism in Austin, Minnesota

> Things weren't handed to us on a golden platter. We worked for
> everything we got through the union. And when I hear people say
> that Mr. Hormel did this and Mr. Hormel did that, that isn't quite
> a true statement. He was a wonderful guy, I'll never take anything
> away from him, but he still was company management. You never
> want to forget that.
>
> —Marie Casey, Austin union founder

On the morning of November 11, 1933, packinghouse workers armed with clubs and pipes swept through the Hormel plant in Austin, Minnesota, and expelled all management personnel from the premises. Union pickets guarded entrances to the facility and persuaded sympathetic truckers and railroad workers to not cross the picket lines with their cargo. In the evenings, the glow of the pickets' bonfires, visible from downtown Austin and the working-class east side, clearly indicated who controlled the Hormel plant. For the workers, abused for years by supervisors and formerly powerless against the company, seizure of the plant was more than simply a method to win the strike. "A lot of suppressed hatred came to the fore in this demonstration," participant Svend Godfredson recalled. Workers beat and forcibly removed hated foremen from the plant, broke windows on expensive cars owned by management, and smashed several time clocks. Austin's nine policemen could do little but watch. One even contributed coal to the fire he shared with the strikers.[1]

The plant blockade established the first successful packinghouse union of the 1930s in the small, one-industry town of Austin. Inspired by the "one big union" ideal of the Industrial Workers of the World (IWW), Hormel workers were able to organize their plant, their town, and eventually their industry. In 1933 they formed the Independent Union of All Workers (IUAW), open to all wage-earners regardless of craft or trade, and used their base in the Hormel plant to organize other workers in Austin's small factories, garages, and retail stores. Hormel employees energetically reached out to industrial workers in the Upper Midwest, encouraging union organization, especially in the meatpacking industry. Along with the independent unions in auto, rubber, and electrical factories, the IUAW was drawn toward the CIO and affiliated in 1937.

Three factors specific to Austin made it possible for unionism to succeed in the Hormel plant several years earlier than in other packinghouses. First, an exceptional "militant minority" composed of leftists from diverse ideological perspectives shared both a firm commitment to industrial unionism and the savvy to develop effective organizing tactics. In 1933 they were able to channel the deep discontent of packinghouse workers into a formidable challenge to company power.

The very formation of the IUAW reflected the larger agenda of its leftist founders: to spark a resurgence of militant unionism and class consciousness. Although most Hormel employees did not share these goals as passionately as the radicals, their immediate concerns were in no way incompatible with the leftist agenda. By placing all packinghouse workers in the same body, the IUAW answered the Hormel workers' need for inclusive unionism that could stand up to the power of the company. In addition, leftists argued persuasively that the IUAW needed to grow in size and develop links with other packinghouses' workers in order to preserve its gains of the early 1930s.

Second, Hormel was a small company extremely vulnerable to an organizing drive in its main packinghouse, unlike the Big Four firms who relied on production from numerous sources. The 1933 strike in Austin completely shut down the company. Moreover, the Hormel family exercised absolute control over their firm. Without pressure from outside shareholders or banks to resist unionism, and in a weak position to oppose a strike in any event, company president Jay Hormel did not resist the IUAW's drive with the same vigor as the larger meatpacking firms.

Indeed, following recognition of the IUAW, Jay Hormel changed from a typical conservative businessman to the "red capitalist," in the words of *Fortune* magazine. "The idea that an employer is the lord and master of his business is an antiquated notion," he told southern Minnesota businessmen in 1937. "Give labor the fair treatment which is its right and labor's right to organize will never harm you." He skillfully turned unionism to his advantage by constructing a wage payment system, the guaranteed annual wage (GAW), which permitted a degree of worker control in exchange for steadily increasing productivity.[2]

Finally, Austin's Hormel workers also benefited from an unusually favorable political climate at the state level. The independent Farmer-Labor Party controlled Minnesota's executive branch during the IUAW's major confrontations with employers. The refusal of FLP governors to order the National Guard into several IUAW strikes greatly facilitated union victories. In addition, the FLP-controlled Minnesota Industrial Commission mediated the initial dispute with Hormel and issued a decree that governed labor relations between 1933 and 1940. The federal New Deal contributed to the Hormel workers' confidence but had little direct impact on their organizing successes.

The unionization of the Hormel plant had dramatic repercussions within Austin's small community. With more than two thousand members at Hormel, the IUAW was able to support organizing drives in other Austin businesses and spearhead a challenge to the political dominance of the town's traditional elite. Although small businesses might be able to defeat a unionizing effort by their own employees, their dependence on the patronage of packinghouse workers gave them little defense against a successful boycott; employers who resisted union recognition faced a precipitous decline in business. The extension of labor organizations throughout Austin's businesses provided a base for successful working-class politics and the election of a Hormel union leader as mayor in 1942.

Throughout the 1930s, the IUAW's one big union provided a common structure and strategy for the leftists and more locally oriented union members. In the early 1940s, however, the stabilization of labor relations at Hormel undermined leftist influence. The 1940 agreement with Jay Hormel linked wages with those paid by national packing companies, shifting the locus of conflict over hourly pay away from Austin. In addition, the long-term contract (with no expiration date) tied the increasing income and benefits of Hormel workers to the growth of the company, undercutting the leftist notion of class conflict. Nonetheless, the dependence of Hormel workers on the gains of other packinghouse workers sustained a more subdued sense of class awareness and kept the union in the progressive wing of the UPWA throughout the international union's existence.

The Making of a Company Town

By 1930, with more than two thousand employees in a town of barely fifteen thousand, the Hormel packinghouse dominated Austin's economy and shaped the opportunities of its inhabitants. Aside from four hundred jobs in the Milwaukee Road railroad yard, the only other wage work in the area was in small food processing plants and service businesses. Professionals and store owners in turn depended on business generated by more than $4 million a year in Hormel wages, and the county government received more than half its income from the packinghouse's property taxes. White-collar Hormel employees and their families made up several hundred members of the town's middle class. The extraordinary importance of the Hormel plant to Austin's vitality and the livelihood of so many residents made labor-management relations a civic, as well as a workplace, issue.[3]

Packinghouse workers formed a distinct and undesirable lower class in Austin, defined by their religion and ethnicity as well as occupation. Middle-class residents proudly traced their families back to New England Yankees and attended Congregational or Episcopalian churches. The Protestant elite controlled the town's only newspaper, filled its professional occupations, owned most small businesses, and dominated municipal politics. In contrast, the all-white packinghouse workers generally were of Irish, German, or Scandinavian extraction and worshipped at Catholic or Lutheran churches. Residential patterns reflected Austin's clear social divisions. The Cedar River, which provided water for the Hormel plant, split the town into two distinct parts. Most packinghouse workers lived in the poor Third Ward east of the river and adjacent to the Hormel plant, whereas the middle class resided on the more prosperous west side.[4]

The town's nominal leading family, the Hormel clan, actually was not closely tied to Austin's elite. George A. Hormel settled there in 1887 and opened a small packinghouse in 1891. The company grew steadily through the first two decades of the twentieth century and entered a dynamic era when Hormel elevated his Princeton-educated eldest son, Jay, to head the firm in the late 1920s. Jay Hormel initiated production of canned ham (the first by an American packinghouse) and devised a sophisticated advertising campaign to overcome consumer resistance to preserved pork. In the early 1930s he followed this success by developing other consumer-oriented processed meats. His most successful new product was spiced pork shoulder packaged in a sandwich-sized can and marketed under the name Spam; sales reached six hundred thousand cans a month in the late 1930s.[5]

For the Hormel workers, Jay Hormel's innovative ideas and the company's prosperity did not seem to improve their lives significantly. "You'd make just enough to pay your room and board, buy a few clothes, and then maybe you'd have a couple of bucks left to go out on a Saturday night and have a little fun," recalled Casper Winkels. "You just lived, that's all." In the sprawling plant, top management had little control over the fiefdoms of production-level supervisors. Workers could be shifted from one department to another, laid off with no advance notice, called in to work an hour in the morning, and then told to come back in the evening to work another hour. Because foremen controlled hiring, promotion, and firing, job security consisted of currying favor with supervisors. "The bosses would tell the workers, 'You bring me a bottle before tomorrow or else I'll fire you,'" remembered John Winkels, Casper's brother.[6]

The depression accentuated the class tensions that already divided Austin's population. Because much of Hormel's growth rested on sales of canned goods, the contraction of consumer spending in the early 1930s had a particularly strong impact on the firm. The company lost money in 1931, and declining sales made hundreds of workers redundant. Rather than institute deep layoffs, Hormel cut wages and shortened hours to share the work. Workers dubbed Hormel's policies "share the misery" because the loss of income made sheer survival difficult. Average weekly pay fell from $23 in 1929 to $19 in 1933, and many workers' incomes plummeted to between $10 and $17 a week. Low wages forced families to rent shabby, uninsulated shacks without plumbing or electricity and to choose in the winter between purchasing fuel or food. Some, unable to pay rent at all, lived in hovels on the railroad right-of-way east of the Hormel plant or in abandoned sheds in the local brickyard. Hormel worker Marie Casey recalled that "we had people that lived in tar paper shacks, we had shanty towns, we had 'skunk hollow,' where people lived in tents." The destitute hobos who shared these quarters, and gathered outside the Hormel plant every morning looking for work, were an ever-present reminder to workers of their fate if they lost their jobs.[7]

The social and economic divisions in Austin clearly emerged in politics. Local businessmen and professionals (along with the Hormel family) were solidly Republican, whereas workers backed Minnesota's unique Farmer-Labor Party at the state level and voted Democratic in national elections. Just before the 1932 elections, Jay Hormel went to each department of the plant, shut down the machinery, and warned his employees, "If you don't vote for Hoover for President and Brown for Governor, you're not going to have a job here." John Winkels, a founder of the IUAW eight months later, recalled that Hormel workers were outraged. Ignoring their employer's advice, more than two-thirds of the Third Ward voters backed Roosevelt and victorious FLP governor Floyd B. Olson in the fall election.[8]

Hormel employees' concerns as workers and as second-class residents of Austin shaped their aspirations and activities during the 1930s. Casper Winkels, who worked at Hormel from 1923 to 1971, expressed in retrospect the complex link between packinghouse workers' desires for better living standards and higher social status. "They wanted more than just a living," recalled Winkels, "I think that's the big reason for organizing the union, to get our wages up so we could enjoy some of the better things in life." Material objectives were inextricably tied to increasing workers' power on the job through union recognition and strict seniority. "If you ain't got seniority, if the boss doesn't like me, he gives me the dirtiest job in the plant," Winkels explained. "That's one of the first things we wanted to get rid of when we organized our union." On a more intangible level, Winkels expressed the desire of Austin's workers to share equally in the abundance of American society and for men to serve as family breadwinners. "Why shouldn't a working man have that right just as well as anybody else?" Winkels asked rhetorically. In the 1930s the militant minority would be able to harness these elemental desires to the program of industrial unionism.[9]

Organizing the Union at Hormel

The "ray of hope" signaled by the electoral victories of 1932, recalled one IUAW founder, encouraged union advocates to "stick their neck out." As news of the passage of the National Industrial Recovery Act and the early industrial confrontations reached Austin, subterranean "whispers and rumblings" spread through the plant. The most extensive conversations took place among the hog-kill workers. Their earnest daily discussions would have decisive importance on the success of a union.[10]

An informal group of hog-kill workers, with close ties to the town's working-class community, emerged as the core of Austin's militant minority. Their central leader, Joe Ollman, reflected the fusion of local traditions and radical politics. Ollman's father had worked in Chicago packinghouses before moving to Austin in the 1910s and opening a grocery store in the Third Ward. Joe started working at Hormel in 1916 and quickly progressed to the most skilled job in the hog kill: splitting the pig's backbone with a heavy cleaver. He was a member of the Amalgamated Meat Cutters in the late teens and joined the small Trotskyist Communist League of America in the early 1930s. In 1933 Ollman's circle included several other left-wing workers of Austin stock who would play a leadership role in the union, including Ray Hubbard, John Winkels, Ardell Nemitz, and Frank Schultz.[11]

Working adjacent to the hog kill, and occasionally joining the lunch-time conversations, was Frank Ellis, foreman of the hog-casings department and a long-time member of the IWW. Before arriving in Austin, Ellis had lived the life of a "boomer butcher," a migratory packinghouse worker able to secure employment in a half-dozen midwestern plants because of his skill. The crippling of his father in a packinghouse accident and Ellis's experiences in several strikes left him with a deep hatred of the packing companies. Hired by Jay Hormel in 1929, Ellis used his position to hire other boomer butchers who were pro-union or perhaps even IWW members. Ellis had contributed to the "whispers and rumblings" in the plant by conducting his own campaign among Hormel workers.[12]

As the IUAW organized over the summer, other left-wing workers assumed central leadership roles. Two Communists who worked in the beef kill, Eddie Folan and Matt Kovacic, brought their key department behind the union cause. Trotskyist Joe Voorhees, a former Duluth school teacher who worked on the loading dock, later became a leader. Svend Godfredson, a Socialist Party member from Chicago, found work at Hormel in the summer of 1933 and became one of the IUAW's tireless stewards. In 1936 he placed its new newspaper on a sound foundation.[13]

Other pro-union workers had received a more conservative training from craft unions. IUAW official Charles Oots, Sr., was a long-time leader of the Coopers Union, and Clarence "Kelly" Running, who oversaw Hormel's electrical work, was an active member of the International Brotherhood of Electrical Workers. Other Hormel employees may well have been influenced by the members of various railroad brotherhoods who lived in the Third Ward.[14]

Many older Hormel production workers also had been members of an Amalgamated Meat Cutters local during World War I. This experience left at best a mixed legacy. Its president, Clarence A. Nockleby, accepted a job in the Hormel front office in 1921, and the local dissolved without consulting its members or returning their money. Nockleby went on to became a company vice president and head of the corporate packing division. The Amalgamated's treachery soured some workers on national labor unions altogether, and Hormel employees who favored unionization showed little inclination to join the Meat Cutters.[15]

While male Hormel employees probably shared Casper Winkle's aspirations for a family wage, the presence of three hundred women in the plant, many of whom were wives, sisters, daughters, and relatives of male workers, encouraged sympathy with women's grievances and support for their right to equal employment. Even though many women supported families, their base pay was 5 cents an hour less than men's. Foremen shifted women into previously male jobs to take advantage of the wage differential and, exploiting their power, "would play around with some of the women . . . trying to get smart with them." The most visible female activist, Helen McDermott, addressed the mass rallies in the summer of 1933 and was a central union leader for the rest of her career at Hormel. Another important leader, Marie Casey, served as a steward in the dry sausage department and sat on the editorial board of the IUAW paper, *The Unionist*. In 1933 the union demanded that "women should receive the same rate of pay as men when they do a man's job." When a small group of male workers circulated a petition in 1936 calling for the discharge of all married women, a heated union meeting of seven hundred overwhelmingly rejected it.[16]

Jay Hormel inadvertently presented union pioneers with an opportunity to break out of their small groups. In July 1933 he instituted pay-check deductions for old-age pensions, life insurance, and the Community Chest, a fund to provide food for the destitute. Supposedly voluntary, the workers actually had little choice but to participate. Hog-kill worker Frank Schultz remembered that "the boss would walk you off the job, get you against the wall, and you knew that never, ever in your life would you make any more money, or get a promotion if you didn't do it!" Workers perceived solicitation for company-supported funds not as potential benefits but as loss of income and evidence of their powerlessness.[17]

The left-led hog-kill gang initiated the revolt against the company. On July 13 a foreman pressed workers to sign authorization cards for the Community Chest drive. "One of the fellows did sign, but the others stood their ground," recalled Frank Schultz. "They told the supervisor to give the fellow back his card, and let him tear it up and to stop trying to force people to sign the cards, or they would not work. The supervisor was thunderstruck by this display of unity and gave the fellow his card back." The successful ten-minute stoppage was an inspiration to restless Hormel workers. "The word spread like wildfire," recalled Schultz, "and was whispered from one end of the plant to another in an amazingly short time." Hundreds responded to a call by the hog-kill workers to come to a meeting in Sutton Park (in the heart of the Third Ward) to discuss formation of a union. Exhortations by Ellis, Ollman, and Helen McDermott persuaded six hundred workers to join the recently charted IUAW. Rallies over the next two weeks brought membership to 2,500. Reflecting the influence of Ellis, the union emulated the IWW by accepting all workers regardless of their place of employment.[18]

In the small town of Austin, the mobilization of Hormel employees ignited hopes among other working people. Hundreds of employees in local service stations, dairies, laundries, hotels, and restaurants poured into the IUAW, along with barbers, painters, and truckers. A July 30 rally and picnic sponsored by the IUAW and the Farm Holiday Association (FHA) drew five thousand workers and farmers to Austin's Todd Park. Termed the largest rally in Austin's history by the local paper, the participants competed in sporting events and heard rousing speeches by Frank Ellis, FHA leader Reed Chaffee, and FLP state representative Otto Goetsch.[19]

These mobilizations reflected a complex amalgam of leftist politics, working-class anger and militancy, support for Roosevelt's New Deal, and a belief that unionization would benefit all area residents. IUAW leaders such as president O. J. Fosso emphasized the benefits of unionism to the town because of the increased purchasing power that higher wages would bring. The union catered to the popularity of the national industrial recovery program among Austin workers by placing the NRA's Blue Eagle symbol on the top of union publications and assigning its members to canvass the town to secure support for NRA consumer codes. Radical leaders such as Ellis were far more concerned with promoting class solidarity and exposing the exploitation of workers by Hormel and local businesses. In a fitting reflection of the union's composite ideology, the IUAW adapted the IWW logo—a globe superimposed with the letters "I. U. of A. W"—and placed it on its publications across from the NRA symbol.[20]

These contradictory ingredients were evident in the September Labor Day parade. To an important extent the event was an affirmation by Austin's working class of their status in an often scornful town. A procession of hundreds of IUAW members down Main Street, led by the Municipal Band, swelled to several thousand as the unionists successfully called on working-class spectators to join their ranks. At the same time, workers indicated their willingness to cooperate with local businessmen and the federal New Deal. One union placard depicted labor and capital riding a bicycle together in the direction of the NRA; the caption read, "Shorter Hours and Higher Wages." A union float with the inscription "For Future Protection for Self and Family" prominently displayed the NRA initials and its symbol, the Blue Eagle. On the union's invitation, businesses strung bunting from their stores, lined the streets with flags, and placed colorful floats bearing their names in the parade.[21]

The rally in Lafayette Park evinced a similar tension. Mayor Hans Marcuson, who sold automobiles, greeted the marchers and praised them for organizing in "an orderly way." The keynote speaker, the Rev. Harry Poll, emphasized that the Golden Rule gave labor the right to organize but warned, alluding to the known differences among IUAW officials, "The moment you call in radical leaders, you will not be able to accomplish anything. In your organization you have conservative leaders and you should keep them that way." Frank Ellis had the final word, however, and vociferously accused Hormel of not complying with the NRA wage guidelines.[22]

As the conciliatory comments by Marcuson and Poll attest, the local elite hoped that by encouraging the moderate wing of the union, working-class insurgency could be steered away from challenges to their authority. The popularity of the IUAW among Austin's working class also encouraged conciliatory strategies by Hormel and mitigated against a sharp, repressive response. Jay Hormel did not try to hinder the union drive by dismissing known organizers as Chicago-based packing companies were doing at the time. He even discussed grievances with union representatives, and corrected the small problems they identified.[23]

The IUAW's demand that it receive a formal role in the determination of wages and working conditions through union recognition and a seniority system, however, precipitated a showdown with the company. Workers grew impatient as Jay Hormel responded to the union's demands with evasive promises to "consider" the request; on the evening of September 22 the IUAW voted to go on strike the next morning to force the company's hand. When Hormel learned of the union's plans, he quickly telephoned local politicians, businessmen, and IUAW officials and summoned them to a conference in the Hormel offices adjacent to the plant.[24]

The extraordinary all-night, face-to-face debate illuminated both Hormel's strategy and the cohesiveness of the working-class challenge to his power. He tried to curry favor with the conservative wing of the IUAW by bitterly attacking Frank Ellis as "a professional agitator, an inciter to riot, untruthful and a red" and praising O. J. Fosso as a "college graduate" who was "an intelligent, fair and upright fellow." Despite the real differences between the two union leaders, the IUAW delegation leapt to Ellis's defense and forced Hormel to discuss the issues that had produced the meeting in the first place. As the plant owner and union representatives argued past dawn on the twenty-third, workers slowly gathered around the meeting room to see if they should report for work. At 7 A.M., "The whistle that should have sounded at this time was silent. Out in the yards men and women by the hundreds were standing." At this point Jay Hormel conceded and signed an agreement recognizing the union and the seniority system. In return, the elated IUAW delegation accepted the principle of arbitration of disputes and directed union members to report for work.[25]

As unions discovered so often in the 1930s, recognition did not necessarily result in actual collective bargaining. Five weeks later, when the IUAW again approached Hormel and asked that their wage requests be submitted to arbitration as provided for in the September agreement, the plant owner refused. "He suggested that we go out and organize the other packing plants first, and then come back and he might consider our request," Frank Ellis recalled. "We told Mr. Hormel that we would organize the other plants, but we needed more money now; higher wages was our problem and competition was his." Angry with the company's refusal to honor its promise, a

November 10 IUAW meeting voted to strike at a future but undetermined date. Immediately after the vote, hundreds of impatient workers marched over to the plant. "We told the sheep kill gang to clean the sheep," participant John Winkels recalled, "and then get the hell out of there because the strike was on." From a makeshift speakers' stand at the main plant gate, Frank Ellis told the workers, "Permit supervisors to take care of the sheep. . . . Give them until tomorrow morning and then let no one in." Workers followed Ellis's advice and took control of the plant in the morning.[26]

The strike stunned Jay Hormel and Austin's elite. They pleaded for Governor Olson to use the National Guard to evict the workers; to their dismay, the FLP governor instead came to Austin himself to mediate. Unable to open his blockaded plant, Jay Hormel admitted defeat. He brought the strike to an end by accepting binding arbitration of the wage dispute by the Minnesota Industrial Commission. The commission granted a 10 percent wage increase to the Hormel workers a month later, less than hoped for but, as Ellis reflected, "Pennies looked big in those days, plus the fact that we got a million dollars of publicity which proved very valuable, not only to our Independent Union of All Workers, but to the entire labor movement."[27]

The Era of the Independent Union of All Workers

Between 1933 and 1937 the one big union umbrella of the IUAW effectively blended the energies of both Hormel's radicals and more locally oriented workers into a dynamic labor organization. Austin's packinghouse workers actively supported a wide range of union initiatives in Austin and nearby towns so that their working-class relatives, friends, and neighbors could also partake of the benefits of collective bargaining. Under the prodding of leftists who contended that the IUAW's gains would be transitory unless it spread unionism to other packinghouses, Hormel workers organized a network of affiliated unions and supporters in the midwestern meatpacking industry. The leftists' strategy reflected their larger agenda: to spark the resurgence of a militant working-class movement in America. Although Hormel workers probably did not fully share this vision, a majority repeatedly demonstrated through their actions that they agreed with its economic logic and the benefits of national industrial unionism. The "Austin orbit" created by the IUAW mirrored similar regional "general unions" centered in urban areas as diverse as Minneapolis, Toledo, and Woonsocket that fused the impetuous mobilization of industrial workers in the mid-1930s with the strategic program of radical union militants.[28]

The union victory of 1933 had a profound effect on Austin itself by altering the balance of power between the town's traditional elite and its working class. "From that time," Svend Godfredson later wrote, "until 1940 there raged near civil war in Austin." Jay Hormel's acquiescence to the IUAW created a foundation of thousands of unionized workers to support other organizing efforts. The *Austin Daily Herald* bitterly complained that the IUAW would "slap down a so-called 'contract'" and threaten to "bring over the Packing House union" to enforce a boycott if firms would not sign a closed shop union agreement. Jay Hormel, for his part, ensconced on a lavish 170-acre estate outside town limits, had little interest in the labor relations problems of Austin's other businesses. As long as his factory operated with sufficient efficiency that he could compete with other packing companies in the national market, Jay Hormel showed little interest in local class conflict. Probably to the frustration of local businessmen, there is no indication that he assisted anti-union alliances of Austin merchants.[29]

The organizing activities of the IUAW in Austin were universally supported among the union's membership, but its forays to nearby towns and packinghouses were more controversial and provoked growing friction between O. J. Fosso and leftist union leaders. Although not necessarily opposed to organizing outside of Austin, Fosso and his supporters did not agree with the leftists' plan to use the IUAW's base in the Hormel plant to launch a national union in the meatpacking industry. As they believed developing a good relationship with Jay Hormel was the key to better conditions in Austin's packinghouse, efforts to build a national labor organization were unnecessary and could hinder the development of cooperative labor-management relations in their town. Although Fosso's extreme position was supported by only a small minority in the IUAW, his suspicions of the benefits of national labor organizations doubtless struck a chord among many packinghouse workers.

The IUAW began to create its orbit even before securing recognition from Jay Hormel. Just two weeks after the initial Sutton Park meeting, the union assigned Frank Ellis and Harold Harlan to respond to many requests for assistance. Over the next year the IUAW established contact with and provided assistance to hundreds of workers seeking to organize their workplace. "We went down there to rank-and-file meetings and told them how we got this and how we done that," recalled John Winkels. "We helped on the picket line." Within three months, the IUAW made two major breakthroughs in nearby Albert Lee, just twenty miles east of Austin. Strikes at the Potter Foundry, employing twenty-one workers, and the much larger American Gas Machine Company plant with more than five hundred employees, secured informal union recognition and wage increases. The IUAW also recruited hundreds of members at the Wilson packinghouse in Albert Lee but was unable to compel the company—with unorganized plants in several other cities—to negotiate. After these initial victories, IUAW members ranged widely across the Upper Midwest, assisting packinghouse workers in Wisconsin, Iowa, Minnesota, and North Dakota.[30]

The momentum of its early victories soon slowed. AFL unionists, heckling and throwing beer bottles, disrupted IUAW meetings in Waterloo, Iowa, and Winona, Minnesota. In 1934 a convention of the Iowa chapter of the Amalgamated Meat Cutters refused to admit an IUAW delegation and recommended expulsion of IUAW members from Amalgamated locals. In Faribault, forty miles north of Austin, an IUAW-led strike in the summer of 1934 at a Wilson poultry plant turned into a prolonged confrontation when the company decided to close the facility rather than negotiate with the union. Sympathy strikes by Wilson packinghouse workers and large rallies of workers and farmers maintained the strikers' spirits but were unable to extract any concessions from the company. In 1935 the IUAW organization at the Waterloo Rath plant collapsed after a premature strike drew support from only a small minority of the workforce. The Albert Lee IUAW, the strongest unit outside Austin, was shaken by a riot at the Potter foundry that resulted in jail sentences and fines for eight union leaders.[31]

These setbacks precipitated a showdown between Fosso's forces and the leftist block led by Ellis, Voorhees, and the hog-kill workers. Fosso accused the radicals of depleting the union treasury to finance a series of unsuccessful strikes and ineffectual organizing drives. "What is the business of the Union?" Fosso asked in a handbill distributed to IUAW members. "Is it to keep in office those whose chief stock in trade is to urge Communism, revolution and strike? Or is it to get for workers that which they want by sensible methods of conference, using the strike weapon only as a last resort?" He proposed reconstituting the IUAW as a decentralized federation and suspending all organizing outside Austin.[32]

Fosso's plan to end the IUAW's aggressive organizing initiatives was applauded by the *Austin Daily Herald,* but a strong majority of union members rejected his arguments. Leftists branded Fosso a "reactionary and a conservative" and effectively pointed out that he was an insurance agent not an industrial worker. In a referendum on the union's direction, the Austin, Albert Lee, and Faribault IUAW units voted to demand Fosso's resignation. The Central Executive Council expelled him in April when he refused to resign. In July the IUAW membership completed the transformation of the union leadership by electing Joe Voorhees to Fosso's old position as IUAW president.[33]

The repudiation of Fosso reflected an important shift in the IUAW. The union's leftist leaders had convinced a majority of packinghouse workers that it was not enough to simply organize their plant and develop a good relationship with Jay Hormel. Increasing their standard of living and securing "some of the better things in life" rested on the capacity of packinghouse workers to unionize their industry. Radicals, always influential in the IUAW, now assumed central leadership positions. In addition to Voorhees in its top post, the new IUAW regional executive council included Hormel hog-kill militants Joe Ollman, Ray Hubbard, and Ardell Nemitz; Communist Jack "Red" Carlson from St. Paul; and two southern Minnesota workers associated with the Trotskyists, Steve Benjamin from Faribault and Ray Hemenway of Albert Lee. The IUAW's Hormel Packinghouse Unit elected Joe Ollman as its president in August 1935 and placed Ray Hubbard and John Winkels on the executive board. Moderate "straight trade unionists," such as Ernie Jacobs, Claude Moore, and T. B. Rockne, remained in powerful union posts but rejected Fosso's local orientation and supported the IUAW's regional organizing initiatives.[34]

The first task of the new leadership was to solidify its base after the destructive infighting with Fosso. IUAW membership outside Austin had been decimated in 1934, and the union even had lost members in the Hormel plant. As in other industrial centers, the working-class insurgency of 1933 and 1934 had subsided, and the IUAW faced the same difficulties as other relatively isolated independent unions.[35] Firmly ensconced in the union leadership, the leftists now had the responsibility of devising new strategies for the IUAW so it would survive.

Inside the Hormel plant, the IUAW sought to enforce 100 percent union membership and use that strength to exercise power over shop-floor relations. Women workers provided the breakthrough that secured a union shop. In January 1936 supervisors provoked the predominantly female sausage department by promoting two male non-union workers to "assistant foremen" and claiming they were ineligible for union membership. At a department meeting, workers decided to "sit down at ten o'clock if nothing happened," recalled chief steward Svend Godfredson. When negotiations faltered the next morning, the workers dramatically "stuck their knives in the table and quit working and sat down." They resumed work after supervisors removed the non-union employees. When the assistant foremen returned to work, they wore union buttons. To avoid any repetition of the incident and further disruptions of plant operations, Jay Hormel agreed to make union membership mandatory for all workers.[36]

Enforcing union power at the shop-floor level is best documented in the hog kill, the core of the Hormel union. In 1933 and 1934 several stoppages organized by steward Ray Hubbard had eliminated non-union workers from the department. In the spring of 1937 Hubbard organized a strike to end management's annoying practice of paying the skilled stickers, headers, and splitters (jobs filled by the radical leaders of the department) unskilled pay rather than the higher level to which they were entitled. The two-day stoppage forced supervisors to meet with union representatives and accede to their demands.[37]

The IUAW systematically extended its presence and influence in the town of Austin as well. Leftists started a weekly paper—aptly titled *The Unionist*—in 1935 to counter the pronouncements of Austin's elite. "It was the first time the revered and sanctimonious judgement of the *Austin Herald* and the Main Street element had been challenged," Schultz later wrote. "To that group, the advent of *The Unionist* was a revolution in itself." Edited by Svend Godfredson and distributed free to IUAW members, the paper served as an influential link with thousands of workers and was the union's voice on problems at work and in the town. Much to their displeasure, Austin businessmen found anti-union deeds prominently criticized, along with the actions of overly uncompromising Hormel supervisors.[38]

An expanded array of union-sponsored cultural activities made the IUAW a center of working-class recreation. IUAW Labor Day celebrations drew thousands to participate in colorful parades, compete in sporting events, and hear speeches by FLP officials, leading radicals, and labor activists. Biweekly dances at the IUAW hall in downtown Austin drew workers and their families to hear Red Walsh's Swing Band, Ray Stolzenberg's Old and New Time Orchestra, and other popular barnstorming groups. Union-organized classes in public speaking and parliamentary procedure facilitated rank-and-file union participation. The Women's Auxiliary, cochaired by Mrs. Joe Ollman, organized talent contests and card parties at the union hall and sponsored several plays performed at the town's high school auditorium.[39]

The IUAW's cultural initiatives in Austin accompanied a renewed organizing effort in local small businesses. In 1936 the union merged several small, nonpacking units into a unified Uptown Workers branch of the IUAW. Under Voorhees's leadership, several strikes in retail and service firms developed into bitter confrontations between their owners and the IUAW. Because there were rarely more than five workers in each business, the financial and moral support Hormel employees provided made "Uptown" workers feel that "they were always surrounded by a sea of supporters." In short order the IUAW won wage increases and improved conditions for barbers, truckers, waitresses, laundry workers, garage mechanics, and retail clerks. Unionism in Austin's small establishments remained insecure, however, because the IUAW was unable to sign closed-shop agreements with all firms in a particular line of business.[40]

As the IUAW rebuilt in Austin, the leftist leaders returned to the problem of expanding its orbit in meatpacking. In addition to its Albert Lee organization, the IUAW had members in a half-dozen packinghouses in Iowa, North Dakota, and Minnesota in 1935. In early 1936 Joe Ollman departed for a three-week swing through Wisconsin, Illinois, Iowa, Kansas, and South Dakota to assess sentiment for organization and establish new contacts with local union activists. Ollman particularly impressed a group of Morrell employees in Ottumwa, Iowa, and a year later they asked the IUAW for assistance. Ollman and other IUAW leaders made the long trip to southern Iowa and spent several weeks providing advice, encouragement, organizing materials, and an IUAW charter. By April 1937 the Ottumwa IUAW local had five hundred members.[41]

In a similar manner, a group of Tobin packinghouse workers in the central Iowa town of Fort Dodge contacted Austin for assistance in late 1936. Several former Hormel employees worked at Tobin, and the leading union activist, Robert H. Schultz, had collaborated in 1933 with IUAW members in an unsuccessful organizing effort at the Madison, Wisconsin, Oscar Mayer plant. Again serving as Austin's emissary, Joe Ollman provided literature and guidance and convinced the Tobin workers to affiliate with the IUAW. During a difficult strike, Tobin workers "wrote a letter to Austin, Minnesota and told them the situation and they sent a check of $250," Schultz remembered emotionally fifty years later, "and that really, really helped."[42]

At the same time as the IUAW expanded its orbit in the Upper Midwest, its leaders were establishing contacts with other independent packing unions and the recently formed CIO. The ineffective strikes of 1934 and 1935 convinced IUAW leaders that their union did not have enough strength on its own to organize the meatpacking industry. Consequently, they worked assiduously to unify the scattered nuclei of packinghouse unionists into a coalition that could establish links with the emerging organizations in the auto, rubber, and electrical industries. In conjunction with the Cedar Rapids-based Midwest Union of All Packinghouse Workers, Voorhees convened a Mason City, Iowa, packinghouse workers conference in January 1936 that drew sixty delegates from seven cities in Minnesota and Iowa. They formed the Committee for Industrial Organization in the Packing Industry and commenced pressuring the CIO to charter meatpacking locals and launch a national organizing campaign in the industry. Much to their chagrin, however, the CIO preferred to court the Amalgamated Meat Cutters in the hope of enticing it out of the AFL. For its part, the Amalgamated attacked the IUAW as "a group of secessionists headed by a few soldiers of fortune" and refused to cooperate with the Austin-Cedar Rapids coalition.[43]

The success of the IUAW's activities in neighboring Albert Lee ironically precipitated the organization's entry into the CIO. The strong IUAW organization included approximately 1,200 members concentrated at the American Gas Machine Company and the Wilson packinghouse, and also foundry workers, truck drivers, and Woolworth's clerks. In March 1937 a strike at the America Gas plant turned violent when sheriff's deputies raided the IUAW headquarters. Deputies fired rounds of tear gas into the small building and arrested fifty-three union members, including Voorhees and the main Albert Lee IUAW leaders. When word of the conflict reached Austin that afternoon, several hundred Hormel workers "got water pipes and gas pipes," John Winkels later recalled, and "a whole caravan went over there." IUAW members attacked the American Gas plant, shattering its windows, destroying stoves and office equipment, and setting a police car on fire. Then the crowd of several hundred "went over to the jail with crowbars" and demanded the release of the detained union members. Some demonstrators pushed through a police line and pressed terrified deputies against the jail door while others tried to break through the prison's exterior wall.[44]

At this critical juncture, FLP Governor Elmer Benson dramatically strode into the jail after racing down from the Twin Cities. He defused the situation by ordering the sheriff to release union members. "The tear gas attack on the union headquarters had no justification whatsoever," he explained to reporters, "and constituted a high-handed assault on the meeting place of workers." Demoralized, the company quickly agreed to reemploy all the workers without discrimination and to formally recognize the union as the sole collective bargaining agent—if it joined a national labor organization. The American Gas unit of the IUAW quickly accepted the deal and affiliated with the CIO.[45]

The April 1937 Albert Lee settlement, although a resounding union victory, sharply posed the question of the future of the IUAW. In all likelihood, promising signals from the CIO persuaded IUAW leaders to accede to the vote of American Gas workers. In late 1936 CIO officials reopened negotiations with the IUAW-Cedar Rapids network of packinghouse unionists. By April, midwestern packinghouse unionists had received strong hints that the CIO soon would enter the meatpacking industry. This time, the hopes of IUAW leaders would be realized. When the Amalgamated Meat Cutters voted on May 10 to remain in the AFL, the CIO immediately began chartering local industrial unions (LIUs) in meatpacking.[46]

Joining the CIO posed risks for Austin unionists because it necessitated refashioning their bonds of solidarity with other workers. This entailed deemphasizing connections rooted in proximity and shared racial and ethnic backgrounds to a more impersonal, industry-based alliance with men and women who were sociologically very different. Historian Peter Rachleff's criticism of the IUAW's decision to dissolve into the CIO emphasizes this element—the way community-based unionism suffered at the expense of industrial unionism. In doing so he neglects how the IUAW's regional focus reflected not only notions of working-class solidarity, but also parochial resistance to associating with workers of different race or ethnicity and faith that Hormel's workers and its owner could reach an accommodation on their own. He also understates the way alliances among workers of different occupations in Austin persisted despite the restructuring of union jurisdictions.[47]

The alliance of leftists and "straight trade unionists" led the IUAW into the CIO because it seemed the best way that Austin workers could satisfy their aspirations for "the better things in life" and that the American working class, as a whole, could advance its political and economic agenda. The tensions between locally oriented workers and the cosmopolitan militant minority are evident in the fragmentary records of the union debate over affiliation. The IUAW's leftists argued that the gains at Hormel would be transitory unless the entire industry was organized and only the CIO possessed sufficient clout to bring unionism to the nation's packinghouses. "To stand still is to die," warned Svend Godfredson in *The Unionist*. "To die is to go backwards. Therefore, we must affiliate." Leftists astutely attached the aspirations of Austin's workers for security and upward mobility to the necessity for a class-based alliance with other packinghouse employees. "Every time that the packing-house workers have asked for an increase in pay, the boss has given the same story. 'I can't pay it unless my competitors do,'" Carl Nilson, a Trotskyist, pointed out in a leaflet distributed to Hormel workers. Organizing the entire industry "will mean more pork chops and pie, better clothes and new automobiles—an improved standard of living for everyone concerned," he concluded. In successive April and May votes all IUAW locals affiliated with the CIO. The Hormel tally was very close—396 to 326. The sizable no vote indicated that many workers still remained skeptical that it was necessary to affiliate with a national labor organization. It would take the accomplishments of the next five years to integrate the independent Austin local, now Local 9 of the PWOC, into the emerging industrial union in meatpacking.[48]

Finishing the Job:
The Hormel Workers in the CIO

Once inside the CIO, Hormel workers systematically completed the unionization of workers within the IUAW's old orbit. Austin organizers assisted PWOC campaigns in South St. Paul and helped the former Albert Lee IUAW local win an NLRB certification election at the Wilson packinghouse in 1940. In Waterloo, Joe Ollman and other organizers from Austin recruited former IUAW members to a PWOC local and arranged for additional assistance from the old IUAW locals in Ottumwa and Fort Dodge. One observer noted that despite formal CIO control of the Waterloo campaign, "It was really the IUAW people." The PWOC easily won an NLRB certification election at Rath in November 1942.[49]

Despite the IUAW's demise, Austin's workers retained their one big union approach. Hormel workers rendered indispensable assistance to a renewed effort to make Austin a 100 percent union town. The IUAW's Uptown Workers branch became CIO Local Industrial Union No. 478, and the former IUAW units now in separate international unions coordinated their activities through a city central labor body. Under the dynamic leadership of business agent and former clerk Eva Sauers, Local 478 spearheaded an organizing drive that swept Austin's retail establishments between 1938 and 1943. As in the IUAW era, packinghouse workers provided essential support for other workers by not patronizing establishments engaged in a labor dispute. Local 9 rigorously enforced boycotts by stationing pickets at unfair establishments, monitoring their patrons, and levying fines against disobedient union members. A national chain might survive the loss in sales due to a union boycott, but no local merchant could maintain a business without packinghouse workers as clients. By 1943 Local 478 had organized the town's dairies, liquor stores, food markets, and many other small businesses. United Auto Workers Local 867 (formerly the IUAW's automotive and garage unit) similarly unionized the town's car dealers and repair shops.[50]

The expansion of union power ineluctably affected town politics. Austin's working class seized the opportunity to preempt traditional elite domination of municipal offices and establish their claim as social equals of the professional and managerial class. Residential separation rebounded to the advantage of workers; with a city-high voter turnout of 60 percent in the mid-1930s, the Third Ward provided a solid base for labor politics. By the late 1930s the working-class vote in the First and Second wards augmented Third Ward totals sufficiently to produce citywide majorities for union candidates.[51]

The nonpartisan municipal election races reflected competition between business and working-class political parties. Although local businessmen universally backed Republicans, all IUAW factions supported the FLP as the party of the Minnesota working class. Democratic candidates for state offices usually received only a few dozen votes in Austin's Third Ward (Table 6). The class-conscious political actions of Austin workers nonetheless remained within the framework of New Deal politics as strong allegiance with the FLP coexisted with consistent support for President Roosevelt. When John L. Lewis endorsed Republican Wendell Willkie on the eve of the 1940 election, Local 9 unionists listening to the broadcast were stunned. Helen McDermott, after the initial shock had passed, took a picture of Lewis off the wall of the union hall and threw it out the window.[52]

The IUAW first entered Austin politics soon after winning recognition at the Hormel plant. Initial gains were limited to election of T. B. Rockne, the first IUAW treasurer, as one of two Third Ward alderman in 1934. In 1938 the union made a major electoral breakthrough. Much to the *Austin Daily Herald*'s displeasure, the Municipal Election Volunteer Committee of Local 9 effectively mobilized workers to vote for a union-endorsed slate. In a heavy turnout, packinghouse union leader Claude Moore took the alderman-at-large position, elected citywide, away from long-time incumbent Walter Tollefson, a Hormel salesmen. Four years later, packinghouse worker T. B. Rockne won a close race for mayor. A decade after Jay Hormel tried to dictate the voting behavior of his employees, packinghouse workers held the top positions in the town's government.[53]

Table 6. Minnesota Gubernatorial Elections, 1934–40

Year	Candidate	Total	1st and 2d Wards	3d Ward
1934	Olson (FLP)	2,947	1,675	1,272
	Nelson (RP)	2,603	2,265	338
	Regan (DP)	486	394	92
1936	Benson (FLP and DP)[a]	3,689	2,206	1,483
	Nelson (RP)	2,758	2,392	366
1938	Benson (FLP)	2,687	1,525	1,162
	Stassen (RP)	3,211	2,753	458
	Gallagher (DP)	272	215	57
1940	Peterson (FLP)	3,920	2,344	1,576
	Stassen (RP)	3,399	2,924	475
	Murphy (DP)	609	448	161

a. Democrats endorsed Benson in the 1936 state election.

Sources: *Austin Daily Herald*, Nov. 8, 1934, Nov. 5, 1936; Mike Holm, *The Legislative Reference Manual of the State of Minnesota, 1937* (Minneapolis, 1937), 302–3; Mike Holm, *The Legislative Reference Manual of the State of Minnesota, 1939* (Minneapolis, 1939), 310; Mike Holm, *The Legislative Reference Manual of the State of Minnesota, 1941* (Minneapolis, 1941), 322.

The triumphs of the Hormel union, however, were bittersweet for the radicals who had played such an important sparkplug role. By the early 1940s most of the union's original leftist leaders no longer lived in Austin. Some had moved to important positions in the PWOC: Frank Ellis directed the Minnesota region, Joe Ollman was part of the union's organizing staff, and Svend Godfredson edited the PWOC's weekly paper, the *Packinghouse Worker.* Joe Voorhees lost his job for allegedly violating the terms of his leave of absence from Hormel, and the company fired Ray Hubbard in 1940 for leading yet another job action. Arbitrators upheld the company's dismissals; without work, both men left town.[54]

The dispersal of the IUAW's radical core was not simply coincidence. In 1940 a long-term labor contract that provided for a new system of wage payment, the guaranteed annual wage, established a firm "rule of law" in the Hormel plant. In place of pay that varied according to the number of hours worked, Hormel employees received regular weekly checks for ½2 of their projected annual earnings. Departments "contracted" to produce a certain volume of work in a year and received bonus checks if they exceeded their quota. Alternately, workers who completed their required output in fewer than eight hours could go home early.[55]

"The company laid no claim to altruism in setting up the plan," its official historian readily admitted. Jay Hormel openly stated his desire to use the GAW to reduce labor turnover and increase productivity. The company president, with the permission of the union, gradually implemented the GAW system in the mid-1930s by letting each department vote individually whether to adopt it. By 1938, 80 to 90 percent of Hormel's workers were on the guaranteed annual wage. Hormel's piecemeal strategy allowed him to circumvent the opposition of leftist union officials who generally opposed the GAW. Frank Ellis attacked it as a form of speedup that would increase workloads. "Mr. Hormel says this plan will make it possible to retain workers about to be laid off," Ellis told the Minnesota Industrial Commission following the 1933 strike. Instead, "it would make a speed-up of work and cause more men to be laid off."[56]

Steady increases in wages and employment levels discredited Ellis's warnings. The workforce grew from 2,300 at the time of the 1933 strike to 3,000 in 1940. Hormel wages consistently stayed above the industry average, and the work week remained shorter than in other packinghouses (Table 7). When a pig shortage curtailed production in 1935, Hormel did not cut the hog-kill gang, and workers received their full annual pay, even though there was not enough work to keep them busy. In some departments, productivity soared; in 1936 the dry sausage division completed its annual quota in just thirty-nine weeks.[57]

Table 7. Weekly Wages and Hours, Hormel versus Industry Average

Year	Wages		Hours	
	Average	Hormel	Average	Hormel
1936	$25.21	$25.34	41.9	37
1937	27.44	29.23	39.4	35.6

Source: "The Name Is HOR-mel," *Fortune,* Oct. 1937, 138.

Although Ellis's exact prediction proved inaccurate, his concern was legitimate. By closely linking workers' incomes with the productivity and competitiveness of the company, the guaranteed annual wage sapped the union's radicalism and militancy. Following the 1940 agreement, job actions virtually disappeared, and arbitration became the central concern of union leaders. In 1941, Local 9 hired an assistant business agent to handle the numerous arbitration cases. Significantly, the union passed over Ray Hubbard (recently fired for leading a stoppage) for the post and instead hired Ray Zerby, a relatively conservative union official. In 1943, Local 9 accepted Hormel's offer to train three employees in time-study techniques. One union official observed that the union eventually "did more to run that operation than anyone in supervision."[58]

Workers overwhelmingly supported the guaranteed annual wage because it satisfied many of the grievances that had produced the 1933 rebellion. It ended the arbitrary rule of the foremen and allowed workers to increase their earnings and regulate the pace of production within the framework of rising company profitability. Marie Casey remembered how her department could hold Christmas parties and other special events during working hours by completing their quota early. Ellis may have considered this a form of speedup, but to Casey it was a treasured improvement over the shop-floor regime of the pre-union era. As once-feared layoffs became a memory, stable employment and reliable paychecks enabled packinghouse workers to use credit purchasing for the first time and move out of their shacks and into modern houses. Workers reveled in the contributions they were able to make to Austin because of the compromise in the Hormel plant. "What we didn't do for this town," Casper Winkels proudly boasted. Because of the income the workers spent in local businesses, "This town just boomed." Living in better homes, enjoying a higher standard of living, and represented by packinghouse workers in local government, Casper Winkels and his co-workers were finally in a position to enjoy "some of the better things in life."[59]

An intrinsic component of this accommodation with the Hormel Company remained a strong awareness of class interests that kept Austin tied to the UPWA and its progressive wing. Despite the GAW's success, the union cadre remembered that the company had not submitted to collective bargaining without a struggle. "We worked for everything we got through the union," Marie Casey reminded interviewers in 1985. Jay Hormel may have been a "wonderful guy," she admitted, but "he still was company management. You never want to forget that." The leftist lesson that the fate of Austin workers was tied to other packinghouse workers endured as an indelible part of Local 9's tradition. With their personal fate bound up with the progress of unionism in the national industry, Austin's workers remained staunch supporters of the PWOC and played a central role in the formation of the UPWA in 1943. Although now in an ancillary rather than vanguard role, the Austin Hormel workers made an essential contribution to the development of industrial unionism in meatpacking.

3

"They Just Had to Deal with the Union": Organizing in the Chicago Stockyards

The fact that the company had to deal with the union was a religion of the workers. And the impetus was such, and the movement was such that in fact, IN FACT, in the plants, they just had to deal with the union, through the stewards who wore the stewards' buttons, the committees of the workers, they just had to do it if they were going to function. So actually, the formal recognition when it finally came down was really a reflection of the fact that was something that was battled through in the plants by the workers.

—Herb March, Chicago union founder

On Sunday, July 16, 1939, sixteen thousand workers from Chicago's mass-production industries jammed the Chicago Coliseum to support the organizing drive in the Chicago stockyards and pressure Armour and Company to sign a national contract. The racially integrated crowd sang union songs and gave a "pandemonious reception" to featured speakers John L. Lewis and Chicago Bishop Bernard J. Sheil as well as union leaders such as the black assistant national director of the PWOC, Henry (Hank) Johnson. Lewis berated the packing companies for maintaining "industrial serfdom" in their plants and promised that "the CIO will stand behind the PWOC in their efforts to bargain collectively." Although Lewis's bellicose statements were to be expected, the stunning appearance of Sheil, the second-ranking member of Chicago's Archdiocese, magnified the rally's impact. Sheil emphatically supported the CIO's efforts in the stockyards by quoting at length from Pope Pius XI's "Quadragesimo Anno" encyclical that endorsed "working men's associations." Drawing on the language of the Declaration of Independence, Sheil declared that a wage that did not provide for sufficient food, clothing, and shelter was "an unjust invasion of fundamental, natural rights." Herb March, a packinghouse union organizer and an acknowledged Communist, added to the meeting's drama by drawing audible murmurs and cheers when he entered the hall, his arm in a sling because of a gunshot wound sustained two days earlier.[1]

The rally, held at the height of the organizing campaign at Chicago's Armour plant, reflected the covalent forces that made up the union assault on company power. The presence of John L. Lewis and workers from other factories targeted by the CIO indicated how rank-and-file organizing in the packinghouses was embedded in a larger workers' movement. The respect accorded Bishop Sheil, March, and Johnson by an integrated audience reflected what was happening on the shop floor of the Armour plant. White ethnic Catholics were cooperating with committed Communists and black workers in the unionization of that facility. In an advertisement published a week after the rally and designed to counter its message, Armour asserted that a national agreement was unnecessary because it already was "continuously bargaining with the CIO" in its Chicago plant. In so doing, management admitted that, by July 1939, "they just had to deal with the union."[2]

Chicago provided the most important challenge to union advocates and, once organized, the fulcrum of working-class power in meatpacking. No union could organize the industry without winning over Chicago's twenty-five thousand packinghouse workers, the largest concentration in the nation. For all of Austin's accomplishments, the unionization of Chicago's packinghouses was the critical breakthrough for industrial unionism in meatpacking.[3]

Subduing the packing firms was a formidable task. Failed strikes in 1904 and 1921 and 1922 left a pall over subsequent organizing activities. Relations between black and white workers, and among various ethnic groups in the packinghouses, were tense because of conflicts at work and in the city of Chicago. Company welfare policies incorporated workers into representation plans and recreation and social clubs and encouraged resistance to unions by providing limited seniority and job rights to experienced employees. In the black community, the packing firms enmeshed important institutions in networks of obligation by financially subsidizing their activities. Within the plants, company harassment, discharge, and blacklisting of union sympathizers were part of the popular folklore of the stockyards, relayed to new employees unhappy with the poor wages and working conditions.

Eventual union successes in the late 1930s and early 1940s rested on unity in action by white and black packinghouse workers in a city where members of different races rarely cooperated. Organizers consistently stressed that the only way all packinghouse workers could attain a better life was by working together, regardless of differences due to ethnicity, religion, race, or sex. Union pioneers reminded blacks of their exclusion from better jobs and pointed out, "You'll never fight your way out of this until you get a union that's going to speak up for you." To whites who harbored racist sentiments toward black co-workers, the PWOC emphasized that "the boss is your enemy. The fellow worker beside you is not the enemy." As in other packing centers, inter-racial unity rested on the union's ability to satisfy the aspirations of all packinghouse workers for material advancement, job security, and power over their workplace.[4]

A carefully constructed "culture of unity" strengthened the inter-racial amity on the shop floor. The PWOC organized integrated social activities such as picnics, dances, and softball teams and desegregated many of the bars near the stockyards. To visually represent their ideology, Chicago PWOC activists adopted a logo of two hands, one white, one black, clasped in a handshake. This symbolism made a deep impression on blacks who the union tried to recruit. "When you joined this union, the first thing you see is a black hand and a white hand," Ercell Allen recalled. "We did things together, black and white."[5]

The roots of organizing during the 1930s can be traced to the actions of three distinct groups who composed Chicago's "militant minority." First, Communists seized the discontent of the early 1930s and the legal openings provided by the New Deal to establish union nuclei in several plants. Second, white ethnic workers who were former members of the World War I-era Stockyards Labor Council reached out to fellow ethnics and brought their communities behind the union. Blacklisted after a strike in 1921 and 1922, they had taken refuge in small meat plants and continued to be a part of the stockyards neighborhood. To a far greater extent than in other packing centers, unionists of the World War I era would play a significant role in the organizing effort of the 1930s. Third, a critical group of black workers joined the nascent organizations, eschewing the aloof stance toward the "white man's union" that had marked black attitudes toward labor organizations in the past. Although older blacks who ignored the picket lines during the strike of 1921 and 1922 resisted initial organizing efforts, those hired during the 1920s and early 1930s were among the first to support a union. The features of this coalition first emerged in the independent unions of 1933 and 1934, but it was the CIO's entry into meatpacking in 1937 that provided the catalyst for the successful organizing drives of the next five years.

Although leftists played a similar sparkplug role in Austin and Kansas City, only Chicago's Communists were able to build a durable organization and retain their influence well into the 1950s. Their immediate membership, and the larger circles of packinghouse workers influenced by Communist notions of class struggle and inter-racial unity, lent a distinctive character to the Chicago UPWA, which in turn would profoundly affect the international union.

The Making of a Divided Working Class in the Chicago Stockyards

When union activists surfaced in the Chicago stockyards in 1933, they had to unravel more than a decade of racial and ethnic conflict among packinghouse employees. Ethnics and blacks shared unskilled and semiskilled meatpacking jobs in an uneasy, and often tense, coexistence. Whites from native-born backgrounds or older immigrant groups dominated the skilled trades and kept themselves apart from the production workers who labored by hand or with a knife. The pattern of class formation before 1930 had created a deeply segmented workforce in the Chicago stockyards.

Most white packinghouse workers lived in the neighborhood colloquially known as "Back of the Yards," immediately south and west of the stockyards. Although investigators decried the area's poverty, its residents tenaciously built stable lives and constructed a thriving ethnic culture, usually invisible to visiting academics and journalists. Packers may have dominated work relations and established the economic limits on sustenance, but workers and their families developed vital survival strategies in the interstices of their neighborhood. The highly organized and cohesive ethnic communities would be an enormous asset to union activists of the 1930s.[6]

Several miles from Chicago's downtown, the Back of the Yards was physically separated from communities to the north, west, and east by a maze of railroad tracks and factories. The area closest to the stockyards consisted of worn, two-story rental properties that stretched monotonously for blocks. Homeowners, composing 34 percent of the area's families in 1930, generally lived several blocks further south in brick bungalows or more solid wooden structures. Although some of the area's worst blemishes had been corrected by the 1930s, infant mortality supplies a useful measure of the neighborhood's status in Chicago. In 1937 fatality rates among children in the stockyards district were double the level in the white, middle-class community of Hyde Park just three miles east.[7]

Packinghouse work was thoroughly integrated into a family economy that rested on the paid and unpaid labor of women and children. Women contributed to family survival in several ways. Teenage daughters were far more likely to work than married women and composed a majority among the two thousand ethnic women who worked in the stockyards in 1930.

Married women generally helped to sustain family income by carefully managing resources and performing housework themselves rather than using new consumer appliances available to the middle class. With the assistance of young children, they tended the family's small garden, canned food, and baked bread. The family economy of the ethnic family required contributions from parents as well as children to maintain the poor but respectable living standards the immigrants had established.[8]

The most important ethnics for union organizers to win over were first- and second-generation Poles. One-third of Back of the Yards residents in 1930, they were the area's most numerous ethnic group, although Lithuanians and Bohemians also created substantial communities, and the Mexican presence increased sharply after 1920. At least five thousand Poles labored in the stockyards in the mid-1930s, making them the largest ethno-racial group of packinghouse workers. Securing the allegiance of Poles, however, entailed influencing a cohesive ethnic community to support a renewed effort to organize the stockyards.[9]

Strong Polish economic, cultural, and religious institutions mitigated against community disintegration and assimilation, even as the growth of mass culture and the evolving habits of the second generation engendered accommodation to some American customs. Only a third of the residents of the Back of the Yards had mechanical refrigeration; most ethnics owned small iceboxes that necessitated daily purchases from convenient neighborhood merchants. Despite the growth of chain stores, Poles and other ethnics continued to patronize more than six hundred small, locally owned grocery markets, butcher shops, and dairies in the neighborhood. As the largest concentration of Poles outside Europe, Chicago also provided exceptional support for Polish culture. Several Polish dailies circulated widely in the city; in 1934 *Dziennik Zjednoczenia* reached 5,600 families in the Back of the Yards area, more than 50 percent of the area's Polish population. Its editors astutely added comics and a sports page to attract second-generation readers. The newspaper *Dziennik Chicagoski* organized its own radio hour in the late 1920s to take advantage of the new medium, and local radio stations competed for Polish listeners in the 1930s with daily broadcasts of Polish-language shows.[10]

The Catholic church remained the most important force for ethnic group cohesion. In the 1930s three Polish-language parishes still served as the "social organ of the community" by organizing a dizzying array of religious and ethnic clubs. Churches especially encouraged social activities such as Polish-language drama and choral clubs and a Polish library, which reinforced Polish culture. To attract the second generation, churches sponsored bowling and basketball leagues and supported a Polish Boy Scout troop that rewarded outstanding scouts with a trip to Poland. Parochial schools constituted the most successful effort to retain the allegiance of the American-born generation. Enrollment grew rapidly at Back of the Yards Polish parochial schools throughout the 1920s and 1930s while attendance at local public schools first stagnated and then actually declined. Despite Americanization pressures from the Irish-dominated Catholic hierarchy, in the 1930s the parochial schools still included four hours of instruction in Polish. The second generation may have listened to the radio and followed American sports, but they remained closely tied to their parents and community.[11]

Poles and other ethnics in the Back of the Yards had provided the main base for the organizing efforts of unions during World War I, but collapse of labor organizations in the stockyards after the bitter strike of 1921 and 1922 left a contradictory legacy. The terrible hardships experienced by packinghouse workers and their families during the long strike soured some ethnics on labor organizations entirely. "I never wanted to hear the word union again in my life," recalled one Polish butcher. The strike also accentuated racism toward the black workers who had crossed union picket lines. "The white butchers hated the Negroes because they figured they would scab on them" packinghouse worker Elmer Benson explained in the 1930s. At the same time, some veterans of World War I-era labor organizations remained resolutely pro-union and part of the stockyards community by virtue of their ability to obtain jobs in the interstices of Chicago's meatpacking industry. These experienced activists would provide an important entrée for unionism into the Back of the Yards in the 1930s.[12]

A "social and cultural apartheid" separated Poles and other white ethnics from their black co-workers. Railroad yards, warehouses, and a hostile Irish neighborhood lay between the Back of the Yards and the South Side black neighborhood a mile directly east. "We only saw the colored when we were at work or coming home," recalled Polish packinghouse worker Gertie Kamarczyk, "we just kept to ourselves and they did too." Deeply entrenched cultural practices influencing residence, schooling, and access to mass culture established even more profound barriers than the mere physical separation of the communities implies.[13]

Racial discrimination in Chicago made meatpacking the largest and most important source of employment for the black community. With close to half of the 4,500 black packinghouse workers in 1930 classified as semiskilled butchers, Chicago's stockyards offered one of the best advancement routes to a respectable working-class status. "To be a top man at Swift's or Armour's meant that you could pay your bills, feed your family, have your kids in clothes and shoes, and have more than a little bit of respect from your neighbors," recalled Lowell Washington, son of a long-time Swift employee. Statistics support Washington's recollection. Although blacks composed no more than 3.4 percent of Chicago's skilled workers in the interwar years, they remained a remarkably constant 30 percent of the packinghouse's production employees. Moreover, pay levels in meatpacking were among the best available to Chicago's working-class blacks. A 1920 study showed that the pay of butchers ranged from $35 to $48 a week, and even unskilled black packinghouse workers earned $22 weekly. By comparison, the top pay for the few jobs open to black men in steel foundries, railroads, and as teamsters hovered at $30. In the mid-1930s, 85 percent of black packinghouse workers still earned between $20 and $30 a week, with 15 percent receiving more than $30. The few highly skilled black splitters and floorsman earned more than $50 weekly, placing them at the income level of black professionals.[14]

It was of lasting significance for the packinghouse workers' union that the family economy of the black community relied far more heavily on the paid labor of married women than was the case in white ethnic households. Black women were three times more likely to seek paid employment than their white counterparts. Even more so than for men, black female packinghouse workers "enjoyed" one of the highest paid jobs open to them. The income of the five hundred black women in meatpacking compared favorably with pay levels of the elite 1.5 percent employed as nurses or school teachers. The importance of packinghouse employment for black women, and the routine experience of paid work by wives, helped make black men especially receptive to the concerns of female packinghouse workers.[15]

As in other burgeoning black communities after World War I, the income of working-class blacks nurtured a thriving society within the confines of rigid segregation. Steady migration from the South brought Chicago's black population to 236,000 in the mid-1930s, most of whom lived in the South Side area dubbed "Bronzeville" by St. Clair Drake and Horace Cayton. The 475 churches claimed a membership equal to almost the entire black population; the larger ones organized athletic teams, schools, employment directories, and entertainment. Residents seeking secular diversions went to Bronzeville's cultural center at 47th and Park. Nearby were two large theaters featuring black performers, the "largest Negro-owned department store in America," and institutions such as Provident Hospital, the Wabash YMCA, and the Parkway Community House that all catered to blacks.[16]

The vitality of Chicago's black community existed behind a wall of unremitting discrimination. Determined white resistance kept Chicago's rapidly expanding black population in a sharply defined narrow band on the South Side and a pocket west of the downtown. By 1930, more than 90 percent of Chicago's blacks lived in areas that were more than 50 percent black. Barely 10 percent were able to own homes, a stark contrast to the fortunes of white workers in the shadow of the stockyards. While infant mortality in the Back of the Yards area was double Hyde Park's rate of 27 per thousand, the average rate for Bronzeville exceeded 82 per thousand, more than triple that of the white, middle-class neighborhoods to the east.[17]

Segregation extended from housing into almost every facet of the life in Chicago, even though discrimination on account of race officially violated Illinois law. School districts deliberately separated black and white students, and white-majority schools generally were newer and more likely to have extensive recreational facilities. Movie theaters outside Bronzeville either banned blacks entirely or restricted them to balcony seats. Shopping in downtown department stores was an uncertain venture; black customers often faced rude employees or outright refusal to render service. Restaurants discouraged black clientele by overcharging for advertised items, serving spoiled food, or simply refusing service.[18]

The combination of white racism and the importance of packinghouse work to the black community made companies such as Armour and Swift influential, and often quite popular, in Bronzeville. In addition to providing badly needed employment opportunities, Chicago packinghouse companies were highly visible supporters of such important community institutions as Provident Hospital, the Urban League, and the Wabash Avenue YMCA. During World War I, packing firms established pro-company Efficiency Clubs at the YMCA and strongly encouraged black workers to join, sometimes awarding promotions to those who became active. The packers' philanthropy was rewarded during the 1921–22 strike, when thousands of blacks crossed the picket lines of white ethnic union members.[19]

The aftermath of the 1921–22 strike entrenched divisions between whites and blacks in the stockyards. Black workers, a negligible presence before 1916, remained employed in high numbers and received promotions into better jobs, largely due to their amply demonstrated antipathy to unions. "We took the Negroes on as strikebreakers in 1921," explained the president of a Chicago packinghouse in the late 1920s, "and have kept them ever since in order to be prepared for any kind of outbreak." In addition to bitterness at strikebreaking by black workers, ethnic men objected to promotions of blacks into butchering jobs previously dominated by whites. "At that time, them Poles wouldn't let you use no knife," recalled Jesse Vaughn, who started work in 1924. "But our foremen, he taught a lot of black butchers." Vaughn's experience reflected tensions produced by shifting patterns of job allocation on the shop floor. The number of foreign-born, semiskilled workers fell by a thousand between 1920 and 1930, whereas five hundred more blacks entered these knife-wielding jobs. While initially increasing conflict among production workers, in the 1930s packing companies would deeply regret the magnified power of black butchers.[20]

Welfare capitalism in the 1920s accentuated fragmentation and allowed packing firms to curry support among employees by encouraging workers to rely on company benevolence for improvements in wages and working conditions. Employee representation councils capped an elaborate system of credit unions, pension plans, stock ownership, and recreational programs designed to encourage allegiance among more senior employees. At the same time, the strict racial segregation practiced by these programs sustained the hostile separation between blacks and whites. Selection of workers to the councils also created workplace leaders who could identify nagging problems without challenging management's authority.[21]

As a system that provided some benefits in a manner that protected managerial authority, welfare capitalism stopped at the door to the foremen's empire. Swift obliquely informed employee representatives of these limits when it warned them to not exceed "your authority" or to create "false expectations in the minds of employes." In fact, the foremen's power over hiring, job assignments, and layoffs often made workers dependent on their supervisor's whims in order to receive welfare capitalism's benefits. Workers were denied vacations and other benefits linked to length of service if they missed more than sixty days of work. In practice, employees "acquired their seniority through the 'half-pint,'" recalled one Armour worker; employment security came from plying foremen with "favors—good cigars, half-pint of liquor." Female workers had little choice but to tolerate sexual harassment. "You could get along real swell if you let the boss slap you on the behind and feel you up," recalled one Polish woman. Frequent layoffs made employee contributions for pensions or insurance an unwise investment, and workers viewed their forced contributions as "a bribe" so they could keep their jobs. Supervisors also routinely required workers to perform unpaid labor after official working hours. Workers termed this practice "working for the church"—a satirical observation that the generous philanthropy of Armour and Swift rested on the unremunerated labor of their employees. The failure of welfare capitalism to challenge managerial control would fuel workers' demands during the 1930s for power through collective bargaining, strict seniority, a grievance procedure, and a steward system.[22]

Although many workers remained unimpressed by welfare capitalism because of its limits, others were more favorably influenced. Some were able to use its programs to correct small problems at work and receive limited, but occasionally useful, nonwage benefits. Representation councils also generated workplace leaders who, in the 1930s, would be the backbone of company efforts to create so-called independent unions as a tame alternative to the CIO. When some of these leaders joined the PWOC, they would in turn form a conservative nucleus that contested with a more militant generation shaped in the "turbulent years" of the 1930s. Welfare capitalism thus entrenched the fragmentation of workers by race and ethnicity; it also established a base for opposition to confrontational forms of unionism. These divisions among workers would prove substantial obstacles to organizers during the New Deal.

The Emergence of Industrial Unionism in the Chicago Stockyards

The crumbling of community and business-sponsored support systems in the early years of the Great Depression weakened traditional loyalties within both black and ethnic communities and placed packing companies on the defensive. "The whole world came tumbling down," recalled Jacinta Grbac, a Croatian whose family's savings were wiped out by bank failures, "and that really radicalized the entire family." All four neighborhood banks in the Back of the Yards district collapsed by July 1932, owing creditors $3 million. A similar crisis hit the black community when Jesse Binga's State Bank closed with outstanding obligations exceeding $1 million. Established fraternal orders and insurance organizations either went bankrupt or refused to make payments to desperate members, and religious charities struggled vainly to fulfill the minimal needs of destitute Chicago residents.[23]

An inconsistent system at best, welfare capitalism's capacity to maintain the loyalty of packinghouse workers to their employers sharply declined under the weight of the depression. Layoffs, three successive wage reductions, and increased production pressures shredded allegiance to the packing companies. "The speed-up was horrible," recalled Herb March, who started at Armour in 1933. "The employers virtually threatened you to make you go." In one case, workers alleged that production quotas for women in Armour's steamy canning department increased 20 percent in four years as weekly pay fell from $20 in the late 1920s to $13 in 1933. The pace and the poor ventilation caused four deaths during the summer of 1934. When one woman complained about conditions, she was discharged with the consent of employee representative C. H. Talley.[24]

The paralysis of established institutions opened a period of social ferment in which radical ideas received a wide and sympathetic hearing. In South

Side Washington Park, white and black unemployed workers gathered daily "to pass the time away" and hear "'jack-leg' preachers joust with curbstone atheists, and Black Zionists break a lance with sundry varieties of 'Reds.'" Participants recalled hearing "inspiring speakers" who proclaimed that "the wealth of this country was so great that there was no need for people to be poor and hungry." Other soapbox orators emphasized inter-racial unity, "that the only way for working people—black, white and whatever—was to organize and break down these racial barriers." Sometimes a speaker would learn that an eviction was in progress and appeal for help. The crowd would then march off to return the furniture of some unfortunate tenant to their apartment. Protests grew more organized under the leadership of Communists and Socialists, who organized unemployed councils in the Back of the Yards and the black community and mobilized thousands in demonstrations to demand government action to alleviate suffering.[25]

The depression and tumult of protest provided both the atmosphere and the initial recruits for advocates of working-class collective action to once again make inroads in the stockyards. As one of the few inter-racial organizations in Chicago, the Communist Party helped bridge the divisions among packinghouse workers and also initiated the process of unionization. Communists were particularly influential among workers active in the unemployed protests of the early 1930s who then secured jobs in packing when employment increased in 1933. Leon Beverly, for example, was an important future black leader of the Armour union whom Communists contacted during protests organized out of the Washington Park forum. Two other Communist recruits from the unemployed demonstrations, Refugio Martinez and Jose Rodriquez, organized among Mexican packinghouse workers. In the Back of the Yards neighborhood, a small group of ethnics, also recruited out of the unemployed protests, methodically expanded their contacts by joining community organizations affiliated with the Catholic church, the YWCA, and the University of Chicago Settlement House.[26]

Chicago Communists received an enormous boost with the arrival of Herb March in the spring of 1933. Only twenty years old, March already was a veteran of mass organizing activity. The son of a Jewish union activist, March grew up in a pro-Socialist Brooklyn, New York, neighborhood. He joined the Young Communist League (YCL) in 1929, and his evident talents earned him a dubious reward. Appointed YCL midwestern organizer over seven states, March left New York City with $5 in his pocket. He hitched rides and rode railroad cars for five days to reach Kansas City, the center of the district. For the next three years, March helped organize unemployed protests in Kansas City and surrounding states and made initial contacts within the area's packinghouses. He met Jacinta (Jane) Grbac at a Communist Party convention in 1932, and the two soon married. Unable to support children on the YCL's "salary," March moved to his wife's neighborhood in 1933 and found work at the Chicago Armour plant.[27]

March brought a practical, down-to-earth tone to Communist organizing in meatpacking. Under the tutelage of William Z. Foster and other experienced Communists, March learned that agitation should dwell on specific issues and grievances rather than ideology. "They even referred to how the Russians did it," he recalled. "First you fight for hot water for tea, then you fight for the tea for hot water, and then you fight for the sugar for the tea." Strikingly handsome, an "outstanding speaker" and "brilliant tactician," March would sink deep roots in Chicago's packinghouses and construct both a union and political organization that lasted for several decades. From a small nucleus of fewer than a dozen in 1933, the packinghouse section of the Chicago Communist Party grew to several hundred by 1939.[28]

March's arrival in Chicago fortuitously coincided with passage of the National Industrial Recovery Act (NIRA). Because many packinghouse workers routinely labored for upward of fifty hours a week, the mandatory reduction to forty hours forced companies to hire more workers. Communists March, Vicky Starr (known at the time as Stella Nowicki), and Joe Zabritsky deliberately "colonized," respectively, the Armour, Swift, and Wilson packinghouses. They found, as March recalled, that despite the weakness of the NIRA's protection of unions, "Workers so much wanted to organize, that when they saw there was a law that you had a right to organize, this encouraged workers to stick their necks out and to begin to fight." The "illusion that they had rights," and the tangible increase in employment, dispelled some of the "fear" that had hung over the packinghouses since 1922. News of the successful November 1933 strike in the Austin, Minnesota, Hormel plant inspired stockyards activists, and some began to display union buttons openly at work.[29]

By 1934 at least five different unions were operating in the stockyards. Communists initiated the Packing House Workers Industrial Union (PHWIU) and recruited several hundred workers, primarily blacks from the Armour plant's killing floors. Arthur Kampfert and other former members of the World War I-era Stockyards Labor Council (SLC) resuscitated the organization and appointed Martin Murphy, SLC president during World War I, to the same position with the revived union. The new SLC was strongest among Polish and white ethnic butchers at small plants, such as Reliable Packing and G. H. Hammond; many probably had been members of the first SLC. A small independent union formed at the Hygrade plant, and the AFL-affiliated Amalgamated Meat Cutters sent a dozen organizers into the stock-yards and claimed eight thousand members. Eight hundred Irish stockhand-lers joined the Amalgamated and won a 10 percent raise with a quick strike in November 1933.[30]

Now that unionism was once again an issue in the stockyards, the legacy of the 1920s retarded progress. Racial divisions remained considerable. White participants in the 1921–22 strike still harbored ill feelings toward black work-ers for crossing the picket lines and then "taking" their jobs. "There was that feeling all the time—resentment," Leon Beverly remembered. The activity of the well-financed Amalgamated aroused suspicion among workers who blamed it for the 1921–22 debacle. "Most would have signed up with the Sal-vation Army before they joined the A. F. of L.," one recalled. As in Austin, the growth of independent unions reflected deep antipathy toward the Amalgam-ated among Chicago's packinghouse workers.[31]

A series of reversals in 1934 and 1935 forced the scattered nuclei of union activists to unify. Union sympathizers were fired in several plants, and the large firms tried to refurbish the credibility of the old representa-tion councils by attributing an October 1934 wage increase to their in-fluence. Workers dismissed for union activity learned to their dismay that NIRA section 7(a) and the new Labor Relations Board had no power to compel reemployment. SLC and PHWIU activists responded by dissolv-ing their organizations and entering the Amalgamated; no doubt the Com-munist Party's abandonment of "dual unionism" facilitated the shift in policy by March and his associates.[32]

Former SLC and PHWIU members quickly found that membership in the Amalgamated would not advance organizing efforts among packing-house workers. In July 1935, Amalgamated Secretary-Treasurer Patrick Gor-man blamed the loss of momentum in the stockyards on workers who "are slow in grasping the necessity for organization to improve working condi-tions and wages." The Amalgamated concomitantly reduced its organizing efforts throughout the meatpacking industry, cut its Chicago stockyards staff in half, and used the money it had saved to increase salaries of vice presi-dents by 20 percent. Kampfert and March secured permission to form an organizing committee but received neither money nor organizers. They asked for help from the Chicago Federation of Labor (CFL), only to be re-buked by Amalgamated representative "Big Bill" Tate, who told CFL dele-gates that the best way to help packinghouse workers was to "refuse to pa-tronize a [butcher] store that does not display the union card." Although CFL leaders were sympathetic, they could do nothing without the Amalgamat-ed's consent.[33]

"We found out that organization didn't want us," black union pioneer Jesse Vaughn remembered thinking after the Amalgamated pulled back from the Chicago stockyards in 1935. "And we didn't want them because they wasn't for the working class of people." Hence, Chicago packinghouse activists closely followed the progress of the newly formed CIO and tried to devise a way to entice it into the packing industry. While the Amalgamated dithered, March, Kampfert, and other activists struggled to bring pro-union workers into an organizing committee that could receive CIO sanction. Several small meetings culminated in the creation of a "Committee of Eighteen" in January 1937. Participants included former SLC leaders Arthur Kampfert and Stanley Srotowski, Communists Les Orear, Vicky Starr, and Frank McCarty, Jesse Vaughn from the small Roberts and Oake plant, and Austin union founder Jack Sechrest, a boomer butcher now working at Armour. After a ritualistic visit to Amalgamated president Dennis Lane, who assured them the time was not right for organizing, the Committee of Eighteen lobbied the CIO to enter meatpacking at the same time as the Austin and Cedar Rapids unions were engaged in a parallel campaign. Asked for proof of their strength, Chicago activists quickly collected two thousand signed cards that said, "I want a CIO union in the meat packing industry." Their pressure was successful. By the fall of 1937 the CIO had issued charters to nine Chicago locals claiming a membership of 8,200.[34]

The CIO's entry into meatpacking, capped by the formation of the PWOC on October 27, 1937, was an enormous boost to the diligent efforts of the stockyard's "militant minority." The credibility of the new industrial union federation was far more important than its financial assistance, which was limited to employing several packinghouse workers. In Chicago, the CIO-affiliated Steel Workers Organizing Committee (SWOC) lent enormous authority to the new PWOC. "The people in the yards waited a long time for the CIO," an Armour worker remembered. "When they began organizing in the steel towns and out in South Chicago, everybody wanted to know when the CIO was coming to the yards." Poles and other East European packinghouse workers were probably familiar with SWOC's efforts to organize their countrymen who lived in the South Chicago steel district. The highly visible welcome extended to black steelworkers by SWOC reassured black packinghouse workers who were considering supporting a labor organization. The Steel Workers directly aided efforts to recruit blacks in meatpacking by contributing one of the most important black leaders to the organizing drive, Henry Johnson.[35]

Remembered by contemporaries as a "fantastic organizer" and a "powerful speaker," Johnson followed a circuitous route to the Chicago stockyards.

Born into a Texas sharecropping family, Johnson later described his father as a "bad nigger" who had joined the IWW while working as a timber worker. After a lynch mob forced his family to leave Texas, Johnson traveled around the country, working as a union plasterer and longshoreman. In the early 1930s he attended City College of New York and received a bachelor's degree. At that time he either joined or become very close to the Communist Party. In 1932 the International Workers Order (IWO), a fraternal organization linked to the Communist Party, hired Johnson. Sent to Chicago by the IWO in 1934, he was hired by SWOC in 1936 and then assigned by the CIO to meatpacking in the fall of 1937, where he became assistant national director of the PWOC. A highly visible speaker, organizer, and writer, Johnson's role in the PWOC demonstrated to black workers that the union was committed to placing blacks at its very highest levels. To whites, Johnson was an important symbol of black support for the union; moreover, his intelligence, eloquence, and literacy provided a powerful antidote to racist notions about the abilities of black people.[36]

Johnson's formal union experience complemented the shop-floor knowledge of black union advocates. "Johnson took us by the hand, told us how to do it," recalled Jesse Vaughn, a close associate of the PWOC leader. At the same time, Johnson's organizing strategy relied on black workers' intimate knowledge of the production process. "Johnson didn't know anything about packing," recalled Vaughn. "He relied on me for that." The dynamic interaction between Johnson and rank-and-file activists like Vaughn is apparent in the union victories at the stockyard's "Little Six" plants, establishments of several hundred workers that catered to the local meat business. While Johnson formulated general strategy and counseled shop-floor leaders on their rights under the Wagner Act, activists recruited white and black workers and orchestrated job actions to pressure management. In several plants, workers on the killing floors used the effective tactic of slaughtering the animals and waiting for the results of negotiation between management and union representatives before removing the animals' innards and placing the carcasses in the cooler. This pressure secured contracts with several small companies in 1938.[37]

These agreements represented an enormous victory, especially "for the old timers who had seen the union crushed so many times," because they represented the first contracts secured by the Chicago PWOC. The agreements also were an important step toward black-white unity in the stockyards. Five of the six presidents of the Little Six locals were black, and their prominence in the union drive received wide recognition in Chicago's black community. Black leaders from the small plants, such as Roberts and Oake union president Jesse Vaughn, tended to be in their twenties or thirties and had entered the yards after the 1921–22 strike. These locals also successfully integrated white workers into what were essentially black-led organizations. Polish women served as stewards in the Roberts and Oake plant, and white men held several executive offices, including the vice-presidency.[38]

The response of black workers to the union's appeal represented a substantial change in their attitude toward labor organizations. But it was the successful efforts to build the union at the huge Armour plant that solidified the Chicago PWOC's inter-racial alliance.

Organizing at Armour

The PWOC's most important target was Chicago's Armour plant, the largest in the stockyards with more than seven thousand workers, two thousand of them black. The union's strategy "was to build a strong network in the Armour plant," Arthur Kampfert later wrote, "to develop leaders in every department." The shop-floor strategy was designed to create a union apparatus that could foster unity between black, white ethnic, white native-born, and Mexican workers by engaging them in concerted activity at the point of production. Union leaders hoped that securing small victories against the company would break through the "fear" that made workers reluctant to join the union and also the "hatred" that had kept them divided.[39]

The nucleus of the Armour union came from the killing and cutting departments, where hundreds of former PHWIU members continued to toil. The integrated group of union pioneers from these areas made the Armour union inter-racial from its very beginnings. Black union pioneers in the hog kill, Al Malachi and Leon Beverly, worked closely with several whites in the adjacent hog cut, including Jack Sechrest, Arthur Kampfert, and Polish butcher Walter Strabawa. Union pioneers in the beef kill included the Rev. Walter Childs, a floorsman and a black member of the SLC during World War I; Peter Davis, a black who had risen from laborer to butcher since starting at Armour in 1925; and Jesse Perez, a Mexican. Perez worked with other Mexican packinghouse workers to recruit their countrymen to the union through an organization (probably influenced by the Communist Party) called the Vincent Tolledano Club. Support for the union among black killing-floor workers helped garner white support because it meant that there would be no repeat of the 1921–22 disaster.[40]

Building inter-racial solidarity infused union strategy beyond the killing floors. After secretive meetings in late 1936 established a skeletal organization, union activity surfaced in February 1937 when killing-floor workers began dispatching racially integrated "flying squads" to other departments. In May, two thousand packinghouse workers attended the CIO's first public rally, and Armour unionists started holding meetings at a Polish bar a block from the stockyards, Sikora's Tavern, whose owner permitted integrated gatherings. The union immediately affected the racial practices of taverns near the stockyards as black PWOC members began to frequent establishments favored by white union members. The union maintained high visibility by holding lunch-time, racially integrated, open-air rallies at Forty-third Street and Packers Avenue in the heart of the yards. Herb March, laid off by Armour for his union activity, became a fixture at these gatherings, speaking from a sound system mounted on his car. For the next twenty years Chicago packing unions would regularly hold rallies at this location, popularly known as "CIO corner."[41]

Initial black support at Armour was not limited to killing-floor workers influenced by the PHWIU. In 1939 the *Chicago Defender,* which had opposed the 1921–22 strike, proclaimed on September 23 that "black workers have learned to raise their heads" in the stockyards and praised the PWOC's actions to "defeat prejudice." The paper observed approvingly that more than twenty black preachers had taken positions as shop stewards in the late 1930s. No doubt ministers of small storefront churches, these men labored in the packinghouse during the week and tended to the religious needs of their parishioners at night and on weekends. Their willingness to serve as departmental stewards was an extension of their concern for their congregation and reflected a deep shift of black sentiment toward the union.

Ethnic production workers and white skilled craftsmen extended the union organization into predominantly white areas of the plant. Joe Bezenhoffer, a Croation and later president of 347 for many years, was a skilled sausage maker who had been fired for leading a strike at a North Side plant before finding work at Armour. Carpenter William Mooney, an Irishman hired by Armour in 1928, used his maintenance job to spread the union message throughout the plant. Young Polish workers Sigmund Wlodarczyk and Joe Poshonka encouraged fellow ethnics to join. George Kovacovic, a Croatian who had migrated to Chicago from the coal fields of Iowa where he had been a United Mine Workers member, also helped build the union among the white ethnics.[42]

Women were slower to join, and female union activists tended either to be Communist Party members, such as Anna Novack in the canning department, or single, such as Sophie Kosciowlowski in the dried beef area. Indeed, the recruitment of Kosciowlowski, who was Polish, to the union is instructive of both ethnic and gender dynamics in the organizing drive. The daughter of a packinghouse worker, she first found work at Armour in 1918 when she was only thirteen. A union member during World War I, she left work to get married, a decision she later called "the biggest mistake I ever made." Divorced after nine years (a difficult decision in her Catholic community), Kosciowlowski was able to get her old job back in 1931. She knew union activist Sigmund Wlodarczyk through family members who also worked at Armour, and through these ethnic networks she became a secret member of the PWOC in 1937.[43]

Armour fought the PWOC drive through a mixture of cooptation and intimidation. The company encouraged former delegates to the Employee Representation Plan, rendered illegal under the Wagner Act, to form an "independent union" known as the Employees Mutual Association (EMA). With their efforts sanctioned and assisted by management, EMA representatives commenced organizing in May 1937. They approached Armour employees during working hours and quickly claimed more than four thousand members. With Armour's evident good will, the EMA secured exclusive collective bargaining rights with the company in September.[44]

At the same time, Armour tried to slow the growth of the PWOC by dismissing leading activists. March and Kampfert had already been laid off in the spring, but they had little seniority and the union was unable to lodge a protest with the NLRB. In November, Armour fired long-time employee Jacob Byra, a Back of the Yards ethnic who had been a union member during World War I. Byra recently had become a steward and recruited most of his ethnic co-workers in the hog coolers. Three weeks later, Armour dismissed beef-kill worker Pete Davis, who was black, when he came to work wearing a huge PWOC steward's button. Inadvertently, the company's actions lent credence to the union argument that management was the "enemy" of all workers regardless of their race.[45]

The CIO fought back tenaciously by using the legitimacy conferred by the law to validate a shop-floor organizing strategy. "The only thing we could do is take the position that [with] the law they had a right to organize," recalled March, the strategist for the Chicago Armour drive. The union recruited members with the stated objective of winning a certification election and took the discharge cases to the NLRB. At the same time, the union asserted rights allegedly guaranteed by the Wagner Act *prior to* actual decisions from the courts or government agencies. "We set up committees and demanded to meet with employers on grievances," recalled March. "When they wouldn't, when we got enough of the workers organized, we'd have work stoppages." The result of this unrelenting pressure may have seemed only "little concessions here and there." But the ability of the union to force the

company "to deal with the union" steadily increased "courage" and "determination" among the workers. The union's artful use of the legitimacy of the
law to build a stubborn and effective shop-floor apparatus created an organizing juggernaut which, as March recalled, "kept on going like a snowball
going downhill."[46]

Throughout 1938, conflict raged in the Armour plant as the CIO extended its steward organization to new departments. Job actions, usually over
the pace of work or application of seniority in job assignments, erupted in
the sausage, canning, sheep-kill, and beef-kill departments. Often the simple threat of a stoppage was enough to reverse the dismissal of a worker or
resolve a small grievance, because the union "picked circumstances carefully
where we felt they would be compelled to yield." Indeed, the very absence
of discharge cases appealed to the NLRB after 1937 reflected the capacity of
the Armour local to halt arbitrary dismissals.[47]

A close look at the dynamics of the union's campaign indicates how its
shop-floor strategy worked in tandem with the development of inter-racial
unity. In June 1938 Armour fired Walter Strabawa for cooking scraps of meat
for lunch. This was a traditional practice by the well-organized pork butchers, who had assigned Strabawa the task for that day. The union sent stewards from several departments to see management and insisted that Strabawa be returned to work. When the plant superintendent rejected repeated
entreaties, the delegation turned on their heels and headed for the door. "All
right you bastards, we'll put him back to work," the superintendent called
out just before the door closed. "He understood what we were saying," recalled March. "Put him back to work or we strike." Black butchers openly
backed Strabawa in the confrontation with management; some even felt
friendly enough to attend his marriage a few months later in a Polish Back
of the Yards church. These significant actions by black workers reinforced
the PWOC's message that "the worker beside you is not the enemy" regardless of race.[48]

Whites reciprocated by supporting efforts to end management's practice
of placing a star on the time cards of black workers, an act that particularly
troubled blacks. "When they got ready to lay off," recalled union founder
Leon Beverly, "all they do is say, 'Well here's a black star, we'll lay this one
off.'" The union took action on the time cards in 1938 after Armour laid off
hog butcher Charles Perry, a black union member with considerable seniority, while white men with less service continued to work. Both white and
black killing-floor workers sat down to protest management's action and
secured a commitment from the company to remove the star and rehire Perry.
Support by white workers for this action deeply impressed black observers

because whites were eschewing past racial privileges in favor of egalitarian employment policies. Such solidarity led the *Chicago Defender* to praise the change among whites "who until recently looked upon Negroes as their natural enemies."[49]

In the fall of 1938 Armour suffered two blows from the NLRB. On September 15, the board ruled that Byra and Davis had been unjustly fired and ordered Armour to reinstate them with full back pay. The NLRB also found that the EMA was a company-dominated labor organization and directed the company to withdraw recognition. A month later, a representation election gave the PWOC 2,840 votes out of 3,418 ballots cast. A majority of the workforce did not vote, however, because supervisors stationed in front of the only polling booth intimidated many workers. On this basis, the company refused to acknowledge the results or rehire Davis.[50]

On the heels of these setbacks to Armour, a wave of violence swept the stockyards, in part instigated by the Amalgamated Meat Cutters. Seeking to halt the CIO's advance in meatpacking, the Amalgamated absorbed the EMA and charted a new local to compete with the PWOC. At the same time, Amalgamated business agent Thomas Devero and other unknown assailants attacked union activists and facilities. A few days after the September 15 NLRB ruling, a bomb exploded in front of the PWOC office; over the next two weeks, Devero and other men threatened and assaulted several PWOC members with firearms and baseball bats. Herb March was the target of two attacks, suffering a broken nose in the first encounter and a gunshot wound the second time. No one was arrested for these incidents except, ironically, March, who carried an unregistered pistol in his car.[51]

These incidents, rather than intimidating union members, "resulted in terrific indignation" among the workers, who saw March's bullet-ridden car, deliberately parked by its owner in front of the Armour plant. Job actions continued unabated, including a "holiday" by 1,100 killing-floor workers in late November to support a stockhandlers' strike. The union also extended its strength into previously unorganized departments. In dried beef, where the union had only a handful of female members, Sophie Kosciowlowski had slowly been spreading union "propaganda" since 1937. Following the 1938 NLRB election, one especially "dictatorial foremen" so antagonized the two hundred women in the department that they marched over to the union hall together and joined. Thirty years later, Kosciowlowski gleefully recalled the astonishment of management the next day. "Everybody, the superintendent, the foreman from other floors, everybody came to look at what happened, women with union buttons on." Their bewilderment reflected how momentum now was on the side of the union.[52]

While the visible apogee to the Armour campaign was the dramatic Coliseum rally on July 16, 1939, an event of more lasting significance for packinghouse workers occurred with far less fanfare two days earlier. Representatives of churches, businesses, community organizations, and the PWOC formed the Back of the Yards Council on July 14 (March was shot on his way home from the founding meeting). Through the council, Catholic union members such as PWOC representative Sigmund Wlodarczyk helped to neutralize conservative religious figures and establish warm ties with younger clerics more open to cooperation with the reputedly left-wing CIO. Perceptive observers had noted the presence of young Catholic priests from Back of the Yards churches at the July 16 rally. Indeed, Bishop Sheil's endorsement of the PWOC at the rally reflected the sentiments of a younger generation of white ethnic clergy who had grown up near, and sometimes worked in, the stockyards. "I knew that the Catholic workers of our district would not join unless the priests said it was right," Ambrose Ondrek, a Back of the Yards priest, later recalled. "So we provided leadership and told our people to join the CIO." Overt support from Back of the Yards religious leaders probably swung wavering Catholic workers into the union camp.[53]

Bolstered by the Coliseum rally and the formation of the Back of the Yards Council, the PWOC finally overcame Armour's resistance to the union. A December 1939 NLRB certification election (held because of Armour's rejection of the 1938 tally) gave Local 347 more than four thousand votes to the Amalgamated's one thousand. A month later, Armour signed a local contract with the Chicago union, providing a guaranteed work week of thirty-two hours, improved vacations, and a grievance procedure. The agreement also ended Armour's hated practice of removing an employee's seniority rights whenever they missed sixty days of work. From its even stronger position, Local 347 consolidated its strength by recruiting workers in remaining unorganized pockets. With a strong union behind them, stewards in the canning room (where four people died from heat exhaustion in 1934) used a job action to force the company to install a cooling system. "This was a big boost to the power of the union," remembered steward Todd Tate. "Guys said, if the union can do that, maybe I want to join." Local 347 had achieved almost 100 percent union membership in the Armour plant by the beginning of World War II. "You just didn't work in that plant unless you supported the union," recalled March. In a scant three years, the PWOC had established a significant degree of workers' power in Chicago's Armour plant.[54]

The victorious Armour drive was the critical breakthrough for the PWOC in the Chicago stockyards. The nucleus of union activists initially constituted in 1933 and 1934 had successfully linked up with the CIO to secure a victory over an intransigent firm. Shop-floor issues provided the common set of experiences around which union organizers could make a case for the benefits of a labor organization. Surmounting mutual suspicions of white and black workers rested primarily on a careful process of building mutual respect at work and confidence that each group would support the other in conflicts with management. The confrontational approach of the union, Local 347 of the PWOC, would persist as long as the Chicago Armour plant remained in operation.

Welfare Capitalism and Industrial Unionism at Swift and Wilson

While welfare capitalism left little mark on the Armour organizing drive, its legacy was far more significant at Swift and Wilson, the two other large plants in the stockyards. At Swift, the pronounced influence of pro-company attitudes among workers hindered initial organizing efforts and shaped the character of the local union when the PWOC finally secured certification. A similar process marked the initial unionizing efforts that created the PWOC local at Wilson, where leaders whose roots were in welfare capitalism were replaced in 1944 by a left-wing group aligned with the Armour local. By the end of World War II, the result was an inter-racial unionism in the stockyards aligned, in its majority, with the left. A strong right-wing minority based in the Swift plant persisted, however, and conflict between left and right would sharpen immensely after 1945.

Swift's retention of many benefits linked to welfare capitalism greatly hindered CIO organizing initiatives during the 1930s. Employees with more than ten years' seniority were protected from layoffs, received modest pensions, and could turn to the company for emergency financial and legal assistance. Swift was far more successful than Armour in transforming its employee representation plan into an independent union, known as the Security League, which had the support of many workers. The Bedaux incentive system also hindered union efforts, especially among women. Through informal work groups in departments such as sliced bacon, Swift employees were able to regulate their work pace and to receive fairly good wages. "What could the union do that they weren't already getting," co-workers asked Vicky Starr when she cautiously suggested that they organize.[55]

To explain to workers what "they weren't already getting," unionists highlighted the main weakness of welfare capitalism: control over wage rates and shop-floor conditions remained completely in the hands of the company. Organizers especially stressed the capacity of a union to ensure that workers received promised benefits. A 1940 issue of the *Swift Flash*, the union's paper, described the union as "insurance against any unforseen detriment to your livelihood, your job." The union attacked abuses by foremen that made workers' lives miserable, such as arbitrary harassment, layoffs not in accordance with seniority, or failure to provide adequate protective equipment. In sliced bacon, Vicky Starr finally won women over to the union after a co-worker died of pneumonia.[56]

At Swift, the key CIO union pioneers were older, skilled workers heavily influenced by welfare capitalism, unlike the leadership cadre at Armour. All accounts credit two skilled white workers in auxiliary departments with initiating the organizing drive: sausage maker Hank Schoenstein and elevator mechanic Ralph Gantt. Although the inter-racial coalition that composed Swift Local 28 was similar in form to the union at Armour, its different roots produced leaders who were strongly anticommunist.

The voyage of Philip Weightman, a black butcher who became the most important union leader at Swift, suggests how welfare capitalism and its limits shaped unionization. Weightman was a highly skilled hog butcher who had turned against unions because of a traumatic experience with the Amalgamated Meat Cutters in 1918. Although a member of its St. Louis local, Weightman was refused service at a union function because of his race. The incident "destroyed my desire for unionism," he later recalled. When Weightman moved to Chicago in 1929, he sought employment at Swift because of its paternalistic policies. "When you work for Swift," he later explained, "you're more of a family." When the PWOC began its furtive initiatives in the Chicago Swift plant, Weightman would have nothing to do with it. Instead, he worked closely with the industrial relations department to field Swift teams in the Wabash YMCA's baseball league. "At that point I was a company man in every sense of the word," Weightman recalled.

While preferring the "family" atmosphere at Swift, the limits to welfare capitalism finally brought Weightman over to the CIO. One day in the late 1930s, the company shocked Weightman by abruptly dismissing a co-worker named Carson. Weightman stunned his foreman by appearing at work the next day sporting several union buttons. Asked to explain his decision to join the CIO when "you got everything you asked for," Weightman responded by pinpointing the fundamental flaw of welfare capitalism. "I could ask you for a new towel, for some more soap in the washbasin," Weightman explained, but if "I had asked you for a raise, could I have gotten that?" The sudden dismissal of Carson could have happened "to any of us." Visibly angry fifty years after the incident, Weightman recalled swearing that "if I can do anything about it, you ain't going to do that to me nor no one else."

Highly respected by other black workers, Weightman's action brought hundreds into the union and transformed a small circle of activists into a credible organization.[57]

Weightman's subsequent career indicates how he meshed a new commitment to industrial unionism with the essentially moderate politics of his youth. Although now convinced that labor organizations were necessary to advance the interests of working people, he nevertheless rejected the radical critique of American society shared by Communists and other leftists in the UPWA. Weightman would become a force in the UPWA through his position as international vice president and head of the grievance department—and one of the most articulate anticommunists in the union. With the solid backing of his old local, Weightman was a central figure in the "right-wing" faction of the UPWA until being defeated for reelection at the pivotal 1948 convention.

Despite the different political inclination of its leading activists, the Swift local emulated Armour's strategy of constructing an extensive departmental steward organization and using grievance committees to broaden participation in the union. As in Armour, the union employed job actions on the killing floors to pressure management to settle grievances. In April 1940, Swift withdrew recognition from the Security League after the NLRB held it was a company-dominated union. The pace quickened at the plant in 1941. The union strengthened its steward organization and mounted regular rallies at the CIO corner, where Swift workers mingled with unionized Armour employees. Victory finally came in January 1942, when PWOC Local 28 defeated the Security League in a certification election. The second major plant in the stockyards had fallen to the PWOC.[58]

The consolidation of a CIO union at Wilson illuminates sharply the conflict between unionists influenced by welfare capitalism and younger workers more favorably impressed by the confrontational strategies of the Armour local. As at Swift, Wilson encouraged former representatives to the employee representation council created in the 1920s to form an independent union, the Employee Representation Committee (ERC). In 1940 the ERC narrowly defeated the PWOC Wilson union (Local 25) in a certification election, primarily because the CIO failed to win sufficient support among white women.[59]

The PWOC secured representation at Wilson only by making an unstable alliance with disgruntled members of the ERC. An internal dispute led several of the ERC's main figures to abandon their organization and join the PWOC. The three key members in this group were Walter Piotrowski, an active member of the Fourteenth Ward's Polish Democratic Club; Dock Williams, an experienced black butcher; and Mary Smith, a white women from the sliced bacon department. Largely as a result of Piotrowski's damning testimony, the NLRB forced Wilson to withdraw recognition from the ERC in 1941. With Armour and Swift organized, PWOC activists descended on Wilson and used advances obtained in organized plants to influence increasingly receptive Wilson workers. As Williams and Smith brought, respectively, older black men and white women into the PWOC, even Piotrowski's sudden resignation when the CIO refused to give him a staff position failed to slow the drive. By April 1942 the PWOC claimed 98 percent membership in the Wilson plant; in December, Local 25 won a second NLRB election by more than two thousand votes.[60]

Not long after the certification election, friction emerged between the former ERC leaders and young black workers who entered Wilson as employment grew because of World War II. While Williams and Smith had brought workers still influenced by the ERC into the PWOC, the new black employees were far more impressed with the leftist leadership of the Armour local and co-thinkers at Wilson, such as Joe Zabritsky, a Communist. In 1944 open conflict erupted between the Williams-Smith leadership and a more militant group spearheaded by Zabritsky and recent black hires Sam Parks and Charles Hayes. The dissidents accused Williams of being a company stooge; he countered by labeling their efforts part of a Communist plot to dominate the packinghouse union. The rhetoric might have been inflated, but the accusations reflected real disagreements over stance of the local union toward management.[61]

Williams finally overplayed his hand by refusing to participate in the CIO's political action campaign in 1944, allowing his detractors to remove him from office. The new leadership of the Wilson local—Parks, Hayes, and Zabritsky—allied closely with Armour rather than with Swift, firmly establishing Chicago-based District 1 as the stronghold of leftist influence in the UPWA.[62]

* * *

By 1943 the Chicago stockyards were union territory. All major plants and many of the small ones were solidly organized and under collective bargaining agreements. Union stewards patrolled the shop floor, using job actions in association with a grievance procedure to influence working conditions. Contracts and seniority governed the larger sphere of relations with the companies. Sophie Kosciowlowski could finally realize her aspiration to be treated with "dignity" by her employer.

Inter-racial unionism lay at the heart of Chicago's success. Although the races remained deeply divided in the city of Chicago, the union principles of mutual aid and support brought white and black co-workers together in pragmatic cooperation at work through their union. After the war, however, the inter-racial alliance would experience strains as blacks became an overwhelming majority of the workforce and pressed unions to become more active on civil rights. A majority of whites would remain union members, but by the 1950s the Chicago UPWA was a black-led labor organization.

Communists played a central role forming the Chicago packinghouse unions and established a solid base for leftist influence in the UPWA. Under March's direction, Communist union members did not neglect the work of developing a substantial sympathetic milieu and building their own organization. The party claimed a membership of several hundred into the 1950s, and its influence spread far outside its nominal members to workers who could see through personal experience the contributions of March and other Communists to the union cause. In alliance with a militant generation of black workers who entered the packinghouses during World War II, Communists would help impel the Chicago UPWA to the forefront of the union's civil rights activity in the 1950s. Operating autonomously from, and sometimes in conflict with, Communist leaders "who didn't know a packinghouse from a pretzel," Chicago Communists avoided many of the mistakes committed by their comrades in other industries and minimized the damage from embarrassments such as the 1939 Hitler-Stalin pact.[63]

As the fulcrum of national union power, the predominantly leftist Chicago district greatly influenced the national union. From their Chicago base, Communists worked diligently, and largely successfully, to support a "center-left" alliance with other local unions in the UPWA who similarly favored inter-racial, democratic, and militant industrial unionism. The influence of leftists in Chicago's meatpacking unions would decisively shape the evolution of the UPWA in the postwar era.

4

"Without a Union, We're All Lost":
The Origins of Packinghouse Unionism
in Kansas City

The fear of the boss, the fear that they would get discharged if they even talked about a union, that was the main obstacle. And then there was, of course, that religious difference and that racial difference, which were obstacles at first but which were all overcome. All of them—simply by showing the people that we all had a common goal to make a decent living, to have a decent standard of living, and this was the way to go, and the only way to go, because without a union, we're all lost. And it's so. It's just that simple. There's nothing complicated about it at all.

—Charles R. Fischer, Kansas City union founder

In the early morning hours of September 9, 1938, workers at Armour's Kansas City, Kansas, packinghouse suddenly seized control of the plant. Strikers blocked the doors, occupied the main stockyards, and streamed out onto the plant roof to shouts and cheers from sympathetic crowds on the sidewalk. Pickets patrolled the plant gate, only admitting Armour executives and other individuals who obtained special permits from the union. Beef-kill workers deserted their jobs and left cattle hanging on the "dead rail" in various stages of dismemberment. When the union admitted supervisors to perform the jobs they usually bossed, company officials complained that the gang "stood around the long belts which convey the slaughtered carcasses to the freezing departments" and made insulting remarks about the foremen's work.[1]

The strike was an extraordinary inter-racial event. Blacks composed roughly four hundred of the one thousand Armour employees who remained in the building for four days. White and black workers, who usually lived in separate environments in Kansas City, had to plan the occupation, eat, sleep, and pass the time waiting for a settlement in the same physical space. In a strictly segregated city, the inter-racial strike community was unique. "It left a unity of friendship that couldn't have been created in any other way," recalled union founder Charles R. Fischer.[2]

The actual issue in dispute seemed small to local observers. The union claimed that management owed five hide cellar workers a total of $22.09 for attending a grievance hearing. How was it that such a small matter would cause workers to seize the plant and risk loss of income, possible arrest, and even dismissal?

The occupation erupted, and was so united, because the grievance of the hide cellar workers resonated with other Kansas City Armour employees. As four of the aggrieved hide cellar workers were black and one Croatian, there was ample motivation for the two largest groups of packinghouse workers to stay in the plant until management yielded. The company's action in the hide cellar dispute was simply the latest in a long series of tactics designed to hamstring the union. Unionists hoped that forcing management to pay the $22.09 would also accomplish a larger objective: to establish union authority over shop-floor conditions and its right to represent workers in disputes with management.

Conscious union strategy before the September confrontation already had established bonds between different racial and ethic groups. The plant occupation consolidated these ties and firmly established inter-racial cooperation at the point of production among packinghouse workers who previously had little or no contact with each other except on the job. The dramatic success of the plant occupation at Kansas City's largest packinghouse, and the positive attention it attracted, opened the way for the construction of similar inter-racial, inter-ethnic coalitions at other plants and the unionization of Kansas City's meatpacking industry.

Characteristics similar to the processes in Austin and Chicago were embedded in the particular features of the formation of packinghouse unions in Kansas City. As in those cities, a distinct group of union activists constituted before the passage of the Wagner Act initiated the process of unionization in Kansas City. Indeed, the IUAW's "Austin orbit" directly touched and influenced Kansas City activists. Similar to Chicago, the pivotal test for the early organizers was to secure support among black workers who had previously opposed unions. Kansas City activists successfully made the concept of inclusive unionism a visible reality by actively involving all ethnic and racial groups in social events, powerful workplace organizations, and common activity at the point of production.

The particular composition of the "militant minority" that initiated organizing in Kansas City lent a distinctive character to the local unions, however. This coalition of Socialists, former mine workers, pro-union ethnics, and race-conscious blacks remained far more stable than in Austin and Chicago, and the same personnel still dominated the local unions in the 1950s and 1960s. They jealously guarded the autonomy of their locals from centralizing pressures exerted by the PWOC and the UPWA and thus were a perennial ally of successive opposition groupings inside the packinghouse workers' national union.

Led by Charles R. Fischer, a skilled mechanic, a group of four Socialists played a critical role bridging the deep divide between black and white workers and penetrating the dense communities of Croatian and other East European packinghouse employees. Socialists recruited recognized leaders from these constituencies into the underground union core and then used racial, ethnic, and workplace networks to reach out from this beachhead into the rest of the plant once the formation of the CIO increased the chance of success. The Socialist message was straightforward: Inclusive, rather than craft, unionism could increase the standard of living for everyone. "We all had a common goal to make a decent living," Fischer explained in retrospect. "Without a union, we're all lost. It's just that simple."[3]

Class Formation of Kansas City's Packinghouse Workers

By the 1930s Kansas City packinghouse workers had created distinct, stable communities in the metropolitan areas on both sides of the Kansas-Missouri state line. Their common bond, however, was limited to experiences on the job; after work, black and ethnic, immigrant and native-born, left for separate neighborhoods, churches, and benevolent organizations. Separation was particularly strict between the races because Kansas City practiced rigid segregation in all areas of life. But the white ethnic groups, although mixing in immigrant neighborhoods, remained internally cohesive communities, still primarily oriented to people with the same roots in the Old World. It would take the shock of the depression and the organizing strategies of Communists and Socialists to establish bonds of common interest and action among the distinct fractions of the packinghouse workforce.

Meatpacking had provided the initial spur for industrial development in nineteenth-century Kansas City and was still the area's largest industry in 1930. The packing industry lined both sides of the flat alluvial river bottoms that stretched along both sides of the Kansas River before it joined the Missouri. All packinghouses were in Kansas; in the mid-1920s eleven plants provided 80 percent of the value produced by Kansas City, Kansas, industrial establishments. Packinghouses operated by all Big Four firms and several smaller concerns made Kansas City the nation's second-largest meatpacking center in the 1930s.[4]

Interspersed through the packinghouse district and nestled in the hills along the Kansas River were the modest residences of the workers drawn by the industry. Successive waves of black and white workers first found shelter in "the Patch," a neighborhood of muddy streets and two-room huts built from boards, tin, and various scraps on Armour property. After 1900, East European immigrants moved into homes in the Kansas hills directly west of the Armour plant; the most famous neighborhood became known as "Strawberry Hill" because of its lush fruit vines. During the same period, black workers moved into separate neighborhoods further north on the Kansas side of the Missouri River or crossed the river to live in Kansas City, Missouri's distinct black neighborhoods. In the 1920s and 1930s, native-born white migrants from the declining midwestern coal regions and Mexicans from the Southwest added to the racial and ethnic mix in the packinghouses and adjacent communities.[5]

Blacks and East European ethnics, later the core of the union organizing drive, were the main sources of production workers for Kansas City's slaughterhouses. Both groups generally earned less than the native-born, Irish, and German workers who held highly skilled knife and maintenance jobs. The numbers of black and foreign-born semiskilled male operatives in Kansas City's packinghouses were roughly equal in 1930.[6]

While packinghouse work was hard, disagreeable, and irregular, the availability of jobs and relatively high pay made it a desirable occupation for working-class blacks. African Americans entered Kansas City meatpacking establishments earlier than in any other urban center. In 1879 hundreds of former slaves fleeing the "restoration" of white rule in the South found work at the understaffed Armour plant. By 1905 black men held 1,500 of the area's 10,500 meatpacking jobs; their numbers grew to 2,000 in 1920, along with more than 250 black women. The willingness of meatpacking firms to hire blacks was a sharp contrast to employment practices elsewhere in Kansas City. In 1929 only one-quarter of the businesses in greater Kansas City employed blacks at all, and they were excluded from skilled trades because most AFL craft unions would not admit blacks to membership. New jobs in the steel, auto, brewing, and chemical industries remained virtually shut to blacks.[7]

Discrimination tempered black opportunity in meatpacking, too. Management polices steered blacks into unpleasant, difficult jobs where, as an Armour publicist explained, "The heat is intense and the smell uncongenial to men of more sensitive disposition." Black men were able to climb into well-paid killing-floor jobs such as splitters and headers but never received promotions into occupations reserved for whites, such as stickers, rumpers, floorsmen, and backers. Although blacks composed 25 percent of all Kan-

sas City packinghouse workers in the mid-1930s, they were disproportionately represented in lower job classifications: 40 percent of packinghouse
laborers in 1930 were black. Yet despite limits on black advancement in
meatpacking, only small numbers of professionals, store owners, Pullman
porters, restaurant waiters, and teamsters earned more than packinghouse
workers.[8]

Dependence on packinghouse employment inclined black workers to
favor management's side in labor conflict before the 1930s. "There is no other
large employer of Negroes in Kansas City which treats colored workmen
with more consideration than does the Armour Packing Company," noted
a contemporary observer. Armour courted black workers by providing year-
round employment, supplying free bathing facilities, and shifting older
employees to easier jobs. In the 1920s the companies expanded their programs to recreational activities, such as sponsoring all-black teams in local
baseball leagues. It was rumored that Armour tried to keep blacks at 25 percent of its workforce because of their aversion to labor organizations; in fact,
blacks composed 38 percent of Armour's hourly employees in 1935.[9]

Once they left the packinghouse, black workers encountered rigid residential and social segregation. "It was almost like two different countries,"
recalled packinghouse worker William Raspberry, "you was just black and
that was it." Segregation of neighborhoods, schools, services, and recreation—by law and by custom—sharply demarcated the separate world of
Kansas City's blacks.[10]

Residential segregation in Greater Kansas City increased as the black
population grew in the teens and 1920s. Local courts enforced restrictive
covenants, and "improvement" associations kept their areas "white territory" by resorting to intimidation and violence if legal methods failed. When
blacks overcame resistance and successfully purchased houses on a previously lily-white block, white homeowners quickly fled to new subdivisions.
The neighborhoods that "went black" tended to be older and dilapidated;
in 1940, 60 percent of the residences in majority black areas of Kansas City,
Missouri, antedated 1900, and one-third only had cold running water.[11]

The growth of mass culture respected Kansas City's color line, and blacks
and whites enjoyed leisure and recreation in racially defined arenas. Barnstorming black jazz musicians, such as Benny Moten and County Basie, made
Kansas City a center for the creative energies of swing orchestras. But downtown jazz clubs only admitted white customers; black music enthusiasts
attended the nightclubs lining Twelfth and Eighteenth streets. Black baseball fans went to see luminaries such as Satchel Paige play for the Kansas
City Monarchs (the dominant team in the National Negro League), while

whites watched future stars Mickey Mantle and Yogi Berra perform for the Kansas City Blues, a minor league team owned by the New York Yankees. Blacks were not admitted to bowling alleys, skating rinks, and amusement parks and were denied access to all public and private swimming pools. Downtown department stores sold goods to blacks but would not let them try on clothing, eat at in-house restaurants, or work as clerks. Strict racial separation extended to movie theaters, the school system, hospitals, churches, hotels, and even the Girl Scouts and the Boy Scouts.[12]

Discrimination inadvertently encouraged the development of a vital and race-conscious black society in Kansas City. A thick web of community institutions produced a rich black culture nurtured by a segregation economy and funded by the wages of thousands of working-class blacks. Blacks built their own hotels and hospitals, and they organized an informal network of rooming houses and restaurants in the homes of black families to counteract exclusion from the white establishments. The *Kansas City Call* served as the voice of the community on both sides of the river, and heavily attended Baptist, Methodist, and evangelical churches provided spiritual solace and organizational common ground. Blacks formed protective associations to defend their homes against harassment and bombings, and huge crowds attended rallies featuring Marcus Garvey in 1922. Books by Harlem Renaissance writers and black Chicago authors such as Richard Wright circulated in the black community and were widely discussed in women's clubs, church discussion circles, and informal reading groups.[13]

Kansas City's separate black society represented both an opportunity and a challenge to union organizers. Scorned by most whites, Kansas City blacks constructed a cohesive community that could be a force to aid or undermine any effort to organize the packinghouses. Solidly entrenched in meatpacking occupations, blacks were courted both by the nascent unions and packinghouse management. With sufficient numbers to decide the outcome of an organizing drive, blacks carefully evaluated the relative commitment of unions and companies to the advancement of their race.

Among white packinghouse workers, the Croatians were the group mostly clearly committed to inter-racial unionism. Croatians shared with blacks both dependence on the packing industry and the experience of discrimination. Croatians and other East Europeans made up 30 to 40 percent of the production workers in meatpacking. But immigrants quickly discovered that "you worked at that time if you knew someone"—and that usually entailed exploiting ethnic or religious connections. At Armour, the plant employment manager—along with other top officials—was a Protestant and member of the Masons. Correspondingly, native-born Protestants generally dominated the skilled, highly paid jobs in the mechanical division. Foremen, generally Catholics of Irish or German extraction and members of the Knights of Columbus, preferred to hire ethnic Catholics. The Croatians, along with other East Europeans, quickly filled the jobs at the bottom of the employment ladder, where in many departments they worked alongside black laborers. Croatians chafed under mistreatment by German foremen who called them "Hunky" rather than by their own names. "That's the way they were treated in those days," recalled Thomas Krasick. "We couldn't complain to nobody because we had no union."[14]

Although Croatians were the largest ethnic group, the first and second generations numbered five thousand in 1930, significant numbers of Poles, Slovenians, Serbs, Russians, Greeks, and Lithuanians worked in the packinghouses and lived on Strawberry Hill. Church organizations and fraternal associations provided cohesion in the multiethnic neighborhood. Immigrants and their children celebrated community ties at picnics, dances, and other festivities and read foreign-language papers that carried news of the old country and the progress of ethnic settlements elsewhere in the United States. Four parochial schools taught the second generation on Strawberry Hill in their parents' languages until forced by a law in 1920 to teach in English.[15]

In the 1920s the formation of families and the expansion of home ownership created a stable if poor community. Women contributed to the family economy by taking in boarders, working in the packinghouses and textile factories near the river, and tending the chickens, vegetable gardens, and fruit trees that many families kept in their backyards. Boarding declined after 1920, but more than half of Kansas City's foreign-born families relied on more than one wage-earner in 1930. The combined income made it possible for many ethnics to acquire a house—a dearly sought objective. Among packinghouse workers, 45 percent of the foreign-born owned homes in 1909, and 78 percent did so by 1930.[16]

An unusual feature of the Croatian community was the influence of the secular, and progressive, Croatian Fraternal Union (CFU). Six Kansas City lodges provided important collective resources such as sickness and death benefits and access to medical care. Members could draw on their insurance to make it through difficult periods. "At one time it was almost like the church," recalled Ann Krasick. "I remember my dad would go to meetings on Saturday night and then he'd come home from the meeting and he'd wake up mama and tell her everything that happened." Although weakened by the depression, the CFU retained its popularity among Croatians. In 1933 the Kansas lodges' membership stood at 3,884, more than 50 percent of the 1930 census total for Yugoslavians in the state.[17]

In response to the economic crisis, the CFU encouraged its members to support trade unions. As early as 1932 the national organization criticized wage cuts, urged members to join "militant labor unions," and recommended that lodges expel scabs and provide strike benefits for members. The CFU endorsed the New Deal and hailed the changes under Roosevelt that helped the "laboring masses . . . continue their struggle for a fairer and more equitable distribution of the things they produce." Local CFU leaders aggressively supported CIO organizing drives wherever there were significant concentrations of Croatian industrial workers.[18]

In Kansas City, packinghouse workers dominated the proletarian CFU. More than one-third of the identifiable lodge officers during the 1930s were employed in meatpacking; between 1936 and 1939, the height of the organizing drive in the Kansas City stockyards, packinghouse workers served as president in five of the six CFU lodges. A few clerks and salesmen were the only white-collar employees active in leadership positions, and no shopkeepers or other businessmen served as officers. Many lodge members also were former union members; in the CFU's ranks could be found veterans of Zagreb craft organizations, the United Mine Workers, and the Amalgamated Meat Cutters.[19]

An astute change in policy by the CFU helped the organization bridge the growing cultural divide between the first and second generation. In 1930 the organization began chartering "English Speaking Lodges" (ESL), where children of the immigrants would feel more at home. Kansas City ESL Lodge 734, the "Jayhawks," cultivated a following among second-generation Croatians by organizing picnics, wiener roasts, and softball teams in the summer and indoor activities such as bowling, plays, concerts, and dances in colder months. In 1939 five thousand turned out to hear the popular CFU-sponsored Tamburitza Orchestra, conducted by packinghouse worker Matt Grisnik, at the organization's forty-fifth anniversary celebration. Befitting the Croatian and American admixture of the event held on July 4, a softball tournament preceded the music. In Kansas City the popularity and success of the Jayhawks allowed the CFU to temper the assimilation of the second generation by organizing them as Croatians to participate in American mass culture.[20]

Careful planning by the CFU shaped the process of Americanization by containing the second generation within the boundaries of an expanding and more diverse Croatian community. This linked the younger generation of ethnic packinghouse workers with their elders, who often had participated in unions during more propitious times. The cohesion of the Croatian community on Strawberry Hill, and its potential to provide a linchpin of ethnic support for an inter-racial union, would be an essential asset of the organizing drive in the late 1930s. And when a small group of Socialists began to seek recruits for inter-racial, industrial unionism, Croatians were among the first to join.

The Development of Industrial Unionism in the 1930s

The packinghouses were the most integrated institution in Kansas City's segregated society; nowhere else did thousands of blacks and whites come together daily for eight, ten, or twelve hours of common activity. Yet strict customs governing job assignments by race and ethnicity obstructed unionism. In the absence of credible labor organizations, workers preferred to rely on their separate ethno-religious networks and contacts within management to keep their jobs and provide openings for family members and other relatives.

The failure of earlier organizing drives also discouraged packinghouse workers from relying on inter-racial workplace organizations to improve their conditions. The 1921–22 strike called by the Amalgamated Meat Cutters received wide support among white ethnics, but most black workers ignored the union's appeal and helped break the walkout. Packinghouse firms successfully established employee representation plans in the strike's aftermath to channel shop-floor discontent into employer-dominated avenues and implemented policies such as limited seniority benefits to encourage loyalty to the company. In the mid-1920s the local Chamber of Commerce boasted, "Kansas City labor is settled and contented. Here there have been only seven strikes since 1898, and none since 1921. Practically all of the existing industries operate on an open shop basis."[21]

A few years later businessmen were less sanguine. The economic collapse of 1929 destabilized relations in Kansas City's packinghouses and undermined the welfare capitalism of the companies. Between 1929 and 1933 three hundred Kansas City firms went out of business, and the manufacturing workforce fell from forty-eight thousand to thirty-four thousand. Employment in meatpacking declined from eight thousand in 1930 to six thousand in 1935—a drop of 25 percent. A shortened work week and three consecutive wage cuts reduced the income of packinghouse workers who were able to escape layoffs. "We were part of the hungry people of the time," recalled Strawberry Hill resident Ann Krasick. The depression, and the intervention of a determined group of Socialists, soon would overturn the system of labor relations that had predominated in Kansas City's packinghouses.[22]

Initially, popular discontent provided a fertile ground for the efforts of

Young Communist League organizer Herb March, who arrived in Kansas City in 1930. Over the next three years, March and other Communists successfully organized an explosive unemployed movement. As in Chicago, Communists tried to translate their success among the unemployed to promote unionism in local factories. March and his comrades distributed a shop paper at the Armour and Swift plants and were able to elicit support among a small group of ethnic and black workers. "We had an informal sort of packinghouse workers union," he recalled. But at this point, before the passage of the National Recovery Act, activists recognized that public activity was suicidal. "It didn't dare meet," March admitted. "You had to be very careful." March's departure from Kansas City in 1933 ended the Communists' initiative in meatpacking, although he put his experience to good use in Chicago.[23]

Four Socialists in the Armour plant subsequently provided the initiative for unions in the Kansas City stockyards. Because all were highly skilled workers of native-born ancestry, they were sociologically similar to union pioneers in other mass-production industries and quite different from the ethnics and blacks who predominated in production jobs. Charles R. Fischer and Howard Rentfrow were powerhouse mechanics, while cooper Clyde Shockey and tinsmith James Lumpkin worked in the machine shop. Fischer and Rentfrow were particularly open about their political affiliation, because both were candidates for state assembly on the Socialist Party ticket in 1936. In the early 1930s, at the same time as the Communists started agitating for union organization, the Armour Socialists were slowly establishing contacts with black and ethnic white workers in their plant.[24]

Charles R. Fischer was the leader of the Socialist group. Fischer's politics owed a great deal to his father, an active member of the International Association of Machinists (IAM), who had moved to Kansas City in the teens after being blacklisted in his native state of Pennsylvania. Although the family was of German extraction, ethnicity did not shape Fischer's politics. Far more influential was his father's participation in Kansas City's Socialist movement; Fischer vividly remembered his father's penchant for speaking from a soapbox to crowds in local parks. Fischer inherited strong social democratic politics from his father as well as a firm belief in the fundamental equality of all ethnic and racial groups. "Prejudice was passé in our house," Fischer recalled, "we just didn't believe in it." He joined the Socialist Party in 1924 at the age of seventeen because they were "fighting for the forty hour week and the eight hour day" and believed in "peaceful revolution, changing the structure of government so that the people on the bottom would be more equalized with the people on top." To the extent that Kansas City's

Socialist heritage was manifested in the 1930s, it was through individuals such as Fischer.[25]

After campaigning for Norman Thomas in 1932 with other Kansas City Socialists, Fischer and his associates in the Armour plant slowly began to assemble a core of union activists representing the different racial and ethnic groups in the plant. By 1935 there were approximately twenty in this small, secret nucleus who were ready and waiting for the opportunity to expand their numbers. Although several years would pass before the union surfaced, the Socialists laid the essential groundwork before passage of the Wagner Act.[26]

They first found allies among a group of former United Mine Workers members who had found jobs in the Kansas City packing industry as mining operations declined in the southern Kansas and Missouri coal fields. The most important recruit among the miners was Orville Ussery, one of the few whites in the hide cellar department, who later became the first president of the Armour local. Two other early allies among the former miners were brothers Cecil and Earl Longden, from Rosewing, Missouri, and, as Fischer recalled, "solid as a rock so far as unions were concerned."[27]

Croatians made up another component of the initial activist core. The Socialists established links with Croatian union supporters and former members of the Amalgamated Meat Cutters through Tony Kostelac. "Tony Kostelac was the main key there," recalled Fischer. Kostelac, who worked in the sweet-pickle cellar, had been strongly influenced by family members who participated in the strike of 1921 and 1922. A leader of the local CFU and highly respected among Croatians, Kostelac served as the local's financial secretary for many years and provided an entrée to the community's social clubs, neighborhood networks, and priests. One of Kostelac's most important recruits was musician Matt Grisnik, patriarch of a clan of active CFU members.[28]

The biggest test for the Socialists, however, was their ability to bring black workers onto the union bandwagon. In 1935 Armour's 570 black employees were concentrated in a few key departments, most notably all three killing floors. Their sheer numbers and critical placement in the labor process made union success contingent on black support.[29]

Deteriorating working conditions during the depression had eroded, but not eliminated, company loyalty among black workers. Favoritism and racist treatment by foremen was a particularly serious problem because Armour employment declined steadily throughout the 1930s and a supervisor's prejudice, rather than a worker's seniority, governed layoffs. Even so, packinghouse work remained one of the best jobs available to black men and women. The packing strike of 1921 and 1922 had created more openings for blacks in jobs previously controlled by whites, and many of these strikebreakers were still employed by Armour in the mid-1930s. In the initial stages of organizing, before the formation of the CIO, a majority of the black workers remained loyal to the company. Veteran killing-floor worker Julius Jacobson rebuffed initial union recruitment efforts. "I ain't never heard where the union did anything for the colored man," he told organizers. His skepticism reflected the experience of Kansas City's black workers with exclusionary craft unions.[30]

The union's first black member came through workplace connections in the hide cellar (later the epicenter of the 1938 plant occupation) when Orville Ussery recruited co-worker Finis Block to the secretive group of union activists. A middle-aged worker widely known in his community as a deeply religious and conservative man, Block's decision to support industrial unionism was a major breakthrough. Born in Arkansas in 1899, Block moved to Kansas City, Kansas, in 1923 and soon found a job at Armour. He left the plant to operate a grocery store but returned to Armour in 1930 when the depression ruined his business. Convinced of the sincerity of union activists, Block tried to persuade black workers that joining with whites in a labor organization would stop the company from "treating them like slaves." He recalled telling black workers in private meetings, "I'm not talking with one of the white men, you're all that's here. I don't need to take this bull. A lot of you been taking it for many a year, and you need protection."[31]

Workplace connections and Block's endorsement helped bring on board Spurgeon Edgerton, an influential black who worked in the sweet-pickle cellar with Croatian Tony Kostelac. Edgerton was a widely respected, race-conscious man who had been active in Kansas City's Marcus Garvey movement and traveled to Liberia in the 1920s on the Black Star Line. He recruited sweet-pickle co-workers John Franklin and Ermon Dixon, as well as Neal Weaver, a "silver tongued lay preacher" who worked in the hog offal department and was until that time an official in the company union. Weaver in turn brought in several co-workers, including the union's first black woman, Sydney Thomas. With this initial support, organizers were able to secure initial backing on the critical killing floors from blacks A. U. Davis, Ollie Reems, George Richardson, and Isaac White.[32]

The inclusive, industrial union strategy of Fischer and his associates was heavily influenced by the successful union in the Austin, Minnesota, Hormel plant. "Austin taught us it is not an impossible task to organize a packinghouse," explained Fischer, "we patterned our effort after Austin." Between 1933 and 1936 Fischer and other Socialists from the Armour plant met several times with IUAW leaders and packinghouse workers from Iowa, Minnesota, and Nebraska to share experiences and facilitate expansion of unions in the industry.[33]

The passage of the Wagner Act and formation of the CIO allowed the Armour's militant minority to greatly expand their activities in 1936 and 1937. Within the plant, the union nucleus employed the CIO's positive reputation to bolster organizing efforts. Fischer recalled that activists "simply pointed out to the rank-and-file the benefits that had been received by the steel workers, by the automobile workers, by the rubber workers and so forth, and it was obvious what the benefits were because it had been done." The CIO's support of inter-racial unionism appealed to black workers jaded by the AFL's history of racial exclusion. "CIO came along and said, well, if you get on a job, from the day you're hired, your seniority starts. And whoever comes behind you, gets behind you. Color has nothing to do with it," remembered William Raspberry. And for the former coal miners in Kansas City's packinghouses, the role of John L. Lewis and the United Mine Workers in the CIO conferred legitimacy on its advocates in meatpacking.[34]

Fischer's reference to CIO accomplishments had a tangible reality for Kansas City packinghouse workers. General Motors workers in a Chevrolet plant on the eastern edge of Kansas City, Missouri, had formed a stable union in 1934 that affiliated with the United Auto Workers (UAW). Armour's Socialists knew UAW members active in the Missouri branch of the party, and Orville Ussery had friends at Chevrolet whom he had worked with in the coal mines. Early in 1937 this UAW local dispatched two auto workers to assist the Armour organizing campaign in response to requests by Ussery and Fischer.[35]

Following the CIO victories over General Motors in February 1937, Armour's militant minority went public, and Local Industrial Union No. 232 (directly affiliated with the CIO) embarked on a highly visible organizing drive. Doubtless the assistance of local General Motors workers, fresh from their victory, enhanced the stature of local unionists. The UAW organizers "brought little pink buttons with UAW on [them]," which union activists distributed throughout the Armour plant. Over the next few months the union extended its organization into departments dominated by white women (margarine, pork trim, and sliced bacon) while consolidating its position among black and ethnic men on the killing floors and the hide cellar, black women in the hog offal, and native-born whites in the mechanical gang.[36]

In addition to its shop-floor strategy, the union employed social gatherings to recruit workers and consolidate inter-racial unity. Union-organized cultural events featuring ethnic and black musicians drew hundreds of black and white packinghouse workers. Between acts, participants cheered speakers who attacked wage cuts and other company policies. By holding these events in the large CFU hall on Strawberry Hill, organizers appropriated the ethnic tradition of social events to the union cause and showed black workers who attended that the union did not permit racial segregation. "Everybody participated, and everybody sat together, there wasn't all this segregation business," recalled Fischer. There were significant limits to interracial socializing, however. "They didn't dance," Fischer recalled adamantly. "That was a no-no, because it was still, in the background of these whites, and some of these blacks, that they didn't like to associate personally. As long as it was for an economic reason, fine, but not in any other sense." Despite the limits to the union's social integration of its members, these probably were the largest unsegregated cultural gatherings in Kansas City at the time.[37]

As in Chicago, packinghouse unionists used the legitimacy of a certification election to provide a focus for the organizing drive. Between the official formation of Local 232 in March 1937 and the election on August 5, CIO activists swept aside company efforts to slow the union's momentum. Armour tried to defuse worker dissatisfaction by rescinding a wage cut and instituting a modified form of seniority. The company also transformed the old employee representation body into an Employees Bargaining Association (EBA). Management tried to confer legitimacy on the EBA by refusing to meet with Local 232 stewards and instead referring grievances to EBA officials.[38]

These delaying tactics proved futile. Neal Weaver, a long-time employee representative, disrupted the company's strategy by persuading almost all the EBA officials to resign and join the CIO. On the eve of the August 5 election, Local 232 consolidated the broad alliance it represented by selecting a balanced slate of union officers. Union members elected Orville Ussery as president and selected two black workers, Weaver and Ollie Reems, to the two vice-presidential positions. Trusted Croatian leader Tony Kostelac watched the union's money as its financial secretary, and the important Grievance Committee was chaired by the man who had started the ball rolling—genial Socialist Charles R. Fischer. Local 232 defeated the EBA by 1049 to 768 in the August 1937 certification election. When packinghouse workers formed the Packinghouse Workers Organizing Committee later that year, the Armour union became Local 15. The vision of Fischer, and the union pioneers, seemingly had come true.[39]

The 1938 Armour Plant Occupation

As was so often the case during the 1930s, NLRB certification did not signify a complete victory for the union or a willingness by the company to accept collective bargaining. At the time of the election, fewer than half the workers in the plant were members of Local 15 and management resisted efforts by the union to establish its authority. A "verbatim record" of negotiations served as the agreement, but, as Fischer recalled, "It was a mess because everybody had their own interpretation on what was said and what it meant." While rejecting the union's demand for strict seniority in hiring, promotion, and layoff, the company did accept the role of stewards and union officials in settling workplace grievances. Under the verbal agreement, a committee of five to nine members was to be compensated for time spent meeting with management over grievances.[40]

Conflict over the union's right to represent workers in shop-floor disputes triggered the September 1938 plant occupation. Tensions built steadily for a year after the certification election as management resisted union efforts to process grievances. Union members were especially antagonized by management's treatment of the Local 15 chief steward Matt Lambie, who faced repeated harassment and was laid off in June despite having seventeen years seniority.[41]

On September 2, five hide cellar workers—four black and one Croatian—stopped work to protest an increase in their workload. Local 15's Grievance Committee, and the five hide cellar workers, spent the entire next day meeting with Armour officials over the issue. Management rejected their complaint as well as union demands to pay $22.09 to the five workers for time spent in the meeting. "When the money was not in their pay envelopes Friday morning," reported the *Kansas City Star*, "the strike was ordered." At stake was the organization's capacity to negotiate, and settle, shop-floor disputes.[42]

Local 15 carefully organized the plant occupation and used it to solidify the union's base. Food and other supplies came from a union strike kitchen and community residents. Workers used ropes to lower buckets over the plant's wall to collect food, drink, and cigarettes brought by strike supporters. Pickets outside the plant gate kept watch for police or potential strikebreakers and built fires to brew coffee for the strikers inside. Twice-daily union meetings kept workers informed on the progress of negotiations and collected dues and initiation fees from many strikers who were not yet members of Local 15.[43]

To build morale and consolidate the strike community, Socialist Jim Lumpkin took charge of the union's Entertainment Committee and arranged for inter-racial performances that drew on the abilities of the workers occupying the plant. "We had some very good musicians," recalled Fischer. "Then there were several guys who had very good voices," including several black baritones and an Irish tenor. A gospel choir composed of black packinghouse workers performed at the union's evening events and entertained workers during the day. Lumpkin wrote several songs especially for the occasion, and workers sang them along with traditional union standards such as "Solidarity Forever."[44]

Sympathy for the strike in Kansas City obstructed Armour's efforts to isolate the union and portray the sit-down as violent and destructive. Because improvements in the standard of living of packinghouse workers would have a positive ripple effect on the community, residents, small businessmen, and public officials in Kansas City, Kansas, were highly supportive of the union's efforts. City authorities rejected company demands to evict the strikers in the absence of a clear danger of violence or a court order certifying that a crime had been committed. Claiming neutrality in the dispute, Acting Mayor George T. Darby successfully pressured the company to negotiate with the union while the plant remained occupied.[45]

In a compromise hammered out under the mayor's watchful eye—the first signed agreement between Armour and Local 15—the company agreed not to discipline workers who participated in the sit-down and to accept arbitration of the hide cellar pay dispute. With the tie-breaking vote coming from a Strawberry Hill Catholic priest appointed by Darby, the arbitration board awarded hide cellar workers the disputed back pay. It also directed the company and the union to split the cost of the meat spoiled during the first day of the dispute.[46]

Following the successful sit-down, Local 15 entrenched itself in departments throughout the plant. "They were forced to negotiate whether they liked it or not. And as a result of that, we signed up hundreds and hundreds and hundreds of people," recalled Fischer. Dozens of well-trained union stewards applied concerted pressure, including stoppages and slowdowns, over hundreds of annoying grievances that management had resisted settling before the occupation. Union officials claimed that they settled 692 out of 778 grievances in 1939—one for every three workers! Numerous disputes over job rights, seniority, and wages resulted in union victories in eleven departments. The union had a particularly dramatic success in May 1939 by forcing management to accept equal pay for equal work by women. Membership reached 1,816 in August 1939 and then mushroomed to 2,700 a year later as overall employment increased. By 1941 there were only fifty non-union workers in the plant.[47]

Local 15's success solidified the joint black, Croatian, and Socialist leadership and vindicated the strategy of inter-racial industrial unionism. Black attendance at union meetings reached 40 percent, a number that matched the proportion of blacks in the workforce, making the union the largest inter-racial organization in Kansas City at the time. Blacks functioned as stewards, union trustees, and elected officials, and Neal Weaver rose to the position of assistant national director of the PWOC for a short time. President Orville Ussery frequently yielded the chair of union meetings to black vice-president Ollie Reems, a far more skilled parliamentarian and public speaker. Tony Kostelac retained the key post of financial secretary for many years. For the rest of the local's history, a balance of blacks and ethnic men and women functioned as stewards, elected officials, and members of union committees.[48]

The Socialists, although small in number, played an indispensable role within the union's leadership. Jim Lumpkin masterminded the union's successful entertainment program throughout 1938 and 1939, and Howard Rentfrow organized its stewards' training classes. Clyde Shockey served as union president after Ussery, and Charles R. Fischer, as chair of the Bargaining Committee, was involved in all negotiations with the company. Fischer was widely known as a Socialist and was unabashed about his political commitments; during the 1938 sit-down he was again on the Socialist ticket, this time for state treasurer.[49]

The union's commitment to gender equality was more limited. The inter-racial cooperation that marked the plant occupation may have been aided by its exclusively male character. The union consciously limited female workers to an auxiliary role. Women "expressed a desire to remain at the plant," reported the local paper, but left after the first day on the recommendation of the men. When women returned in the morning, "expecting to reenter," they were halted by company guards, "which, apparently, met with the approval of the men strikers." Subsequently, women's participation in the sit-down consisted of preparing meals at the union commissary and delivering supplies to the men inside the plant. Doubtless the absence of women removed a potential source of tension between black and white men, but it also left women out of the pivotal event that consolidated the union leadership team. Although the Kansas City packinghouse locals, as was generally the case in meatpacking, firmly supported equal pay for equal work and included women in leadership positions, the change in relations between the sexes was not as dramatic as the change in race relations.[50]

Organizing Other Kansas City Packinghouses

Success at Armour opened the way for union activists to organize other packinghouses along the Kansas River. Features similar to the Armour drive emerged in the union drives at Cudahy and Wilson: the leadership roles of Croatian and black workers, the use of job actions to establish union authority over working conditions, and utilization of the National Labor Relations Board to protect union organizers and hold a representation election. In May 1940 the PWOC easily defeated the Amalgamated Meat Cutters at the Cudahy plant by a vote of 813 to 19, and the union secured certification at the Wilson packinghouse in 1942. Along with successes at Meyer Kornblum and other small meat factories, Kansas City PWOC membership exceeded five thousand by 1943.[51]

The PWOC's one failure in Kansas City was at the Swift plant. In July 1943 the PWOC lost badly to an Independent Packinghouse Workers' union formed by former leaders of Swift's company union. The independent union subsequently affiliated with the National Brotherhood of Packinghouse Workers (NBPW), an organization entirely based in the Swift plants. Despite repeated efforts in the 1940s and 1950s, the UPWA never was able to displace the NBPW in Kansas City Swift.[52]

Racial divisions largely explain the PWOC's defeat at Kansas City Swift. The NBPW retained strong support among white workers who were never persuaded that adversarial industrial unionism was preferable to company paternalism. By and large, white workers retained confidence in the Swift management and shied away from the PWOC as a union too inclined to go on strike. "Instead of my foreman and I talking, and iron it out," Martha Richardson, a white Swift worker, complained that grievances at the CIO-organized Cudahy plant invariably meant "the whole department went out." The PWOC's inter-racial unionism especially antagonized whites who preferred racial privilege to equal employment opportunity. Supervisors allowed the informal hiring and promotion networks of religion, ethnicity, and kin to remain in place, thus favoring entrenched white groups in the production jobs. Highly paid jobs such as ham boning and sliced bacon remained all-white throughout the 1950s.[53]

While whites favored the NBPW, black Swift workers generally supported the CIO. The unwillingness, or inability, of the NBPW to correct managerial abuses on the shop floor or to alter the traditional racial allocation of jobs alienated most black workers. "The Independent union can't do nothing," complained one black butcher. Another criticized the union representatives as "too close to the foreman." Theodore Purcell's study of Kansas City Swift in the 1950s supports these impressionistic statements. The NBPW had fewer stewards and filed far fewer grievances per worker than equivalent UPWA unions, and it never cooperated in national strikes against Swift. Unlike UPWA unions, it did not file grievances over job loads and work schedules and rarely contested promotion practices. In fact, there was no Grievance Committee at all.[54]

The laxity of the NBPW toward shop-floor relations had clear racial dimensions. "When a Negro comes to Swift & Company, the ceiling is very low," commented one black worker. "If you're looking for a promotion . . . well these positions are never here." With its predominantly white base, the NBPW had no desire to alter traditional limits on black employment. In the 1950s, when UPWA locals in Swift's packinghouses ended employment discrimination against black women, the independent union made no effort to terminate the informal ban in the Kansas City plant.[55]

The white domination of Local 12, and its cozy relationship with management, created a persistent—although minority—pro-CIO group in the Swift plant that was almost entirely black. Swift's paternalistic style and active support for NBPW, however, limited the PWOC's backing to between 30 and 40 percent of the workforce. "Where Armour would say: 'You do this and you do that,' and that's all there is to it," complained a black CIO supporter, Swift "might come along and use a little different tack, or pat the guy on the back, or offer him a little concession, or say we're all one big happy family." Despite repeated attempts, the PWOC never was able to persuade white Swift workers to embark on the inter-racial and adversarial unionism that other Kansas City packinghouse workers had embraced.[56]

* * *

With the exception of Swift, by the mid-1940s CIO unionists in Kansas City's packinghouses had transformed power relations in their workplaces. Unions enforced strict seniority in layoffs and promotions, regulated departmental job loads, won extended vacation plans, and secured wage increases. The inter-racial locals were the most impressive accomplishment. Black workers, who remained suspicious of many labor organizations, fully participated in and actively led the packinghouse unions. Croatians and other ethnics accepted blacks as equals in the union, even though there was little social interaction away from the workplace except among a few leaders. A workforce that had been fractured along racial, ethnic, and religious lines for fifty years now cooperated in a union to improve their lives.[57]

The leadership cadre that emerged from the struggles of the 1930s remained in place for most of the 1940s and 1950s, invigorated by infusions of younger workers whose experiences motivated them to take on union responsibilities. As in Austin, however, the early radicalism of the local unions faded after 1940 as Socialists such as Fischer became liberal Democrats. Ironically, packinghouse workers still regarded Fischer and his compatriots as

Socialists and never withheld support or sympathy because of their radical taint. These factors, taken together, instilled a powerful progressive, inter-racial, and independent tradition that Kansas City locals expressed within the PWOC and UPWA into the 1960s.[58]

The experience of Kansas City's packinghouse workers was in many ways typical of other multiracial meatpacking centers that unionized in the 1930s. The workplace was the only arena in which workers could initially meet and establish a relationship of trust, cooperation, and mutual support. From work, union advocates reached out through ethnic and racial networks into internally cohesive neighborhoods of packinghouse workers, employing a sophisticated combination of establishing authority on the job and creating an inter-racial community through union events. As in Chicago, it was through cooperation on the job that black and white workers began the process of building mutual trust and respect. Charles R. Fischer's adage, "without a union, we're all lost," expressed in simple but elegant terms the bedrock of inter-racial unity in the Kansas City stockyards.

5

"We Had to Have Somebody Behind Us": The Origins of Packinghouse Unionism in Sioux City, Iowa

> I don't think we could have accomplished what we did accomplish without having the backing of John L. Lewis and others in the union. We knew that we had an organization behind us. Otherwise, it wouldn't have been any point of even trying to organize 'cause we'd have been beaten down. We had to have somebody behind us.
>
> —Jennie Shuck, Sioux City union founder

When CIO organizer Harmon R. Ballard arrived in Sioux City on June 6, 1937, with instructions to initiate an organizing drive in the local packinghouses, he faced a difficult task. "The Trades and Labor Assembly sent me a letter asking me to refrain from organizing any units here," he recounted in a contemporary magazine. "Every day during our first week, a policemen was stationed at the elevator on our floor. Two to four officers were detailed at every meeting we held in Teutonia Hall for a week." The Sioux City business elite, highly dependent on the packinghouse industry, feared the effects of unionization and no doubt encouraged the police surveillance. Hostility from local AFL unions reflected the deep division in the national labor movement. And Ballard quickly found that Sioux City's packinghouse workers were totally unorganized.[1]

Opposition from the AFL and local businessmen was beyond his control, so Ballard concentrated on his organizing responsibilities. He quickly established contact with packinghouse workers who wanted to bring the CIO into their plants, and hundreds attended a mass meeting on June 24. In August the CIO issued a charter to Local Industrial Union No. 389, with jurisdiction over Sioux City's meatpacking industry.[2]

Ballard's experience illustrates the dynamics of the process of union formation in Sioux City packinghouses. Unlike Chicago, Kansas City, or Austin, there was no cohesive proto-union group of workers who had undertaken organizing in the packinghouses before the CIO-initiated drive in 1937.

This was due to several factors specific to Sioux City. First, its geographic isolation on Iowa's western border kept it outside of regional networks of packinghouse unionists in the mid-1930s. Second, because meatpacking was by far the most important local manufacturing business, there were no unionists from other mass-production industries who could assist the packinghouse workers. Third, no organized left-wing group had sufficient membership in the packinghouses to push for unionization. And, finally, a devastating strike in 1921 and 1922 and an abortive organizing drive in 1934 and 1935, both led by the Amalgamated Meat Cutters and Butcher Workmen, weighed heavily on the attitudes of pro-union workers and made them reluctant to risk reprisals without better hope for success.

Similar to other meatpacking centers, however, the organizing drive the CIO initiated in Sioux City depended on and was led by a distinct "militant minority" of local packinghouse workers. Their strategy, developed under the guidance of Ballard but given shape by the workers, shared important basic features with the rank-and-file organizing techniques elsewhere in the meatpacking industry. Union activists identified workplace grievances that cut across differences in race, ethnicity, and sex. They built strong steward systems and used job actions to empower workers and undermine managerial authority on the shop floor. Organizers adroitly tapped ethnic, familial, and neighborhood networks of packinghouse workers and brought respected group leaders into the center of the organizing drive. And they used the National Labor Relations Board to give legitimacy to their efforts and made NLRB certification a focus for membership recruitment. Through these activities, they hoped to convince co-workers that a labor organization would provide more job security and opportunity for economic advancement than existing company structures and informal employment networks.

Ballard's successful June rally, attracting hundreds of workers only two weeks after he arrived in Sioux City, reflected the CIO organizer's ability to establish contact with existing subterranean circles of pro-union packinghouse employees. Three discernible groups furnished early support. Russian workers, because of their sheer numbers in unskilled production jobs and their readiness to support unionism, were the linchpin of ethnic backing for the CIO drive. Blacks, although a relatively small number of packinghouse workers, supplied indispensable support on the strategically important killing floors. Finally, a small coterie of workers with prior union experience, usually native-born or from more established immigrant groups (Irish, German, or Scandinavian) and working on higher-paid skilled jobs, provided essential leadership as well. Ballard's arrival was the trigger that encouraged union activists to surface, because they were unwilling to launch an organizing drive until they had support from a powerful and reliable national labor organization. Without the CIO's backing, explained union pioneer Jennie Shuck, "We'd have been beaten down. We had to have somebody behind us."

As they had hoped, Sioux City's union pioneers received indispensable assistance from the CIO. Its program of industrial unionism provided an organizational vehicle to unite the different fragments of the local workforce. The CIO's national structure buttressed the efforts of Sioux City's union activists by providing an alliance with other segments of the industrial working class. Successes in auto, steel, and other industries legitimized the shop-floor organizing strategy of local union leaders. The link with the Packinghouse Workers Organizing Committee magnified the power of Sioux City workers by establishing contacts with packinghouse workers who labored in the plants of the same national companies in other locations. By creating bonds between Sioux City's fledgling unions and locals that had already achieved union recognition, PWOC organizers were able to argue convincingly that victory was indeed possible. Together the CIO and the local union leaders were able to overcome the perceptions of isolation and powerlessness that made packinghouse workers reluctant to join a labor organization.

The Formation of a Meatpacking Community

The CIO's initiative reflected the importance of Sioux City to the national packing industry, especially to pork production in Iowa. Located at the junction of the Missouri and Floyd rivers, the city's capacity to serve as a processing hub linking the rich farming belt of the Upper Midwest with eastern sales outlets made it Iowa's largest meatpacking center in the twentieth century. In 1929 Sioux City packinghouses killed 40 percent of Iowa's total hog slaughter and employed 30 percent of the state's meatpacking workers (Table 8). That same year, Sioux City's seven meat establishments contributed two-thirds of the value of local manufacturing and employed three thousand workers, more than a third of the city's industrial workforce. Approximately 2,500 worked at the Armour, Cudahy, and Swift plants (Wilson did not operate in Sioux City). The economic health of the city revolved around the hundred-acre complex of pens and slaughterhouses built on the fork of land between the rivers.[3]

The growth of the packing industry profoundly influenced Sioux City's social structure. At the very bottom were migratory workers who entered the city every fall looking for work during seasonal hog rush. When meat-

Table 8. Pork Packing in Sioux City and Iowa

Year	Sioux City[a]	Iowa[a]	Percent Sioux City
1881	47	955	5
1891	655	1,820	36
1901	725	1,991	36
1911	874	2,053	43
1921	1,255	3,099	40
1926[b]	1,771	4,379	40

a. Figures are in thousands slaughtered.
b. Iowa's next largest pork center in 1926 was Ottumwa, with 675,000 hogs slaughtered, 38 percent of Sioux City's total.
Source: H. H. McCarty and C. W. Thompson, "Meat Packing in Iowa," *Iowa Studies in Business* 12 (June 1933): 125–26.

packing employment declined in the spring, they left to seek jobs harvesting the products of the Midwest's vast agricultural hinterlands. More permanent workers attracted by the industry came from Russia, Southern Europe, and Asia and generally dominated the production jobs in the packinghouses. Older immigrant groups (generally Irish, German, and Scandinavian) filled jobs in the booming building trades, took positions as machinists and railroad workers, or worked in highly paid knife and skilled trades jobs in the packinghouses. Some were able to became small businessmen, primarily building contractors and storekeepers. The native-born Protestant founders of Sioux City remained the dominant group, however, by virtue of their control over the city's professions, newspapers, banks, insurance companies, and large firms. The city developed a clear social ecology, with the older immigrant groups and native-born settlers residing in the rolling hills back from the Missouri River while the new immigrants lived in neighborhoods near the water. A family's economic progress could be measured by the distance of their home from the riverside industrial district.[4]

Sioux City's packinghouse production workers generally lived in the Bottoms, the flats near the Missouri and Floyd river junction adjacent to the packinghouses and other manufacturing enterprises. Most residents before the Panic of 1893 came from Ireland, Germany, and the Scandinavian countries, but after 1900 the East and South Bottoms became a polyglot neighborhood where recent immigrants from Europe and Asia, migrants from the American plains, and blacks from the South lived and worked. They were physically separated from downtown Sioux City to the west and north by multiple railroad tracks and from the East Side suburbs by the Floyd River. The stockyards, perched along the Missouri River shore, defined the southern border of the neighborhood and provided most of the employment for its residents. Pinned between the Floyd and the Missouri, Bottoms residents faced devastating floods in 1892, 1936, and 1952 during the high-water months of March and April.[5]

A large number of churches and associated fraternal organizations provided organizational cohesion to the ethnic communities. At least nine churches linked to specific ethnic groups serviced the Bottoms. Lithuanians attended St. Casimir Catholic, the Polish went to St. Francis, blacks worshipped at a Baptist Evangelical church, and the Greeks, Syrians, and Jews had their own religious centers. Sioux City's larger Irish churches outside of the Bottoms controlled the Catholic parish, but the recent immigrants regulated affairs in their own religious institutions. The Poles were especially religious and were the only immigrants beside the Irish to support a parochial school.[6]

Russian packinghouse workers contributed the most important group of union pioneers in 1937 and 1938 because of their community's particular history as well as their place in Sioux City's immigrant culture. The Russians composed the largest immigrant group in the Bottoms neighborhoods. The first and second generations numbered approximately three thousand, evenly divided between Jewish and Russian Orthodox worshipers. The Russians formed a cohesive community on their own while living intermixed with other immigrants. On days off from work, relatives, neighbors, or friends from the packinghouse would visit, drink coffee or home-brew, talk, and play cards. Children attended neighborhood schools with Poles, Lithuanians, Syrians, and blacks, played together in mixed groups, and later dated and married across ethnic lines. Interaction among ethnics at work and in the community forged close bonds and helped develop mutual respect. Jennie Shuck, a founder and leader of the Cudahy union, later explained, "We didn't have to be told in school that all these people are just as good as you are—we learned to live with them all."[7]

Compared to Sioux City's other ethnics, however, the Russians were far less tied to their church and more open to union activity and radical political ideas. Most non-Jewish Russians were at least nominal members of the Russian Orthodox church in the East Bottoms. Although they would crowd its small hall for religious celebrations, parishioners did not treat the priest as an important community leader. Factional divisions among Russians were played out as church politics and usually resulted in replacement of one priest by another, followed within a year by another change in personnel. Between 1916 and 1940 at least fifteen different priests filled the church's pulpit. In contrast to the Russians' casual attitude toward their religious leader, Lithuanian and Polish priests lasted ten or twenty years and were powerful influences in their respective communities.[8]

Weak church authority over civil affairs facilitated the efforts of leftist and pro-union Russians to recruit fellow immigrants to their cause. In 1919 local parishioners deposed priest C. Zakrevsky because of his vocal attacks on radicalism and unionism. "Czarism and priests like Zakrevsky have kept Russian people in darkness for hundreds and hundreds of years," explained a Russian packinghouse worker in a letter to the local paper. "Zakrevsky is a former servant of the czar." In November that year, many Russian packinghouse workers stayed home from work to celebrate the second anniversary of the Bolshevik Revolution. These same workers were active members of the Amalgamated Meat Cutter locals until a disastrous strike in 1921.[9]

With this tradition, there was a pool of Russian packinghouse workers willing to join a labor organization that exhibited both the determination and the resources to have a reasonable chance for success. With his CIO credentials, and a long history of activity in the Iowa United Mine Workers, Ballard attracted several influential Russians willing to build the union among ethnic production workers. One especially important early leader was Armour worker John Davidchik, whose large family was active in the local Russian church. Several of his sisters worked at Swift and helped spread the union among the women in their plant. Davidchik became the vice president of Local 389 in July 1937 and played a leading role in Sioux City's packinghouse unions into the 1970s.[10]

At Cudahy, Ballard's principal Russian recruits were Jennie Shuck and her father, Vladimir Zenkovich. Zenkovich was an army scribe and schoolteacher from Minsk who emigrated in 1907 to avoid further military service. He was an unusual man for the immigrant Russian community—a well-educated freethinker who refused to attend church. "People had letters from the old country that they couldn't read, they'd come over to have him read them, or have him write a letter for them," recalled his daughter. Literacy was not useful for advancing an immigrant's career in Sioux City, however, so he found work at the Cudahy plant and became one of the highly skilled butchers on the beef kill. He joined the Amalgamated Meat Cutters and participated in the strike of 1921 and 1922 and was still working in Cudahy's beef kill in 1937.[11]

Zenkovich's wife died in childbirth in 1915, when Jennie, his eldest daughter, was only six. When she turned a "tall" fifteen in 1924, her father asked Jennie to go to work to help support the family. Married in the early 1930s to Paul Shuck, another Russian Cudahy worker, she continued to work and closely followed the progress of industrial unions, especially the rise of the CIO. When Ballard began organizing in Sioux City, the Zenkovich and Shuck families were among his first recruits at Cudahy. Jennie used her knowledge of Russian, Polish, and Lithuanian to draw the immigrant women in the plant into the union, while her father and her husband encouraged the men on the killing floor to support it. She became a charter member of the local, its first recording secretary, and one of the PWOC's leading female organizers during World War II.[12]

Black workers made up the second key group of CIO union pioneers in Sioux City. Some lived intermixed with other residents in the South Bottoms, but most resided in a distinct neighborhood on the near West Side. Blacks had filled the lower rungs of the employment ladder, serving as porters, helpers, and occasional laborers, since steamboats had first called on the town's docks in the late 1850s. Their numbers in Sioux City grew from 305 in 1910 to 1,139 in 1920, with particularly rapid growth during World War I as dozens found jobs in the packinghouses for the first time. Nonetheless, a color line remained, and black men were limited to work in the distasteful rendering operation and the dangerous killing floors. By 1925 almost 50 percent of Sioux City's employed blacks worked in the packinghouses. "The black community totally depended on packing," Jennie Shuck observed, "they were either a packinghouse worker or a shoe shine boy."[13]

Sioux City was not hospitable toward its black residents. Racial prejudice, discrimination, and segregation were widespread, especially among the older immigrant groups and the native-born elite. Blacks mixed freely with the new immigrants in the Bottoms neighborhood, and their children attended the same schools, but their territory in Sioux City proper was strictly circumscribed. Whites fled when the black community expanded in the teens, 1920s, and 1930s, selling their homes as soon as a black family moved onto their block. Blacks were restricted to the balconies in local theaters and were well aware of the informal limits to their movements. A park on West Third Street bordered the black neighborhood but was unsafe for blacks to use in the 1930s "If you did, you'd be liable to get your head whooped," recalled Sam Davis, a teenager at the time, "because it was the white district."[14]

Black workers generally were early supporters of the union but played a subordinate role in the formation and subsequent leadership of locals. They made up between 5 and 10 percent of the packinghouse workforce in Sioux City, with close to one hundred at Cudahy, around thirty at Armour, and fewer than fifteen at Swift, the smallest plant. At Cudahy, well-known Golden Glove boxer Clayton Johnson, along with fellow beef-kill workers Johnny Shores and Dewey Cardwell, were among the first to join the union. At Armour, early union leader Elder "Mojo" Owens was one of three cattle splitters and a highly respected figure on the South Bottoms. Blacks who entered the plants as strike breakers in 1921 tended to oppose the union, but their numbers were quite small.[15]

The most visible and influential black leader was Arthell Shelton, a Swift beef-kill worker who served as recording secretary of inter-plant Local 389 and became the first president of the Swift union. Known as "Sweet Potato" among his contemporaries, Shelton's past is mysterious. He began working at Swift in 1930 and lived in the South Bottoms neighborhood. By reputation he was a tough character; it was whispered among packinghouse workers that "Sweet Potato ain't no-one to mess with." Once active in the union, Shelton was attracted to leading black activists from Chicago's packinghouses, especially Hank Johnson and Jesse Vaughn. Fragmentary evidence suggests that Shelton either joined or was very close to the Communist Party.[16]

The final cluster of union pioneers was a mixed group of radicals and former union members led by Cudahy worker Bruce Nolan. Nolan worked as a migratory agricultural laborer for much of the 1920s and had encountered the IWW in his many travels. He briefly owned a dairy farm outside Sioux City and participated in the confrontational Farm Holiday milk strike of 1932, only to suffer foreclosure on his land in 1933. Destitute, he was able to get work at Cudahy by claiming to be a hog splitter, although he had no packinghouse experience. Ballard easily drew him into the organizing drive. "I was a rebel here in town," Nolan recalled, "it wasn't a time to compromise."[17]

Several years before Ballard's arrival in Sioux City, Nolan had established a network of union activists at Cudahy who were concentrated in the mechanical division. The group included Tom Morley, a former IWW member; Frank "Fox" Lavenger, a 1921 strike veteran; Berth Madison, a Scandinavian with union experience; and Pete Gaaul, a former member of the International Association of Machinists. Through Nolan, Ballard was able to bring the entire group into Local 389.[18]

Despite the influence of a few individual radicals, leftist organizations as such did not play an important role in the organizing drive. The Communist Party sent several organizers to Sioux City and had considerable influence inside the PWOC apparatus but was unable to recruit more than a handful of workers. The Socialists had fewer than ten members—holdovers from the teens and a few who joined during the early 1930s—and no contacts among industrial workers. The IWW left a stronger mark on packinghouse workers than either of these groups, but individuals who were influenced by it, such as Nolan and Morley, acted as individuals and not an organized leftist force.[19]

Older ethnic and black workers who had participated in the strike of 1921 and 1922 also backed the CIO drive. Embittered by the strike's defeat, they were highly suspicious of the Amalgamated and initially wary of the CIO. They interacted with a younger generation in the plant from their respective neighborhoods and had considerable influence on the course of events in the late 1930s. "People were going to listen to them," recalled Nolan, "it was a case of convincing them that this was going to be a union that was different."[20]

As a general rule, women were slower to express support for the union. Only exceptional women without children and from active union households, such as Sophie Ferdig at Swift and Jennie Shuck at Cudahy, played a leadership role in the early stages. Recruiting women to the union simply as members, however, was not difficult once success seemed possible. Jennie Shuck brought her entire hog-casing department into the union and had particular success among the immigrants, "especially these older women who came over from the old country. They knew what degradation [was] and how they were treated back there by the landowners."[21]

The union pioneers who provided leadership for the organizing drive of 1937 and 1938 were a diverse group bridging ethnic, racial, and gender lines. As leaders of their respective constituencies, they brought networks of followers into the PWOC and persuaded community leaders, notably black and white clergy, to come out publicly in support of unionizing the city's packinghouses. The hundreds of workers attending the PWOC's rally on June 24, 1937, reflected both the close links between the union pioneers and their supporters, and the attractiveness of the CIO to these restless workers. Nonetheless, they still needed to overcome the tactics of the packing companies, which had been carefully honed in the past to defeat organizing drives.

The Roots of Unionism in the 1930s

Any effort to bring the internally divided immigrants and blacks together in industrial unions had to overcome the weight of previous defeats and the determined efforts of the companies to win the loyalties of their workers. In 1921 and 1922 the collapse of the national strike by the Amalgamated Meat Cutters destroyed the union locals that had flourished during World War I. Despite determined resistance by Sioux City's packinghouse workers and passionate support from the entire Bottoms community, hundreds of sheriff's deputies allowed the companies to operate their plants at reduced levels. Residents of the Bottoms, never in a secure economic position, suffered terribly during the long strike fought during sub-zero temperatures. "The 1921 strike devastated this part of Sioux City," recalled Jennie Shuck, "I knew that we were hungry, our shoes were soled and half-soled and half-soled again because Dad didn't have the money." In early February, union mem-

bers had little option but to endorse the "settlement" proposed by Amalgamated leaders: "Back to work, those who can get a job, and if you don't get a
job you're out of luck."[22]

The collapse of the strike left a bitter memory. Of the 1,200 workers who
reapplied for work, only 250 were rehired. Many left the area completely.
Bitterness toward the packing companies, and the union that had failed, sunk
deep roots into Bottoms residents who struggled to recuperate their losses
over the next few years. A contemporary writing in the 1930s observed, "Yet
today, more than fifteen years since, the packing house strike is vivid in the
memory of some men who were never rehired, unemployed except for occasional odd jobs."[23]

In the aftermath of the strike, packing companies devised a network of
welfare policies designed to encourage loyalty. Employment security
through limited seniority systems, vacations, and social activities such as
athletics sought to reduce turnover among more seasoned employees and
engender pro-company attitudes. A business-sponsored sandlot baseball
league and weekly boxing matches between clubs of packinghouse employees drew large crowds in the mid-1920s. Sioux City's minor-league baseball
team even collapsed in 1924 because business-sponsored sporting events
drew away many its fans.[24]

The packing companies also installed plant conference boards as a mechanism for worker representation that did not challenge managerial authority. At Swift, for example, seven employee representatives elected by workers and seven from management met periodically to pass motions and
discuss problems in the plant. Swift traffic manager Frank Logman served
as chair throughout the 1920s and 1930s and could cast a deciding vote in
event of a tie. Motions required only a simple majority for approval, but
decisions on grievances took a two-thirds vote. With these rules, management could prevent any action that conflicted with their plans while having
a mechanism for ascertaining discontent on the shop floor. Armour and
Cudahy had similar arrangements.[25]

Participation in the conference boards reflected a pragmatic decision by
packinghouse workers who had no viable alternatives. Although small
matters might be resolved in meetings between worker representatives and
management, basic company policies toward employees were not negotia-
ble. Seniority was only one of several criteria for rehiring laid-off employees and the arbitrary power of the foremen still defined shop-floor relations.
Low pay, irregular hours, frequent layoffs, and harsh working conditions
remained major grievances that could not be rectified through management-
dominated conference boards. "There's no point complaining about it, or

trying to take up a grievance about it, because you might get fired," recalled Jennie Shuck. "You had no security, no job security at all."[26]

The depression, and declining income for packinghouse workers, removed the material basis for packing companies' cooptative policies. With Sioux City's economy hinged to meatpacking, "Everybody was suffering except the bootleggers," recalled Jennie Shuck. "Men were laid off by the hundreds and, of course, the packers they were taking advantage of that." Wage cuts and short hours cut income drastically, and families survived on food grown in their backyards and fish and small game caught along the river. Packinghouse workers welcomed the distribution of free milk by local Farm Holiday Association members in August 1932, and several were jailed for joining the blockades farmers established on roads leading into Sioux City.[27]

Local discontent and passage of the National Industrial Recovery Act enabled the Amalgamated Meat Cutters to establish locals briefly in the three major plants. The organization quickly evaporated when the packing companies refused to negotiate with the unions and the Amalgamated would not call a strike to demand union recognition. After widespread layoffs in late 1934 and a small wage increase, workers dropped out of the Amalgamated in droves and left the locals an empty shell by May 1935. "Everybody knew it was because of the organization that these packers got so big-hearted all of a sudden," complained labor columnist Harold Sturgeon, "but the packers chalked up the credit to the Plant Conference Board company union."[28]

In the organizing drive of 1937 and 1938, unionists sought to convince workers that the PWOC could succeed where the Amalgamated had failed. They argued that industrial unions could provide more material benefits and employment security than company-sanctioned mechanisms and pointed to the victories of the CIO in other industries. The union pioneers drew on the local packinghouse workers' desire to develop power inside the plants against company domination and appealed to their common interests at work, regardless of differences in race, sex, language, or church. The combination of workplace grievances and the possibilities of success, organizers hoped, would be enough to overcome the defeats of 1921 and 1922 as well as of 1934 and 1935.

For families without savings and dependent on regular weekly wages, the potential benefits of the union had to be balanced against the risks of membership and the alternative forms of representation and advancement that employers sanctioned. Supervisors strongly encouraged employees to join "independent" unions and permitted officials of these organizations to collect dues in the packinghouses during working hours. Family and ethnic networks, reinforced by fraternal orders such as the Masons, provided hiring and promotion tracks for workers who had connections to foremen. Given these alternatives, the union's appeal of advancement through united collective action did not necessarily meet a favorable reception.[29]

Once Ballard consolidated Sioux City's union pioneers into a coherent group, local packinghouse workers led the organizing drive. Activists went door to door in Sioux City's Bottoms neighborhoods during the summer of 1937, recruiting packinghouse workers into Local 389 regardless of who employed them. Organizing within the plant was furtive and conducted in dressing rooms or on breaks in order to avoid the watchful eyes of company unions, stool pigeons, and supervisors. Union advocates promised to secure higher wages, fringe benefits, and job security through seniority, a powerful shop steward system, and a collective bargaining agreement. H. R. Ballard coordinated overall union operations, but the CIO sent no more paid organizers to Sioux City, leaving local packinghouse workers largely to their own resources.[30]

Although particular characteristics shaped each plant's organizing drive, several general patterns emerged. First, in all three facilities the killing-floor men were the first to join, and the union used this base to support organizers in other departments. Second, the union tried to assert its presence on the shop floor as soon as possible, either through wearing CIO union buttons, appointing stewards, or presenting grievances. Third, when the companies resisted tacit or explicit recognition of the union, organizers used job actions to force consideration of their demands.

Organizing at Sioux City Swift

All the packinghouses resisted the union's organizing drive, but Swift's management was by far the most intransigent. At Armour and Cudahy, the unions gradually were able to increase their strength through a series of job actions and struggles over grievances. At Swift, the company refused all union overtures and provoked a major strike lasting from September 29, 1938, through January 1939. A detailed NLRB investigation into the strike provides extraordinary insight into the process of unionization at Swift.[31]

For the first nine months of the organizing drive, between June 1937 and March 1938, the union grew slowly at Swift by expanding its core on the beef, hog, and sheep killing floors despite persistent harassment and intimidation by company supervisors. Arthell Shelton, with ten years of experience in the beef kill, served as the overall leader of the Swift unionists. Sam Malinosky, a Russian veteran of the 1921 strike at Cudahy, was the first person to join in the hog kill, and Earl Sutherland, another South Bottoms resident, start-ed the union in the sheep kill. By the end of 1937 the killing-floor workers "got to wearing their badges," recalled Alvin Edwards, "and the foreman, he was about nuts. Of course, the company was on him to get everybody to take their badges off, and they wouldn't do it."[32]

A major obstacle to the CIO drive was the strength of the Employees Security League (ESL), whose leaders were former employee representatives to Swift's Assembly. Swift granted exclusive recognition to the ESL in June 1937 and signed a contract with it that merely reprinted policies that the company had implemented unilaterally in 1934. Swift management dis-cussed grievances with ESL representatives and allowed its stewards to col-lect dues and recruit members during working hours while denying simi-lar privileges to the CIO.[33]

CIO unionists at Swift contemptuously dismissed the ESL as a "sewing circle" that had no power to compel management to recognize workers' grievances. They systematically undermined the ESL and expanded their base by demanding recognition of CIO stewards and their right to represent workers in negotiations with management. On the shop floor, the ESL steadi-ly lost ground because its representatives proved unable to resolve shop-floor problems and unwilling to use pressure tactics against managerial intransi-gence. In the eight months before the September strike, as the company union's ineffectiveness became apparent, the CIO recruited key ESL leaders, extended their organization into old ESL strongholds, and isolated remain-ing ESL activists.[34]

In April 1938 management's refusal to meet with Local 389 leaders over plant grievances brought a new wave of workers into the CIO. Henry Jans-en, a former Assembly representative, resigned as ESL steward in the beef kill in early April and joined the CIO. Seventeen more beef-kill workers joined in rapid succession, including ESL steward Harold Flea, giving the CIO thirty-three members out of thirty-nine in the department. Large num-bers of workers also joined from the curing cellars, beef casing, stock food, and sanitation. In the hog cut, Alex Malinosky, the brother of hog-kill work-er Sam Malinosky, joined the union in early May despite repeated harass-ment for wearing a CIO button. At the end of June 1938 the union had 157 members, 35 percent of the plant's workforce.[35]

Swift workers also were well aware that the PWOC was gaining strength at other packinghouses. Next door at Armour, unionists had secured NLRB certification and were able to settle grievances through job actions and pres-sure by stewards. On June 26, 1938, a "victory parade" sponsored by Local 389 and the Women's Auxiliaries drew a thousand packinghouse workers and union supporters in a march through the center of town. Workers carrying signs and placards surrounded large colorful floats built by union members, while a marching band led the enthusiastic throng. Speakers included national PWOC leader Hank Johnson and local union officials, along with Sioux City Mayor Daniel F. Loepp and two city council members.[36]

In the summer of 1938 the largest group of non-union workers in the Swift plant, aside from the mechanical division, were the white ethnic women in the sausage and casings departments. Only two had joined by the end of June, although almost twenty men from those departments were union members. A few women in the sausage department joined in early July, but the real breakthrough came on August 1, when seven women and two men signed union cards on the same day. This group included Mary Borschuk, a Russian from the South Bottoms and future financial secretary of the local, and Lucille Cramm, later a member of the Bargaining Committee. Women in hog and sheep casing started to come into the union after John Davidchik's sister Zena joined in late August. On September 1, 62.5 percent of the workforce in these predominantly female departments were union members, higher than the percentage for the plant as a whole.[37]

In September, as the Swift union consolidated its hold in many departments and organized new, previously weak areas, pressure grew on management to meet with CIO representatives. Workers in the loading dock, pork trim, beef cooler, and beef cut streamed into the organization, and union membership approached 100 percent on the killing floors. This dynamic growth created problems for the union, which was caught between an immovable management and pressure from new members to settle shop-floor disputes. "Every membership meeting that we have," complained Shelton in 1938, "the workers are always having grievances, and some grievances that have been standing for a year or two, we can't get them settled and we don't have any way of discussing them."[38]

The conflict came to a head in late September. Typically, the particular dispute that precipitated a showdown involved both pay and union authority over shop-floor conditions. Ernest Seward, a hog-kill steward, complained to the union that his pay had been cut because of a transfer into another department. His foreman rebuffed the grievance, and the plant superintendent refused to discuss the dispute with the department's Grievance Committee. Infuriated, the union membership voted to go on strike in order to compel management to meet with union committees.[39]

At 10 A.M. on September 29, close to a hundred killing-floor workers stopped work and demanded that Swift recognize the authority of the CIO's Grievance Committee. Contrary to union leaders' optimistic expectation of a quick victory, management rejected the union's demand to negotiate. As the debate proceeded for several hours under the shadow of cattle, pig, and sheep carcasses in various stages of dismemberment, the killing gangs remained on the floor, surrounded company personnel, and prevented foremen from continuing the slaughtering process. Soon the animals started to spoil, and adjacent departments ground to a halt in support of the stoppage.

In the early afternoon Swift informed the killing-floor gangs that they either had to resume work or leave the premises, or else they would be fired. Workers ignored the threat, maintained the occupation of key departments, and paid no attention when supervisors distributed discharge slips. Any possibility of compromise was eliminated in the late afternoon when the Woodbury County sheriff, acting at Swift's request, arrested seventeen union leaders under Iowa's conspiracy laws. Women workers left the plant at 4:30, but most men remained until 1 A.M., when they learned the sheriff planned to return and make more arrests.[40]

On the day of the strike, 291 workers, 65 percent of the production employees, were members of the union. Many who were not in the CIO participated in the stoppage and joined the union immediately thereafter, including three former ESL leaders. The twenty-one identified union leaders had an average of eight years' seniority and came from the three killing gangs, the hog and beef cuts, and the sausage and casings departments. The 165 discharged workers were all CIO members and included the Swift union's central leaders and workers from the strongest union departments.[41]

For Swift workers, other packinghouse unionists, and the CIO in Iowa, the strike in Sioux City became a test of the strength and determination of the new industrial unions. Statewide CIO councils in Iowa, Nebraska, and Minnesota declared a boycott of Swift products, and CIO locals in Des Moines donated fifty tons of coal. The women's auxiliaries of the Swift and Cudahy locals operated a strike kitchen, relying on donations of food from local merchants and farmers. The PWOC toured Swift striker Alice Kozlowski through Chicago and other packing centers to raise money for the Sioux City struggle.[42]

The decisive struggle, however, was waged on the streets in front of the Swift plant. Union picket lines shut the packinghouse for the first three weeks of October. The Sioux City police, under the authority of labor-backed commissioner of public safety Harold Sturgeon, did not (or could not) enforce a court injunction against mass picketing. Swift negotiators, who steadfastly refused to rehire the discharged workers or meet with union committees, tried to break the strike by organizing a back to work movement. Led by ESL president Clarence Johnson, strikebreakers twice attempted to enter the plant on October 18. Strikers repelled the first group of scabs after the police pulled back from a confrontation, but later in the day, under the protection of the Woodbury Country sheriff's deputies drawn from neighboring rural areas, the strikebreakers broke through the picket lines. Deputies armed with riot batons, water hoses, and tear gas fought a pitched battle against a thousand enraged strikers and supporters from the Bottoms neighborhoods who tried to storm the plant and evict the scabs. Quiet returned the next day after National Guard troops armed with rifles and fixed bayonets excluded pickets from the area adjacent to the packinghouse.[43]

The strike lost strength after the October 18 riot. The National Guard and sheriff's department allowed strikebreakers to enter the plant, and forty union leaders were jailed in December for riotous behavior and other felonies. Large rallies bringing hundreds of CIO unionists and packinghouse workers from other cities could not counteract the dwindling financial resources of the young union and its unemployed members. Swift rejected one proposal after another, including plans to establish impartial arbitration boards of varying composition. In December the women's auxiliary spent the last of its money organizing a Christmas party for the families of the Swift strikers.[44]

In January 1939 the NLRB trial examiner's intermediate report bolstered the union by finding Swift guilty of illegally supporting the ESL and refusing to bargain with the CIO. The examiner ruled that the CIO indeed represented a majority of Swift's employees on September 29 and that all discharged workers had a right to their jobs because of the company's unfair labor practices. With this leverage, the union offered to call off the strike if Swift promised to rehire 101 of the 165 discharged workers with back pay but without any seniority. NLRB attorney Lee Loevinger tried to dissuade the union from making this deal, but Don Harris informed him that "the union feels forced to accept this because of the financial condition of both the organization and the individual members." When Swift agreed to the offer in late January, the strike officially came to an end.[45]

Despite brave words to the public and to its members, the strike shattered the union organization at the Swift plant. Central union leaders such as Shelton and most of the killing-floor workers lost their jobs permanently. Rehired strikers lost all seniority and job rights and often were sent to poorer jobs than those they had held previously. CIO membership fell to just over a hundred at the Swift plant, and the intimidated group did not resume the organizing drive. In the spring of 1940 the NLRB ruled that even though Swift had illegally dominated the ESL, the CIO union had engaged in an unlawful plant occupation prohibited under the Supreme Court's recent

Fansteel decision. Hence, the NLRB overturned the trial examiner and held that the workers who had stayed in the plant had been legally fired. This edict ended the last hope of the sixty-four discharged workers not covered under the union's settlement with Swift.[46]

Victory and Accommodation in
Sioux City's Packinghouses

Left on their own, the Swift workers would not have been able to rebuild their union after the 1938–39 strike. Although the NLRB had identified the local as representing a majority of the workers on September 19, 1938, it also had sanctioned the dismissal of the union's strongest members. Indeed, its 1940 decision stated that the union no longer represented a majority of the Swift workers, removing any legal pressure on management to negotiate. The NLRB's ruling complemented the repression of mass picketing by sheriff's deputies and the National Guard, drawing on farmers and small businessmen in Woodbury County outside of Sioux City. The hostility of government agencies and non-working-class residents paralleled the experience of packinghouse workers in 1921 and 1922 and, all other factors being equal, would have discouraged a renewed organizing drive.

This time, however, Swift workers were not on their own. The alliance with other packinghouse workers, in Sioux City and other midwestern meatpacking centers, provided sufficient support for them to make a dramatic comeback in just three years. In 1939 the PWOC National Office hired several former Swift union leaders, and Sioux City's other packinghouse locals forced their companies to employ qualified butchers discharged by Swift. With close to two thousand union members, the Cudahy and Armour locals were able to sustain the remaining union members at Swift and support renewed efforts in 1941 and 1942 to rebuild the local. Tony Stephens, a paid organizer and former Swift worker discharged in the strike and convicted of a felony, led the PWOC drive in 1942 that resulted in a successful April certification election. A tight labor market due to World War II no doubt helped as well but was not sufficient by itself to spark a new organizing initiative.[47]

The strength of the Armour and Cudahy unions was critical to the victory at Swift. Locals at both plants sent large numbers of members to help the smaller Swift union block entrances to the plant, and several Armour and Cudahy workers were arrested as participants in the October 18 riot. In December 1938 the Armour union shut down the plant after management fired union president Clarence Knox for circulating a petition. After two hours the company accepted union demands to rehire Knox and his supporters without discrimination and settle outstanding grievances. A few days later, it was Cudahy's turn to feel union power as 120 union stewards brought the plant to a halt for fifty minutes by blowing whistles at the start and end of the job action. There were few non-union workers in either packinghouse by February 1939.[48]

The capacity of the union to organize Swift workers and hold on after a disastrous defeat vindicated the rank-and-file organizing strategy of the union pioneers and their alliance with the CIO. The PWOC's perseverance after the strike, and its successes at other plants, showed Sioux City's packinghouse workers that the new industrial union was not going to disappear after a defeat and abandon its members, as the Amalgamated had in 1922 and 1935. Bonds of mutual class interest, forged through common action against company power, held even after a serious setback and proved strong enough to overcome the resistance of the packing firms.[49]

The accomplishments of Sioux City's packinghouse workers need to be balanced by acknowledging the boundaries that their unions accepted. The defeat of the Swift strike severely inhibited the development of the social unionism that evolved elsewhere in the UPWA by weakening the role of black workers within Sioux City meatpacking locals. The departure of Arthell Shelton from his home town eliminated the most prominent black union leader, and the deal accepted by the PWOC disproportionately hurt blacks because they were concentrated on Swift's killing floors. Black workers never again played a central leadership role in Sioux City meatpacking locals, although they remained strong supporters of the organization. After World War II, local unions experienced little internal pressure to engage in anti-discrimination activities because black workers were marginal to union leadership and remained fewer than 10 percent of the workforce. As a result, Sioux City locals lagged on civil rights issues in the late 1940s and 1950s compared to the rest of the UPWA.

The weakness of the Sioux local on civil rights in turn inhibited progressive stands on gender issues. Because there was little internally generated activity on racial issues, women did not have allies in their efforts to influence local unions as was the case elsewhere in the UPWA. Women remained active as shop stewards in all locals, but there is little evidence of other influence in the Sioux City locals. At Cudahy, Jennie Shuck felt pushed out of union activity by Bruce Nolan, and she left the packing industry in 1949 when her husband contracted cancer. Her anger at Nolan, and what she perceived as resistance to women's participation, was still palpable in an interview forty years later. When Sioux City locals did make advances for women and blacks in the 1950s they were largely the result of victories secured elsewhere.[50]

The dismissal of 154 Swift CIO members, sanctioned by the NLRB for exceeding "the bounds of permissible union activity," also influenced union members by clearly defining the contours of acceptable union conduct and the sanctions for breaking those rules. The evident importance of the NLRB and local political authorities on the success or failure of organizing efforts reinforced interest in and support for a political party that could affect the actions of local, state, and federal governments. PWOC organizers especially encouraged the desire for political action among immigrant packinghouse workers by arranging classes for them to prepare for naturalization examinations, and helping the new American citizens register to vote. But in the context of the 1930s, rank-and-file working-class political involvement flowed into the Democratic Party rather than incipient efforts to form an independent third party.[51]

Democratic Party influence, especially the popularity of President Franklin D. Roosevelt, doomed an attempt by progressive newspaper editor and former Sioux City mayor Wallace Short to establish an Iowa Farmer-Labor Party in the 1930s. The new party had an impressive start in 1934; as the FLP's candidate for governor, Short received more than 30,000 votes statewide and 5,555 in Woodbury County. Competition with the Democrats and internal fissures prevented the FLP from building on its initial showing, however. When the FLP polled fewer than ten thousand votes in 1938 it lost the official ballot status it had attained in 1934. In Woodbury County, the FLP's strongest base, Short's vote fell to 1,747. Perhaps more telling was the poor showing of the FLP candidate for Woodbury County sheriff in the November 1938 election in the midst of the bitter Swift strike. He received only 378 votes in Sioux City despite popular dissatisfaction with the activities of the incumbent Democratic sheriff who was at that time escorting strikebreakers into the Swift plant.[52]

Iowa Democrats isolated the FLP simply by agreeing with its positions and asserting that with its national structure the Democratic Party was in a better position to win reforms favorable to the working class. In 1934 the FLP placed a full-page advertisement in Short's paper, the *Unionist and Public Forum*, declaring, "It Takes a New Party to Meet Some New Problems." "We are informed that we have a new deal, but we are *afraid the dealers are the same old crowd with the same marked deck*," it warned. In the next week's edition, Iowa Democrats responded that "the ideals and aims of the Democratic Party are in harmony with the aims and ideals expressed in the Farmer-Labor Platform—ideals that OUR PRESIDENT is seeking to achieve for the mass of the common folk." To FLP supporters the ad cautioned, "LET'S NOT DIVIDE OUR STRENGTH and allow reaction to triumph next Tuesday." Indeed, as the Iowa

FLP faltered in the late 1930s because of internal divisions, appeals for unity behind Roosevelt's party became more compelling.[53]

As the Democratic Party consolidated its base in Sioux City's working class, it drew leading FLP figures away from Short's organization. Daniel F. Loepp, the FLP candidate for county attorney in 1936 and a popular labor lawyer, successfully ran for mayor in the nonpartisan 1938 municipal elections with the backing of prominent Democrats. Harold Sturgeon, former managing editor of Short's paper, won the important position of commissioner of public safety in the same election. Loepp and Sturgeon, who owed their positions to a mobilized and active working class, vigorously supported the packinghouse union during the 1938 Swift strike as well as efforts by the Teamsters to organize local bakers and truck drivers—but as Democrats rather than FLP members. The revitalized Democratic Party made Sioux City's labor unions major players in regional politics, especially after World War II. But its support also reflected a willingness by workers to conform to the New Deal system of labor relations.[54]

With their successes at the workplace and their ability to make the packinghouse workers a powerful political force in Sioux City, the PWOC enabled the Bottoms residents to achieve economic security and community respect. The steward systems established in the 1930s remained strong, and the Sioux City locals participated fully in the shop-floor struggles of the 1940s and 1950s. These significant accomplishments, however, have to be placed within appropriate limits. Sioux City packinghouse locals did not carry much social unionism beyond the war years; activity outside the workplace in the 1950s consisted primarily of political action designed to support the local Democratic Party. And after the initial organizing surge ended, both women and blacks found it difficult to use local unions to address their particular concerns unless the international union brought pressure to bear on local leaders—as it would in the 1950s.

The accommodation reached in Sioux City is effectively conveyed in how the PWOC unions participated in a 1942 Labor Day parade. Although the CIO and AFL jointly sponsored the march, PWOC contingents dwarfed the AFL turnout. Cudahy Local 70 took first place for its float, which read "Help Uncle Sam Pull the Load. Buy War Bonds" and was drawn by a costumed Uncle Sam. Motorized military units flanked the labor union members and their patriotic floats, a fitting symbol for the new relationship of protection and oversight between the federal government and the new industrial unions in Sioux City's packinghouses.[55]

6

"So That Your Children Will Not Have to Slave as We Have": The Struggle for an International Union

The Packinghouse Workers under the banner of the streamlined CIO organization has been the only organization in the history of the meat packing industry that has gone over five years of life. I hope this organization will stand as long as we have a meat packing industry; and that your children and children's children will not have to slave in those packinghouses as we have slaved in the past.

—Arthur Kampfert, speech to 1943 UPWA convention

For three days a pall had hung over the October 1943 founding convention of the United Packinghouse Workers of America-CIO. While the meeting transacted routine business, a constant swirl of behind-the-scenes caucuses tussled over who would become the leaders of the new organization. Suddenly, on the last day of the convention, the logjam broke. The disputing factions reached a compromise, and the CIO abandoned efforts to hand-pick the leaders of the new international union. Euphoric delegates realized that the last obstacle had fallen to the establishment of an international union. Despite the press of business, packinghouse workers showed their respect for the retiring PWOC leaders—who they had so often vociferously criticized—by demanding that they address the convention. After several had spoken, Sioux City delegate Jennie Shuck asked Arthur Kampfert to take the floor, because he had been "fighting for the Packinghouse Workers for a great many years." In an emotional moment, Kampfert reminded his audience of the destruction of the unions after World War I and the recent strife that had almost split the PWOC. He implored the delegates to maintain a "unity of purpose" and elevate the living standards of packinghouse workers so that your "children and children's children will not have to slave in those packinghouses as we have slaved in the past." The packinghouse workers in attendance applauded mightily at this heartfelt sentiment that, through unity, they could look forward to a better future for themselves, their families, and the entire working class of people.[1]

The establishment of a democratic international union in meatpacking was a prolonged struggle. The union's genuine rank-and-file roots outside of the CIO made it difficult to create effective cooperation among the very different groups of workers and local unions from many plants. At the same time, packinghouse workers had to fend off the creation of an international under the overly firm guiding hand of the CIO. CIO officials such as Philip Murray and Allan Haywood drew on their experiences with the Steel Workers Organizing Committee (SWOC) for a model upon which to base a future UPWA. They pictured a centralized organization whose leaders would be resolutely loyal to the CIO and its policies. Whether the officials of a future UPWA would have roots in the meatpacking industry and a real base among the union's members was an entirely secondary criteria to CIO officials.

Despite many disagreements over particular issues, packinghouse workers generally shared a different vision of their future international union. They wanted to balance the need for a national structure to confront packing companies with protections that the international union apparatus would remain under the control of local unions and not become a power unto itself. Accustomed to being able to judge the quality of their immediate leaders through personal observation, local union activists wanted the future officers of an international union to come out of the packinghouse industry and have a track record they could evaluate. In short, packinghouse workers fought to achieve an international union and a leadership that was both responsive to and responsible to local unions.

Agreement among local union leaders, however, was not an easy process. Strategic disagreements and parochial allegiances to regional leaders hindered cooperation. Factional struggles consumed the PWOC between 1939 and 1943 and at times threatened the very fabric of solidarity between local unions. A close examination of these struggles, however, illustrates that similar concerns informed the actions of local unions that might occupy opposite sides of a dispute at a particular moment. In particular, local unions repeatedly demanded that control over contract negotiations and all other union activities rest with individuals familiar with the industry and accountable to packinghouse workers. It was the special contribution of Austin leaders Joe Ollman and Frank Ellis, supported by the former IUAW locals in Minnesota and Iowa, to formulate an astute strategy that united often-feuding local unions. In 1942 and 1943 Austin's program forged sufficient unity among packinghouse workers so they could control the circumstances, terms, and results of the UPWA's birth.

* * *

The powerful local unions in midwestern packinghouses faced a dilemma in the late 1930s. Although firmly rooted in their plants, they were unable to secure national agreements with the packing companies. The locals hoped that the PWOC, formed in October 1937, could increase local unions' bargaining power by creating institutional links among packinghouse workers in different areas who labored for the same national firms.

The bureaucratic structure of the PWOC was an impediment to these aspirations. It was an organization literally controlled from the top down. The CIO appointed the members of the Organizing Committee's national directorate, and regional PWOC leaders were in turn installed by the PWOC national chair. Most of these men were drawn from other industries and had little knowledge of conditions in meatpacking. The "coal miners," as they were derisively dubbed by union pioneers, compounded their ignorance by retaining tight control over the PWOC and resisting the rank-and-file involvement practiced by local unions. The autocratic style of PWOC national chair Van A. Bittner, a long-time United Mine Workers leader, particularly clashed with the democratic sensibilities of packinghouse unionists. The complaints of Mason City, Iowa, activists were typical. They accused Bittner of being "a dictator" who ensured that "no packing members of the Packinghouse Workers were given anything to say about the policy of the Packinghouse Workers Organization." For packinghouse workers, consolidating their position in the anti-union industry was indissolubly linked to the establishment of a democratic international union.[2]

Discontent with the PWOC's hierarchical structure began to crystalize in 1939 over efforts to secure a national agreement with Armour. A meeting of PWOC local union delegates that preceded the celebrated July 16, 1939, Chicago rally resolved to shut down Armour if the company continued to resist a national agreement. With strong locals certified in fifteen plants that composed the central pillars of the company's operations, packinghouse workers felt they were in a strong position to compel Armour to sign a collective bargaining agreement. CIO-appointed PWOC leaders shrank from the confrontation, however, fearful that a strike could fail and that a prolonged conflict might undermine their control over the organization. Without consulting local union delegates, on August 19, 1939, Van Bittner agreed to let individual Armour plants sign agreements with local unions rather than hold out for a national contract. At the same time, the PWOC prohibited local unions from engaging in job actions without permission from the national office.[3]

Local agreements did not satisfy union founders or the unions they led. Armour plant superintendents avoided discussions over substantive issues by claiming (probably correctly) that they did not have the power to alter wage levels or determine company policies regarding seniority. Although management agreed to meet with union stewards over grievances—already a common occurrence—the agreements provided little additional leverage for the union. Kansas City Armour leaders complained that workers were losing confidence in the union because their local contract was "being violated daily by management." Instead of the hoped-for links among workers in different plants of the same national firms, Armour locals had "not been able to obtain proper information concerning local situations and organization process in other communities," thereby "crippling" their capacity to extract concessions at their plant. The reverberations of Bittner's action did not become apparent immediately, but important leaders of Armour locals would emerge as anti-CIO dissidents in the early 1940s.[4]

Ongoing conflict between Armour locals and the PWOC national officers paralleled explosive internal struggles over the influence of the Communist Party. The August 23, 1939, Hitler-Stalin pact provided Van Bittner with a ready excuse to uproot the Communist Party from its strong position in the PWOC's apparatus, especially in Illinois, Iowa, Nebraska, Minnesota, and Texas. Included in the fall 1939 purge were PWOC national director Don Harris, Chicago District director Herb March, regional organizers Tony Stephens and Kermit Fry, and perhaps as many as six other PWOC staffers with ties to the left. Bittner also fired Joe Ollman, even though the Trotskyists had roundly condemned the German-Soviet agreement. He assigned former Iowa UPWA official J. C. "Shady" Lewis to implement his orders in the PWOC's Iowa-Nebraska District 3. "I have never found a dirtier mess in my experience in the trade union movement than we have found here," Lewis told Bittner. "It was a hot bed for the comrades."[5]

Indeed, Communists in District 3 had managed to infiltrate the PWOC apparatus. In contrast to the approach of Chicago Communists, who first developed a base among packinghouse workers before taking leadership posts, Harris and his circle used their positions within the PWOC's structures to recruit packinghouse workers to the Communist Party. Their overbearing, and often clumsy, bureaucratic actions antagonized many union pioneers, especially in Cedar Rapids and Omaha. Harris particularly angered local unionists when he instructed them to consult regularly with Communist officials who had no formal position in the PWOC. He also placed several well-known Communists on the PWOC staff while dismissing at least three paid organizers and former packinghouse workers who resisted his efforts to control the district. The clashes between the Omaha Armour local and Harris turned its leaders into strong anticommunists, and they applauded J. C. Lewis's "clean and thorough job in District No. 3 in cleaning out the Reds."[6]

Behind the fierce rhetoric, there were striking parallels between District 3's criticisms of the Communists and attacks by other locals on Van Bittner's bureaucratic behavior. Unions occupying opposite sides in the PWOC's internal alignments actually articulated similar concerns: the sudden change of staff personnel, which disrupted organizing drives; imperious directives from PWOC officials, which were not subject to modification or approval by local unions; and the use of non-packinghouse workers as organizers. For example, the anti-Bittner Kansas City locals complained that PWOC organizers were incompetent "stoolies" appointed because of their loyalty to the CIO rather than their organizing ability. In a similar vein, the anticommunists in District 3 protested that "you had to be a member of the Communist party" to become an organizer, and the ones hired by Harris had "split and hurt Packinghouse Workers." Accusations that Van Bittner's "coal miners" controlled union policy were matched by complaints from Omaha that Harris told locals to follow directives from Communist Party officials with little knowledge of the industry. "We don't need that," explained Nels Peterson in a message that could have as well attacked Van Bittner. "We have a Local Union for it." Yet, despite similar underlying concerns, the particular configurations of resentment at bureaucratic PWOC behavior engendered deep conflict among local unions.[7]

The divisions in the PWOC almost destroyed the fledgling national union. The internal struggle in 1939 and 1940 slowed organizational growth, and most election victories merely ratified the successful recruitment drives of local unions. Despite sixteen certification victories in 1939 and 1940, PWOC membership stagnated around twenty thousand over the two-year period (Table 9). With the PWOC leadership unable to deliver the goods by expanding the organization's national base, their legitimacy among local unions steadily declined, and agitation for packinghouse workers to take control of their union increased.[8]

After two years of growing tension, open warfare erupted in 1941. Triggering the factional struggle was the decision of assistant national director Hank Johnson to support Republican Wendell Willkie, the candidate endorsed by John L. Lewis, in the 1940 presidential election. Although nominally a dispute over politics, Johnson evidently hoped to use the growing

Table 9. PWOC Membership, United States, 1938–43

	1938	1939	1940	1941	1942	1943
January		21,834	21,134	23,836	55,962	59,432
February		19,742	20,356	23,622	55,630	60,750
March		19,120	21,218	24,278	44,860	49,496
April	1,372	17,102	19,624	24,705	45,546	53,502
May	8,462	16,678	19,152	17,411[a]	46,522	58,372
June	10,204	17,800	21,120	22,034	44,502	91,510
July	10,324	18,754	19,568	24,130	47,070	68,708
August	11,972	21,170	20,172	34,002	49,532	66,356
September	12,630	18,884	19,522	33,892	57,212	
October	16,914	18,692	21,104	43,356	45,006	
November	19,256	19,006	18,778	43,886	53,948	
December	19,564	18,380	23,878	50,570	52,310	

Note: Membership figures are based on receipts of per capita tax from local unions. This may understate membership in the early stages of the PWOC because the union did not require locals to remit payments until they had solidified.

a. The height of the dues-withholding movement.

Sources: "Receipts, PWOC," UPWA Papers, box 1, folder 7; Lewis J. Clark to Philip Murray, September 10, 1942, CIO, ST 66; James Carey to Haywood, June 25, 1943, CIO, ST 67; Financial Reports, PWOC, September 1942 through August 1943, CIO, ST 67.

tension between Lewis and other CIO officials to challenge Van Bittner's control over the PWOC. The CIO "re-assigned" Johnson after he sent telegrams to local unions, declaring himself the personal representative of "our great leader, John L. Lewis" and urging them to vote for Wilkie. He was then fired after refusing to accept an assignment outside of Chicago. Dismissed as well were Johnson's two closest allies, prominent black organizers Arthell Shelton and Frank Alsup. Shelton had been a leader of the Sioux City Swift strike in 1938 and 1939 and, at the time of his dismissal, was orchestrating a dynamic drive at the Chicago Swift plant. Alsup, a skilled boomer butcher from Cedar Rapids, had served as the director of Minnesota-based District 2 since 1937. All three were reputed to have links with the Communist Party and probably survived the 1939 purge by virtue of their popularity among black workers. Hired by District 50, a catch-all division of the UMW, the three men encouraged supporters to consider joining the mine workers if the PWOC did not respond to the concerns of packinghouse workers.[9]

The dismissal of Johnson's group, and their subsequent effort to promote affiliation with District 50, split the packinghouse union and generated seemingly bizarre factional alliances. Opposing Johnson were the Communists in Chicago Armour Local 347, the anticommunist Omaha unions, the Iowa locals in District 3 and, to a certain extent, Local 9 in Austin. Supporting Johnson were the St. Paul unions, Chicago locals that opposed the influence of the Communist Party, and, to some degree, Kansas City-based District 4. It was a strange configuration: Communists fought Johnson, formerly linked with their party, and supported a PWOC leadership that had purged Communists scarcely a year before. Trotskyists in Austin strongly opposed the pro-District 50 orientation of St. Paul Trotskyists, and anti-Communists in Omaha lined up on the opposite side of their putative co-thinkers in Chicago. A perplexed James Carey, assigned by the CIO to mediate the dispute, was baffled by the factional configurations. "This does not seem to be a fight between lefts and rights," he observed. "The lines are drawn a lot of different ways."[10]

Carey's confusion was understandable. The alliances did cross ideological lines and made little sense to observers ignorant of the patterns of union formation in meatpacking. As in the conflicts of 1939 and 1940, the shared aspiration of packing locals for a democratic union found expression in different strategic positions. The profound short-term disagreements in 1941 were sufficient to drive a wedge between those who ostensibly held similar political views, and to unite packinghouse workers who had immense ideological differences but shared the same strategy for constructing a democratic national union. Untangling the alignments within the PWOC over the Johnson affair requires attention to the specific history of particular locals and regions rather than the political ideology of their leaders.

The obviously racial dimensions to the dismissals of Johnson, Alsup, and Shelton particularly disturbed a loose network of black leaders based in Chicago. They viewed the removal of Johnson as a blow to black influence in the PWOC and white support for Van Bittner's action as evidence of racism. Johnson had supplied the tangible link with the CIO for blacks who headed several Chicago locals, most notably Jesse Vaughn at the small Roberts and Oake plant and the team of Richard Saunders and Burette King at the 1,500–member Armour Soap Works. With the help of Johnson and Alsup, these Chicago workers had established a small midwestern network of black packinghouse workers. The purge of Johnson's group sundered their connection to the national organization and weakened their confidence in the union's commitment to racial equality. Soon after Johnson's dismissal, leaders of four Chicago locals complained, "How can PWOC officials expect us to explain to our membership that there is no discrimination in our Union, when Mr. Van A. Bittner and his officers have fired the three best Negro organizers in our Union?" The black Chicago leaders were able to take control of the joint Chicago PWOC Council by forming an alliance with opponents of the Communist Party.[11]

The St. Paul locals at the Armour, Cudahy, and Superior packinghouses were close allies of Saunders and Vaughn because of their ties with Frank Alsup. Because Alsup had served as the Twin Cities-based director of District 2 from 1937 to 1941, he provided the primary connection with the CIO for St. Paul packinghouse workers. Already angered at Bittner's actions in the Armour negotiations, it is not surprising St. Paul unionists exploded after Alsup's dismissal. They deluged the PWOC with letters and resolutions calling for the resignation of Bittner and the reinstatement of Johnson, Alsup, and Shelton "until such time as we have an international union and elect our own officers." In order "to bring some pressure to bear on the national office," the St. Paul locals promised to withhold per capita dues payments to the PWOC until their demands were met, and they urged other locals to do the same. Trotskyists in the Armour local, led by Milt Siegel and Martin Schempf, provided the most vocal leadership for St. Paul's actions. Boyd Collins, the black president of the Superior local, backed the call for suspending per capita payments, because "the longer we play around with them [the PWOC], the longer they will stall."[12]

In District 4, dominated by large Armour locals in Kansas City, Kansas, St. Joseph, Missouri, and East St. Louis, Illinois, Bittner's failure in 1939 to press for a national Armour contract had already soured them on the PWOC leader. Unlike the St. Paul and Chicago unions, however, District 4 locals had little personal allegiance to Johnson's group, and all supported Roosevelt in 1940. Significantly, they used the events of 1940 and 1941 to call for the resignation of Bittner without an equivalent demand to rehire Johnson and Alsup. Their major objectives were completion of the organizing drive in packing, securing contracts in the Big Four chains, and formation of an international union "democratically controlled by the workers who have a right to elect their own officers and representatives." Despite their differences with other opposition locals, District 4 worked closely with St. Paul to spread the per capita withholding movement to other midwestern packinghouse unions.[13]

The anti-Johnson alliance was even more heterogeneous. The District 3 locals that had supported Bittner's earlier purge naturally applauded the dismissal of Johnson, whom they viewed as a Communist. Echoing their earlier attacks on Don Harris, they accused Johnson of using "his connections and influence through the Communist Party not for the purpose of building unionism but for the purpose of trying to secure self-control and domination of the Unions that make up the PWOC." There also are intimations—in a manner that substantiated the suspicions of Vaughn and Saunders—that the Omaha unionists blamed Communists (and, implicitly, Johnson) for pressure to mix socially with blacks, something they strongly opposed. In addition, Omaha maintained close ties with Cedar Rapids and its primary leader, Lewis J. Clark, because of assistance they had received from the Midwest Union of All Packinghouse Workers in 1936 and 1937. Because of their role persuading the CIO to enter meatpacking, Cedar Rapids primarily identified with national PWOC leaders. Sioux City's positive relationship with CIO organizer H. R. Ballard, another mine worker and strong supporter of Van Bittner, put them in the pro-administration camp. The loss of the Swift strike of 1938 and 1939 removed Arthell Shelton and his allies from the scene and thus precluded links with Johnson's group through that connection.[14]

In Chicago, the experienced activists who had struggled so hard to bring the CIO into meatpacking fought Johnson's efforts to swing the locals they had constructed into District 50. They had been active before the entry of the CIO into meatpacking and thus did not view Johnson or Shelton as indispensable. Instead, to veteran organizers such as Arthur Kampfert, Johnson's efforts to split the PWOC made him "another Homer Martin," a reference to the United Auto Workers president who left the CIO for the AFL. The disruptive debates at union meetings and withholding of per capita payments even antagonized some black workers who had been drawn in by the initial core of union activists. "Every meeting that you go into, they take these meetings over," complained Pete Brown, president of Local 23. In his view, "the Johnson group are out to destroy the gains that Negroes who work in the packing industry now have."[15]

Johnson's actions also alienated him from his former comrades. Herb March and other Communists always had maintained a distant relationship with Johnson, a putative but secret Party member. "Hank Johnson was a Communist," recalled March. "He was an opportunist, that's the problem." Chicago Communists genuinely feared that a split in the PWOC would be a historic setback to the organizing efforts to which they had contributed so much. They also realized that Johnson's actions presented the Communists with a golden opportunity to reestablish their influence inside the PWOC after the 1939 purge.[16]

Herb March played a critical role in this episode. He successfully used his popularity to undermine Johnson and entrench Communist influence in the PWOC. After Bittner dismissed March from the PWOC in 1939, the CIO deliberately removed him from Chicago by assigning him to the Bethlehem Steel drive at Sparrow's Point, Maryland. A curious turn of events brought him back to Chicago in the nick of time. Suspecting March would turn against the PWOC after this treatment, District 50 hired him away from the steel drive and sent him to Chicago with instructions to bring Local 347 onto the side of Johnson. Instead, once back in Chicago, March employed his influence among Armour workers to support the PWOC. He personally struck a major blow against Johnson by dramatically appearing at a Local 347 meeting in February 1941 (just days after returning to the city) and defeating the pro-Johnson forces who had controlled the union in the initial stages of the controversy. March's action forced CIO leaders to accept the influence of the Communists in Chicago's PWOC. The new accommodation occurred well before the June 22, 1941, German invasion of the USSR sealed the renewed alliance by turning the Communists into enthusiastic supporters of American involvement in World War II.[17]

Although March's action was a material blow to Johnson's faction, Austin Local 9's position sealed their fate. As an advocate of a democratic, international union since 1935, Austin had as little sympathy for Bittner's bureaucratic behavior as it did Johnson's efforts to pull packinghouse locals into District 50. Austin attacked Bittner's "indiscriminate hiring and firing of PWOC personnel," (a clear reference to Johnson and his associates) and criticized efforts to withhold per capita as a "disruptive movement [that] can bring no possible good to packinghouse workers." With this centrist position, Austin tried to use the controversy to weaken the CIO's hold over the PWOC rather than secure Johnson's reinstatement.[18]

Local 9's initiative created an unusual public schism among Trotskyists. Joe Ollman and other Austin-based Trotskyists forcefully argued against the efforts of their St. Paul comrades to withhold per capita payments from the PWOC. Instead of fighting for the jobs of individuals (presumably Johnson and Alsup), Ollman urged opposition locals to develop a plan "to build an international from the ground up." Drawing on Austin's experience of enticing the CIO into meatpacking, he warned the impatient St. Paul dissidents that "unless we have an organized group of packinghouse workers to go into a constitutional convention, the same bureaucrats in the PWOC will tell you what to do. They will be an organized group and the only way you can defeat an organized group is with another one."[19]

Austin's alternative was a sustained fight within the PWOC for an international union. Backed by former IUAW affiliates in Fort Dodge and Ottumwa, Iowa, in 1941 Austin presented the only step-by-step procedure for forming an international. Its program, developed by Joe Ollman and Frank Ellis, projected holding several national conferences before an actual founding convention. At these conferences, packinghouse workers would elect committees composed of local union representatives to prepare a constitution and set the convention's agenda and rules. Ollman and Ellis hoped that these preparations would enable packinghouse workers to control the founding convention. Until that time, Austin and its allies advanced a "power-sharing" arrangement in the PWOC whereby elected "policy committees" of local union representatives would exercise power jointly with CIO-appointed officials. Ultimately, the Austin program would set the terms under which the UPWA formed.[20]

As the internal struggle intensified, CIO leaders were deluged with delegations and letters from disgruntled PWOC factions. Dozens of packinghouse workers descended on the November 1940 Atlantic City CIO convention to air their complaints and lobby delegates. A few months later, a pro-Johnson caucus from twenty-four local unions arrived uninvited at SWOC's Pittsburgh office on April 3. They barged into the SWOC building and compelled Philip Murray and Alan Haywood, in the midst of tense negotiation with Bethlehem Steel, to hear their complaints. Murray pleaded ignorance of the situation in meatpacking because he had just assumed the presidency of the CIO. In view of the "state of emergency" in the PWOC, however, he designated Haywood and James Carey his "personal representatives" and directed them to conduct hearings into the dispute and make appropriate recommendations.[21]

The subsequent April 14 and 15 investigation in Chicago drew two hundred packinghouse workers from both sides of the Johnson controversy. Presided over by CIO leaders Carey and Haywood, virtually every packinghouse worker who attended expressed an opinion on the crisis in the PWOC. The pro-Johnson faction repeated their criticisms of Van Bittner's leadership and demanded his resignation. Taking a plank from Austin's program, they advocated the formation of a provisional national executive board composed of representatives from major packing centers and followed by a national conference to adopt a constitution for the future international union. Johnson's opponents did not defend Bittner's record and admitted that his responsibilities in the Bethlehem drive consumed most of his attention. Carey candidly admitted, "It is hard to charge a man for mismanagement when he hasn't been in the thing."[22]

The willingness of the CIO and the anti-Johnson faction to sacrifice Van Bittner provided the basis for a settlement sufficient to reduce internal divisions, although not entirely satisfactory to either side. By the end of the hearings, both Carey and Haywood were dropping clear hints that there would be a shake-up in the PWOC structure because "the present machinery does not respond to the needs of the Packinghouse Workers." In addition to the persuasive testimony of many workers, the CIO worried about the dues-withholding movement. In May, per capita receipts fell 30 percent as locals representing more than seven thousand workers placed their dues in escrow accounts in order to pressure the CIO. With Johnson and Alsup prepared to offer charters in District 50 to dissident packing unions, some action had to be taken to avert a destructive split in the PWOC.[23]

In early May, Philip Murray "reassigned" Van Bittner to other duties in the CIO and installed PWOC District 3 director J. C. Lewis as the new national chair. Murray rebuffed dissident demands for democratic control over the PWOC, however. Instead, he simply authorized Lewis "to select representatives to assist him." Lewis, aware of the extent of dissatisfaction within the union, appointed packinghouse workers to various PWOC posts, including some previously dismissed in 1939 and 1940. He restored Tony Stephens to the organizing staff and Herb March to head Chicago-based District 1, confirmed former Austin business agent Roy Franklin as District 2 director, and appointed Cedar Rapids leader Lewis J. Clark as PWOC vice chair. The unlikely alliance between the anticommunist Lewis and Chicago Communists brought cries of protests from Chicago unionists who had supported Johnson largely to weaken March's influence.[24]

J. C. Lewis and the CIO no doubt hoped that placing known packinghouse leaders in responsible positions in the PWOC would mollify the advocates of more internal democracy and deflect agitation for the formation of an international union. Their objectives were moderately successful: by July, the per capita withholding movement had collapsed, and even the most intransigent locals in St. Paul resumed dues payments. Many locals remained unhappy with the absence of internal democracy in the PWOC, however, and unionists in St. Paul, Chicago, and Fort Worth retained links with District 50 for several years.[25]

Although PWOC members who continued to cooperate with UMW District 50 worried PWOC leaders, the sorry ending to the Johnson, Alsup, and Shelton group eliminated any threat from that quarter. As a result of an internal District 50 dispute, Shelton shot Alsup and Johnson during an October 1944 UMW hearing, killing Johnson, who was only forty. It was a tragic end for a man who had once played such an important role in the Chicago stockyards. Shelton served many years in jail for the murder, and he and Alsup never resurfaced in the union movement.[26]

The new PWOC chair also took immediate steps to resolve the issue that had started the factional tensions in 1939: securing a master agreement with Armour. Doubtless attentive to the fragile situation in the PWOC, Lewis included local union representatives in the new Armour negotiating team. This was an important advance for the power of local unions within the PWOC and a democratic form ultimately incorporated into future negotiations. As in 1939, Armour objected to signing a national contract, prompting the PWOC to break off talks in July 1941 and recommend "a general strike throughout the Armour and Company packinghouse chain" to local unions. With meat production increasing because of U.S. aid to Great Britain, the PWOC hoped that a threat to strike would bring the National Defense Mediation Board (NDMB) into the negotiations. Their estimation proved correct. A week later the NDMB formally intervened in the dispute and pressured Armour to accept a national contract.[27]

Union and company representatives reached an agreement on the historic pact, the first national collective bargaining agreement in the history of the packing industry, on August 8, 1941. Signed in September after locals had an opportunity to discuss and vote on it, the one-year agreement covered twenty thousand workers in fifteen plants. It provided for a small wage increase, paid vacations, departmental seniority, and, most important of all, exclusive recognition of the PWOC. Cudahy signed a similar agreement on November 1 that covered ten thousand workers in seven plants and contained a maintenance-of-membership provision. Less than two months later, the PWOC scored another important victory: Armour, Cudahy, Swift, and Wilson agreed to settle a suit brought by the union under the terms of the 1938 Fair Labor Standards Act. The companies agreed to pay millions in back overtime pay, covering the period from October 24, 1938, to November 24, 1941. The national agreements and increased employment levels in packinghouses brought PWOC membership to fifty thousand by December 1941, double the union's size over the past two years and a striking comeback from its precarious state in April. It was an auspicious first six months for the new PWOC leadership—and an important lesson that participation of local unions in contract negotiations augmented the union's bargaining power and reduced internal dissension.[28]

Lewis's success at the bargaining table raised his star in the PWOC, but there still was considerable dissatisfaction with his tight control over the union's operations. Muted rumbles from the IUAW Austin-Fort Dodge-Ottumwa alliance, St. Paul, District 4, and Detroit locals in the last half of 1941 indicated that many local unions were not satisfied with Lewis. Sharp protests from Armour and Cudahy locals erupted in February 1942 when Lewis repeated Van Bittner's mistake and reopened the Armour and Cudahy contracts for negotiations over wages without first convening a meeting of affected locals. In May, he bent to the pressure from local unions and agreed to the formation of a ten-person National Policy Committee. Drawing on the model of recent negotiations, caucuses of locals representing, respectively, the Armour, Cudahy, Swift, Wilson, and independent plants each elected two representatives. A national delegated conference on May 3, 1942, instructed the Policy Committee to "guide" Lewis in future negotiations.[29]

External events suddenly undermined J. C. Lewis's position. In May 1942, the simmering dispute between John L. Lewis and Philip Murray broke into the open and severed the bonds between the UMW and the industrial union federation it had spawned. The dispute placed J. C. Lewis, a veteran UMW leader, in an untenable position, and in mid-July he chose his long association with the mine workers over the CIO and resigned from the PWOC. The CIO replaced him with Sam Sponseller, a former Flat Glass Workers official, elevated Roy Franklin and veteran Chicago Armour leader Oscar Wilson to the PWOC national board, and designated Lewis J. Clark as its secretary-treasurer. The Policy Committee remained in place, but with its power still restricted to contract negotiations. Rank-and-file input remained limited to periodic "consultation" among CIO-appointed leaders and local union delegates at district conferences, with the agenda confined to, once again, wage and contract issues. The CIO made vague promises, however, to call a national wage and policy conference as a "forum" for local union representatives and hold a constitutional convention "at some future time."[30]

Unlike Lewis, whose competent management of the PWOC and long record in the UMW accorded grudging respect from packinghouse workers, Sponseller had no personal following and was an unpopular choice to head the union. "We didn't like what he stood for," recalled Boston union founder Jesse Prosten. "Sponseller represented the roots of the bureaucracy that was starting to develop within the labor movement of the 1940s." District 3 locals were infuriated that longtime Cedar Rapids leader Lewis J. Clark had been passed over in favor of Sponseller. With the support of Omaha and Sioux City unions, Cedar Rapids Local 3 complained that "a man from packing should be the head and chairman of the Packinghouse Workers Organizing Committee." The powerful Chicago locals, including the usually antagonistic Armour and Swift unions, joined the protests along with Austin Local 9. Sponseller particularly antagonized Chicago's race-conscious black workers by only hiring white secretaries in the PWOC national office. "There was a degree of discrimination by Sponseller in the national office that we weren't going to tolerate," recalled Chicago Swift leader Philip Weightman.[31]

Opposition to Sponseller's appointment created a broad alliance inside the PWOC to press for an international union. Districts 1 and 3, no longer as internally divided, now held a similar attitude toward the PWOC leadership as the older opposition groups in Districts 2 and 4. Even Sioux City, a solid CIO supporter thus far, joined the dissident forces; local union leaders complained in 1942 that "the PWOC, through its District Directors and Field Representatives exerts a dictatorial force over all the local unions." Cedar Rapids endorsed the program first formulated by Austin in 1941, notably the creation of an elected body of packinghouse workers to draft a constitution and rules for a founding convention. Frustrated by the limits on discussion at official district conferences, Fort Dodge initiated a widely attended but unsanctioned meeting of midwestern locals to discuss forming an international union. Held despite desperate attempts by Sponseller to block the gathering, the September 13 conference demanded that the PWOC hold a national policy convention sixty days after the National War Labor Board (NWLB) decision on the union's wage demands. The resolution provided that the conference would in turn lay the groundwork for a constitutional convention. Bowing to the inevitable, in November the PWOC accepted the Fort Dodge plan.[32]

"They finally capitulated and allowed us to have our own union," recalled Herb March, but "they didn't necessarily want us to select our own leadership." Once the CIO conceded the principle of an autonomous packinghouse union, the struggle in 1943 shifted to the form in which an international would be constituted. The model for most CIO leaders was the highly centralized United Steel Workers of America (USWA), founded in May 1942. Philip Murray and other CIO-appointed SWOC leaders had simply taken over as the USWA's first officers, where they exercised tight control over the new union's operations. The CIO hoped that Sponseller and the packinghouse workers appointed to PWOC positions would perform a similar role in a future UPWA. "You can't walk by yourself in this particular instance any more than a babe that has not yet been able to learn to walk without the assistance of his mother's hand," CIO official Fullerton Fulton warned impatient packinghouse workers. Sponseller praised the method used to establish the USWA and attacked the notion of constructing some "new-fangled machinery" to create a UPWA. Murray and Haywood also were determined to prevent the Communists, based in District 1 and East Coast District 6, from having much power in an international union.[33]

By February 1943 the Austin plan had support from all areas and became an effective alternative to the CIO's efforts to mold a new packinghouse union in the image of the steel workers. At the February 1943 wage and policy conference, District 3 locals, with support from Kansas City and St. Paul, introduced a resolution condemning PWOC leaders "not elected by the rank and file" whose policies "have not followed the wishes of the rank and file members." Arguing that the time was right to adopt "a definite program" for forming an international union, the locals proposed that a committee with representatives elected from each district draw up the constitution and rules for the founding convention. Although Sponseller blocked passage of the resolution in February, a similar proposal passed a second wage and policy conference in July.[34]

The formation of the powerful Constitutional Convention Committee in the summer of 1943 reflected the victory of Austin's original 1941 plan. Empowered to draw up a constitution and establish basic convention rules, it allowed packinghouse workers to design their organizational structure and founding meeting outside of the CIO's control. The large committee included key leaders from the various regional groupings of packinghouse workers and thus was able to forge a consensus on the structure and objectives of the new international union. The draft constitution created an international executive board that had four officers selected at union constitutional conventions, as well as directors from each of ten regions elected by the locals in their area. The preamble, which bore March's style, was unique to the packinghouse workers. Its key clause read: "We recognize that our industry is composed of all nationalities, of many races, of different creeds and political opinions. In the past these differences have been used to divide us and one group has been set against another by those who would prevent our unifying. We have organized by overcoming these divisive influences and by recognizing that our movement must be big enough to encompass all groups and all opinions."[35]

Common work on the constitution encouraged joint efforts to bring a slate of candidates to the convention who, if elected, would be responsible to packinghouse workers. The leadership question dominated the October founding convention and overshadowed the routine adoption of the draft constitution. A caucus of locals from Districts 1, 2, 3, 4, and 6—informally dubbed the "Iowa group"—endorsed Lewis J. Clark for president, Frank Ellis and Philip Weightman for the two vice presidencies, and Meyer Stern for secretary-treasurer. The CIO and a minority of PWOC delegates favored current PWOC officials Sponseller for president, Oscar Wilson and Roy Franklin for vice presidents, and Ed Roche from East St. Louis for secretary-treasurer. The candidacy of Stern, a Communist, particularly worried CIO leaders and conservative PWOC unionists.

The night before the election, Alan Haywood summoned supporters of each slate to his hotel room in order to force a compromise. CIO leaders knew that the Iowa group could easily defeat their candidates and wanted to avoid a humiliating vote. Haywood offered to withdraw the CIO-supported slate if the Iowa group would accept Roche in place of Stern, and he threatened to withhold the promised CIO charter unless they complied. Despite Haywood's threat, the Iowa group refused to budge. When the delegates reconvened next morning, "Alan Haywood was coming to the platform to stop the convention," recalled Philip Weightman. "Just as Haywood was taking the platform to speak, Meyer Stern handed him a note of withdrawal. Otherwise we wouldn't have had an international union." With Stern's disputed candidacy resolved, the convention elected the slate of Clark, Ellis, Weightman, and Roche by acclamation and joyfully adjourned. The delegates were pleased with their successful struggle to establish and control their own union.[36]

The UPWA leadership team reflected the coalition of local unions that composed the new international. Cedar Rapids and Austin, represented by Lewis J. Clark and Frank Ellis, secured their positions due to their role bringing the CIO into meatpacking in 1937 and establishing the UPWA in 1943. Philip Weightman's selection mollified the Chicago Swift local, always suspicious of the Communist presence at Armour, and was a significant statement to wary black workers that they would have a representative and an advocate at the highest levels of the new union. Weightman and Ellis were not simply titular office holders; Ellis supervised the union's organizing activities, and Weightman directed the grievance department. Ed Roche, added as the price for the CIO's support, made no strong impact on the union and lasted only three years.

The structure of the UPWA International Executive Board (IEB) permitted the strong regional characteristics of UPWA locals, especially leftist influence at the local level, to be reflected in the national union. Although Communists held no executive offices, Communists Herb March and Meyer Stern, the directors of Districts 1 and 6, exercised considerable influence at the highest levels of the organization, often in alliance with Vice President Frank Ellis, an old Wobbly. At the same time, the directors who represented the strong local unions in Iowa and other midwestern states were willing to cooperate with the left despite political disagreements. The most important centrist leader was District 3 director Tony Stephens, a Sioux City Swift union founder discharged in the strike of 1938 and 1939. Often this left-center bloc had an ally in Fred Dowling, an active social-democrat and the director of Canadian District 10, an almost completely autonomous UPWA region. Relatively conservative southern directors A. J. Pittman and Grover Hathaway, a minority at the 1943 convention, retained a strong voice in the UPWA through the solid support of their districts. They occasionally could enlist the cooperation of independent-minded District 4, whose directors usually came from the Kansas City Armour local, and Glenn Chinander, director of District 2. The very diversity of the groupings in the international leadership, and the changes in directors that occurred at almost every convention, mitigated against any one faction becoming dominant in the international union.[37]

The complicated, internecine struggle for a democratic union began the

UPWA's trajectory away from the pattern of development of other main-stream CIO unions. The capacity of packinghouse workers to force the CIO to grant an international union charter on their terms reflected the authentic rank-and-file base of the local unions that composed the heart and soul of the UPWA. The result was an international union permeable to rank-and-file influence because the locus of power rested at the lower echelons of the organization. One specific result of the struggle against Van Bittner, the establishment of "chains" of local unions in the plants of the same national firm, created a critically important channel for union democracy. By creating tangible connections among local unions in different regions of the UPWA, the chains became a vehicle for local union cooperation and power that would spread considerably beyond periodic contract talks.

The formation of a democratic UPWA largely fulfilled the objectives of the union founders who hoped to establish an industrial union capable of confronting national firms while remaining under the control of packing-house workers. Arthur Kampfert, in his remarks to the founding convention, articulated the delegates' hope that their creation would ensure that the divisive forces that tore the unions apart after World War I would be contained by the consensual binding ties of the UPWA. But their construction would be sorely tested during the next five years. The pressures of world war, the cold war, and a difficult strike in 1948 would threaten the very existence of the UPWA and its capacity to ensure that "your children and children's children will not have to slave in those packinghouses as we have slaved in the past."

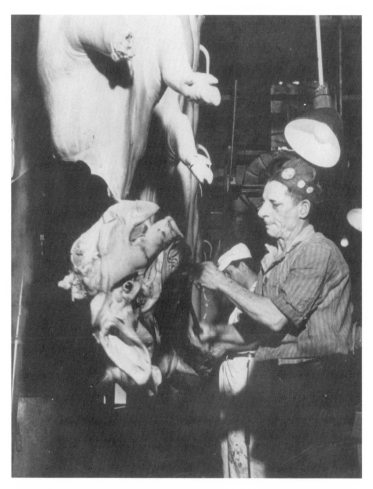

A "header" on the pork-kill line, ca. 1947. (State Historical Society of Wisconsin, WHi (X3) 50700)

Workers blockade the Austin, Minnesota, Hormel plant, November 1933. (State Historical Society of Wisconsin, WHi (X3) 50702)

Meeting announcing formation of the PWOC. National Chair Van Bittner is speaking; to his immediate left are Don Harris and Hank Johnson. (State Historical Society of Wisconsin, WHi (X3) 50701)

Herb March signing placard of Kansas City delegate at the July 16, 1937, mass rally in Chicago. March's arm is in a sling because he had been shot two days before when he left the founding meeting of the Back of the Yards Neighborhood Council. (Herb March)

The 1944 send-off rally in Chicago for UPWA leaders going to Washington to pressure the National War Labor Board for a wage increase. (Herb March)

Opposite: Herb March speaking to noon-time rally in Chicago stockyards, ca. 1946. (Herb March)

UPWA International Executive Board, March 1946. Standing (left to right): unidentified, Meyer Stern, Grover Hathaway, A. J. Pittman, Norman Dolnick, A. J. Shippey, Ralph Baker, Joe Ollman, Fred Dowling, Herb March, and Ralph Helstein. Seated (from left to right): Philip Weightman, Lewis J. Clark, Frank Ellis, and Lewis Roach. (Herb March)

Noon rally at "CIO corner" in Chicago stockyards, 1947. (Herb March)

Chicago delegate Sophie Kosciowlowski speaking at UPWA's tumultuous 1954 convention. (State Historical Society of Wisconsin, photo by Les Orear, WHi (X3) 50573)

Negotiations with Armour and Company, 1960. The two Armour representatives are on the left, facing the UPWA negotiators. The participation of many unionists in negotiations was typical of the UPWA. (State Historical Society of Wisconsin, WHi (X3) 50571)

Committee on problems in the South meets during the first UPWA anti-discrimination conference in 1951 to prepare program recommendations for the national conference to approve. Field representative Emerson Mosely is at the blackboard. Immediately next to the blackboard is Jareutha Coleman, Local 28. (State Historical Society of Wisconsin, photo by jo banks, WHi (X3) 50703)

District 1 Education Committee, ca. 1950. (State Historical Society of Wisconsin, photo by jo banks, WHi (X3) 50704)

UPWA picket Jesse Prosten participates in protest against racial violence in Trumball Park homes, ca. 1955. (State Historical Society of Wisconsin, WHi (X3) 50572)

PART 2

"All That Capitalism Would Allow": The Era of the United Packinghouse Workers of America

Once the CIO won all that capitalism would allow it . . . sitdowns and mass struggle gave way to union administration, dues collection, labor board briefs, detailed negotiation. The swivel-chair tribe began its own long-lasting sitdown in union office. This tribe rode to office on the broad shoulders of Lewis and the backs of the agitators, the militants, the reds. Once they arrived they turned—dutifully, patriotically, devoutly—to kick in the face those on whom and over whom they had scrambled.

—Len De Caux, 1970

The formation of the United Packinghouse Workers of America in October 1943 marked a dramatic expansion in the class-based alliance between different racial and ethnic groups of packinghouse workers. Wresting control of the UPWA from reluctant CIO officials allowed workers to extend their union's policies to the limits of "all that capitalism would allow" in postwar America. The power of local unions over the international union apparatus mitigated against the loss of democracy and shop-floor power characteristic of other CIO unions in the 1940s and 1950s and kept the UPWA's "swivel-chair tribe" in check. As a result, black workers and white progressives were able to weave their influence, earned through diligent work in the pre-CIO period, into the fabric of the new organization. The result was a union strongly based on the shop floors of the nation's packinghouses that was able to expand its program of social unionism in the 1950s into unparalleled cooperation with the emerging civil rights movement.

The particular course of industrial unionism in meatpacking reflected a complex interplay between government policies, strategies of the industry's firms, and the struggles of workers on the shop floor and the picket line. The focal points of conflict shifted several times in the life of the UPWA; in each phase, however, control over work and remuneration were the central contested arenas. During World War II, close federal supervision of labor relations created a three-cornered struggle as workers tried to use government regulation to entrench union power at the same time that companies sought to leverage the patriotic calls for sacrifice to tame union strength on the shop floor. Immediately after the war, leading packing firms tried to take advantage of new legal restrictions on labor to roll back the advances of the union, first at the bargaining table and then in a nationwide strike in 1948. With the companies frustrated in their efforts to dislodge the UPWA from the industry, conflict in the 1950s took the form of a guerrilla war over the pace and intensity of work on the shop floor. At all points these struggles were lineal descendants of efforts by packinghouse workers during the organizing era to exercise control over their work and increase their share of the industry's wealth.

In general terms, the pressures on packinghouse workers differed only in degree from those workers experienced in other American mass-production industries. After World War II, large firms in auto, steel, and electrical industries also abandoned efforts to eliminate labor organizations in favor of strategies designed to encourage "responsible" unionism that would refrain from challenges to managerial prerogatives. De Caux's complaint, written in 1970, is a measure of how well American corporations succeeded in their objectives.[1]

Despite similarities, the distinctive features of the postwar meatpacking industry made for important differences in labor-management relations. Packing companies were far less reconciled to unionism than their confederates in other industries because they were steadily losing market share in an increasingly competitive environment. Reducing labor costs and reasserting control over work remained central features of managerial psychology as new insurgent firms employed innovative production methods to take growing chunks of the national market. At the same time, the "chains" of local unions, uniting workers in different plants of the same national firms, gave packinghouse workers a considerable resource with which to maintain pressure on a reluctant industry. Packing companies faced a union that was far more democratic than its compatriots in other industries, and able to survive the labor movement's efforts to destroy dissident organizations in the late 1940s and early 1950s. The resulting clash between stubborn companies and a democratic labor organization helped reinforce traditions of inter-racial unionism and shop-floor militancy inherited from the 1930s.

The UPWA's efforts were complicated by competition from other labor organizations. There is no doubt that the UPWA was the major architect of pattern bargaining in meatpacking, represented the vast majority of workers under master agreements, and was the dominant union in the Big Four firms. Yet two other unions could not be ignored. The independent National Brotherhood of Packinghouse Workers (NBPW) represented approximately 25 percent of Swift employees, and the AFL-affiliated Amalgamated Meat Cutters and Butcher Workmen had close to nine thousand members in Armour and Swift plants (Table 10). The Amalgamated also represented an additional fifty thousand packinghouse workers in small independent plants, predominantly on the East and West Coasts.

Even though the UPWA dominated the Big Four, the other unions had sufficient strength to weaken its efforts. During the UPWA's 1948 strike, meat production from plants represented by the NBPW and Amalgamated prevented the walkout from measurably affecting national meat supplies. Relations among the unions reached a low point following the strike, as the NBPW and the Amalgamated unsuccessful raided dozens of UPWA-organized plants. Slowly the UPWA reduced tensions with the Amalgamated by establishing coordinated bargaining efforts and signing a no-raiding agreement. The two organizations almost merged in 1956, but negotiations collapsed at the last minute.

The main obstacles to the merger reflected fundamental differences between the two organizations. When UPWA negotiators insisted on guarantees that its grievance, wage-rate, and program departments would continue to deliver the same services to packinghouse workers, Amalgamated officials walked out and called off the merger convention. They felt the UPWA's demands would compromise and undermine the authority of the central Amalgamated officials. At issue was whether the UPWA's industrial union structure, and the responsiveness of its apparatus to the shop-floor concerns of local unions, would continue under the Amalgamated. To the UPWA, the critical need for labor unity was not worth placing the "swivel-chair tribe" in complete control of the union that represented packinghouse workers.[2]

The UPWA's evolution after World War II suggests that a range of possibilities was open to the industrial unions that emerged from the 1930s.

Table 10. Big Four Master Agreements, 1951

Union	Number of Plants			Number of Workers		
	Covered	Armour	Swift	Covered	Armour	Swift
UPWA	70	15	27	60,000	24,650	18,680
Amalgamated	22	11	11	7,700	3,700	4,000
NBPW	9	—	9	7,900	—	7,900

Sources: U.S. Department of Labor, *Directory of National and International Labor Unions in the United States*, Bulletin 1127 (Washington, 1953), 22; Lawrence R. Klein, "Wage Chronology No. 7: Swift & Co., 1942–1948," *Monthly Labor Review* 69 (July 1949): 25–26; U.S. Department of Labor, *Collective Bargaining in the Meatpacking Industry*, Bulletin 1063 (Washington, 1952), 12; membership data, UPWA Papers, box 497, folder 7.

There is no doubt that the postwar strategies of manufacturing firms, along with the actions of state and federal government, dramatically shaped the playing field for labor and foreclosed many opportunities. Within the confines of "all that capitalism would allow," however, the UPWA followed an unusual path. Its capacity to retain shop-floor power and social unionism, and its alliance with the early civil rights movement, provide tantalizing glimpses of the options that remained available to the labor movement in postwar America.

7

"We Are Not Asking for Favors": World War II and the Consolidation of a Democratic UPWA

It was amazing how quickly they were able to absorb the whole concept from the other workers who were there. We had the experience of building our union up through the period of the war which involved this constant stoppage, slowdown, fight around issues, constant militancy around issues was at the heart of the functioning of the union. As a result, the rank and file was unusually militant, and had a strong feeling of the union being their organization.

—Herb March

Even under normal conditions the July 1944 UPWA convention in Omaha would have been tense. The National War Labor Board (NWLB) had placed the union's wage demands on hold, frustrating workers who had hoped for rapid improvement in their income at a time of labor shortages. Packing firms had seized on unsanctioned walkouts throughout the country to oppose union demands and ask the government to remove union security provisions from the national agreements.

The conditions under which the UPWA conducted its deliberations, however, were far from normal. When black delegates arrived at the convention hotel they were denied accommodations and directed to use the service elevator to reach meeting rooms. The Arrangements Committee, chaired by District 3 director Tony Stephens, had made the terrible mistake of not inquiring into the hotel's racial policies. "They were beefing, and I don't blame them," recalled an Omaha activist.[1]

The UPWA acted quickly to avoid a walkout by incensed black workers. The union immediately moved the convention to the Omaha UPWA hall, where delegates met for four days in sweltering 100–degree weather. White members checked out of the discriminatory hotel, and delegates of both races stayed in the homes of Omaha UPWA members because there were no integrated public accommodations. On the floor of the convention, Stephens accepted responsibility and apologized to the black delegates, admitting that the incident "opened our eyes in Omaha to something we never knew existed here before." The union's prompt actions averted a break in its interracial alliance; however, the incident provided blacks with an opportunity to remind UPWA members of their power. There would have been no agreements with the Big Four companies "if it hadn't been for the Negro joining with you then," pointed out Kansas City delegate Roy Calvin. "We are not asking for favors. We will take what is coming to us."[2]

Calvin's statement aptly summarized the dynamics of race and class in meatpacking during World War II. The UPWA did not count on government regulation during the war to provide improvements in pay and working conditions. It was the widespread informal shop-floor bargaining of packinghouse workers, sanctioned by the union, that corrected many local grievances, strengthened the UPWA's hand in formal negotiations over wages and benefits, and integrated new employees into the shop-floor structures of local unions. Black workers, whose absolute numbers increased as a result of the recomposition of the labor force, became even more powerful inside the UPWA. With their influence in local unions facilitated by the continued importance of shop-floor bargaining, World War II accentuated the capacity of black packinghouse workers to use the UPWA as a vehicle to combat discrimination. As a result, the union emerged from World War II with its militant practices and in-plant structures intact and the power of black workers considerably augmented.

The ability of local unions to establish a UPWA under their firm control was a critical reason for the union's behavior during World War II. The power of local unions rendered the new international leaders highly sensitive to rank-and-file pressure that could upset the balance of forces within the union. This placed the locus of power within the UPWA at the lower levels of the organization and gave local unions considerable influence over the actions of the international leadership. Weakness of central authority in the UPWA also mitigated against the formation of a union bureaucracy capable of containing rank-and-file self-activity and enforcing its will on stubborn local unions. Indeed, UPWA officials who adopted policies that conflicted with the wishes of local unions found they had little power to enforce their decisions.[3]

The dynamics of the packing industry provided an additional impetus for the UPWA's development during the war. As in other industries, contract and grievance negotiations entailed complex entanglement with the bureaucracy created by the government to manage labor relations. But more so than in industries such as auto and steel, the upper management of the packing companies remained bitterly opposed to unionism as such and only signed national contracts under the direct pressure of the federal government. They resisted settling grievances through official channels and then called on the NWLB to remove union security measures, especially maintenance of membership and the dues check-off, when local job actions erupted. At the same time, enormous production pressures for the war effort encouraged frontline supervisors to reach informal accords with union stewards and individual work groups, resulting in an increase in union power over the pace and intensity of work. These dynamics mitigated against union officials employing coercive measures to control workers who were making the advances through informal negotiation on the job that the union was having difficulty achieving at the bargaining table.

The articulation of industry and union dynamics gave the newly formed international union insufficient capacity to enforce its authority on recalcitrant members and adopt measures subordinating local unions to the national office. Consequently, the war years had a very different effect on the UPWA than mainstream CIO unions such as the UAW and USWA, where government regulation encouraged and aided the efforts of central union leaders to exert their control firmly over the activities of local unions. The very weakness of the young union's central bureaucracy, and the concatenation of conflict with packing firms, caused the UPWA to emerge from the war with the authority and independence of local unions fully intact.[4]

The retention of power at the lower echelons of the union was encouraged by the manner in which the UPWA capitalized on, rather than suppressed, shop-floor unrest. Participation in work stoppages familiarized new packinghouse workers with the union's prewar techniques of exercising power at the point of production and equipped them to use similar methods after 1945. "It was amazing how quickly they were able to absorb the whole concept from the other workers who were there," recalled Herb March. Integration into the union's shop-floor structures also created bonds between the World War II generation and their local unions and helped them develop, as March later explained, "a strong feeling of the union being their organization." The war years thus generated a new cohort of union activists to reinforce the generation who had started the organization. Immediately after the war, these workers had the training, the motivation, and the institutional opportunity to reinforce the UPWA's shop-floor structures and the power of the local unions. The attitude of UPWA leaders made the critical difference. Their willingness to appropriate the rank-and-file militancy rather than repress that discontent channeled the energy of new workers into support for the UPWA's "oppositional infrastructure."[5]

The war years also had an impact, albeit less dramatic, on gender relations within the union. In a manner similar to other industries, increased
labor demand brought women into jobs that previously had been the province of men. The UPWA advocated paying women the same rate as men who
had previously performed the job. The union's stance was only in part designed to protect the income of women; it also preserved the traditional distinction between male and female spheres of work. The approach left a mixed
legacy. Layoffs at the end of the war reestablished the prewar pattern of labor market segmentation, but the seniority provisions in union contracts
enabled women to reenter the packinghouses in traditionally female jobs
relatively quickly. Employment and income gains were particularly important for black women who entered the industry in large numbers and at some
packinghouses where they previously had been excluded. As with male
workers influenced by the shop-floor turbulence, the World War II generation of women, especially blacks, would be a strong force pressing for gender equality at work and within the union in the 1950s.

The election of Ralph Helstein to the union presidency in 1946 symbol-
ized the effect of the war years on the UPWA. Helstein's election was the
result of the local unions looking for a more talented leader than Lewis J.
Clark while maintaining the balance between different political and regional currents. Although not a packinghouse worker, Helstein was intimately
acquainted with rank-and-file workers in the Midwest, knew the conditions
in the plants, and was committed to maintaining the social unionism of the
1930s in the increasingly difficult 1940s. A lawyer who had worked with
many Minnesota CIO unions, he also had the virtue of not being tied to any
particular union faction. The dilemma of the fiercely independent packinghouse union choosing a lawyer to lead it did not seriously trouble Helstein's
supporters, because it was the local unions who remained the true power
in the organization.

Government Regulation, Shop-floor
Turbulence, and Wartime Strikes

Once the UPWA moved its 1944 convention to the Omaha union hall,
delegates were able to concentrate on the troubling problems of wartime
strikes and stalemated negotiations between the union and the packing companies. During World War II, bargaining in meatpacking became a three-
cornered contest between the young union, the packing firms, and the National War Labor Board (NWLB). After 1942, packinghouse workers had to
present their wage and contract demands to the NWLB as well as the com-

panies, requiring union representatives to spend months in Washington, D.C., lobbying board members. The long delays hindered efforts by union leaders to use the war to consolidate the UPWA's base in the meatpacking industry in preparation for the inevitable outbreak of industrial conflict once overseas hostilities ended.

Although union certification and national contracts with major firms (Swift and Wilson signed master agreements in 1943) reduced management's arbitrary authority during the war, industrywide working conditions had not fundamentally changed. In 1941 packing was the fifth most dangerous industry in the country, with an average weekly wage of $26.84, about $10 less than in the auto industry. The average wage, however, was a statistical fiction. Wage rates for the same job varied wildly and irrationally from company to company in the same city and among plants of the same company in different areas. Complex geographic differentials created separate wage structures for the "near" South, "far" South, western plants, "river" plants located in the interior, and "metropolitan" plants in large centers such as Chicago and Kansas City. An 11–cent-per-hour differential between male and female jobs lowered the entire wage structure for women.[6]

The power of the NWLB severely hindered union efforts to improve these conditions through negotiations with management. Formed out of the wreckage of the National Defense Mediation Board, the NWLB had the authority to intervene into labor-management relations, unlike the NLRB, whose powers were limited to the terrain of union recognition and unfair labor practices. The NWLB could control wage increases, approve or reject contracts, insert clauses into collective bargaining agreements, and rule on grievances. A tripartite board with representation from employers, the AFL and CIO, and the "public" (in reality, labor relations specialists), the NWLB was not afraid to use its power. It altered wage agreements 58,794 times during the course of the war. An analyst noted, "For the first time in the history of the United States nearly three million employees could not obtain wage increases even though the raises were agreed to by their employer."[7]

A surge of employment bringing tens of thousands of workers new to industrial conditions into the packinghouses added a powerful destabilizing agent to shop-floor conditions. The labor force increased by more than fifty thousand in three years; depending on the local area, employment grew between 30 and 100 percent at the same time as many male workers entered the armed forces. To fulfill government orders, packinghouse firms hired more white and black women, black men, whites from rural areas, older workers previously outside the labor market, and even Italian prisoners of war. As wages in packing lagged in comparison to other war industries, constant hiring was unable to increase employment to the levels that the government and the companies desired. In the fall of 1943 the War Manpower Commission complained that low employment levels had held hog slaughter below desired levels; to save time, most meat for overseas consumption was not being boned despite the shipping expense.[8]

Long hours by packinghouse workers were the only solution to inadequate employment levels, and overtime pay partially compensated for the lower hourly rate. By the end of the war, average weekly pay in packing reached $44.54, a 65 percent increase over 1941 and only $2.36 less than in auto. On the average, however, packinghouse workers labored forty-seven hours a week to earn their money, compared with the thirty-nine-hour week for auto workers. On an hourly basis, packinghouse workers earned 95 cents to auto workers' $1.20.[9]

The NWLB's policies on wages and acceptable union behavior posed impossible constraints on the meatpacking union. The first NWLB ruling on the union's demands, issued February 9, 1943, denied the PWOC's request for a general wage increase. Under the guidelines of Little Steel formula that governed wartime wage increases, the board used a tortured rationale to argue that packinghouse workers already had received the maximum permissible raises. It agreed with the union's objections to the industry's chaotic wage structure but issued no rulings and instead encouraged labor and management to settle disputed job rates through the grievance procedure. The only substantive benefit awarded the union were union security provisions—maintenance of membership and the dues check-off—which the board inserted into master agreements over the objections of packing companies. As in the other industries, the board added union security to meatpacking contracts in order to "insure responsible leadership and enable that leadership to maintain proper discipline."[10]

The board's decision provided little incentive for the packing companies to negotiate with the union and resolve grievances. Over the next two years there was virtually no progress on wage differentials, and union contract demands in 1943 and 1944 were referred to the NWLB, where they languished until 1945. Grievances faced the same fate. In the middle of the war, the NWLB received ten to fifteen thousand grievances a month from all industries. By mid-1944 hundreds of grievances from packinghouses, some more than a year old, remained on hold in the NWLB office. The result, in meatpacking as in other industries, was widespread unsanctioned job actions. "It has been necessary for the union to take direct action, sometimes, to settle minor grievances," commented one Kansas City government official on local conditions in meatpacking. "In practically every instance where direct action was taken for a short time, the unions involved did get their grievances adjusted."[11]

Wartime strikes in meatpacking affected virtually every plant in the Big Four companies as well as many independent firms. Rather than "wildcats," as they are often incorrectly labeled, they were a form of concerted shop-floor bargaining. Typically, strikes were short job actions by a particular department, led by informal leaders of the individual work group, union stewards, or at times local union officials. Usually striking workers remained in their department in a form of the sit-in. "How can you replace a worker who's sitting on his job, especially if he's carrying a knife?" noted Sioux City Armour leader Clyde Wensel. At times, departmental actions could spark plant-wide strikes, especially if management tried to discipline workers who initiated the dispute. Truly spontaneous walkouts were rare and usually limited to non-union workers unfamiliar with conditions in a packinghouse, such as seven Kansas City workers who struck to protest low temperatures. Job actions generally occurred only after company inflexibility on grievances eliminated all other options for the affected workers.[12]

The cattle butchers in East St. Louis provide a clear example of these shop-floor dynamics. The plant's beef-kill gang engaged in a prolonged dispute with management over the pace and organization of slaughtering operation. Experienced floorsman Dewitt Weary and other butchers kept the pace of slaughtering to sixteen and a half cattle an hour when Armour wanted seventeen and a half. At one point the foreman suspended the workers when the gang refused to increase its work tempo. UPWA President Clark pressured the local union to accept the higher rate, and at the 1944 convention he publicly attacked the beef-kill gang for stopping work "before notifying anybody in the International." The workers seem to have accepted the increased pace for a short time, but within a year the beef-kill was once more embroiled in stoppages and slowdowns.[13]

Stoppages also frequently erupted when management altered established work patterns to fill special military orders without providing additional help or paying workers a rate they deemed appropriate. Employees who refused to perform the new job assignments routinely received suspensions or even discharges. In one case, Armour suspended ham-boners in Mason City who refused to bone pig shoulders (which yielded less meat than hams) for a military order unless they received a better pay rate. The union's only legal avenue was an appeal to the NWLB—which could take more than a year, during which time the company would continue the practice. It is hardly surprising that so many locals resorted to job actions to enforce their interpretation of shop-floor practices, even though there was no contractual language authorizing their actions.[14]

There is a curious, and significant, gap between the UPWA's formal support for the labor movements's no-strike pledge and the extent of shop-floor unrest. The union endorsed the no-strike pledge at its founding convention and reaffirmed its position in 1944 over the opposition of a small number of local unions. More important, rank-and-file workers overwhelmingly supported the war effort and, often having relatives and friends in the armed forces, genuinely desired to do their part for an Allied victory. Many UPWA members volunteered for military service, and those who remained at work religiously purchased war bonds and actively participated in patriotic celebrations. Austin Local 9 sponsored a huge victory rally in 1942, and Chicago's Armour, Swift, and Wilson locals each won the Army-Navy E for Excellence awards for high productivity. St. Joseph, Missouri, Armour workers even staged a walkout because a Jehovah's Witness refused to buy war bonds.[15]

Yet even where union leaders strongly opposed wartime strikes, as in the Communist-led Chicago Armour local, job actions were easily as extensive as in other plants. St. Joseph workers, willing to shut down their plant to protest the lack of patriotism of a Jehovah's Witness, nonetheless participated in the same type of job actions typical of other packinghouses. The contradiction between ideology and practice was similar to that noted by Martin Glaberman in the auto industry, where a majority of auto workers engaged in unsanctioned job actions "in a period when a referendum was indicating close to two-to-one opposition to wartime strikes."[16]

A closer look at shop-floor dynamics at the Chicago Armour plant unravels this apparent contradiction. Reflecting the Communist Party's World War II politics, Herb March and other Communists from Local 347 were vocal supporters of the no-strike pledge. On the shop floor of the Armour plant (and other Chicago packinghouses where they had influence), however, Communists followed a far more tolerant practice. Indeed, Armour's killing floors, with large numbers of Communist Party members, were the most militant departments in the plant. "We told the guys to avoid [stoppages]," recalled March, director of District 1 during the war. "But if you got an obstinate management, and they won't do anything, the guys are understaffed, they want to get the production out, they start giving the guys hell—and they wouldn't take it."[17]

A protracted struggle erupted in April 1944, for example, when management removed a union ballot box, used for a steward's election, in the hog-kill department. Union stewards protested the company's action because the long working hours made it difficult for the union to conduct elections at their meeting hall. Backed by the gang, stewards threatened to halt work in the hog kill at 3:30 P.M. after eight hours, rather than work the scheduled ten, unless the company ceased interference with in-plant union elections. Three emergency grievance meetings during the course of the day failed to win any concessions from Armour. At 3:19, the hog-shacklers stopped work in support of their stewards' demands, and the entire gang remained on the floor. When the shacklers resumed work at 3:55, at the request of stewards, the killing gangs refused to dress the hanging pigs. There was no more slaughtering that day, and the hogs already on the dead rail spoiled.

The job action apparently was successful. No workers were discharged, and the company ceased efforts to interfere with union elections conducted in the plant. The reaction of union officials was significant. Stewards, without the sanction of higher officials, initiated the stoppage as a way of bringing pressure on management outside of the grievance procedure. Jesse Prosten, a Communist and the international's representative in the dispute, placed the blame on the company at the same time as he tried to persuade the men to return to work. "The membership in the department was losing faith in the grievance machinery," Prosten pointed out to Armour officials, and "this was the culmination of Company practices that would lead to nothing else but chaos and anarchy in the plant." Rather than disciplining the workers involved, Prosten explained in an internal union report that his primary concern was preventing the departmental conflict from "touching a match to a tinder box" and escalating into a plantwide walkout.[18]

The unsanctioned job actions generally provoked a similar dynamic. Higher-level union officials, formal supporters of the no-strike pledge, in fact tolerated departmental stoppages and tried to turn them to the union's advantage. "The employers would attempt to say to you, we won't deal with you as long as you're stopped," recalled March. "Our position would be, look, you got to give us some indication about what is going to be done about this or else we won't be able to convince them to go back to work." At Swift, Vicky Starr had similar recollections. "Thank God some people turned their heads when some of these things happened." As "a steward or something like that, not a top official, we could do this and get away with it." Todd Tate, an Armour steward in the canning department, confirmed Starr's observation. "Sometimes the supervisors would be pushing too hard, they would mistreat somebody, and the whole gang would stop. We didn't have to ask the president or nobody else."[19]

The justification of the union activists for job actions mixed support for the war effort with pragmatic working-class self-interest. Drawing on the wartime rhetoric of sacrifice, workers used their employers' allegedly selfish actions as justification for interfering with production. "It wasn't just a one way street," pointed out Mary Salinas, a Mexican-American Fort Worth leader. "If they were able to violate their commitment, what would be wrong with us violating ours, too?" Unionists further defended their actions within the confines of the nation's patriotic needs by carefully distinguishing between a job action in one department and striking an entire plant. Frank Wallace, a steward in Fort Worth Armour, didn't consider departmental stoppages a "violation of the pledge, because they didn't last long enough to cause any major problems." When Sam Sponseller visited the Omaha Cudahy plant to discuss repeated stoppages with union leaders, local president Walt Mason recalled telling him, "We're not striking. I don't see no picket out there." The distinction was not simply rhetorical; production losses due to a short departmental stoppage could be made up rather quickly. "The only thing we were concerned about is we didn't want a general strike to come, because it could have," recalled March. "The workers by and large took a lot of crap because they were interested in helping to win the war."[20]

The packing companies documented the stoppages and pressed the NWLB to lift the union security provisions from UPWA contracts. Their demands, transmitted through government agencies, prompted UPWA leaders to make formal requests that local unions halt the job actions. Polite investigation of the incidents by General Counsel Ralph Helstein was intended to make locals aware of the companies' allegations. "We'd send a nice letter back to them," recalled Richard Saunders, a Chicago unionist, "telling them we'd investigate right away and we did—we never did come up with nothing, but we'd investigate."[21]

Efforts by President Clark to use the union apparatus to halt the job actions and discipline striking workers proved a dismal failure. Clark resorted to threats in only two cases, both involving plantwide strikes. North Bergen, New Jersey, Local 214, ordered by Clark to take disciplinary action against strikers, fined each participant $1 and donated the money to the Allied Relief Fund. Indianapolis Local 43, threatened with an International Executive Board investigation for a three-day stoppage unless it disciplined strikers, resolved that the loss in pay for the workers involved was penalty enough. The international took no further action when the local simply reaffirmed the no-strike pledge. There is no evidence that the UPWA formally investigated a local union for engaging in unsanctioned job actions despite its power to do so under a 1944 convention resolution. Although the international union lobbied locals to halt stoppages, the grievance department admitted that "on many occasions, [it] had to go into situations where strikes were pending to assist the local union leadership in settling disputes." It is striking how the grievance department, headed by the relatively conservative Philip Weightman, emulated the pragmatic accommodation of Communists to shop-floor discontent.[22]

The response of the UPWA to the wartime strikes offers a sharp contrast with developments in the UAW, where the international union increased its power over local unions in an effort to suppress the job actions. In 1943 the NWLB denied maintenance of membership to UAW Chrysler unions because local officials had not enforced the no-strike pledge. Under this pressure, the UAW International Executive Board decided in 1944 to bypass local union officials, investigate job actions directly, and impose disciplinary measures against workers and union leaders involved. In rapid succession the international terminated unsanctioned strikes by workers in UAW Locals 600, 490, and 235 by unilaterally removing the unions' officers and appointing officials who were willing to administer the no-strike pledge more strictly. Nothing comparable took place in the UPWA.[23]

The success of shop-floor bargaining, an organic continuation of the UPWA's prewar strategy, reinforced union strength at the point of production and prevented the strictures of the no-strike pledge from sapping rank-and-file union involvement. The militancy underlying the job actions tended to turn the local unions and structures within the international into channels for sentiment from the base rather than transmission belts for orders from the central office. Frank Ingersoll, president of St. Joseph Armour Local 58, tried to explain the shop-floor reality to an exasperated Lewis J. Clark. In response to repeated entreaties to curtail strikes, Ingersoll plaintively complained, "Company Encourages work stoppages by settling grievances after workers stop work, Instead of settling them before they walkout." Ingersoll was simply explaining what many stewards already knew: Job actions—even the threat of one—were an effective way to extract concessions from front-line supervisors.[24]

The pressure from below was so powerful that by 1945 the scattered opposition to the no-strike pledge inside the UPWA spread throughout the organization, as it had in the auto workers union. At the 1944 UPWA convention, opponents of the pledge from Indianapolis, East St. Louis, St. Paul, and Omaha made their views known but did not vote against a resolution that reaffirmed the union's opposition to strikes during the war. In 1945, with military victory seemingly assured, patriotic support for the war effort no longer exacted the same restraint. In February 1945 Clark reported to the IEB that a majority of Big Four locals were asking the board to repeal the no-strike pledge and conduct an industrywide strike vote. A few weeks later, an angry District 2 convention "disemboweled" international officers for their support of no-strike pledge and replaced recently drafted Director Glenn Chinander with leftist Joe Ollman. "The delegates that did most of the hollering are veterans of World War 2," Ollman explained to the IEB. The conference unanimously resolved to fight to overturn the no-strike pledge at the next UPWA convention. Grover Hathaway, director of southeast District 9 and a supporter of the no-strike pledge, admitted that "the thinking of the people in District No. 2 is not too far from the thinking in my district."[25]

Rather than suppress the sentiment against the no-strike pledge, UPWA leaders used shop-floor discontent to break the stalemated NWLB negotiations. On February 2, 1945, Director of Economic Stabilization Fred Vinson blocked a scheduled ruling on the UPWA's wage case by limiting the NWLB's authority to grant fringe benefits. The outrage of packinghouse workers at Vinson's action "threatened seriously to disrupt the entire operations of the industry." A hastily assembled conference of local unions dispatched a delegation of forty-five packinghouse workers to Washington. Against the background of ongoing job actions and sentiment to terminate the no-strike pledge, they buttonholed government officials and forcefully reminded them of the unrest in the nation's packinghouses. "There can be no doubt of the effectiveness of this action," reported UPWA General Counsel Ralph Helstein to the UPWA's 1946 convention. He dryly noted that "representatives of local unions throughout the country rendered invaluable service in creating a necessary atmosphere."[26]

Pressure from local unions secured a favorable NWLB order on February 22, 1945. The board denied a general wage increase, under the Little Steel formula, "but the rest of the order was a gold strike." The board increased weekly guaranteed pay from thirty-two to thirty-six hours and ordered daily instead of weekly calculation of piece rates. As weekly hours had plummeted in early 1945, longer minimum hours were a particularly welcome boon. The board accepted union arguments that the company should provide tools and clothing and pay for time spent donning work garments and sharpening knives. Because there had been little progress resolving wage inequalities through the grievance procedure, the NWLB established a Meat Packing Commission (MPC) to settle the issue.[27]

The NWLB decision, and resistance of the packing companies to a final settlement, intensified internal pressures to end the no-strike pledge. Impatient UPWA members continued their unsanctioned job actions, including a plantwide walkout by Kansas City Armour workers on March 31. In late May, a majority of the International Executive Board resolved to take a strike vote—in violation of the no-strike pledge—in order to extract a better settlement from the packing companies. Communists Herb March and Meyer Stern were the only vocal opponents of the board's decision.[28]

Before the union needed to implement its new policy, the packing companies gave in to the UPWA's major demand for retroactive pay—a provision the meat cutters had already conceded. Although the Amalgamated accepted February 1, 1945, as the effective date for increases, the UPWA generally secured retroactive payments on fringes, inequalities, and wage differentials to 1944—and earlier in some cases. This "gold strike," as the union later called it, was a result of the willingness of UPWA leaders to harness rank-and-file discontent and not a "favor" granted by the government. The back pay garnered from the agreement netted UPWA members $40 million.[29]

The Meat Packing Commission provided other important benefits for the union. Over the objections of the business representatives to the NWLB, the MPC was empowered to standardize wage rates in the Big Four and independent packinghouses. Composed of representatives from the industry's three unions, the five largest companies, and two public members (including commission chair Clark Kerr), the MPC engaged in a thorough review of meatpacking's wage structure. Over a two year period it evaluated a hundred thousand jobs in one hundred plants and ordered companies to provide wage rate information to the union. Local unions checked company claims by conducting their own job evaluations and then forwarded the results to the UPWA's representative on the MPC (who also headed the union's wage rate department).[30]

Despite initial reluctance, the companies participated in a cooperative manner because it was an unusual opportunity to reorganize widely varying wage patterns on the terms of the dominant firms. For the union, it was an ideal chance to fundamentally improve the wage-rate structure of the industry and allow for greater shop-floor control over the content and pay levels of jobs. To replace meatpacking's anarchic wage structure, the MPC sorted all hundred thousand jobs into twenty-five wage brackets, placed at regular intervals of 2½ cents. Typically, this aided the union, because a job paid a lower rate at one plant was raised to the level of the highest rate for the same task. Hourly raises that resulted from the process averaged 1.8 cents, and some job rates increased 15 cents. UPWA members received $15 million in retroactive pay as a result of the MPC decision, and future annual wage expenses for the packing firms increased an estimated $5 million.[31]

Packinghouse workers gained more than pay increases as a result of the MPC's ruling. Standardization of the wage structure facilitated the UPWA's efforts to regulate shop-floor conditions. Greater knowledge of the industry's national pattern of remuneration gave the union the capacity to bargain over work loads and pay levels for particular jobs, not merely overall wage levels. The wage rate department, created largely to centralize wartime information on wage inequalities, became a fixture in the international and an important service agency to union locals. Future disputes over work loads and job rates in one plant now had the authority of the entire union, because the UPWA tried to enforce the principle that the wage paid for a job should be the same regardless of who performed the work or what plant it was in. The MPC, however, only standardized wages within the preexisting geographic regions, thus preserving the pay differential among plants in different parts of the country. It also institutionalized the lower wage structure for female workers by establishing separate seniority and job lists for men and women. Aggressive union actions over the next decade would be necessary to eliminate the historic wage inequalities of the meatpacking industry.[32]

Reconstituting the Packinghouse Workforce

The institutional advances of the UPWA during World War II rested on the capacity of the local unions to incorporate thousands of new workers into union traditions and structures. Aided by maintenance of membership and the dues check-off, persuading new workers to join was not that difficult. "They joined the union or they didn't come through the gate," recalled a leader of the Sioux City Armour local. In fact, packing companies protested in vain when strong locals vigorously enforced 100 percent union membership. The UPWA's brand of unionism, however, depended on active rank-and-file support rather than simply formal membership. As in the organizing era, the unions secured rank-and-file loyalty by actively working to protect workers' interests on the shop floor. This was especially important during the war, because the long delays entailed in the NWLB negotiating process made it difficult to secure short-term material benefits for new employees. The level of union activity on behalf of its members during and immediately after the war trained these new workers in the UPWA's militant approach and drew many into the union's shop-floor apparatus.[33]

Patterns of inter-racial unionism inherited from the organizing era shaped the UPWA's policies toward World War II-era black workers. Black employment increased dramatically during the war, heavily influenced by historic discriminatory patterns in major industrial centers. Employment restrictions against blacks in war-bloated metal industries allowed white packinghouse workers to move into better-paying defense jobs and shunted blacks looking for work into meatpacking. "Everybody that wanted good money quit packinghouses," recalled Ann Krasick. "All the white people went to work in these wartime industries." Packinghouses were the only war-related factories to employ blacks at levels equal to or greater than their proportion in the area's labor market. Blacks composed more than 50 percent of the UPWA's membership in Kansas City and Chicago by the end of the war.[34]

The opportunities for blacks in the packinghouses, and their representation by UPWA locals, differed considerably from the experience of blacks with the unions that had bargaining rights in metal industry plants. Kansas City provides a good example. There, blacks entering the Armour plant "were well-accepted, given all the rights of any other person," recalled Charles R. Fischer. To fill positions of whites who had vacated their jobs, blacks received union training in skilled powerhouse jobs and various semiskilled positions. In contrast, only 165 blacks, employed solely as custodians, worked at three UAW-organized auto plants in Kansas City employing 4,600 workers. The UAW admitted blacks but would not permit them to transfer to production jobs. At the huge North American Aviation and Pratt and Whitney plants on the city's outskirts, the AFL-affiliated International Association of Machinists and management amicably agreed to restrict blacks to menial jobs. The IAM refused to admit blacks and insisted that they join the Service Employees union regardless of job classification. As was the case nationally, the UPWA fully defended the rights of black members, the UAW simultaneously admitted blacks and enforced their marginal positions in auto plants outside Detroit, and the IAM excluded them altogether.[35]

The union also supported new women workers, but its actions were qualified by efforts to avoid changes in the traditional sexual division of labor. Although women had worked in meatpacking since the late 1800s and composed 20 percent of the industry's workforce in the 1930s, the war brought more into the nation's packinghouses. Many took positions in the rapidly expanding canning departments, while others moved into jobs in the killing and cutting operations previously performed by men. Companies exploited the lower female wage scale by paying women who performed traditionally male jobs a lower rate. Often firms justified paying less by small changes in the work process that reduced the amount of heavy lifting, but much of the time the simple presence of a woman seemed justification enough. Generally, men did not object to the use of women when jobs truly were vacant but resisted when the companies cut wages or displaced experienced men.[36]

A dispute in the Kansas City Armour plant illustrates how union support for equal pay for equal work protected the sexual division of labor at the same time as it increased wages for women. During the war, employment of women in the plant doubled to nine hundred, 25 percent of the its swollen workforce. Women moved into the previously male preserve of ham-boning in 1942, a department whose pay levels were among the highest in the plant. Men were amazed to see "women swinging them heavy hams around," recalled Charles Fischer. "They were just as fast as the men." Although a male ham-boner had received 86½ cents per hour for trimming outside skins and knuckles, two women who now performed the job each earned 55 cents per hour. Men who remained in the department were assigned to different jobs often paying less than 60 cents per hour, compared with earnings of 80 cents or more in 1940. Many men either transferred into other areas where they could earn more or quit entirely and found work at the Swift plant.

Local 15 responded by protesting management's wage cuts as well as alteration of the boundaries between male and female jobs. Union representatives pointed to the speed of the men who had been displaced and the seemingly irrational use of two women to perform a job previously held by one man when their combined pay exceeded the rate of their predecessor. "Take a look at the operation now and see who is guilty of laying down on the job," they asked, "The employees? or Management?" The local accepted placement of women on male jobs "when men are not available" but protested "the Company's attempt to replace men with women on certain jobs where it is unnecessary in order to lower wages." Local 15 thus qualified acceptance of new women workers, and equal pay for equal work, with the proviso that they should only perform traditionally male jobs when there were no men "available" to do so. After the war, ham-boning once again became an exclusively male department.[37]

UPWA locals, which had favored equal pay for equal work in the 1930s, followed the same policy during World War II. As in Kansas City, the union combined defense of existing wage levels with protection of the established demarcation between male and female jobs. It is notable that this policy aroused no open opposition from male or female workers or even significant attention at union gatherings. As with black workers, the union's stance toward women reflected principles firmly established in the organizing era. Beginning in May 1942, the union filed more than a hundred equal pay for equal work grievances, protesting every instance it could document of women receiving lower pay than the men who had previously performed the job. The Kansas City Armour local alone filed more than fifty of these grievances. Arbitrators typically split the difference between the male and female rates, raising women's pay to a level halfway between their previous earnings and the old male rate. Union actions secured substantial wage increases for women workers in traditionally male jobs.[38]

Union initiatives were especially important to hundreds of black women who sought to escape traditional employment barriers during World War II. Kansas City and Chicago packinghouses provided rare job opportunities for black women, but management restricted them to a narrow range of tasks. Most of the nation's packinghouses would not hire black women at all, despite the labor shortage. In both cases, these employment patterns were rooted in pre-union practices and enjoyed the support of a significant group of white women in lily-white departments who benefited from the exclusion, partial or total, of black female labor. In Chicago and Kansas City, the union was able to increase the number of black women packinghouse workers as well as expand the range of jobs they could perform. In Omaha, the union engaged in a successful campaign with the local NAACP chapter, under the leadership of Rowena Moore, to force Armour to hire black women for the first time. The net result was a significant increase in the number of young black women in midwestern packinghouses.[39]

Although the substantial breakthroughs for black women would not come until the 1950s, their growing numbers during World War II established a critical base for postwar activism. The experience of Addie Wyatt, the UPWA's preeminent black women leader in the 1950s and 1960s, provides an example of this pattern. Born in Mississippi, she obtained a job at the Chicago Armour plant in 1941 at the age of seventeen. Not long after starting work, the union used the seniority system to prevent Wyatt's foremen from replacing her with a newly hired white woman. When she became pregnant a few months later, Wyatt's fear of losing her job was dispelled by the union, which had secured unpaid maternity leave for female employees. These union actions on her behalf persuaded Wyatt to attend a Local 347 meeting. "I saw a picture that I have never been able to forget," she related forty-five years later. "Here were workers who were learning . . . how to band together to improve their lives through collective bargaining, political and social action. And I wanted to be a part of it." After the war, Wyatt was the most articulate representative of black women who had entered the industry during World War II and became union stalwarts in the 1950s.[40]

With the sharp fluctuation in employment at the end of the war, the UPWA's enforcement of seniority ensured that the contract shaped the reorganization of the packinghouse workforce. Heavy layoffs in 1945 displaced many wartime hires, but as employment grew rapidly in 1947 to the same level as during the war workers could choose to use their seniority to reenter meatpacking. World War II veterans, as in other CIO-organized industries, earned seniority for the time they spent in the military. Black veterans immediately stepped back into their jobs and found their seniority helped them transfer to better, higher-paid positions. White veterans benefited in a similar manner, although many were able to find employment elsewhere and never returned to meatpacking. While layoffs affected black workers who had entered the plants during the war, they were able to return to the packinghouses. "The blacks stayed because the union was in there," recalled Virginia Houston, hired at the Kansas City Armour plant during the war. "Your seniority meant something to you."[41]

Women effectively used seniority to retain employment in meatpacking, but severe layoffs pushed them out of "male" jobs and returned them to traditional female (and lower-paid) tasks in the booming prepared foods areas. At the same time as overall employment fell 25 percent at Kansas City Armour in 1945, the number of women in the plant dropped 40 percent. When employment levels rose in 1946 and 1947, seniority accumulated during the war was sufficient for most women to use their recall rights to return to work. Increasing employment and enforcement of seniority not only protected the women who had first gained entry to meatpacking jobs during the war but also reestablished the firm division between the sexes within packinghouses.[42]

The recomposition of the sexual division of labor in meatpacking to its prewar pattern was a setback for women, but the UPWA treated them equally under the terms of its contracts and constitution. Indeed, the movement of women back to female departments was a direct result of strict union enforcement of seniority, especially the opportunity for black male veterans to reclaim their old jobs. Although Fort Worth Armour worker Hattie Jones "didn't feel it was fair" that women were pushed out of knife jobs and into a new frozen food department after World War II, "I don't think we would have got to work any if it hadn't been for the union. They did give us a square deal: they let us go back in there, hold our seniority. All the women that had been laid off got to go back into this new department." In contrast, UAW locals after World War II often did not enforce the seniority provisions in the contracts that gave women the right to return to work after layoffs.[43]

The black men and women who entered the packinghouse during World War II had a profound effect on the UPWA. They emerged from the war more militant and assertive than blacks of an older generation. In part, the tight labor market minimized the fear of unemployment and encouraged them to resist management. "For them to tell me, 'you're fired,' hell, that was like an everyday word," recalled Eunetta Pierce. "I didn't care; I'd go find another job." For men who served in the armed forces, the military experience provided an additional impetus. The World War II veterans who had fought under segregated conditions were no longer willing to observe patterns of racial deference that their parents' generation had tolerated. "Guys came out of the military and they didn't give a damn about the Ku Klux Klan," recalled Richard Saunders. "You had a breed of people who said, hell, I'm entitled to this—I want it!" After returning from the European theater, "I couldn't see myself being discriminated against the way we were," Eddie Humphrey explained. "We died, our blood had been shed for this country, and I felt . . . that instead of crumbs, we want us a slice of the pie." Where present, the World War II generation of black workers would become pillars of the UPWA's shop-floor apparatus and instrumental in the union's postwar anti-discrimination initiatives. Conversely, meatpacking centers that did not experience black in-migration during the war, such as Sioux City and Austin, tended to lag behind the rest of the union in their commitment to social unionism in the 1950s.[44]

The Consolidation of Union Power and Union Democracy

The UPWA emerged from the maelstrom of World War II more powerful in the packinghouses and more responsive to its membership. Instead of the decline in internal democracy that accompanied the institutional stabilization of the UAW, the UPWA's enhanced national strength depended on the integration of local unions into its national structure and activities. The fifteen Armour plants included in the 1941 agreement grew to twenty-four by 1946; the Cudahy master agreement covered eleven plants, and the Wilson and Swift contracts each included eight. The UPWA also scored important victories in NLRB elections against NBPW locals in Des Moines and St. Paul. American membership reached ninety thousand by the end of 1945, with an additional ten thousand in the growing Canadian district. Unlike World War I-era packing unions, the UPWA was able to consolidate its wartime gains into a durable and powerful national organization.[45]

The destructive aftermath of World War I was on the minds of union leaders as demobilization began in the summer of 1945 and the UPWA prepared for direct negotiations with the meatpacking companies. "We can't afford to mess around much longer," Frank Ellis warned the IEB in 1945, "that is the thing that defeated the meatcutters after the last war." Aware that the government would soon no longer serve as a buffer between it and the packing companies, the UPWA resolutely began to make preparations for a strike. Within the packinghouses, the UPWA engaged in a concerted campaign to recruit non-union workers, especially in plants represented by relatively weak locals. The UPWA tried to build public support for a national strike by stressing the compatibility of labor's demands with the interests of the larger community. Union publicity highlighted the huge profits earned by the companies during World War II and their capacity to grant higher wages without increasing prices. Improving the living standards of the "working man," the UPWA contended, would help "commerce, industry and all of us prosper."[46]

The UPWA stressed both the patriotic contributions of its members and the low wages in meatpacking to support a demand for a 25 cent increase. "We packinghouse workers did our share during the war," UPWA locals pointed out in a leaflet distributed in Omaha's stockyards district. However, as union publicity explained, the decline in overtime earnings in 1945 caused packinghouse workers' pay to plummet. Adjusted for inflation, weekly earnings fell 9.5 percent between January 1944 and the fall of 1945. World War II veterans in the UPWA's ranks made especially powerful appeals. Sioux City veterans poignantly complained, "We can't buy an automobile for even twice the price that we sold ours for when we left for the service; our apartment or house is rented to someone else for a much higher amount per month than we paid." The veterans asked their community for "support in our efforts to secure the wages which we so desperately need and certainly deserve."[47]

The UPWA membership was ready for a showdown with the packing companies. Job actions, which had declined for a short time after the June 1945 settlement, again spread through industry once the August IEB meeting formally withdrew the no-strike pledge. There were five stoppages in September and October at the Chicago Armour plant, and the tenacious East St. Louis cattle-killing gang engaged in seven job actions between September and December. The packers adamantly refused to meet the union's wage demands and only offered a 7½ cents increase. Local unions voted by a 20 to 1 ratio to authorize a national strike. At the December IEB meeting, no one disagreed with Meyer Stern's assessment of rank-and-file attitudes: "Our membership is insisting on a strike if we don't get a substantial wage increase."[48]

The positive impact of the war experience is apparent in the manner the UPWA organized and conducted its strike in 1946. The strike apparatus constructed by the union was designed to forge a broad consensus on strategy and tactics in its first effort to stage a national work stoppage by dozens of local unions. A special conference of local union delegates in December 1945 firmly established local union control over the strike. Overall "questions of policy in relation to the strike" were the province of an eighteen-person Strike Strategy Committee elected at the conference. It consisted of the four international officers, influential district directors such as March and Ollman, and representatives from the Armour, Cudahy, Swift, and Wilson chains and major independent plants. UPWA General Counsel Ralph Helstein and Education Director Svend Godfredson also served on the body. Larger committees composed of local union representatives conducted the negotiations with their respective companies. To ensure local union authority over and cooperation during the strike, the conference resolved, that "no offer of settlement shall be accepted by any negotiating committee until it is cleared by the strategy committee, which in turn will call a conference of Local Unions before making a final decision."[49]

The conference's decisions guaranteed that the UPWA's local unions would have the information and institutional power to control the preparation, execution, and termination of the strike. Equally important were the efforts of the union to organize the strike on the local level. In addition to promoting community outreach, the Strike Strategy Committee asked Herb March to prepare a strike manual for local unions. March's widely distributed guide emphasized rank-and-file involvement in the strike and suggested concrete techniques to accomplish this task. The manual urged UPWA locals to create large strike committees reflecting the diversity of the workforce, with one representative for every fifty union members. To make full use of the membership, March urged locals to maintain pickets twenty-four hours a day, with mass picketing once a week, and to organize food distribution and other activities out of the union hall. "Never should the idea be developed that you have enough people for your activities and therefore a large portion of the strikers can stay at home," the manual warned. "When people are idle and not involved in any specific thing to help win the strike, demoralization begins to set in."[50]

When the UPWA and the Amalgamated Meat Cutters struck the nation's packing industry on January 16, 1946, it was at the height of the postwar strike wave. There were contemporaneous strikes underway in auto, steel, electrical, and other industries. The strike was highly effective, curtailing meat production by 50 percent and threatening widespread consumer shortages. As a result, the government moved rapidly to end the walkout. Just ten days into the strike, President Harry S. Truman used his power under the War Labor Disputes Act to take control of the packing companies and order a return to work by the UPWA and the Amalgamated.[51]

Dozens of local union representatives assembled hurriedly on January 25 to consider the UPWA's response. The union faced a federal order to return to work, and their only compensation for suspending the strike was to await a commission ruling not binding on the packing companies. UPWA leaders were well aware that General Motors and U.S. Steel recently had rejected recommendations by similar government fact-finding bodies and doubted that the packers would act any differently. "Previous experiences with the delays of government boards," an official union history noted, "made UPWA officers reluctant to abandon history's most effective packing-house strike without something a bit more concrete."[52]

Local union delegates decided to defy the government. Paraphrasing John L. Lewis's famous dictum, Vice-President Weightman told inquiring reporters, "You can't skin a cow with a bayonet." Under the watchful eyes of the delegates, Lewis J. Clark telephoned Secretary of Agriculture Clinton P. Anderson and informed him that the union needed, at minimum, a firm commitment that the National Wage Stabilization Board would implement the commission's findings. Without guarantees, Clark warned Anderson, the UPWA would not return to work. Delegates waited in Chicago for Anderson's response and informed locals calling for instructions to "sit tight" and remain on strike. At 8 P.M. the UPWA received a telegram from Anderson providing the assurances for which the union had asked, and the strategy meeting ordered a return to work pending the commission's findings. A few weeks later, the commission followed the pattern established in the steel strike and awarded the UPWA a 16 cent increase, one penny more than the Amalgamated's settlement. Although many local unions approved the agreement under protest, arguing that they deserved a 25 cent raise, it was still the "greatest single increase ever won in the packing industry" and the first successful national meatpacking strike.[53]

The participation of local union representatives in all phases of the 1946 strike spelled the end for Lewis J. Clark's reign as UPWA president. By all accounts an incompetent and weak leader, he was an "emperor without clothes" by the end of the strike. Local union delegates on the Strike Strategy Committee were so dissatisfied with Clark's performance that he was removed as chief union negotiator during the course of the conflict. "Clark was a nonentity," recalled union staffer Norman Dolnick, originally hired by Clark. "He didn't know how to negotiate. He didn't want to negotiate. He just wanted all the honors and the perks that go with being president." To Jennie Shuck, who remained sympathetic to the UPWA's first president, "Lewis Clark was a good man but he didn't really have the ability." Leaders from Chicago, St. Paul, Kansas City, and Sioux City all retrospectively criticized Clark's performance in the 1946 strike.[54]

There were other factors behind the removal of Clark at the UPWA's 1946 convention. Beginning in September 1945, Clark tried to use anticommunism to undermine Herb March's position in District 1. Clark rebuked March for publicly supporting the Farm Equipment union in a jurisdictional dispute with the UAW and for publishing an article in the *Daily Worker* discussing the Communist Party's activities in meatpacking. Clark received assistance from Vice-President Weightman, whose Swift local was a bitter opponent of March, and Secretary-Treasurer Ed Roche. In lengthy responses designed "to set the record straight," March reminded Clark and Weightman that the Communist Party was active in meatpacking before the formation of the CIO, "and bore the brunt of firings, black-listing and police terror." Accusations of Communist influence were designed, March charged, to "mould a portion of the board into a clique" in order to prepare a move at the next convention "to exclude Communists from full participation in our union." Clark's red-baiting no doubt worried influential union officials who feared internal fratricide could weaken their young organization.[55]

Sometime in the spring of 1946, dissatisfied UPWA leaders began to consider replacing Clark with the talented general counsel Ralph Helstein. Born on December 11, 1908, Helstein had graduated from the University of Minnesota law school in 1934 and immediately joined the staff of the National Recovery Administration. After a few months in Washington, he left the NRA and opened a private practice in Minneapolis, where he became legal counsel for several CIO unions, including the PWOC. Introduced to Austin packinghouse workers by Eddie Folan, a Communist, Helstein was Local 9's chief legal counsel during the 1940 negotiations that led to the historic guaranteed annual wage agreement. Appointed general counsel of the Minnesota CIO in 1939, he moved to Chicago in 1942 to fill a similar post for the PWOC. He was the UPWA's main spokesperson in World War II government hearings and replaced Lewis J. Clark as the union's chief negotiator during the 1946 strike.[56]

In his many speeches and writings, Helstein expressed a deep liberal belief that all groups, regardless of race, national origin, or political views, deserved equal rights and civil liberties. Reflecting a social-democratic inclination, Helstein viewed the labor movement as a force "to advance the interests of its membership but, in a broader sense, to advance the interests of the entire community." Although extremely skilled in the legal dimensions of postwar labor relations, Helstein had deep reservations about the dependence of labor unions and their leaders on government agencies. "A trade union cannot be an instrument of the state if it is to fulfill its responsibilities," he told a Toronto audience in 1953. "It must be free to criticize and to challenge policy and program at all levels."[57]

Through his various jobs for the packinghouse union, Helstein had met and impressed UPWA leaders in Austin, St. Paul, Chicago, and Iowa—the union's heartland. The 1946 strike increased his stature throughout the organization, as local union delegates favorably noted his "guts" in the tense showdown with the government. At the 1946 convention, St. Paul unionist Milt Siegel nominated Helstein as a union president able to lead the UPWA in the "tougher battles" ahead, "not only as negotiator and administrator, but I know he will be able to cope with any situation." Other supporters described him as "above reproach" and "a man above 'isms,'" and even opponents praised his abundant talents. Although accounts vary, Helstein later credited Joe Ollman with first suggesting he run for president. Also encouraging Helstein's candidacy was the director of Canadian District 10, Fred Dowling, and Herb March, Jesse Prosten, and Meyer Stern, who were Communists. "Who the hell would have thought of a lawyer," recalled Jesse Prosten. "But he was trusted and he was an honest guy and he was a liberal guy."[58]

It was to Helstein's advantage that he was neither rooted in one of the regional groups that made up the UPWA nor beholden to any particular current for his position in the union. Hence he was a candidate whose selection promised to maintain the union's militant character while preserving the delicate equilibrium between different regional and political groupings.

By the time the convention opened in Montreal on June 3, rumors were swirling about Helstein's candidacy. The District 1, 2, 6, and 10 group backing Helstein had picked up support for their candidate from Districts 3 and 4 before the convention, largely due to Clark's amply demonstrated incompetence. Several CIO leaders attended and aggressively lobbied against Helstein. "President Murray's eyes are upon you," Allan Haywood pointedly told delegates in his opening address. In a clear sign of support for Clark, Haywood complimented "your officers, every one of them, for the splendid cooperation they have given." Clark's backers granted that the UPWA president had "made mistakes" but opposed electing a lawyer to lead the UPWA. "Brother Helstein has done a good job as our legal advisor," explained a delegate from Detroit Local 69. "We want to retain a man who is a packinghouse worker at the head of our organization." Vocal opposition to Helstein was largely concentrated in the Omaha, Cedar Rapids, and Chicago locals that favored Clark's efforts to curtail leftist influence in the UPWA.[59]

As the debate proceeded toward the end of the third day of the convention, it was apparent that Helstein had the votes to defeat Clark in a head-to-head contest. Supported by all delegates from Districts 2, 6, and 10 and a majority from Districts 1, 3, and 4, Helstein had at least six hundred votes among the convention's 943 delegates. Probably fortuitously, the convention adjourned for the evening before taking a vote, and the caucusing continued through the night in elevators, hotel rooms, and local bars. Haywood threatened March and Prosten that the CIO would remove Lee Pressman as its general counsel if the Communists persisted in supporting Helstein. In addition to pressure from the CIO, Communist Party Trade Union Commission chair George Morris ordered March and other Communists to withdraw their support from Helstein. Summoned to Morris's hotel room to hear this directive, March exploded. "George, go scratch," he recalled saying. "I'm a member of the National Committee and I'm directing you to keep your nose out of our goddamn business. We're going to go through with this."[60]

By the next morning a deal had been worked out to avoid humiliating Clark. The UPWA president withdrew his name from nomination, and Helstein received the unanimous vote of the convention. In return, Clark ran unopposed for secretary-treasurer, replacing Ed Roche. In his acceptance speech, Helstein reminded his critics, "I have been with this organization now for some years and during that period I think I have come to know the people, I think I have come to know the problems in the plants." Setting a tone that he would hold to tenaciously, the new union president told the convention, "Until every man is judged on his own merits, irrespective of other considerations, we cannot hope to achieve a democratic society in which all people will enjoy the fruits of their labor."[61]

Helstein's victory cemented the UPWA's World War II gains. The union had installed a leader skilled in the complex mechanics of postwar collective bargaining and also deeply committed to maintaining a democratic, politically diverse organization open to rank-and-file influence. Helstein's victory firmly established UPWA independence from the CIO and the dominance of the union's center-left coalition. His election also reflected the UPWA's impressive accomplishments since 1943. The union had navigated the conflicting pressures of state regulation and shop-floor unrest in a manner that extracted important concessions from the packing companies, both in formal contractual terms and in the day-to-day relations between work groups and their supervisors. New workers had been educated in the union's philosophy and integrated into its shop-floor structures. Local unions remained the dominant force in the organization, allowing the centralization necessitated by pattern bargaining to be balanced by the active participation of union cadre.

"I knew we had to make a turn," reflected Herb March on the struggle to elect Helstein. "It made for an unusual union. The packinghouse workers became a union under Helstein—for a time at least—in which there was tolerance of all sorts of viewpoints, and democracy in a true sense." Indeed, the contrast between the UPWA and the UAW in 1946 is palpable. Elected UAW president three months before Helstein, within two years Walter Reuther would restrict leftist influence and rank-and-file participation in his union. In a press conference just after his victory, Reuther declared that he would "isolate the 10 percent [of the UAW] which has outside loyalties. We are interested . . . in trying to break up and isolate a small disciplined minority." In 1946 the UPWA bore more resemblance to the "left" unions in the CIO such as United Electrical, Farm Equipment, and the Food and Tobacco Workers. Over the next two years, the paths of the UPWA and mainstream CIO unions would diverge sharply, and the "turn" taken by the UPWA at the 1946 convention would become increasingly important to its health and survival.[62]

8

"Something New Is Added":
Surviving Labor's Cold War, 1946–50

During the war we had to submit to their demands because we
had to get the meat to the Army and the Navy. But the war is over,
and as the Lucky Strike advertisements say, "Something new is
added." The fact is that there is not now a friendly administration
begging for them, who can make us give them more than is war-
ranted from the merits of the situation.

—Wilson and Company Vice-president James D. Cooney, 1948

These people are back in the plants fighting with all that is in them
to regain what they lost. However, they are more militant people,
they are more fighting people than they ever were before. I think
it is a job that we have to do, to go back and pick out those people who are willing to work, and who found out during the strike
that they had to work where they had been complacent before
that, and had done nothing except attend local union meetings
and pay their dues and said nothing. We should pick these people out and put them into leadership.

—Russell Lasley, Waterloo packinghouse worker, 1948

Testifying before a House subcommittee chaired by right-wing Michigan
Republican Clare Hoffman, Wilson packing executive James D. Cooney vent-
ed his anger at a union whose power his company bitterly resented. Wilson
had only signed a contract with the UPWA in 1943 under the direct order of
the NWLB and had doggedly fought the union's strength on the shop floor
throughout the war. Cooney's sympathetic audience encouraged unusual
candor by a packing executive. Hoffman's committee had strayed far from
its nominal jurisdiction over expenditures in executive departments to investigate allegations of union-initiated violence in the UPWA's recent strike.
To the committee, Cooney outlined his firm's view that with the ending of
the war "something new is added" to labor relations in meatpacking. Without the protection of a "friendly administration," he promised that the packing industry, now with the support of federal and state governments, would
either tame the UPWA or destroy it.[1]

Cooney was not the only one to believe that something new had been added to labor relations in meatpacking. A month after his testimony, Russell Lasley, a black union leader from Waterloo, Iowa, took the floor at the UPWA's discordant 1948 convention during a debate on the recent strike. Convention delegates were fully aware of the particularly explosive situation that had faced Lasley's local. While trying to drive through a mass picket line in front of Waterloo's Rath plant, a black strikebreaker had killed a white striker. As hundreds of union members saw their comrade fall to the ground, they erupted in rage and stormed into the plant, seizing and beating the workers inside. The Iowa National Guard, equipped with tanks and rifles, had restored order—and permitted strikebreakers to cross picket lines unscathed.

Lasley, elected a union vice president later in the convention, appealed to delegates to look ahead and plan for the future rather than dwell on what had passed. Above all, he urged them to rebuild the union by drawing on the participants in the 1948 strike, who now were a "more militant people" and no longer "complacent" toward their union. To Lasley, what had been added was a new generation of union cadres whom the union could integrate into its leadership and shop-floor "oppositional infrastructure."[2]

The conflicting expectations of Cooney and Lasley reflect both the shift in labor-management strife in meatpacking immediately after World War II and the continuities in the arenas of conflict. Although leading packing companies cooperated with other firms in the National Association of Manufacturers (NAM) to roll back labor's advances of the late 1930s and war years, they tended to be extremists among their compatriots. Management psychology may have played a part, but competitive pressures provided a more immediate spur. Unlike the dominant companies in the metal and electrical industries, meatpacking's Big Four experienced a steady decline in their market position as medium-sized firms such as Hormel grew considerably and entirely new companies entered the industry. Profit rates remained in the traditional range of 1 to 2 percent of sales, giving management no release from the pressure of maintaining control over the throughput of product in their plants. Indeed, because the modern facilities of upstart firms employed more efficient production methods, the Big Four needed to improve labor productivity and restrain wages simply to maintain their leading position. Wilson may have been the most intolerant of the Big Four, but the same pressures operated on them all.[3]

For their part, packinghouse workers fought to retain, and even expand, their inroads on traditional company prerogatives. From the perspective of the shop floor, management's efforts to exert unregulated control over the organization and pace of work appeared unchanged. Packinghouse workers shaped by the organizing struggles, and who enjoyed the relatively lax labor discipline of the war years, were not inclined to abandon their gains. To their advantage, unlike the workers in the auto and steel plants, their international union also was committed to retention of power on the shop floor. Hence the efforts of packinghouse workers and their union to retain control over work were unusually strong at the same time as the companies they faced were particularly determined to take back what they had lost.

The basic conflict over power inside the plants was ineluctably shaped by the cold war and the deteriorating environment for labor in postwar politics. The confluence of legal pressures on unions, especially the Taft-Hartley Act, with anticommunism decisively affected the entire American labor movement. Unions that resisted the legal constraints of the postwar period were hounded by government investigations of Communist influence, prevented from using the protection of the Wagner Act and the National Labor Relations Board, and raided by other labor organizations. Government repression and attacks by other unions decimated the eleven leftist labor organizations that the CIO expelled in 1949 and 1950; their well-known fate was a potent reminder to unionists of the terrible costs that resistance entailed.

Within the very real constraints of the period, the UPWA devised a distinctive response to postwar challenges. In the critical period from 1947 to 1950, it managed to avoid the expulsions from the CIO that hamstrung the so-called left-led unions as well as the bureaucratization of internal life characteristic of the UAW. Political diversity, avenues for rank-and-file involvement and influence, and a strong shop-floor union structure all remained durable features of the UPWA into the 1960s. Communists and other leftists remained active in the union and received unqualified support from the international union when they faced investigations by the federal government. The UPWA's great achievement was to survive the postwar pressures on labor without severing its roots in the insurgent unionism of the 1930s.

The UPWA, however, did not emerge unscathed. The events of 1947 through 1950 weakened both its left and right factions and placed the center—especially President Ralph Helstein—in a more powerful position. The defeat of its 1948 strike forced the union to comply with the Taft-Hartley Act and resulted in the resignation of Herb March from the International Executive Board, although he remained influential in the union by virtue of his continued association with the Chicago Armour local. Nonetheless, the UPWA's capacity to preserve shop-floor power, leftist influence, and internal democracy placed it in a category by itself among postwar unions that faced the same array of state-imposed limitations. Its ability to integrate packinghouse workers into shop-floor structures gave the union a forum to counter the conservatism of the postwar era. The payoff would come in the 1950s, when the UPWA would greatly expand its commitment to social unionism and civil rights.[4]

The UPWA's Crucible: Taft-Hartley and the 1948 Strike

In February 1947, reflecting back on the successful fall 1946 negotiations, President Helstein seemed puzzled by the outcome. "I cannot still understand," he told the IEB, "the relative ease with which the packers consented to maintenance of membership and in many respects improved it. Obviously, they wanted to avoid a strike—the question is why?" Answering his own query, Helstein speculated that the packers were concentrating on passing antilabor legislation in Congress and delaying a showdown until new restrictions on union activity would hamper the UPWA. Very simply, the companies were waiting for a more advantageous moment in which to do battle.[5]

Helstein was well aware that meatpacking's Big Four shared the objectives of other leading industrial firms to, as Howell Harris has noted, "reduce the scope of union influence" and eliminate "direct action tactics on the part of workers." The wartime labor shortage and the strike wave of 1945 and 1946 had greatly weakened managerial control over the shop floor in meatpacking and other industries. By the end of the war, shop-floor discipline unraveled as "the worker became the boss" because of the labor shortage and the successful departmental job actions. Despite the postwar decline in employment, strong work gangs, especially on the critical killing floors, were able to continue established informal practices. In the Waterloo Rath plant, for example, hog-kill workers only labored thirty minutes out of every hour, and employees in several departments openly played cards on the job in defiance of foremen's orders. During the summer of 1946, killing-floor workers struck over job loads, work assignments, and attempted discharges in Chicago, East St. Louis, Oklahoma City, New York City, Omaha, St. Joseph, and St. Paul. In many strong departments UPWA stewards were the real authorities on the shop floor.[6]

A "Union Responsibility Clause" submitted by Armour to the fall 1946 contract negotiations succinctly detailed company objectives. The clause would have prohibited union employees from controlling or limiting the pace of production and banned strikes during the term of the agreement. It would have made the union liable for damages caused by a work stoppage and given the company authority to discharge employees "instigating, fomenting, actively supporting or giving leadership" to the strike. "The effect of the Company's proposal," noted an internal union analysis, would be to prohibit workers from exercising shop-floor power "and to subject them to punishment . . . in the event they attempt to remedy the Company's arbitrary increase of their work load or job standard." Armour also sought to prohibit union members from respecting the picket line of another union, supporting the boycott of a product, or refusing to handle goods received from another plant engaged in a labor dispute. Taken together, the Armour proposals were a recipe for reducing the union to a marginal influence in the packing plants and relegating it to the limited terrain of wages and benefits.[7]

The UPWA had a completely different vision of postwar labor relations in meatpacking. It projected stabilizing labor relations and reducing shop-floor disorder in exchange for economic benefits and entrenched union power over the pace and organization of work. The UPWA's nominal objective was to extend Hormel's guaranteed annual wage plan throughout the industry because it would simultaneously increase wages and be of "great practical benefit" to companies by placing industrial relations "on a sound and stable foundation." Similar to other CIO leaders who wanted to consolidate labor's influence in postwar America, the UPWA's social democratic objectives included reaching a stable accord with the dominant firms in the industry.[8]

The UPWA also aspired to institutionalize existing de facto union power at the point of production, however, by expanding the parameters of collective bargaining to include the pace and intensity of work. Its insistence on retaining shop-floor power was an element not included in the corporatist schemes offered by Walter Reuther and Philip Murray and mitigated against an accommodation with the large packing companies along the guaranteed annual wage model. Although willing to accept a structured grievance procedure in place of job actions, the union defended "the inherent right of workers to negotiate with management upon all working conditions affecting them including such important questions as work load, job standards, etc." That objective would prove far more than the Big Four firms were willing to tolerate and preclude the development of "labor peace" in the meatpacking industry.[9]

The contracts signed in late 1946 satisfied the UPWA's dual objective to establish "a more stable relationship between management and workers" and preserve union strength on the shop floor. The general objectives and particular features of Armour's Union Responsibility Clause were decisively rejected. In fact, the contracts stated "that all grievances shall be handled,

whenever possible, by the departmental steward" and permitted union representatives to respond to disputes during working hours. The Armour contract explicitly excluded disputes over job loads from arbitration, giving the
UPWA full authority to strike over those issues while the contract was in
effect.[10]

The limited concessions the UPWA made were in line with resolutions
passed with wide support at union conventions and did not compromise its
objectives. In accordance with a position adopted in 1946, it accepted the
"customary" contract provision that there should be no strikes or job actions
while a grievance was being processed. It also agreed to arbitration as the
terminal step in the grievance procedure, a union objective since 1944. As
later union practice would demonstrate, these concessions did not severely
hinder the exercise of power over production. The absence of strictures
against workers engaging in labor disputes protected informal shop-floor
bargaining and other practices designed to ensure the companies "respected the agreement as well." Local unions subsequently found the clause limiting strikes a minor obstacle to the use of shop-floor pressure. Writing the
union's "oppositional infrastructure" into the collective bargaining agreement also guaranteed that departmental stewards—not distant, full-time
union officials—would be the workers' voice in daily shop-floor labor relations. Packing companies had been unable to turn the union apparatus into
a means for controlling the rank and file.[11]

The UAW's response to quite similar demands from the auto industry
provides an illuminating contrast with the UPWA. In the 1946 Ford contract,
for example, the UAW accepted a clause permitting dismissal of workers
leading or "actively supporting" unauthorized strikes. The UPWA blocked
a very similar provision. While the UPWA designated stewards who labored
on the shop floor as the primary union representatives, the UAW reserved
processing of grievances to committeemen on the union payroll. The UAW's
measures encouraged, in Martin Halpern's judgment, "the separation of
plant officials from the rank and file and the building of a union bureaucracy" by cooperating with the efforts of firms to curtail workers' power over
production.[12]

If the packing companies were to relax the union's grip over the work
process, they would have to do so without the assistance of the international or the cooperation of the rank and file. In all likelihood Helstein was correct that the meatpacking industry hoped new government measures would
aid its efforts to qualitatively weaken the UPWA. Anti-labor laws already had
spread at the state level during World War II, but the passage of the Taft-
Hartley Act in June 1947 encoded the objectives of firms to restrict the pow-

er of the new industrial unions. Accurately described by Nelson Lichtenstein as "a climax to and a symbol of the shifting relationship between government and the unions," Taft-Hartley restricted the ability of labor organizations to exercise power at the point of production. It banned secondary boycotts and sympathy strikes, permitted the federal government to impose mandatory sixty-day strike delays, and made unions subject to severe financial penalties for defying the NLRB or engaging in a series of newly defined unfair labor practices. In addition to these constraints, the act required union officials to file affidavits stating that they were not Communist Party members, and made access to the certification machinery of the NLRB contingent upon compliance with these new rules of behavior.[13]

Taft-Hartley and other anti-labor legislation constituted a grave threat to the UPWA and its gains over the past ten years. The restrictions on strikes and boycotts, and penalties for exceeding the legal limits on union activity, imposed constraints on the union that the packing companies had been unable to secure through collective bargaining. District 2 Director Joe Ollman astutely noted that making compliance with Taft-Hartley a precondition for access to the NLRB gave the government a "club" to hold over the head of local union leaders who "might object in a militant manner to any kind of practice that is being put over on them." The affidavits threatened the positions of many leftist UPWA leaders and, as Ollman observed, fanned internal factionalism by giving anticommunists "an opportunity of purging certain people and certain elements in our own union and driving them out of positions of leadership."[14]

A July 15 conference of local union delegates resolved that the UPWA would not comply with the affidavit requirements and would "shun any use of the law." Characteristically, the UPWA projected strengthening the union's shop-floor structures in order to prepare for the new challenges immediately ahead. Admonishing the packing companies that "we will see to it that our contracts are enforced," the union urged locals to reinforce their steward systems. An International Executive Board circular warned that "the success with which the steward system functions will largely measure our ability to withstand the union-smashing pressure" of Taft-Hartley, and the organization department initiated a national newsletter designed to keep stewards apprised of developments in the industry.[15]

Initially, the UPWA's opposition to Taft-Hartley corresponded with the official stance of the entire labor movement. Resistance by organized labor, however, collapsed in October when the AFL voted to comply and the CIO adopted a formal position of "neutrality" on the act's provisions. When the UAW agreed to submit to Taft-Hartley's requirements in November, active resistance to the "slave labor" law collapsed except among a small number of unions that had significant leftist influence.[16]

Compliance with Taft-Hartley by the rival Amalgamated Meat Cutters, and the unraveling of CIO resistance, set the stage for far-reaching debates at November 1947 and January 1947 IEB meetings over whether the UPWA should conform to the new law. The disagreements were triggered by the NLRB's refusal, in September 1948, to certify the UPWA at a Jacksonville, Florida, Swift plant because the international had not filed the requisite affidavits. A right-wing faction of board members pressed for compliance because they feared weaker sections of the union could not sustain a campaign of resistance to Taft-Hartley in the event of raids by the Amalgamated and independent unions. Their leading spokesperson, Vice-president Philip Weightman, argued that "the question that should be uppermost in . . . our minds here is whether or not our union can exist without using the machinery set up under the National Labor Relations Board. Unless we are able to use that machinery, in my opinion our union will be destroyed." Not stated, but no doubt an underlying factor in the debate, was the golden opportunity for anticommunists in the UPWA to eliminate Herb March, Meyer Stern, and other leftists from the union.[17]

Leftist board members opposed compliance and attacked Weightman's belief that the UPWA could protect itself by bending to pressures from the government. "We have only one protection, and that is the strength of our organization," warned Herb March. He argued that succumbing to the Taft-Hartley Act would hurt the UPWA by encouraging union members to rely "on a prop that is not going to be there to keep them up." Frank Ellis and Joe Ollman, not personally endangered by the affidavits, nonetheless opposed compliance for similar reasons. In prosaic packinghouse language, Ollman characterized the filing of affidavits as "the electric prod" being used by anti-labor forces to drive labor into the "slaughtering pen" of the Taft-Hartley law. Echoing March, he stressed that compromising in order to maintain access to the machinery of the NLRB "does not get us the kind of protection that we think we are going to get." Despite deep doctrinal differences, the left-wingers on the International Executive Board articulated a clear view that maintenance of the union's internal vitality was more important than accommodation to the new restrictions on union activity.[18]

UPWA President Helstein, backed by Fred Dowling, Lewis J. Clark, and Tony Stephens, articulated a centrist position that compliance might be unavoidable but must nonetheless be fought as hard as possible in order to educate the membership on the deteriorating relationship between the government and labor. Arguing that the main purpose of Taft-Hartley was "to put the government of the United States on the side of big business," Helstein rhetorically asked right-wing board members, "Are we to believe that the law designed for the purpose of destroying us is going to help us?" If the union did not state clearly that the law would be used to attack the union movement, "The workers are going to say, why weren't we told that this is what we had to expect?" Uncomfortably aware of the real danger of raids, Helstein conceded that the UPWA might not be able to sustain attacks at its weaker flanks without access to the NLRB. When and if that transpired, he would support compliance. It was essential, however, that the union's characteristic determination in negotiations—"that we are never willing to admit that the company's last offer is really their last offer"—not be forgotten in the confrontation with the government over Taft-Hartley. The union might have to sign the affidavits "in self preservation," but it shouldn't "defy the whole pattern of our union's conduct in other matters and jump into this thing until we are actually forced to do so." Although more willing to compromise than the leftists, Helstein shared their judgment that the union's survival rested on its support among rank-and-file packinghouse workers.[19]

By a narrow 6 to 4 margin (with the centrist group abstaining) the board voted in November to comply with Taft-Hartley. Internal resistance to filing the affidavits, however, blocked implementation of its decision. Districts 1, 3, and 6 refused to cooperate on the grounds that the board's edict illegally nullified the vote of the delegated July conference. Frank Ellis, clearly unhappy with the board's decision, warned local unions not "to get back into the rut of running to the Labor Board with all our troubles" at the same time as he informed them of the International Executive Board's action. Although a "Taft-Hartley Board" election might be necessary, Ellis informed local unions that *"every other method must be exhausted first."* No doubt influenced by this internal discontent, Helstein adopted a loose interpretation of the board's vote. He asked the four executive officers, but not the district directors, to file affidavits, thereby protecting March and Meyer Stern.[20]

Relentless pressure from the federal government made it impossible for Helstein and his centrist group to straddle the issue, however. In December the Department of Labor ruled that the UPWA remained out of compliance with Taft-Hartley because all International Executive Board members had not signed affidavits. Determined to make the union comply, right-wing board members demanded at the January 1948 board meeting that the IEB take whatever steps were necessary to comply, including the removal of March and Stern. As both men refused either to sign the affidavits or resign, Helstein's bloc faced a dilemma. The board could not remove the two Communists without violating the union constitution (because they were elected by their districts), and the union could not comply with Taft-Hartley as long as they remained board members. At this critical juncture Helstein's centrist group sided with the board's leftists against the demands of the right-wing. By a 10 to 6 margin, the board referred the issue of district directors filing the affidavits to the next convention. The union's democratic structures had prevailed over government pressure to uproot leftist influence.[21]

The UPWA's debates over Taft-Hartley took place under the shadow of another major confrontation with the packing companies, only this time without the cooperation of the rival Amalgamated Meat Cutters. In accordance with the 1946 agreements, the UPWA reopened its contracts in December 1947 and asked for a 29 cent wage increase. In late January (before the International Executive Board's debate on Taft-Hartley) the UPWA learned that the Amalgamated had settled for a 9 cent increase. Despite fears that it could not shut down the industry while plants organized by the Amalgamated and the NBPW remained in operation, the UPWA refused to accept the "tail wagging the dog" and stuck to its wage demands. In February a conference of local union representatives authorized the board to call a national strike.[22]

Taft-Hartley, and other problems associated with noncompliance, seriously hindered execution of the strike. The debate over Taft-Hartley had delayed strike preparations by absorbing the union's attention during the fall hog rush. The now-mandatory sixty-day strike notice, filed in mid-December, gave packing firms plenty of time to increase inventories in preparations for the stoppage. The fear of raids by other unions cast a pall over strike preparations. Helstein bravely suggested that the union could campaign for a "no union" vote if challenged in an NLRB certification ballot, but the UPWA really had no strategy to counter that threat. Moreover, on the eve of the scheduled March 16 walkout, President Truman appointed a commission of inquiry (provided for under Taft-Hartley) and asked the UPWA to suspend the strike. The union refused and labeled the president's request tantamount to asking for "sacrifice by one party, and only one party" because the commission had no power to compel the companies to settle with the union.[23]

The strength—and weakness—of the UPWA's 1948 strike was its almost exclusive reliance on the union rank and file. To the union's disadvantage, the strike was not part of a broad national campaign by CIO unions; indeed, the UPWA's resistance to Taft-Hartley placed it visibly at odds with the mainstream of the labor movement. In turn, the union's isolation stimulated considerable efforts to mobilize its rank and file in order to win the strike. The union reinstituted strike mechanisms employed in 1946, including national and local strike strategy committees, and it issued a revised version of March's strike manual. Daily bulletins, supplemented by occasional telegrams, kept the widely scattered locals apprised of important developments. During the course of the two-month stoppage literally thousands of packinghouse workers would actively participate in some form of concerted strike activity. Although there were pockets of opposition to the strike, national balloting registered that an overwhelming 90 percent were in favor of a stoppage against the Big Four firms.[24]

Although the national political environment was quite hostile to unions in 1948, local community support for the UPWA seems to have been as strong as in 1946. In Chicago, Catholic churches in the Back of the Yards neighborhood and Protestant congregations in the black community donated food to the strikers. Churches and local merchants provided food, credit, and other resources in Cedar Rapids, St. Joseph, St. Paul, Omaha, and Fort Worth. The Omaha police department openly sympathized with the strikers, and the acting police chief made a highly publicized donation of $200 to the union. Striking UPWA members from Sioux City secured donations and support from individuals and small businesses by going door to door in their community and nearby small towns. Sioux City packinghouse workers shared Omaha's success at getting the municipal authorities on their side. "We were in with the sheriff's department," recalled Cudahy leader Grant Holbrook. Largely through the efforts of the Sioux City and Omaha locals, the National Farmers Union and several other farm organizations publicly criticized the intransigence of the packing firms and endorsed the union's demands.[25]

To encourage membership participation, local unions used their strike headquarters to create programs that responded to the emotional and material needs of UPWA members and their families. Monetary support from community organizations, other unions, nonstriking UPWA locals, and the UPWA national office provided sufficient funds to maintain soup kitchens and provide emergency financial assistance. Each local area formed welfare committees to dispense relief money, provide counseling, and assist workers who owed rent or were unable to make payments on other debts. In Omaha, a union entertainment committee organized evening plays, movies, and wrestling matches.[26]

Financial support from nonstriking UPWA locals was central to the union's strategy. Workers outside the Big Four had a substantial stake in the 1948 walkout because their wage rates generally were tied to the pattern established in the national master agreements. In fact, nonstriking locals donated the bulk of the money used for food and other relief measures. The Austin Hormel local alone contributed $131,558 and "adopted" the families of St. Paul strikers arrested by police. In District 1, nonstriking locals contributed $26,204 to the Chicago-area strike fund—more than received from the UPWA national organization or any other source.[27]

Unlike the 1946 dispute, the packing firms aggressively tried to undermine the strike by bringing scabs and strikebreakers into their facilities. "Armour and Company just dug in their heels," recalled one participant. The companies sent letters to striking workers, warning they would be fired if they remained on strike. Foremen individually contacted workers and tried to persuade them to return. In Chicago the packers used trucks and railroad cars to bring strikebreakers past the massive union picket lines. In Chicago, Omaha, St. Joseph, and Fort Worth the packing firms housed strikebreakers in their plants.[28]

Efforts to halt strikebreakers regularly brought hundreds, at times thousands, of UPWA members to mass packet lines. The daily confrontations occasionally erupted into violent clashes. Pickets cursed at strikebreakers, rocked their cars, and promised to "deal with them" later. In Winona, Minnesota, UPWA pickets halted scabs by following a car of strikebreakers inside the plant gate. "They were laughing like hell until we opened the doors, pulled them out and beat the shit out of them," recalled Henry Giannini. With evident glee he added, "No one else went through." Sioux City union members patrolled a key bridge linking the Bottoms neighborhood with the stockyards. When Armour president Clyde Wensel sought to stop a strikebreaker, the man put a knife at Wensel's throat. Fortunately, Elder "Mojo" Owens, a black kill-floor worker, backed him up. "I said, 'Look behind you, sir,'" Wensel recalled telling the strikebreaker. "There was Owens with a baseball bat." The bridge remained under union control.[29]

Legal restrictions and police repression seriously interfered with union picket lines. By the of the strike the UPWA had been served with fifty injunctions restraining picketing and other strike activities. "If there were any cities where such injunction were not issued, I don't at the moment know where they were," Ralph Helstein told the union's 1948 convention. Local police arrested hundreds of union members for ignoring the injunctions and committing other alleged infractions. Chicago unionists contended with a force of a thousand police who used squads of club-wielding officers to escort strikebreakers through picket lines. In late April, Chicago UPWA member Santo Cicardo was killed by a truck that police allowed to speed toward a union picket line at Armour's Soap Works plant. In Kansas City, a violent police assault on April 23 wrecked the Cudahy union hall, injuring more than fifty pickets and bystanders. Strikers in several places blocked railroad tracks to prevent shipment of cattle into the plants. Police arrested ninety Omaha Armour workers who employed this tactic.[30]

The strike remained solid for the first month, but small groups of union members began trickling back to work in late April. The initial problems with scabs reflected relatively weak union allegiance among particular groups rather than economic pressures. Eyewitness accounts generally agree that scabs were most likely to be middle-aged white men and women in weak union departments, such as the relatively well-paid workers in sliced bacon and the mechanical division. Swift plants generally had more problems with scabs than the other chains, even though pay levels were the same. At Chicago Swift, for example, where workers were far more impressed with company paternalism than at Armour and Wilson, strike participation was notably weaker than elsewhere in the Chicago district. More favorably inclined toward their company than other workers, these employees generally were less willing to risk their individual economic status for uncertain collective accomplishments.[31]

The major force weakening the strike in April was lack of cooperation from the other meat industry unions rather than cracks in the UPWA's ranks. With the Amalgamated and NBPW remaining on the job, the UPWA completely halted meat production only in Omaha and Sioux City. In April, production in Iowa, Minnesota, and Kansas City fell about 50 percent, and in Chicago approximately 30 percent. More important, on a national basis cattle slaughter fell 20 percent and hogs just 10 percent. Continued operation by independent firms and vastly increased production by Amalgamated and Brotherhood plants allowed the packing industry to alleviate the worst effects of the UPWA's strike and avert the sharp decline of aggregate meat supplies that had provoked federal intervention in 1946.[32]

Six weeks into the strike, a company ultimatum threatened to turn the trickle of scabs into a flood. The Big Four firms announced in late April that they would unilaterally implement the 9 cent raise on May 3. Workers who remained on strike past May 10, they warned, would forfeit pensions, seniority rights, and vacations.[33]

The largest clashes of the strike erupted the week following the May 10 deadline, as hundreds and sometimes thousands of strike supporters confronted strikebreakers in dozens of cities. Workers in Albert Lee overturned the cars of scabs attempting to enter the Wilson plant. Union members in St. Paul defied a court injunction and blockaded the main entrance to the stockyards. Pickets repulsed several police charges, overturned cars, and used their fists to disperse scabs. A riot erupted in Waterloo, Iowa, after Fred Lee Roberts, a black scab, fatally shot white union member Chuck Farrel in front of the plant. Despite these dramatic mobilizations, any initial success was fleeting. The governors of Iowa and Minnesota called out the National Guard in response to the disorder; within a few days the fixed bayonets of troops protected scabs in Waterloo, Albert Lee, and St. Paul from angry UPWA members.[34]

Despite strong resistance in some centers, the company deadline caused the weakened strike to disintegrate rapidly. On May 11 the Chicago stock-handlers broke with international union policy and unilaterally signed an agreement. Herb March accurately observed that the action "had the same effect as dropping a sledgehammer between the eyes as far as a strike is concerned in Chicago." Within a few days, 1,500 workers crossed the picket lines at the Chicago Swift plant, along with six hundred at nearby Armour. Although the Iowa and Omaha locals in District 3 remained fairly solid, the strike collapsed rapidly elsewhere. Hundreds returned to work in Kansas City, Fort Worth, Oklahoma City, Atlanta, and Los Angeles. In the southeast region, Director Grover Hathaway reported that "the whole district wants this strike settled." On the East Coast, Meyer Stern reluctantly admitted that the stockyards settlement has "seriously affected morale."[35]

"The company just outlasted us," Charles Hayes later observed. Dependent on local union resources and donations from other labor organizations for the strike fund, the UPWA simply could not sustain the declining strike any longer. District 1 raised $113,486 for its strike fund, an average of only $5.50 for the twenty thousand striking workers in that region. Many UPWA members exhausted their savings and lost cars, homes, and other goods purchased on installment plans. The $69,000 received from the CIO and affiliated unions scarcely made a dent in the strikers' needs. Henry Giannini, whose St. Paul Cudahy local was willing to remain on strike, reluctantly accepted the necessity to return to work because further decay of the strike elsewhere "would destroy the international." After four days of intense debate, on May 19 the National Strike Strategy Committee accepted the companies' 9 cent offer and directed locals to return to work so packinghouse workers could "rebuild our union."[36]

The UPWA's weakened state, and vulnerability to raids, ended the debate over compliance with Taft-Hartley. The union emerged from the strike seriously in debt and with more than seven hundred members discharged. It faced dozens of legal cases arising out of picket line violence, as well as the danger of losing NLRB certification at many plants because of election petitions filed by the Amalgamated Meat Cutters and various independent unions. American membership declined from a hundred thousand at the beginning of the strike to around sixty thousand in its aftermath. In this situation, Meyer Stern signed the Taft-Hartley affidavit, and Herb March resigned as District 1 director. In an uncompromising statement published in the June 11 *Packinghouse Worker,* March warned that other unions "who took the 'compliance' road, also stopped fighting for higher wages and better working conditions." March stated clearly, however, that he was resigning of his own accord for the sake of the union because continued resistance to filing the affidavits "could only have led to a bitter inner union conflict, at a time when our union must be united to beat back the attacks of the packers and the raiding of other unions."[37]

From its weakened state the UPWA made a extraordinary recovery that later assumed a legendary character inside the organization. The most immediate threats were two dozen certification elections against the Amalgamated Meat Cutters and scattered independent unions. In a tribute to its continued popularity in the strike's aftermath, the UPWA won every single one, usually garnering three or four times the vote totals of its opponents. UPWA publicity proudly defended its efforts to win a larger raise and effectively accused the Amalgamated of sabotaging its efforts. "Its a FACT," a UPWA leaflet told Birmingham Armour workers, that the UPWA negotiated "the first master agreement." The Amalgamated, on the other hand, "sold their membership—and all packinghouse workers—down the river for a 9 cent raise." The UPWA also played on its reputation as a fighting union and the Amalgamated as a pro-company organization that had abandoned packinghouse workers in the past. A Cedar Rapids leaflet pointedly reminded workers that after the 1921 strike, the "Amalgamated 'sold-out' the membership and *did nothing* to get the workers their jobs back." The UPWA, on the other hand, would fight to get everyone "back to work" and "show the Amalgamated what a 'real union' really is like." A national leaflet prepared by the organization department (and probably drafted by Frank Ellis) combined these themes. It promised workers "we won't lick boots here!" and claimed that the UPWA failed to win more money "because at the critical moment [Amalgamated officials] Gorman and Jimerson put the knife in *your back!!*"[38]

The UPWA also made good use of a *Life* magazine spread on the Amalgamated's lavish fiftieth-anniversary celebration that abutted a photo essay on the UPWA's 1948 strike. While the story on the UPWA showed St. Paul strikers battling with the police and the National Guard, a full-page photo of the Amalgamated event featured well-dressed male union officials ogling a scantily clad woman. The UPWA took full advantage of the clear counterposition of the two union's priorities. A leaflet to Atlanta Armour workers used the *Life* stories to point out that while the UPWA "was battling on the picket lines," Amalgamated officials, as their "reward for scabbing," had consumed 216 cases of beer and two tons of meat and received eight hundred gold compacts, a thousand gold cigarette cases, and twenty-two thousand roses. Noting that the $225,000 spent for the spectacle came out of the Amalgamated's treasury, the leaflet asked workers whether they wanted their dues money to go for lavish parties or to improve the wages and working conditions of packinghouse workers. "We have made gains for the last ten years only because we have been willing to fight the packers," the union explained. *"We shall never become a company union for the packers such as the AFL has been for the last 50 years!!!!"* The election results were a clear indication that tens of thousands of rank-and-file packinghouse workers were swayed by these arguments.[39]

Wilson posed the greatest challenge to the resurgent UPWA. Unlike other packing firms, Wilson refused to sign another master agreement in August when the existing contracts expired. "There never was any chance to settle this strike with Mr. Helstein and his associates," declared Wilson Vice-president James D. Cooney just days after the union offered to return to work for 9 cents. "This union is infested with Communists and Fellow Travellers." On the shop floor, supervisors tried to reclaim the control over production that they had exercised before World War II. As in the old days, foremen ignored seniority in making job assignments, and workers with decades of experience were "shifted by the Company like they are wandering Hogs, Cattle, or Sheep." In the hog kill of Wilson's Chicago plant, a gang that killed three hundred hogs per hour before the strike had their quota doubled. Similar speedup occurred in other departments, along with other forms of petty harassment. In once case, foremen fired a worker for sitting down while his machine printed labels, a practice the union claimed "he has been doing for several years."[40]

Company actions inadvertently corroborated the UPWA's claim that a union was "the only thing that stands between us and the old slave day conditions that formerly existed." Leaflets repeatedly invoked the deterioration of working conditions since the strike and rhetorically asked, "Would CIO allow the foremen to act like they were 'Tin Gods' and the workers were trash under their feet?" By the spring of 1949 the UPWA had racked up huge majorities in certification elections at all seven Wilson plants. Many workers who were not union members—and even some who scabbed during the 1948 strike—voted for the UPWA, an eloquent testimonial to the effectiveness of its propaganda. "We won," recalled discharged Chicago Wilson worker Charles Hayes, because "the people realized that they couldn't work for Wilson without a union." In May the union's resurgence received a boost when a stoppage by hog-kill workers in the Chicago plant once again forced Wilson to meet with UPWA stewards over grievances.[41]

In 1949 the sticking point remained Wilson's refusal to sign another master agreement. It would allow its plants to sign local contracts but wanted to break out of the pattern bargaining structure of the meatpacking industry. Wilson's position was unacceptable to the UPWA because the master agreements were essential to the union's national bargaining power. To bring additional pressure on the company, the union launched a national boycott of its products. UPWA members distributed hundreds of thousands of leaflets to consumers, cleverly conveying its grievances against the company and carrying the campaign's primary slogan: "The Wilson label disgraces your table." One humorous palm-sized handbill portrayed a dog backing away from a tray of Wilson dogfood. "I got self respect," the leaflet had the dog say. "I won't eat . . . Wilson meats." While they distributed leaflets, union supporters wore aprons with enormous letters imploring "Don't Buy Wilson Products." When several entered a large Chicago store that carried Wilson meats, participants dryly reported that there was "quite a bit of interest on the part of the shoppers and a great deal of concern on the part of the manager." In September 1950 Wilson finally backed down after a threatened national strike and signed a master agreement with terms similar to those accepted by other companies.[42]

Subduing Wilson was only one aspect of a larger effort by the UPWA to reestablish shop-floor organization and reinstate discharged workers. The presence of scabs, ranging from a few dozen to several hundred, complicated the union's efforts because those workers could not be counted on to support its policies. The bitterness of union members toward workers who crossed picket lines was palpable. By all accounts, former strikers "made their lives miserable." In Fort Worth, "There were some individuals, employees, that some of us never completely forgave," recalled Frank Wallace. Waterloo leader Charles Mueller, some forty years later, still resented workers who crossed the picket line in 1948. "The first thing that come to my head is, yeah, that guy scabbed in '48, and it makes him a lower form of worm to me." To Omaha workers, "You could steal $100,000, they'll forgive you," recalled Vic Meyers. "But you walk by that picket line and they'll remember their name."[43]

"Boy, they sure got rid of them when they went back," recalled one Omaha activist. Despite the watchful eyes of supervisors, in the shop-floor environment UPWA members could employ many techniques to force scabs either to join the union or leave the plant. Union members ostracized scabs and engaged in various forms of intimidation. "We'd just ignore them and they didn't get treated right," recalled Helen Zrudsky. "So they'd either come in or get out." Within a few months, American UPWA membership grew by 50 percent, from a poststrike low of sixty thousand back to ninety thousand, its level before the brutal 1948 conflict.[44]

The UPWA's capacity to save the jobs of more than seven hundred work-ers fired during the strike was an enormous boost to its popularity. The union's diligent efforts also provided a clear contrast with the Amalgamat-ed's abandonment of its members in 1922. Within nine months, the griev-ance department secured reinstatement of 90 percent of the discharged em-ployees. Jesse Prosten, under attack for his Communist views, was the main union negotiator in these efforts. In 1949 an International Executive Board report praised Prosten's efforts as "one of the most outstanding performances ever seen in any union." He later explained that his accomplishment rested on the willingness of many local union leaders, fired without cause and prob-ably entitled to back pay, to waive monetary claims if their companies would rehire all the workers who wanted to return. "Sacrifices were made by the guys who recognized they might have won a thousand dollars," recalled Prosten, for the purpose of "getting everybody back." The union also was highly successful at securing acquittals, or only nominal fines, for hundreds of UPWA members arrested during the strike. In Kansas City the UPWA even won $11,300 in damages from the police department for their raid on the Cudahy union hall.[45]

The UPWA's rapid recovery was the result of the continued vitality of its shop-floor structures in key departments and plants. The heart and soul of the union, the killing floors and cutting departments in midwestern and metropolitan packinghouses, remained solid and highly organized. "Going back in there was just like you had a weekend off," recalled Sioux City kill-ing-floor worker Alvin Edwards. "That's one thing that saved the situation," explained Omaha leader George Fletemeyer. "They had a steward system." Shop-floor strength was a critical aid to union efforts to reinstate discharged workers. The St. Paul Cudahy local used a plantwide slowdown to compel management to rehire forty-one workers. Armour plants used slowdowns, and threatened a national strike, if the company refused to reemploy work-ers and give them full credit for seniority. "We said to them," recalled Mary Salinas, "'We're not any weaker than when we left. In fact, we're stronger.'" The numerous certification elections, as in the 1930s, provided a focus for building union support and strengthening the steward system.[46]

In the many areas where the union's shop-floor strength had been seri-ously disrupted, the union rebuilt by consciously drawing on the "cream of the crop": UPWA members whose leadership qualities had emerged during the course of the strike. Some local unions, especially those which had se-vere problems with scabs, took several years to reestablish their plantwide apparatus. Even strong locals had to rebuild to a certain degree. To strengthen weak areas, organization department head Frank Ellis urged local unions to approach rank-and-file members who had demonstrated their commitment during the strike and "work such men and women into permanent positions of leadership and responsibility." Following this approach, locals recruited individuals such as Max Graham in Omaha, Charles Mueller in Waterloo, and Virginia Houston in Kansas City, people first drawn into union activity during the 1948 strike. All three became stewards within a year and later served as local union leaders. The UPWA's brush with catastrophe had made them appreciate "what they could have lost." On balance, the 1948 strike brought a new generation of cadres into local union structures.[47]

For black workers who entered meatpacking during and immediately after World War II, the 1948 strike encouraged greater commitment to the UPWA. Unlike the debacle of 1921 and 1922, which drove deep fissures between blacks and the packinghouse union, the 1948 strike reinforced interracial unity. "Blacks and whites were just like two black-eyed peas," recalled Eddie Humphrey. "We were all in the same pod. We were all after the same thing." A 1949 survey showed that 96 percent of UPWA locals felt that black strike participation was as good as, or better than, the activity of whites. The most impressive example was in Waterloo, where the killing of a white striker by a black scab produced none of the racial conflict that might have occurred two decades before. In fact, Charles Pearson, a black union activist, observed that in the confrontations with police and the National Guard, "It seemed like the people in the street drew closer together, the black and the white unified. Well, hell, we're goin' lose our jobs if we don't combine and stay together." The UPWA's recovery from the strike in turn amplified the power of blacks as the union assiduously drew young black men and women into its shop-floor structures.[48]

Rather than the crushing blow to the UPWA that the packing companies had hoped, the 1948 strike and the union's rapid recovery actually augmented its bargaining power. Charles R. Fischer, who at the time considered the strike "the worst mistake we had ever made in our life," later credited it as the turning point for the UPWA. "It taught the company a lesson. They lost millions of dollars out of that deal, and they knew we could do it again if we took a notion to do it. So then out of that, in later negotiations, came sick leave, came expanded vacations, came hospitalization, came the pension plan. All of that. It was a result of the '48 strike."[49]

Contractual advances in the immediate aftermath of the strike support Fischer's statement. Just three months after the union returned to work, the UPWA signed one-year agreements providing for another general 4 cent increase. Its 1949 contracts included severance pay for the first time, special increases to plants in the South and rural areas, and wage improvement by increasing the spread between brackets from 2½ to 3 cents. In the Armour agreement, the union successfully fought to retain clause 95E, which permitted strikes over job loads while the contract remained in effect. By 1950, with Wilson's acceptance of a new master agreement, the UPWA had stymied the efforts of packing companies to tame or eliminate the union.[50]

The struggle of 1947 through 1950 confirmed the analysis of the UPWA's center-left bloc that the union could only survive the postwar reaction against labor by maintaining the strength of its organization on the factory floor and its popularity among rank-and-file packinghouse workers. The legacy of the 1948 strike was only partly the strike itself; the capacity of local unions to reestablish their shop-floor organization and resist raids by other unions determined the long-range impact of the national walkout. As UPWA president Helstein later recalled, "Our people found they could get involved in that kind of a fight, take a beating, and come back from that beating and make the companies toe the line." Instead of workers asking, "Where were our leaders?" as Helstein had feared, the UPWA garnered new respect from its rank and file for its courage, determination, and material successes, and it defeated the efforts of packinghouse companies to return shop-floor relations to the pre-union era. "If we hadn't struck in '48, we probably would have to strike in '51 or '52," explained Max Graham, whose union activity stemmed from experiences in 1948. What was "added" to labor relations in meatpacking was, in his words, the "strength" for the UPWA "to roll on through the 1950s." In subsequent years the workers who composed the "generation of '48" would provide new union stalwarts for the UPWA.[51]

Factionalism and the UPWA's Center-Left Coalition

The UPWA's struggle with the packing companies between 1947 and 1950 occurred during one of the most intolerant periods in American history and triggered explosive internal conflicts over Communist influence in the UPWA. The obstacles caused by noncompliance with Taft-Hartley and the UPWA's weakened state immediately after the strike initially fanned attacks on Communists inside the union. The union's ultimate decision to reject a purge of the left proved to be another critical watershed for the UPWA. By protecting the right of union members to act on a range of political opinions, the UPWA kept open channels for rank-and-file influence and thus greatly facilitated the expansion of social unionism in the 1950s.

Internal tensions were exacerbated because of the international conflict over communism and domestic repression against Americans linked with the Communist Party. While the UPWA was on strike, the Marshall Plan passed Congress. Later that summer ten Communist Party leaders were indicted under the Smith Act, and Whittaker Chambers lodged his famous charges against Alger Hiss. As the UPWA recovered from the strike, the McCarran Act established the Subversive Activities Control Board, thirty-two states passed laws barring "subversives" from public employment, and Joseph R. McCarthy delivered his first tirade against Communist influence in the State Department. Inside the labor movement, the CIO expelled eleven international unions with a total of 1.5 million members. Rival unions tried to mobilize anticommunism sentiment in their raids against the UPWA in 1948 and 1949. The Amalgamated promised packinghouse workers that its officers "cannot be a communist or communist sympathizer," and an independent union in Chicago accused Wilson leader Sam Parks of wearing "red underwear" and being on the Communist Party payroll.[52]

By the late 1940s, however, the pattern of development of the UPWA mitigated against a purge. The left's undisputed role in the creation of packinghouse unionism and its diligent actions on behalf of UPWA members discredited right-wing arguments that Communists were not loyal members. The preservation of the UPWA's shop-floor infrastructure had provided a positive frame of reference for packinghouse workers to evaluate the contributions of radicals inside their union. This was especially true for black workers who appreciated the support of leftists for action against discrimination. The need for unity in order to navigate the difficult period after the strike also made a purge seem ill-advised. The willingness of March and Stern to make survival of the UPWA their first priority, even at the cost of Communist influence, no doubt impressed UPWA members. Consequently, unique among CIO unions, the UPWA remained heavily influenced by the left and avoided expulsion from the CIO.

Appeals to anticommunism failed to win the support of a substantial minority in the UPWA, much less a majority. Although packinghouse workers, especially East European Catholics, no doubt shared a repugnance for Soviet actions in occupied Europe, they also were deeply suspicious of politicians and union leaders who seemed more intent on uprooting Communist influence than advancing workers' rights. Sympathy for the American government's stance that communism was a threat to democracy did not necessarily translate into intolerance toward leftists inside the union. Typically, Sioux City Swift union leader Jimmy Hilsinger called the charges of Communist influence in the UPWA "a vicious, slanderous campaign to remove a leadership that's trying to do the job properly." Communists could rely on the shared experience on the shop floor and the picket line to shield them from the brickbats of anticommunism. "It didn't come down to me that they were Communists," recalled Omaha leader James C. Harris, "but that they were fighting for the working people."[53]

The key group resisting the siren song of anticommunism was the centrist "broad middle" in the UPWA, the industrial unionists in the UPWA's midwestern heartland who, in Norm Dolnick's pithy phrase, "didn't give a shit about the left and right fight, they just wanted a good union." To these workers, the performance of union leaders meant far more than their putative political views. "What is it that they've done?" Omaha leader Darryl Poe would ask when charges of Communist influence were leveled against the UPWA. "Don't tell me what they are, what did they do?" In Cedar Rapids and Omaha, where union leaders were outspoken opponents of leftist UPWA officials and staffers, anticommunism failed to excite the rank and file. "It never meant anything to me because you're working with all these people and you know them," recalled Jeanette Haymond, a Cedar Rapids steward for many years. "In fact, you hardly heard any discussion down in the plant about anything like that." Omaha steward Max Graham recalled that there was "a lot of that red-baiting." But "most of my interest was what went on in the plant. So some of this other thing, you'd almost have to be an officer."[54]

The preservation of structures for rank-and-file involvement provided a framework in which union members could evaluate the contributions of leaders known to be Communists. March and Prosten, the most prominent Communists in the union, never hid their beliefs. "I have always disdained to conceal the fact that I am a Communist," wrote March in his 1948 resignation statement published in the union's newspaper. March, who had risen from Armour's shop floor in the early 1930s to his leadership position, always retained respect for his unwavering commitment to the rank and file. "Herb would deal with the issues," recalled long-time critic Richard Saunders. "The heck with what he was." Jesse Prosten, who criss-crossed the country after the 1948 strike restoring discharged packinghouse workers to their jobs, also benefited from his personal relationship with many union members. "We were part of the people we worked with," he recalled. "I was some fucking nut who was a Red as far as they were concerned, but I was the guy who produced for them. Because it was a rank and file operation, you couldn't bullshit them about what a guy was doing or wasn't doing." Anticommunists in the UPWA always ran into the obstacle that it was difficult to attack Communists and other leftists for conduct deleterious to the union. "Economics is the main thing," pointed out St. Joseph leader Bill Webster, "and nobody done more to raise the packinghouse workers economic standards than Jesse Prosten."[55]

Black workers, especially the increasingly influential younger generation, were an important bulwark against anticommunism. Most seemed unswayed by accusations of Communist influence in the UPWA. In Chicago, "It didn't ring a bell with them," recalled Charles Hayes. To blacks in St. Joseph, "It was no big deal," reflected Bill Webster. Black workers also respected the indefatigable efforts of Communists and other leftists to advance the union's anti-discrimination policies. "By damning them, you're actually making the Communists heroes," a Waterloo black worker observed sarcastically. Sam Parks praised March and other Chicago Communists for "standing out as an example to white workers cooperating and working with blacks," and he credited the left with a "hell of a contribution" to the civil rights struggle. Even Philip Weightman, a staunch opponent of Communist influence in Chicago, shared the respect of other black workers for the left's commitment to racial equality. "I might not have been as aggressive as I was if it hadn't been for them," he later admitted.[56]

A final and necessary ingredient defeating anticommunism in the UPWA was the personal stance taken by union president Ralph Helstein. Despite the obstacles to anticommunism flowing from the packinghouse union's particular history, Helstein could have followed Walter Reuther's example and brought the centrist "broad middle" into an alliance with the UPWA's right wing rather than its left. Helstein's refusal to do so reflected his belief that accepting reactionary demands to suppress dissent and expel leftists would undermine the labor movement's ability to challenge vested interests. "The labor movement has been a traditional rallying point of the forces of the common people of the world," Helstein told delegates in his forceful opening speech to the UPWA's tumultuous 1948 convention.

> It must continue to fight to perform that role. It must continue to fight for the rights of its members—it must continue to fight for tolerance, for freedom of thought, freedom of religion, for equal rights and opportunities for all regardless of race, creed, color or opinion. And it must fight for those rights in the nation as a whole and within its own ranks. It must fight for those rights against the vigorous opposition which has now been generated by the forces that are the traditional enemies of the labor movement. Of course, it is harder to struggle than to surrender.[57]

To play a progressive role in society, Helstein believed that the labor movement had to "struggle" against, rather than "surrender" to, conservative pressures to enforce conformity in its own house.

Anticommunist agitation grew steadily in the UPWA between 1946 and the 1948 strike. At the time of the 1946 convention, the UPWA International Executive Board criticized the widespread circulation of anticommunist material by some locals and warned the union membership of "the dangers inherent in generalized attacks which fail to offer anything constructive, that only call names." By 1947 relations had deteriorated so much in District 1 that a third of the locals had ceased participating in the left-influenced council that governed the region. That year local unions in Los Angeles, Salt Lake City, and St. Paul inserted provisions in their local constitutions prohibiting Communists from holding office.[58]

The center-left majority tried to cool the factional strife. The board refused to approve the constitutions of local unions that prohibited Communist participation in leadership, and the 1947 convention passed a "statement of policy" that attacked "the present wave of witch hunt hysteria as the weapon of reaction and monopoly whose goal is to destroy the trade union movement." At the same time, in a style characteristic of other CIO unions, the resolution deplored "recent attempts to influence our actions" and, in a slap at the Communist Party, declared, "We will make our own decision free from outside influence." These minimal efforts bought time but in no way ended internal tensions.[59]

The decision of Henry Wallace to run for president on a third party ticket in December 1947 added fuel to the factional warfare. Wallace's support among packinghouse workers reflected a deep disillusionment with the policies of Harry Truman and congressional Democrats. "We don't want a Republic party and Truman either," a St. Paul packinghouse worker wrote Ralph Helstein. "Wallace is a better man like Roosevelt." Truman particularly antagonized labor by asking Congress for broad power to break strikes, including the authority to draft strikers into the army. Indicating an openness to political action outside the two-party system, the 1946 and 1947 UPWA conventions encouraged local unions to support candidacies that would lead in the direction of an "independent political party." Notably, support for the resolutions came from the anticommunist Chicago and St. Paul Swift unions as well as leftist locals. Sympathy for Wallace among packinghouse workers reflected deep dissatisfaction with the political direction of the Democratic Party and was not simply a manifestation of organized leftist influence.[60]

UPWA members who supported Wallace were thus entirely within the spirit and the letter of union decisions. Ralph Helstein encouraged this sentiment. In a widely publicized speech, the UPWA president told a District 3 convention in February 1948, "If the facts are as they are today, I will cast my ballot for Henry Wallace." Wallace attracted considerable support from Iowa and Chicago UPWA locals. Sioux City Cudahy local president Bruce Nolan served as treasurer of the Iowa Progressive Party and was a delegate to its July convention, along with fellow union founder Berth Madison. Paul Robeson, campaigning for Wallace during the UPWA's 1948 strike, received a warm reception from Waterloo Rath workers when he joined them on the picket line and addressed a packed union meeting. In Chicago, "practically all our pickets were wearing Wallace buttons," recalled Herb March.[61]

The UPWA's tolerance of pro-Wallace activities by union locals and officials directly conflicted with CIO directives and thus added to internal political tensions. In January 1948 the CIO executive board sought to curtail Wallace's influence in the labor movement by directing regional CIO bodies and affiliated international unions to support Truman. CIO leaders denounced Wallace as a tool of the Communist Party whose sole contribution would be to elect an anti-labor Republican as president. The CIO's activities had an enormous influence inside the UPWA because Wallace needed at least CIO neutrality to mount a credible alternative to Truman. UPWA members who remained highly critical of Truman, and who favored a labor party, pulled back from Wallace because of his connection with the Communist Party and the fear of splitting the labor vote. "I suppose if a legitimate third party or labor party would have been formed at that time I think I would have joined it," reflected Henry Giannini. "I didn't think he was a legitimate third party person who could start a third party and lead it." Critics of the Helstein leadership viewed continued tolerance of pro-Wallace activity by union officials as yet more proof of its capture by the left.[62]

Conflict over Wallace's candidacy was the final stimulus to the development of a motley anti-administration alliance at the June 1948 UPWA convention. A coalition of anticommunists, critics of the recent strike, and opponents of the Wallace campaign tried unsuccessfully to wrest control of the union from Helstein's center-left bloc. Calling themselves the CIO Policy Caucus, the dissidents shared a common target and not common politics. Two of its candidates, incumbent Vice-president Weightman and District 8 Director A. J. Pittman (who ran for secretary-treasurer), were leaders of the right-wing faction on the International Executive Board. The candidacy of Austin union founder and *Packinghouse Worker* editor Svend Godfredson for the union's presidency moderated the right-wing tinge of the Policy Caucus and broadened its appeal. "I, as a person coming from the shop, had the right to be a candidate," Godfredson later recalled. "I didn't want a union established where the president didn't need any opposition, where everything was decided beforehand." Charles R. Fischer and the Kansas City-based District 4 supported the opposition, primarily because of their criticism of the recent strike rather than because of diligent anticommunism. Although Godfredson and Fischer later claimed that they would not have eliminated Communists from the union, the right-wing component of the opposition would have dominated the union's top offices and almost certainly led to a purge of leftists.[63]

The weakened state of the union, and recriminations over the collapse of the 1948 strike, framed the struggle at the convention. Angry delegates pilloried the international officers for poor technical and strategic planning, and several called for "straightening out" the leadership. Right-wing delegates tried to build a bridge between anticommunism and anger over the strike's failure by criticizing the officers for opposing full compliance with Taft-Hartley. If the board had not bent to the "personal interests of one or two members," argued District 2 Director Glenn Chinander (in a clear reference to March and Stern), "we would have been in a better position to strike." Although explicitly anticommunist delegates were a distinct minority, their arguments threatened to link the strike's failure with the laxity of the Helstein leadership toward Communists and thus lay the basis for a purge.[64]

Administration supporters used the evident need for unity to counter the opposition's complaints. "Now, criticism is easy," pointed out a Local 15 member whose Kansas City union had opposed the strike, "but is it helping any?" Delegates cheered Frank Ellis when he attacked efforts to find a "scapegoat." "I was out fighting," he told delegates. "I am willing to take my responsibility. Are you going to take yours?" Russell Lasley pointed out that as a result of the strike, many union members "are more militant people, are more fighting people than they ever were before." Instead of wasting time "quibbling and quarreling," he urged delegates "to put down their jealousies" and develop a program for rebuilding the union. Given the weakened state of the organization, Lasley's arguments carried considerable weight among pragmatic delegates worried over the union's survival.[65]

The defeat of the opposition slate confirmed that the center-left coalition retained majority support among union members. Helstein, Ellis, Clark, and Lasley (supported by Helstein against Weightman) narrowly won, with support from the union's "broad middle" (especially in Iowa), social-democrats in Canada, and left-influenced locals in New York, Chicago, and Minnesota (Table 11). Although opposition leaders remained directors of their districts, Weightman lost his UPWA post and was immediately hired by the CIO. Not long after the convention, the victors fired Godfredson and several staff members for their continued activities in support of the CIO Policy Caucus. Henry Giannini, an important opposition figure in St. Paul, admitted, "We got too big for our britches, and decided we were going to clean house. Instead, we got cleaned out."[66]

Table 11. UPWA Election Results, 1948 Convention

Office and Candidates	Pro-Administration	CIO Policy Caucus
President	683.23	527.22
(Helstein-Godfredson)	(56.4 percent)	
Vice-President I	648.43	563.04
(Ellis-Kampfert)	(53.5 percent)	
Vice-President II	621.16	591.17
(Lasley-Weightman)	(51.2 percent)	
Secretary-Treasurer	654.29	552.71
(Clark-Pittman)	(54.2 percent)	

Source: *Proceedings, Fifth Constitutional Convention of the United Packinghouse Workers of America,* 157, 178, 207.

The resolution of the Wallace issue set the tone for the subsequent containment of differences in the UPWA and avoidance of outright conflict with directives from the CIO. As a result of the forceful intervention of CIO officials, the Resolutions Committee withdrew a proposed motion that would "neither endorse nor condemn the Third Party." In its place, the convention simply endorsed established CIO policy. Because delegates already had returned the Helstein leadership to office, the difference was largely semantic. Supporters of Wallace continued their activities without interference because the officers were not obliged to make the policy of the international binding on local affiliates or union members. As the Policy Caucus quickly learned to its dismay, UPWA leaders had no intention of using the union apparatus to enforce conformity with CIO directives. At the same time, formal endorsement of CIO policy protected the UPWA by minimizing the CIO's leverage for intervention into its internal affairs.[67]

Reverberations of the 1948 convention continued for another two years and left the Helstein leadership in even firmer control. In August a CIO Policy Caucus meeting drew sixty local officials from Chicago, St. Paul, Kansas City, the Southeast, and the West Coast. The conference voted to urge locals to withhold per capita payments until the international rehired discharged staff members and suppressed pro-Wallace activity by local unions and UPWA officials. It was a disastrous step for the opposition. Only a few participants actually implemented the conference's decision, and their resistance quickly crumbled when the international placed an administrator over Chicago Local 28, the leading dissident group, for violating the UPWA constitution by withholding dues. As a result, many local leaders who initially supported the CIO Policy Caucus withdrew, and it collapsed by the end of 1948. Charles R. Fischer, who attended the group's Cedar Rapids meeting, refused to participate in the dues-withholding movement. "There's times in the function of organized labor where you're in a position where you can't fight both ends against the middle," he recalled. Indeed, the disruptive actions by the CIO Policy Caucus were a striking contrast to the hard work of Jesse Prosten to restore discharged union members and the willingness of Meyer Stern and Herb March to remove themselves as an obstacle to the union's recovery.[68]

Using language that stressed the need for working-class unity, administration supporters devastatingly attacked the Policy Caucus's "sabotage" of the union's efforts to recuperate from the 1948 strike. They pointed out that the AFL had used the controversy in its leaflets during raids on UPWA plants, and that the packing companies' trade journal had approvingly reported on the Cedar Rapids meeting. A leaflet distributed to Local 28 members called the local's incumbent officers "traitors to the Union and traitors to you" because they were trying to "split and wreck our Union in the face of problems that packinghouse workers are confronted with." Reflecting the opposition's isolation, delegates to the 1949 UPWA convention roundly criticized the dues-withholding movement and voted by a 3 to 1 margin not to seat the right-wing officials of Local 28. On the floor of the convention, Omaha leader Nels Peterson, one of the union's most strident anticommunists, sided with Helstein and attacked the "unprincipled and factional opposition" for their "disruptive" campaign. Two district directors who had supported the Policy Caucus, Glenn Chinander and Grover Hathaway, also opposed seating locals who had withheld per capita payments. An election in Local 28 held soon after the convention rejected the incumbent right-wing officers in favor of a group that promised to support the international union.[69]

Isolated within the UPWA, the anticommunist dissidents appealed to the CIO. Following the expulsions of several leftist unions at the CIO's 1949 convention, opposition leaders in the UPWA secretly asked CIO President Philip Murray to support their faction. Although unwilling to expel the UPWA, he agreed to speak at the union's 1950 convention to drum up support for a resolution barring Communists from serving as union officials or holding staff positions. In his address, Murray savagely parodied UPWA President Helstein's speaking style and viciously attacked communism as "a conspiracy of the most filthy nature." His rhetoric reached a fever pitch when he defended the expulsion of the United Electrical workers from the CIO. "There was our mare's nest, there is where all the deviltry reached its lowest level. . . . They had them on their payroll, every district, every area, clever cunning scoundrels, many of who had never worked a day in a factory in their lives, trained in the hard field of dictatorship, accepting the dictates of their masters and carrying their filthy, dirty, lousy policies into the councils of their own trade union."[70]

Murray's frenzied exhortation was to little avail. His depiction of Communists as foreign agents rather than committed union activists conflicted with the experience of many UPWA members. "Politically, everybody knows where I stand," Jesse Prosten pointed out from the convention floor in an emotional response to Murray. "When I go to a local union to settle a grievance I don't ask anybody whether he is a Republican or a Democrat or a Communist," he reminded delegates, who were well were aware of Prosten's diligent work for the union. To Murray's charge that Communists like Prosten were "trained" in "dictatorship," he said simply, "If I am deported I am deported to Brooklyn. If I think differently I learned what I learned in the public schools of America." Behind the scenes, the Resolutions Committee worked out a deal to quash efforts to purge Communists. Helstein's supporters agreed to withdraw the administrators from two locals that had withheld per capita payments if opposition groups halted their efforts to bar Communists. Although the differences remained, organized anticommunism subsequently abated.[71]

* * *

The result of these tumultuous events was a union that made limited concessions to anticommunism without surrendering its internal democracy and diversity. Herb March was the major casualty of the period. Hired by the international as a field representative after resigning as district director, he was fired by Helstein in January 1949 under direct pressure from the CIO. "At worst, as things stand now, I'll go work for my local," March recalled telling Helstein at the time. "But the question is, what's happening to you? Where is your principle?" Saul Alinsky and other Helstein associates criticized his actions as "craven behavior." In his defense, Helstein pleaded that in order to "save the union" he had to make concessions to the CIO, and March was "too heavy a load to carry."[72]

Helstein and his centrist, social-democratic current were the major beneficiaries of the factional turmoil. Although leftists remained a force within the union, they were weakened at its highest levels. March remained influential in the union as an employee of Local 347, but his replacement as District 1 director, liberal Wisconsin unionist Harold Nielsen, was a minor figure on the International Executive Board. In addition to March's departure, Frank Ellis retired in 1950, and a tragic recurrence of tuberculosis forced Joe Ollman to abandon union activity for several years. Ellis's successor as union vice-president and head of the organization department, Tony Stephens, was a Helstein protégé whose heavy-handed behavior was an unpopular change from the style of the old Wobbly. Ollman's replacement, Glenn Chinander, was a firm opponent of Helstein and leftist influence in the union.[73]

Leftists retained their influence at the lower levels of the organization. The union staff remained studded with radicals. Much to the anger of the union's right wing, in 1949 the UPWA hired former United Electrical workers member Leo Turner as a District 1 field representative and former Progressive Party official Charles Fischer as Helstein's administrative aide. The union retained Communists Prosten and Orear, as well as Trotskyists Milt Siegel and John Janosko. Communists remained the dominant force in the Chicago UPWA and were influential in several other locals throughout the 1950s. In fact, the international not only tolerated but also actively defended leftists who remained in its midst. When the House Un-American Activities Committee (HUAC) summoned March and other Local 347 leaders to testify in 1952, the international paid for its general counsel, Eugene Cotton, to organize their defense. In contrast, the UAW used a HUAC investigation of Local 600 officers that same year to attack Communist influence in its largest dissident local and to remove its elected officials.[74]

Although the UPWA's retention of internal democracy and diversity constituted a significant divergence from the UAW and the CIO's mainstream unions, its survival and continued vigor offers an unfortunate contrast to the so-called left-led unions. Refusal to file the Communist affidavits for at least two years and expulsion from the CIO in 1949 and 1950 destroyed the weaker of the left-wing unions and placed those which survived in a vulnerable position. The largest leftist union, the United Electrical workers (UE), lost half its membership between 1949 and 1951 because of raids launched by other labor organizations, especially the CIO-endorsed International Union of Electrical Workers (IUE). The UPWA's concessions, including the dismissal of March from the international staff, reflected a hardheaded estimation of unionists who opposed a conservative turn in the labor movement and saw, all around them, a rain of blows against militant unions. By doing so the Helstein leadership minimized the opportunity for the union's opposition faction to split the UPWA and seek CIO endorsement for a competing, anticommunist union, as had occurred in the electrical industry. The UPWA would have been far less able to advance its members' interests had it failed to comply with Taft-Hartley and been expelled from the CIO.[75]

The UPWA entered the 1950s scarred but unbowed by the struggles of the immediate postwar period. Notwithstanding personnel shifts, its tradition of shop-floor unionism remained embedded in the organization's practice and supported by its dominant leaders. The UPWA had preserved democratic structures in the organization and maintained the coalition of local unions with different political persuasions and social composition. During the 1950s advances in collective bargaining would reinforce the national, inter-racial coalition despite serious stresses, strains, and some losses. As a result, channels for rank-and-file expression and demands remained open, and even expanded, as a new challenge galvanized the union during the 1950s: the fight against racial and sexual discrimination.

9

"This Community of Our Union": Shop-floor Power and Social Unionism in the Postwar UPWA

> Organized labor can be one of the most powerful instruments to do away with this evil that confronts our nation that we refer to as segregation and discrimination. It is certainly true that the forces that are anti-Negro are by and large anti-labor, and with the coming together of the powerful influence of labor and all people of good will in the struggle for freedom and human dignity, I can assure you that we have a powerful instrument.
>
> —Martin Luther King, Jr., at 1957 UPWA conference

> We have within this group, this organized group, this community of our union, established folk-ways and mores and customs and methods of life that perhaps do not conform to the normal pattern existing in this country today. But they do correspond to this pattern which we believe is right as a matter of human decency and which we know to be absolutely essential in terms of the betterment of the membership of our organization, and we will not tolerate any attack on that pattern of life which has been established within the community of our union.
>
> —Ralph Helstein, 1949

On October 3, 1957, the Rev. Martin Luther King, Jr., told the UPWA's third Anti-Discrimination Conference, "We have broken loose from the Egypt of slavery. We have moved through the wilderness of separate and equal, and now we stand on the border of the promised land of integration." In his famous uplifting intonation King urged the rapt delegates to further action. "We must not rest until segregation and discrimination have been liquidated from every area of our nation's life." To sustained cheers from hundreds of black, white, and Mexican-American packinghouse workers, UPWA President Ralph Helstein presented King with an $11,000 check to fund the ambitious voter registration drive of the newly formed Southern Christian Leadership Conference (SCLC).[1]

King's appearance climaxed an eighteen-month campaign by UPWA officials and local unions on behalf of the Montgomery bus boycott and the SCLC. International union officials publicized the boycott within the UPWA, helped King obtain northern backers, and were the only AFL-CIO unionists to participate in the formative meetings of the SCLC. In the South, packing-house workers reportedly "were on fire" in support of the boycott. Two Montgomery UPWA locals rendered "day to day" assistance, and northern packinghouse workers contributed thousands of dollars.[2]

By necessity, the UPWA relied on local unions to raise money for the SCLC because the international organization did not have large cash re-serves. Addie Wyatt, a black Chicago union leader new to the staff, received the difficult assignment of traveling to predominantly white local unions in Indiana, Wisconsin, and Ohio to appeal for donations. Her task was to con-vince northern white packinghouse workers that they would benefit from enfranchising southern blacks and ending racial segregation. Although white members often were cynical at first, local after local voted to donate to the SCLC after Wyatt explained "what they had in common in doing so."[3]

King's appearance at the 1957 UPWA conference was neither empty sym-bolism nor an aberration. It reflected a convergence between the emerging civil rights movement and a labor organization that had initiated its own aggressive anti-discrimination efforts well before the Montgomery bus boy-cott. Beginning in the late 1940s, UPWA locals fought an aggressive campaign to end discriminatory practices in the packinghouses and communities where union members lived. The UPWA was the only AFL-CIO union aside from the overwhelmingly black Brotherhood of Sleeping Car Porters to back King's efforts actively in the 1950s. The rapidity with which UPWA mem-bers responded to the Montgomery bus boycott, and the enormous degree of support for the struggle from a majority white union, reflected a deep commitment to the principles of racial equality and justice.[4]

The UPWA's initiatives provide an especially sharp contrast with other AFL-CIO unions. The formal commitment to racial equality on the part of most labor organizations did not translate into a challenge to the discrimi-natory customs of the plants under their jurisdiction; indeed, there is con-siderable evidence that CIO-affiliated unions often fully participated in the replication of those practices. Unions whose racial policies were more sim-ilar to the UPWA's generally were expelled from the CIO.[5]

The UPWA's civil rights initiatives took place in a hostile environment in which racism and racial segregation remained commonplace. The union could not displace racist attitudes generated by forces outside its plants, but it could and did build on the material necessity for an inter-racial alliance among workers to provide an alternative set of values that stressed the essential equality of all races. "This community of our union," Ralph Helstein told a race relations institute in 1949, has "established folk-ways and mores and customs and methods of life that perhaps do not conform to the normal pattern existing in this country today." He emphasized that the union was committed to these "customs" because they are "absolutely essential in terms of the betterment of the membership of our organization." The UPWA ethos of racial equality certainly had a moral component, but its effect on the attitudes and practice of white workers grew out of the tangible necessity for inter-racial cooperation if labor were to exercise power in the meatpacking industry. Because the UPWA remained a majority white organization, its civil rights program could not have advanced without white support. The UPWA's achievement, in the 1950s, was to move beyond an inter-racial alliance that treated blacks and whites as equals to one that challenged the racist norms of American society.[6]

Aggressive civil rights activity rested on a firm foundation of shop-floor unionism. The strong steward system and use of semilegal job actions allowed it to engage in considerable shop-floor bargaining over the pace and organization of work. A strong union apparatus that incorporated both black and white also provided a common nexus for inter-racial activity and experience that was generally absent from American society during the 1950s. Exercise of shop-floor power usually was defensive in nature, in the sense Michael Mann defined, "to attain a measure of creativity and control within the given work process."[7] In the 1950s, however, the union turned its entrenched defensive power into an offensive weapon that secured additional concessions from the packing firms and altered the traditional racial division of labor.

Mobilizations against racism in turn encouraged women inside the union to organize. The unequal treatment of women, especially the male-female wage differential, could not be ignored in the context of anti-discrimination activity designed to address racist patterns. Moreover, black women who mobilized around issues of race were acutely aware of their gender interests and used the sympathy of black male unionists and existing women's networks to place demands on the UPWA. Although the union never responded as dynamically to women's concerns as it did to racial issues, it nonetheless provided a vehicle for women to organize among themselves, to secure material advances, and to generate a proto-feminist awareness of the deep gender distinctions in society.

There were distinct limits to the UPWA's social unionism after World War II. The internal democracy and local union autonomy so critical to success also acted as a brake on national policies that conflicted with the sentiments of large segments of the membership. In the North, predominantly white locals often were only grudging supporters of the anti-discrimination campaign. In the South, some union leaders opposed implementation of the anti-discrimination program and sought to disaffiliate from the international union when strongly pressed to do so. The tension between union democracy and social unionism was a particular problem for women when they advocated policies that conflicted with long-standing masculine assumptions embedded in union traditions. Although they had strong union support for elimination of the differential between wages for males and females, women's efforts to alter the sexual division of labor inside meatpacking plants encountered considerable resistance from men. Such tensions were unavoidable. Without the opportunity for the rank and file to influence their union, the UPWA would not have remained a dynamic and progressive labor organization.

Chains, the Shop Floor, and the UPWA's New "Militant Minority"

The 1948 strike finally broke the resistance of packing firms to the UPWA. "We learned one thing out of the strike," recalled Eddie Humphrey. "If you bloody a guy's nose good enough and let him know you been in a fight, he don't want to bother you no more." Although conflict continued over wage costs and control of production, it devolved into a guerrilla war of position and maneuver at the bargaining table and on the shop floor. Only a short strike in 1956 against Swift disrupted what could appear superficially as a decade of labor "peace." Yet workers from all major packing centers recall endemic conflict on the shop floor. Periodic eruptions produce records that document the peak flashpoints of shop-floor bargaining.[8]

It remained far more difficult for meat producers to pass higher labor costs on to consumers than in the nation's metal-based industries. Meatpacking became increasingly competitive in the 1950s as the Big Four firms steadily lost market share, and labor costs remained one of the few variables nominally under management's control. "Material costs, to quite an extent, are governed by market conditions," one company president reminded an industry conference in 1948. He urged packing executives "to find some method of bringing our rate structure into line" and counteract "the growing tendency toward a reduction in output of the individual worker in our plants." After Wilson's surrender in 1950 ended resistance to pattern bargaining, company efforts concentrated on lowering labor costs and increasing productivity through manipulation of the wage structure and incremental changes in the production process.[9]

Union objectives directly clashed with company strategies. The UPWA worked assiduously to take wages out of competition by eliminating contractual wage differentials and standardizing work loads and job rates. At the bargaining table, the UPWA sought to eliminate the geographic differentials that allowed some southern workers to earn 40 percent less than northern workers under the same contract. Through the grievance procedure, the wage rate department, and the steward system the UPWA closely regulated changes in job content or volume that could imbalance the wage structure. Union pressure in contract negotiations and on the shop floor was designed to increase the share of the industry's earnings that went to employees.

Efforts to equalize wage costs reinforced the UPWA's social unionism. Its commitment to ending wage differentials made it receptive to pressure from female members to eliminate the gap between the base wage of men and women. Its efforts to raise southern wages to the level of northern cities bolstered the union's inter-racial alliance; white Birmingham packinghouse workers, for example, secured handsome pay increases because of the support of black union members in Chicago. In this manner the pragmatic economic strategy of the union helped create space for the initiatives of blacks and women in the organization.

The organizational nexus for exercise of the union's shop-floor power was the webs of shop steward organizations connected into "chains" of local unions in the same plants of national firms. The chains served as means to link day-to-day defensive activity of stewards with the periodic offensives of the union at the bargaining table, and provided a palpable connection between rank-and-file workers and the union apparatus. Although there is no evidence of by-laws or constitutional definition of the powers of chains, their authority over relations with their respective firms was not questioned by any union leader or faction.

Chains actually predated the UPWA, and as master agreements became the dominant factor setting wages and working conditions they became very powerful within the union. Chains originated during the late 1930s from efforts by local unions, especially in Armour and Cudahy plants, to control negotiations with their firms. Packinghouse workers insisted, "We're going to run our own show," recalled Herb March. "And so we projected the idea of chain conferences." The self-governing nature of the chains resulted in the first representative national body in the PWOC, the 1942 Policy Committee, being constituted from representatives of chains rather than geographic ar-

eas. The ad-hoc union committees that oversaw the War Labor Board negotiations, as well as the 1946 and 1948 National Strike Strategy Committees,
were composed of chain representatives. The union institutionalized their
power during the 1950s by holding biannual wage and contract conferences at which chains prepared for the upcoming negotiations. The powerful
chain organizations mitigated against the potential for national contracts to
stifle the autonomy and power of local unions.[10]

Composed and controlled by local union leaders who usually still
worked in their plant, chains provided a particularly important cohesive
element that held the UPWA's disparate locals together. "When you make
one big chain organized, then you got somebody behind you on the other
end," explained Cedar Rapids steward Frank Hlavacek. "You ain't alone."
The regular contacts among local union leaders ensured that political differences did not obscure their common economic interests. Right-wing Cedar
Rapids leaders worked with Chicago leftists Sam Parks, Carl Nelson, and
Charles Hayes in the Wilson chain, just as Omaha anticommunist Nels Peterson met with Communists Leon Beverly and Sam Curry from Chicago's
Armour local. Delegates at chain meetings also established personal bonds
that facilitated regular communication and solidarity among locals. "Out of
those negotiations you got some pretty good friendships," recalled Swift
leader William Nolan. Although local union representatives often squabbled
among themselves, they respected the will of the majority. "When we took
a vote, if you lost, you kept your mouth shut and went along," recalled
Emerson Dappen from Omaha Armour. "It was all done in a democratic
process."[11]

The chains provided a means for local unionists to participate actively
in the formulation of contract demands and the negotiating process. Between
1953 and 1955 the chains in the Big Four firms met thirty-one times. Typically, local unions collected desired contract improvements from their mem-
berships and brought these to biannual conferences that distilled the demands into broad national objectives. Chain meetings then set the agenda
and priorities for their particular firm before opening negotiations. Local
union representatives participated in the national negotiations and convened
another chain meeting to vote on a contract before submitting it to a referendum vote of the membership. Although UPWA officials Helstein and Prosten generally were the primary union spokesmen, the presence of between
forty and one hundred local leaders during negotiations was not merely
window-dressing. "We all participated," recalled Cudahy leader Henry Giannini, a long-time critic of the union leadership.[12]

Local union representatives made their presence felt as the company started to yield on a few issues but resisted on others. The UPWA delegation frequently recessed to discuss company counterproposals and would vote whether to accept them or press for more. "We'd have a knock down, drag out fight . . . whether we were going to take it or what we were going to do," remembered Dappen. In one case, Swift locals debated among themselves whether to make one last effort to further reduce the southern wage differential. "Omaha and St. Paul said no way," recalled Loren Callender, a Sioux City Swift leader. The Sioux City local then lined up support from three smaller Swift plants and outvoted the two big locals. The delegation went back into negotiations and won its demands.[13]

The participatory character of chains made them a particular powerful vehicle for standardizing wage rates. The effort had two dimensions: ending industrywide geographic and female differentials and standardizing rates for the same job performed in many plants. During negotiations, women, southern union members, and representatives of plants suffering from wage inequalities pressured union negotiators to demand that companies eliminate differentials. "They stood their ground, that our people are just as skilled, what they produce, we get the same price for, and they pay the same dues," recalled L. C. Williams, a Fort Worth Armour worker. Beginning with the 1949 contracts and continuing throughout the 1950s, the UPWA secured special increases for women and for workers in southern and rural plants in order to establish a single national base wage. The UPWA's wage rate department coordinated the far more complex problem of standardizing pay rates for individual jobs by methodically collating wage and job load data supplied by local unions. In contract talks local unions and the wage rate department's staff person would use this detailed information to secure raises for individual jobs in plants that were below the standard level. In both cases, chains served as the UPWA's organizational junction between the shop floor, local unions, and the national organization and made negotiations a conduit for often-complex pressures from the rank and file.[14]

The local unions on which the chains rested continued throughout the 1950s to engage in considerable shop-floor bargaining outside of the nominal collective bargaining process. As in the 1930s and 1940s the union sought not only to increase wages and benefits but also to exercise control over the front-line relationship between workers and supervisors. Sam Davis, a Sioux City hog-shackler and steward, observed that if "you don't do it like that, you ain't got a union," a reflection of the UPWA cadre's consensus their labor organization needed to do more than simply engage in collective bargaining to maintain rank-and-file loyalty. The union also had to have the means to restrict the power of supervisors, who "can't give you a penny in wage increases," as Todd Tate pointed out, but still could "mess you around" and make life miserable on the job. Control over work remained as strong a union objective as it had been in the organizing era.[15]

Chains reinforced the shop-floor power of local unions by creating regular lines of communication that could be tapped to support each other in conflicts with management. The relatively small Swift locals in Sioux City, Des Moines, Evansville, and Denver, for example, stayed in close contact. "If one of us got into trouble," recalled Loren Callender, "a phone call went out to those four locals and we could feel within an hour or two they had met with their local management and if they hadn't got a satisfactory answer, they were on the street all at the same time." The Swift chain was not at all unusual. When the Oklahoma City Armour management fired the local union's Grievance Committee, word spread rapidly through the chain. Within a few hours, other Armour local union leaders had met with management in their plants and threatened to strike unless the Oklahoma City workers were rehired. The demands secured reinstatement of the discharged union leaders.[16]

Preservation and reproduction of the departmental steward system provided the core of the UPWA's shop-floor infrastructure. "We want our stewards to act as the arteries of our membership," St. Joseph union member Rosalie Widman explained to a District 4 conference in 1950. "If Department Stewards are acquainted with the Local's activities and policies they will be able to cultivate interest and understanding of our members in the plants." Union policy was to maintain one steward for every ten members, and most local unions were able to have at least one for every twenty or twenty-five workers. The union's objective was to have a representative in every department so the labor organization could influence day-to-day conditions. In the years immediately after the 1948 strike, many workers took their first step toward greater union activity by taking over from older workers who often were union founders. "It was still kind of a popular thing," recalled George Fletemeyer. "A guy could get a little recognition being a steward." Stewards in turn used workplace meetings in dressing rooms to involve the entire department in discussions over a company practice or plans to respond to a particular problem. A departmental steward organization thus allowed a local union to establish a viable relationship with rank-and-file packinghouse workers who might never attend a union meeting.[17]

Union classes trained stewards in the history of unionism in meatpacking, the structure and characteristics of the industry, the union's anti-discrimination program, its contract provisions, and its grievance procedure. Originally designed by Svend Godfredson, UPWA courses combined information on industrial relations with history to give stewards a broader sense of their role. A sheep-kill steward, who was black, praised Godfredson's training session for teaching him that "I'm not just a steward of the people who have problems on the sheep kill, but I am the guardian and steward of all the rights workers have won." The program continued under Godfredson's successor Louie Krainock, trained at Highlander Folk School, and then by Myles Horton, Highlander founder. In 1951 alone, more than 1,300 stewards and union officers attended union training sessions. A stewards' bulletin, started that year, had an internal circulation of five thousand. After Horton's departure in 1953, a program department headed by Richard Durham continued the union's leadership training program.[18]

A tightly organized steward structure allowed the union to use the grievance procedure in conjunction with job actions to influence the content and pace of work. While UPWA locals would resort to job actions, they generally preferred to use the grievance procedure. When companies repeatedly violated union rights and abused the grievance procedure, however, local unions showed little reluctance to employ slowdowns and stoppages. "It was a weapon that we had and we could use," recalled an Omaha union leader. In this sense, most job actions were for the purpose of ensuring that the grievance procedure worked to the advantage of the union, rather than the company, by allowing workers to regulate shop-floor conditions without having to resort to direct action on a regular basis.[19]

Job actions usually erupted, as one local union leader recalled, when "we couldn't get something straightened out." A front-line supervisor might alter established work patterns, sparking a slew of grievances, or a company superintendent would resist resolving shop-floor disputes at the lower levels of the grievance procedure. "That's when you run into these slowdowns and stoppages," recalled Fletemeyer, president of Omaha's Swift local, "because they finally get the opinion that that's the only thing that's going to move some of these people off their dead end." Disagreements over work loads and job standards provoked most job actions, with a significant number also arising from workers' efforts to enforce seniority and reverse disciplinary measures. Callender, a chief steward, said that in the Sioux City Swift plant, if "we weren't getting our grievances settled, the message got out, 'Hey, slow it up a little bit, let's see if we can't get some of these things resolved.' Or we'd walk in and say, 'You've got till noon to get another meeting set up with us, or there won't be any work this afternoon.'" A flagrant discharge, though, would often arouse an immediate response in strong locals. "The hell with that," recalled Dappen. "We ain't going through no damn grievance procedure."[20]

Taft-Hartley, which required prior notice of strikes, and the contractual restrictions on job actions forced local unions to organize stoppages covertly. "Our main whip was to catch them with their pants down," recalled Sam Davis, "they can get ready for you when you let 'em know what you're going to do." The techniques that local unions developed for organizing illegal job actions protected officials from retaliation. "You had to make sure that when you did, that the people said, 'Hey, it was not the action of our leaders in the plant, it's our action,'" recalled Loren Callender. In many plants union leaders used nonverbal signs, such as tipping their caps a certain way or crossing their arms while walking through the plant, to let stewards know that "spontaneous" job actions were in order. "You weren't supposed to do that under the contract," explained Emerson Dappen. "If I came in the morning and decide that something is really wrong, all I'd do is lay my hat on the boning table and the whole damn department stop." In one of many examples of these staged "unsanctioned" job actions, the local union at G. H. Hammond in Chicago held a plantwide stoppage to halt pressure on older workers by one supervisor. At a union meeting to plan the action, the local president reminded members, "I'll be there and I'm going to tell you to go back to work—but you better not!" Through such astute tactics UPWA locals regularly employed strong shop-floor structures to circumvent the postwar restraints on direct action.[21]

Work stoppages and slowdowns generally emerged out of a process of negotiation between individual work groups and the local union. Union officials had to be careful in evaluating the extent to which an aggrieved department could or should receive support from workers elsewhere in the plant. In the best instances, "We got it from the rank and file," recalled Kansas City Armour steward Nevada Isom. "If the rank and file wanted to slow down, they would have to prove it, and we would back them up." If the union moved too sluggishly, stewards might initiate actions on their own, leaving officers little choice but to support them. There were cases where "the members just resisted and they rejected some things that the company would put on them," Addie Wyatt remembered. "If the leadership didn't move fast enough, you'd find the workers out in front of you." Similar to the dynamics of World War II stoppages, union leaders generally reacted to department job actions by pressuring management to settle grievances rather than repressing the initiative of the rank and file. "They had their own department," explained James Samuel, a Chicago Armour steward. "They had to do what they had to do."[22]

Enforcing union power at the point of production made the packing companies accept widespread informal shop-floor bargaining. Workers justified their actions by claiming they were simply enforcing rights guaranteed by the contract and refusing "to be disrespected." In fact, UPWA contracts only gave the union authority over job loads and not the organization or pace of work. Workers interpreted their rights broadly and asserted that an increase in a job's production standard, a reduction in the number of employees in a work area, or an increase in the pace of production constituted a change in job load. Union strength on the plant floor allowed packinghouse workers to expand the formally constituted "rule of law" in their workplaces beyond rights actually encoded in their contracts.[23]

The killing floors, the centerpiece of union power and the key department in the plant, exercised the most control over the production process. Stewards in Chicago's Armour plant used a stopwatch to regulate the pace of the hog kill. In St. Paul, Armour killing-floor workers deliberately allowed their knives to go dull if management ignored the union steward who regulated the speed of the killing process. In Cedar Rapids, workers sabotaged machinery when the company placed locks on the mechanism to prevent stewards from controlling the speed of the continuous chain. Sam Davis used his critical position as a hog-shackler to control the pace of slaughtering at Sioux City Armour. "They knew better than to yack-yack with us," he explained. If supervisors unduly pressed the hog-kill gang, he would slow down and warn, "I'm not going to catch no hogs till you get that straight back there." As the source of product for the entire plant, union regulation of the killing floor's tempo produced daily conflicts with management.[24]

The killing floors represented the apogee of workers' shop-floor power. At the other end of the scale were departments in which incentive payment systems stimulated rivalry rather than solidarity, such as in the largely female pork trim and sliced bacon areas. Workers on individual piece rates might resist job actions because of the effect on their pay, and ignore contractual lunch and rest breaks in order to make more money. Slowdowns were the most common form of job action, but even then the union had to gauge carefully whether it had sufficient support among pieceworkers. While the extent of a local union's shop-floor authority ranged between these extremes, the killing floors remained the critical link because they provided meat for the entire plant.[25]

The international union supported, encouraged, and relied upon the capacity of local unions to engage in job actions. In one case, the international praised Chicago Armour hog-kill workers who struck in July 1949 when company officials refused to discuss an increase in chain speed. An internal union newsletter approvingly noted, "Other departments at the Chicago plant got the 'bug' about fighting speedup and some adjustments were made." A few years later, *The Blade,* District 3's publication, favorably reported that gut-pullers in the Mason City Armour plant walked out when the company increased the production standard. The dispute ended favorably for the union when the company placed another worker in the department.[26]

Clause 95E in the Armour master agreement complemented widespread semilegal shop-floor bargaining by allowing the union to initiate local job actions. The contract provision excluded job loads from arbitration and permitted work stoppages following a twenty-four-hour notice. In 1951 the international gave wide publicity to repeated strikes over job loads by the freezer gang in the St. Joseph Armour plant. At issue were loads on the hand trucks used to move meat—as high as 1,100 pounds on the two-wheel carts and 1,700 pounds on four-wheel vehicles. "The company wanted as much as they could get on the gondolas without it falling on the floor," recalled departmental steward Buford Thompson. The union wanted to reduce the loads by a third, both to make the work more humane and protect employment levels. Management's resistance to settling the dispute led to several "unofficial" strikes and then three stoppages under clause 95E. Local 58 finally settled the dispute on its terms when the entire plant walked out for three days in May. Delegates to the UPWA's 1951 wage and contract conference applauded the local's action, and the union highlighted its successful struggle in District 4's newsletter and the UPWA national stewards' bulletin.[27]

The strength of local unions and the cohesion of the chains allowed the UPWA to develop a new tactic to pressure packing firms during contract talks—the "stop and go" strike. Rather than employ a national stoppage, the UPWA relied on the strength of its local unions, usually in the Cudahy and Armour chains, to orchestrate rolling, "spontaneous" strikes in different plants of the same firm during negotiations. Probably devised by Herb March, stop and go strikes entailed a series of short departmental walkouts in one plant complemented by simultaneous stoppages in other cities. The strikes exerted financial pressures on management by making it hard for the companies "to plan production," while workers were able to draw their full paychecks. In this manner, the UPWA turned the defensive shop-floor bargaining of its strong unions into an effective offensive weapon that minimized economic pressures on members.[28]

The nominally spontaneous stop and go strikes doubtless were coordinated and initiated by the international union to overcome company resistance at the bargaining table. Local union representatives on the chain negotiating teams, hoping to "jar the company loose," would contact their union and instruct it to begin job actions. In Kansas City, for example, the officers of the Armour local would call in "stewards from every department, and tell them what the negotiating committee had told them, and go back in there and tell them people what to do, and don't do no more and no less." In Omaha, Armour union leaders would stand outside the plant gate and nod to particular groups of workers to indicate it was their turn "to turn the heat up" on the company. One day stoppages would leave livestock sitting overnight; if management tried to compensate by reducing its purchases, the union would work several days without a job action, forcing the company to release workers early while having to pay them a full week's guaranteed pay. In January 1952, Chicago Local 347 alone pulled twenty departmental strikes to support the union's demands for a 6 cent raise.[29]

The UPWA's tactics in the 1952 contract negotiations made full use of the shop-floor pressure it could apply through the nexus of chains and shop steward organizations. Talks deadlocked in the summer when Armour made settlement of other issues "contingent upon the elimination" of clause 95E from the contract. The company's refusal to bargain stalled negotiations with other firms because the UPWA advised Armour that 95E "was not on sale for any price." Rather than extend the contract after the August 11 expiration date, the union allowed the agreement to lapse and instituted its own work rules at Armour and Cudahy plants. Local unions refused to perform any overtime or Saturday work (except in the power and refrigeration areas), held incentive pay jobs down to the minimum standard, and "set their own job loads based on the principle of a fair day's work." In addition to the highly publicized slowdown, local unions employed stop and go strikes and followed a secret policy of refusing to work with nonunion employees.[30]

Time was on the side of the union. "October is here—the hogs are coming," reported the organization department after several weeks of union pressure. "Company offers are getting better. BUT, THEY STILL AREN'T GOOD ENOUGH!" With the fall hog rush in full stride, packing companies tried to counterattack. Several plants locked out their workers, and Armour ceased deducting dues from workers' paychecks. Such measures proved counterproductive. At Armour, making stewards collect dues reinforced links between the union apparatus and thousands of workers engaged in the job actions; in fact, per capita receipts rose 18 percent in September over the previous month. Moreover, closing plants was precisely what the companies could not afford, with hogs flooding the stockyards. After shutting the St. Joseph plant for several days, local management verbally accepted the union work rules "and asked only that they be notified in advance if any new additional rules were added to the list."[31]

Company resistance crumbled in mid-October. On October 18, Cudahy accepted the union's terms, and Armour capitulated ten days later. The outstanding economic advances of the contracts were a pension plan and overtime pay on Saturday, regardless of total hours worked in a week. The union retained clause 95E, won a commitment by the company to supply job load information, and secured a September 1 expiration date, better for the union because it was closer to the hog rush. In addition to a general 4 cent raise, the two-year contract included wage reopeners every six months and significant correction of geographic differentials and inter-plant inequalities, and it cut the female differential from 9 to 5 cents. The UPWA justly claimed that it was "the biggest package since 1946." It also was a resounding victory for the UPWA's mutually reinforcing structures of industrywide chains and shop-floor steward organizations.[32]

The 1952 negotiations also illustrate how union structures could serve as a conduit for black influence. As a result of rank-and-file pressure from black workers, union negotiators secured agreements from Armour and Cudahy to remove all signs enforcing racial segregation in their southern plants. During the Armour chain meetings that set negotiating priorities Fort Worth representative L. C. Williams urged northern packinghouse workers to use the upcoming contract talks to end segregation in southern plants. After a District 1 conference endorsed Williams's strategy, Chicago Armour delegates Herb March and Sam Curry successfully amended the bargaining platform submitted by the International Executive Board to the UPWA's 1952 convention to include the desegregation plank. Local union representatives on bargaining committees ensured that the demand stayed on the table during the heated fall 1952 negotiations until the packing companies acquiesced.[33]

The union's shop-floor structures and struggles produced a new generation of union cadres during the 1950s. Although only a small minority were political radicals, they shared the commitment of the older generation of union activists to unions as an instrument that could uplift and protect "the working class of people." The St. Joseph freezer stoppage, for example, was lead by black workers Buford Thompson and Bill Webster, who had found employment at Armour after World War II. Webster was a World War II veteran and son of a floorsman who worked at St. Joseph's Swift plant. Hired in 1947, he was drawn into union activity after serving on the picket line during the 1948 strike. An active rank-and-file participant in the 1951 freezer department stoppages, Webster was one of many younger workers who found the UPWA's shop-floor unionism compatible with their own desire for equality, justice, and better working conditions. Later a union officer in the 1960s and 1970s, like many UPWA members Webster retained a strong belief in unionism. "Without it I think that they would almost still be in the dark ages," he ruminated in 1986. "It's the only lobby that working people have."[34]

Webster's story easily could be multiplied, varying only in details. Virginia Houston and Nevada Isom at the Kansas City Armour plant, Loren Callender in Sioux City, Addie Wyatt and Charles Hayes in Chicago, Charles Pearson and Charles Mueller in Waterloo, Betty Watson and Max Graham in Omaha—these workers, black and white, composed the generation of union activists upon whom the union relied to carry on the militancy of the 1930s in the changed circumstances of postwar America. And for many, the UPWA provided a unique opportunity to organize against racial and sexual discrimination.[35]

The Advance of Social Unionism in the 1950s

The channels for rank-and-file influence in the UPWA led to an acceleration of the organization's social unionism. The new union militants rose out of their departments to become stewards, officers, and members of important union committees. They pressed their concerns inside chain meetings, at UPWA conventions, and the biennial wage and contract conferences that set negotiating priorities. Beginning in 1953, the union attached anti-discrimination and women's conferences to the contract meetings. These sessions, attended by hundreds of UPWA members, allowed rank-and-file leaders to raise their priorities and forge links with like-minded activists in other UPWA plants. As participants in critical contract sessions, blacks and women on the chain negotiating committees watched carefully that their particular interests were not sacrificed during the last frantic hours of all-night bargaining sessions. The institution of union democracy, which had survived the difficult postwar years, now expanded to allow union members to make a strong imprint on their organization's objectives.

The UPWA's social unionism was in turn reinforced by sympathetic national leaders such as Ralph Helstein who believed that unions should be part of a broad progressive movement for social reform. In 1953 the International Executive Board urged UPWA members to engage in a "continuous participation in the broad range of community affairs, such as fights for rent control, anti-discrimination, charitable drives, etc. The union must become identified in the minds of the community as an outspoken, vital force." These general directives influenced the priorities of union staff and elected officials who, as Chicago Armour steward Todd Tate recalled, made a concerted effort "to educate the membership and involve them in activities which were designed to bring about a greater level of consciousness." Advocates of social unionism in local areas found they could use the international union's bureaucracy to pressure their unions to oppose discrimination in their plant and community. "If you hadn't something going on, they'd call the roll on your ass," recalled Jimmy Porter, a black activist about Waterloo. "This was *mandated*, it wasn't something that just passed, and your district director was going to have to account for what you've done." Although access to the halls of power was an asset to the union's anti-discrimination activists, it also would in time produce resentment by local unions suspicious of the international union's meddling in local affairs.[36]

The UPWA's expanded anti-discrimination program was forged in the immediate aftermath of the 1948 strike. Previously, the union had made few advances beyond simply the principles of egalitarian treatment of black union members. As an organization, the UPWA consistently spoke out against lynching, race riots, and other forms of anti-black intolerance. But aside from scattered local initiatives, local unions generally did not alter the existing racial division of labor within the packinghouses or patterns of discrimination in adjacent communities.[37]

In an effort to hold the union together in the wake of the 1948 strike, Ralph Helstein asked John Hope II of Fisk University to conduct a race relations survey of the organization. Helstein's motivation was straightforward: "I felt there had to be something affirmative going on outside of an area in which the companies could screw us." The surveys graphically depicted the extent and limits of the UPWA's inter-racial coalition. On the positive side, they confirmed high levels of black union participation: Blacks were stewards in 83 percent of UPWA locals and held executive board positions in 73 percent. There were alarming signs of racial prejudice and segregation, however. More than 30 percent of white members objected to working with a black in the same job classification, and 90 percent of southern whites supported segregated eating facilities. Whites filled 96 percent of the Bureau of Labor Statistics' forty-four meatpacking job categories, whereas blacks were present in only 54 percent. In many cases, blacks and whites dressed in separate locker rooms; in the South, they used separate drinking fountains, lunch rooms, and other facilities in accordance with prevalent Jim Crow laws.[38]

On the basis of these findings, the UPWA's 1950 convention adopted a comprehensive anti-discrimination program and established an anti-discrimination department, headed by Vice-President Russell Lasley. The union also made a significant decision to alter and strictly enforce a nondiscrimination clause that had appeared in all UPWA contracts since 1941. Instead of simply prohibiting discrimination against employees, the international demanded that the packing firms add the word *applicant*. Potentially, this gave the union the power to halt hiring discrimination against blacks.[39]

Although the international union apparatus provided a lever for anti-discrimination activity, the independent initiatives of local unions determined the extent to which the UPWA's programs were put into practice. "It was up to the local people to say, 'this is what's hurting me here,'" explained Anna Mae Weems, a dynamic black leader of Waterloo, Iowa's packinghouse workers. In this respect the union's expanded anti-discrimination program relied on and reinforced the "oppositional infrastructure" of local unions. In areas such as Kansas City, efforts to apply the anti-discrimination program revealed weaknesses in local shop-floor structures and led to concerted efforts to rebuild the steward system. In locals with a white majority, international policies provided considerable leverage for black activists to use the union apparatus for civil rights activity.[40]

If the international's programs provided the lever, Chicago packinghouse locals were the fulcrum for expanded civil rights activity by local unions elsewhere. The black majority unions at the huge Armour, Swift, and Wilson plants, employing more than ten thousand workers, were the keystone to the UPWA's industrial power. White UPWA members probably winced at Sam Parks's aggressive "super-militancy" and Herb March's open Communist views, but the union's ability to secure national contracts unquestionably rested on the strength of the Chicago locals. By engaging in a wide range of anti-discrimination activities, Chicago locals established the precedent for, and directly encouraged, civil rights initiatives in other cities.

The UPWA's expanded anti-discrimination program had three broad areas. First, unionists identified discriminatory practices in their own plants and tried to correct them. This included integrating lily-white departments and dressing rooms and ending hiring discrimination against black women. Second, locals attacked discriminatory practices in their communities, primarily restrictions on black access to bars, restaurants, and public facilities and also employment restrictions by local businesses. Finally, packinghouse workers consciously worked with and influenced community-based organizations, especially the NAACP.

Within their plants, local unions began a concerted campaign to integrate all-white departments by encouraging blacks to use the seniority provisions in UPWA contracts. White opposition proved particularly strong among male workers in the mechanical division and women in the sliced bacon department. Local union leaders generally informed reluctant white workers to "either work with them or you find another job," recalled Nevada Isom. "That was spelled out to them and they cooperated very nicely." In Fort

Worth, white women in sliced bacon stopped work to prevent black women from entering the department. Local union president Mary Salinas bluntly informed them that "they were going back to work and accept it as it was, and if they weren't satisfied they could just quit." Hog-kill workers struck in the Kansas City Wilson, Chicago Wilson, and Waterloo Rath plants to secure management's cooperation with the union's effort. Union victories were truly impressive. Within five years black men and women broke through deeply entrenched racial barriers in dozens of plants.[41]

Closely linked with departmental integration were union efforts to use the "applicant" contract provision to end hiring discrimination against black women. Chicago's majority black locals were the first to use this clause. In 1950 the Swift union arranged for both black and white women to apply for jobs and carefully monitored the employment office to determine the company's response to the applicants. While white women were courteously ushered into a back room, interviewed, and then hired, company officials brusquely turned black women away with the excuse that there were no openings. The local filed a grievance against Swift and won a landmark ruling requiring the company to hire the black women with back pay from the date they had initially applied. The international union widely publicized the Chicago victory and pressed other local unions to follow a similar strategy. In a historic advance for black women's employment opportunities, the union forced dozens of plants in all major packing centers to follow Chicago Swift's example. As with plant desegregation, it took local initiatives to translate international policies into practice.[42]

The campaigns of UPWA locals against discrimination by packinghouse companies encouraged an impressive level of community civil rights activity. Indeed, prior organizing experience of recently hired black women such as Rowena Moore in Omaha, Anna Mae Weems in Waterloo, and Addie Wyatt in Chicago provided natural leaders for these efforts. Union members targeted problems that had long angered blacks and remained prevalent in the 1950s: housing segregation, refusal of businesses to serve or employ blacks, and restrictions against black access to schools and recreation. Most of these union-initiated civil rights drives predated the Montgomery bus boycott.[43]

Chicago UPWA members mobilized repeatedly during the late 1940s and early 1950s to support the right of blacks to live in new neighborhoods and public housing projects. When thousands of whites rioted to protest black families moving into the Trumball Park Homes, UPWA members went door to door in the project, telling blacks that the union would support their right to live there and encouraging whites to accept their new neighbors. Through its steward system, the union brought black and white union members to picket city hall and demand that the Chicago Housing Authority accept black tenants at Trumball Park. Protests organized by the UPWA and other organizations in the mid-1950s helped to prevent racist forces from driving black families out of the housing project.[44]

Simultaneously, Chicago UPWA activists carried on a campaign against discrimination by South Side businesses that relied on black purchasing power but would not hire them. "We were reaching the point now where you're not going to continue to take our money if you're going to treat us this way," recalled Charles Hayes. Sam Parks and Hayes sat in at a Goldblatt's Department Store near the stockyards, where black UPWA members could purchase merchandise but not be served food or employed outside of janitorial positions. There was a fiery confrontation when packinghouse workers remained seated at the lunch counter after being refused service. "Sam raised so much hell I think the walls were vibrating," recalled Hayes. Once Goldblatt's and the Drexel Bank acceded to union demands, other South Side businesses soon fell into line.[45]

Chicago was not the only UPWA center to fight racism in the community. In Kansas City, packinghouse workers participated in a broad groundswell of opposition to Jim Crow customs. They fought to end segregation in swimming pools, municipal parks, schools, and public accommodations and to terminate employment discrimination by retail businesses. Interracial delegations of packinghouse workers organized by Marian Simmons, a UPWA official, pressured stores along Minnesota Avenue—the main shopping street in Kansas City, Kansas—to serve and employ blacks. In the late 1950s UPWA members supported consumer boycotts and participated in daily picket lines against discrimination by Kansas City, Missouri, department stores. By the early 1960s, civil rights protests had opened employment and access to many heretofore segregated Kansas City services and businesses.[46]

In Waterloo, Iowa, packinghouse workers launched an impressive assault on patterns of community racism. They mounted a systematic campaign to end restaurant discrimination against blacks by planting white and black members in the same establishment and then suing owners who refused to serve blacks. Packinghouse workers also picketed and organized boycotts of department stores that refused to hire blacks. "If they didn't hire no blacks, then we didn't buy," recalled Robert Burt, a union founder. In the small town of Waterloo, Local 46 successfully altered the very fabric of community race relations.[47]

Anti-discrimination activism by UPWA members spilled over to and influenced other civil rights groups, especially the NAACP. Union aggressiveness intersected with the efforts of NAACP Labor Secretary Herbert Hill to increase working-class membership in the middle-class-dominated organization. "When we got active, the NAACP was called a 'tea sipping' organization, silk-stocking," reflected Todd Tate. With the cooperation of international UPWA leaders, local union stewards recruited thousands of UPWA members to the NAACP. In Chicago, Omaha, and Waterloo, packinghouse workers took over local chapters that black professionals had previously controlled.[48]

In areas with overwhelmingly white social composition and relatively weak black leadership, the anti-discrimination program had far less impact. Without pressure from black members, white union leaders rarely challenged the traditional racial division of labor inside packinghouses or engaged in community civil rights activity. In Sioux City, where the black population had decreased after World War II, there was little union civil rights activity except for occasional protests against police brutality. Predominantly white St. Paul was another weak spot, aside from the passage of a local Fair Employment Practices Act in 1956. National campaigns, such as ending hiring discrimination against black women, did spill over to Sioux City and St. Paul, but they did so because of legal precedents established elsewhere. The anti-discrimination program never touched the Austin Hormel plant, which remained all white. These shortcomings were the obverse side to the UPWA's impressive successes: Local initiatives, not pressure from the international office, determined the extent of the anti-discrimination program.[49]

The anti-discrimination initiatives depended on the active support of a critical minority of white members and tolerance from the union's white majority. The active participation of white union cadre was indispensable, even though they comprised probably no more than 10 percent of the white membership, usually stewards, officers, or members of union committees. They rendered critical institutional support inside the union, participated in integrated public protests, and provided the bodies for carefully crafted tests of discriminatory practices. Union challenges to employment discrimination, for example, depended on the cooperation of whites who could testify that they obtained jobs denied to blacks. Without this evidence, "All you had to do is say, 'this didn't happen,'" explained Charles Pearson. "We couldn't break the barrier if we went in to break it alone." The progressive racial attitudes of union activists in turn favorably influenced larger numbers of whites to support the anti-discrimination program more passively.[50]

The union's commitment to breaking down segregation inside the plant was designed not only to advance blacks but also to produce more tolerant attitudes among whites by creating an inter-racial environment at the rank-and-file level. Henry Giannini's assertion—"I can't see how anybody can work side by side in a plant and discriminate against somebody"—reflected a pragmatic working-class opposition to racial discrimination and tolerance of racial difference generated by integrated work situations. Betty Watson, a white Omaha leader, employed the same logic when she explained, "We worked together, we did the same work. So why should they be treated any differently?" As a steward at the Kansas City Cudahy plant, Marian Simmons found that integration of the women's departments and dressing rooms reduced racial tensions. "We became friends," she recalled. "We had sort of a family going among the women, the blacks and the whites." There even were cases of whites who initially opposed integration of their department but later elected black stewards and union officials. "They needed me for their grievances," recalled Anna Mae Weems, who became the steward in sliced bacon not long after breaking the color line. "They looked to me as someone to protect their rights." By strengthening the bonds of mutual material interest, UPWA activists believed that workplace integration could change the racial attitudes of whites.[51]

In the South, where integration violated both laws and social customs, the union primarily emphasized shared economic interests. The UPWA's reduction of the gap between northern and southern wages in part reflected a strategy to retain southern whites' allegiance. "When we consider the differential between the average wages of workers in the North and their fellow workers in the South, it is clear how discrimination robs white workers," a 1953 union pamphlet pointed out. "Discrimination lowers the wages, not only of all Negro and all women workers, but it robs all white men, too." Hard numbers supported the UPWA's rhetoric. When the union signed its first national contracts in 1941, the hourly pay of some southern workers was 40 cents compared to a northern rate of 72½ cents—a difference of 44 percent. By 1953 those same southern workers were receiving hourly pay of $1.37, only 8 cents or 5 percent less than northern workers. The union never hesitated to point out that it was support from Chicago's majority black locals that made it possible for southern whites to catch up to the pay of northern blacks.[52]

"I'm not going to say we broke down the social barriers which they had," admitted Ralph Helstein. "But there is no doubt that in terms of the union itself there was a lot of change that took place." Although the union's efforts by no means eliminated deeply entrenched racial attitudes, its material accomplishments provided a powerful incentive for southern whites to tolerate the union's inter-racial creed. The limits to the changes in racial attitudes of white members, accurately summarized by Helstein, should not negate the UPWA's important accomplishment. The union successfully brought large numbers of white workers to support—even if they did not participate in—its civil rights initiatives.[53]

The UPWA's anti-discrimination program represented a significant expansion of social unionism. Rather than simply respond to instances of racism, the union sought to uncover and correct patterns of discrimination in its plants and adjacent communities. The union's shop-floor structures and chain organizations provided conduits for blacks to influence their locals and the international union and persuade white workers to support action against discrimination. Its aggressive polices contrasted starkly with the laxity of mainstream CIO organizations and represented an "opportunity found and kept" by its black members in a manner paralleled, to a far lesser extent, only by industrial unions expelled from the CIO.[54]

The Women's Movement in the Postwar UPWA

The acceleration of the UPWA's anti-discrimination program directly encouraged mobilizations of women throughout the union. Despite significant accomplishments, however, union initiatives on women's issues remained hamstrung by the union's masculinist language and assumptions. Although women composed 20 percent of the packinghouse workforce, many male workers retained the belief that women were temporary wage-earners who were in the labor market for exceptional reasons. The UPWA reinforced these views. "During the war, often more than one member of the packinghouse worker's family took a job," a union leaflet explained in support of its 1946 wage demands. "Now the women are going back into the home and the children are back in school where they belong." The UPWA routinely buttressed its wage demands with income calculations that assumed only one family member worked, even as union leaders repeatedly defended women who entered the labor force because of material needs. While criticizing union members who believed that "women work only for the purpose of being able to buy luxuries," Helstein also proudly broadcast the union's objective to secure the family wage. "We believe firmly in the right of a worker to have assurances of an annual income adequate to meet his needs and the needs of his family," he told the UPWA's 1950 convention. The UPWA's commitment to equal rights for women remained constrained, in a manner dissimilar to its civil rights activism, by deep-seated assumptions among its male members that women should play a subordinate role at home and in society.[55]

The counterbalance to the UPWA's masculinist bias were forms of female solidarity based in networks constituted at work and in the community. The sex-segregated nature of packinghouse work provided an institutional basis for women leaders to emerge out of predominantly female processing departments. Although few women rose to the higher levels of the union, there were many female stewards and members of local union committees, such as the executive board and bargaining committee. Male unionists, while retaining firm control of the organization, encouraged female representation at the departmental level. Male Omaha leaders recruited a young Betty Watson to become a steward, for example, "because so many times a woman does not want to relate her problems to a man." Convention resolutions in 1952 and 1954 affirmed that it was union policy for women to be represented on all union committees, at all conferences and conventions, and among a local's officers.[56]

The contribution of strong union structures to women's participation can be seen particularly clearly at several small Chicago plants. Illinois Meat and other small facilities in the Chicago stockyards had unusually high proportion of women workers because of the pork processing work that dominated the plants. Women's groups regularly met at the union hall to discuss problems at work as well as to socialize and play cards. Leadership training sessions also attracted black women to the union hall, where they learned the union's history and the mechanics of collective bargaining. These strong networks helped black women assume top union offices. Established women leaders in Illinois Meat Local 56 drew a young Addie Wyatt into union activity by bringing her to UPWA women's conferences. "We were inspired by what we heard," she later recalled. Elected Local 56 vice president in 1953, Wyatt assumed the union's presidency a few months later when the incumbent resigned. She subsequently joined the union's staff, where she became a national example of black women's activism in meatpacking.[57]

The Kansas City Armour local also illustrates the power of workplace networks among black women, who were highly active in the local at the departmental level and consistently served on the union's Bargaining Committee and Executive Board. To resolve "some problems just among the women," they caucused on their own and created a formal Women's Committee in 1952. Black women provided an essential source of pickets and political support within the Kansas City UPWA for Marian Simmons and her campaign to eliminate discrimination along Minnesota Avenue.[58]

The women's networks in Chicago and Kansas City were mirrored in other areas of the union and reached a national scale through biennial women's conferences during the 1950s. Women in Austin, Sioux City, Waterloo, Omaha, Fort Worth, and Cudahy, Wisconsin, recalled participating in all-women's groups that discussed union issues and workplace concerns and organized social events. "We would have coffee and we would talk and exchange ideas about what could be done in the plant or what they would like to see put into the next contract," recalled Mary Salinas. "It was a good place for women to get started in union leadership," recalled Lucille Bremer, a president of Waterloo Local 46 in the 1980s. "It's where I started."[59]

National conferences allowed women activists to meet each other, share ideas, and form friendships and political alliances. In addition to facilitating the efforts of women to incorporate their demands into the union's negotiating priorities, the conferences served as a "watch dog over the district officers to push the programs." Firm, long-lasting friendships formed among the women who were struggling for the same objectives. Wyatt formed a close bond with Ruth Haynes, a black sugar worker from Baltimore and other determined women leaders from around the country. "These were the women who inspired me," she recalled, "and encouraged me to take the legacy and run with it and pass it on to the next generation of women." Although men also attended the conferences, de facto women's caucuses reflected the women's space that these events opened. "The cocktail party that is being held this afternoon is on behalf of all the women delegates," President Helstein announced to the 1957 national conference. He pointedly added, "The males, I think, will be conspicuous by their absence."[60]

The most striking reflection of increased women's activism in the 1950s was the rapid end to the historic male-female differential in meatpacking. "WE WANT THAT $8 MILLION!" screamed a headline in District 3's newsletter during the 1952 "squeeze" on the companies. "By paying women 9 cents an hour less than men, the packers have been able to make almost 8 million a year in extra profits for themselves." As the union frequently noted, the lower base rate reduced the entire female wage structure. In 1946 not a single woman in the Sioux City Swift plant made more than 75 cents an hour, whereas a third of the men exceeded that level. Although some women feared they would be replaced with men if they earned the same pay for the same work, the pressure from women's committees and conferences to end the differential ensured that this demand remained on the negotiating table. At the May 1952 convention, female delegates used a resolution on the wage differential to press the union to put its principles into action. "It is very nice to sit here convention after convention and agree with us women, but yet you sit back and don't do a darn thing when you go back into that plant," complained Omaha delegate Gisela Koubsky. "We want action. We don't want words." This pressure no doubt helped chain bargaining committees be more resolute when they pressed the companies to reduce the wage differential in the fall negotiations. The 1952 agreements were the first reductions in the differential, and a schedule of raises secured in 1956 eliminated the gap between the base male and female rates.[61]

Pressure by women also secured provisions in the master agreements to protect pregnant women from job discrimination. Although a few locals had won these clauses in the 1940s as part of local agreements, they became national policies in the 1950s. Women could receive an unpaid leave of absence for as long as a year, and up to eight weeks at half pay while pregnant, under the sick-leave provisions in UPWA contracts. Although not compensating women adequately for pregnancy (and considering it an illness rather than a natural condition), the provisions won wide praise from female union members and helped many by guaranteeing their jobs after a leaving work to have a child.[62]

Relatively low leadership participation by women reflected the limits on their power within the UPWA. Although fairly strong at the shop-floor level, in 1955 only sixty-five women were officers in the union's eighty largest locals, and 80 percent of these held minor positions such as recording secretary. Only one, Mary Salinas in Fort Worth, served as a union president. Just 10 percent of the delegates to the 1954 convention were women, and there were but eight women on the union's seventy-two-person staff. The only district that approached proportional representation was predominantly black District 1.[63]

Barriers to women's participation reflected how a male culture permeated union structures. "A man works from sun up to sun down; a women's work is never done," complained Velma Otterman Schrader, a Waterloo union founder who became inactive in the union during the 1950s after having three children. Despite consistent pressure for child care at union meetings, there is little evidence of measures taken to facilitate participation by mothers. Women active in the union often had to brave an unpleasant, and sometimes hostile, environment. A panel at the 1955 women's conference attributed low women's participation to lack of attention by local unions to "home problems" such as child care, the "sloppy, disorganized, even rowdy" conduct of meetings, and "the gossip and rumors that are often circulated about active union women." Women may have been able to organize within the UPWA and receive support as workers, but the union itself remained a decidedly masculine institution.[64]

The Limits on Social Unionism in the UPWA

The longstanding power and autonomy of local unions and the pressure of women and blacks on the international to implement its social agenda created an inherent tension in the UPWA's social unionism. Reflecting how the UPWA apparatus remained permeable to rank-and-file influences, demands by female and black workers could spur the international union to fight against racial and sexual discrimination. At the same time, local unions that responded sluggishly to the union's accelerated social agenda bitterly resented increasing pressure from the central office. Some local leaders viewed new policies against discrimination as merely an excuse for aspiring bureaucrats to expand their power. Paradoxically, the retention of union democracy created pressures that encouraged the international to reduce local union autonomy. This dynamic also could hinder the UPWA's social unionism, because forcing locals to implement policies they opposed contradicted UPWA traditions and entailed very real dangers of weakening the union by fanning internal dissension.

These complex tensions are apparent in two episodes: conflict over implementation of the union's civil rights agenda in the mid-1950s and tensions over changes in the sexual division of labor in the 1960s. In both cases, black and female union members pressed the international to pursue policies that other packinghouse workers strongly opposed. Southern white workers may have been persuaded of the need for inter-racial unionism, but many balked when black workers used the union's anti-discrimination program to challenge traditional boundaries between black and white. Male workers, willing to have female union members receive the same pay and the same protections as men, objected when women began to call for changes in the traditional distinctions between male and female jobs. These cases illustrate how the mores and customs accepted by the "community of our union" also had clear boundaries.

Open conflict over the union's civil rights program erupted in November 1952 following implementation of the agreement to desegregate plant facilities in the South. The most dramatic revolt occurred in Fort Worth, where a group of racist white workers demanded that management reimpose segregation in the cafeteria and locker rooms. Aided by the aggressive intervention of the international union, a coalition of black, Mexican-American, and white workers remained supportive of plant desegregation and repelled a campaign by an all-white slate to take over union offices in January 1953. The plant remained desegregated, in violation of existing Jim Crow ordinances. Although unsuccessful, the revolt in Fort Worth indicated that many southern white workers had gone along with the union's anti-discrimination program only so long as it did not affect social relations between black and white.[65]

The UPWA did not wait for the opposition to seize the initiative. In May 1953 local unions and UPWA officials filed charges against Adrian McKinney, head of the UPWA's Southeast ninth district, for participating in a union social affair that allegedly excluded blacks. The union's action caused a furor in the labor movement. McKinney's supporters claimed the UPWA was simply using its anti-discrimination policies as an excuse to oust a staunch anticommunist, and a group of southern CIO officials helped McKinney by persuading the CIO to launch an investigation into Communist influence in the UPWA. The struggle ended in a stalemate. A CIO committee absolved the UPWA of charges of Communist influence, and in return the union suspended disciplinary proceedings against McKinney even though evidence strongly suggested that he was guilty of the charges.[66]

While union leaders engaged in diplomacy, turmoil and racial tensions rocked southern UPWA locals in 1953 and 1954. Southern district directors McKinney and A. J. Pittman encouraged a rebellion by southern white members against the international by attributing its integrationist policies to Communist influence. The international union's response to this challenge was telling: It used the union apparatus to encourage southern black workers, generally more supportive of the international than whites, to assume leadership roles.[67]

The rise of George Thomas, a black Fort Worth leader who replaced Pittman as District 8 director at the UPWA's 1954 convention, is a good example of how the union bureaucracy encouraged greater union participation by blacks. The international cultivated Thomas, a highly respected president of his local in the late 1940s, as an alternative to Pittman by placing him on the staff and assigning him to other areas in the Southwest District. All accounts confirm that southern blacks and Mexicans viewed Pittman as an opponent of the union's anti-discrimination principles and openly welcomed a more dynamic leader. Because the district was only 35 percent black, Thomas also had to secure white support to defeat Pittman. Apparently, he did so by showing, though personal contact, his commitment to advance the union in a manner that benefited all races. "It was a time when they forgot the guy's color and looked specifically at his qualifications and what he was able to do for all of us," recalled Fort Worth unionist Frank Wallace.[68]

One of Thomas's main jobs was spurring blacks to become more assertive in their local unions. Encouraging black participation simultaneously advanced the UPWA's anti-discrimination policies and weakened southern white opposition. For example, Thomas worked with other UPWA leaders to encourage blacks to play a stronger role in several large sugar locals in the Mississippi delta. Although black sugar workers formed the overwhelming majority of the membership, a small group of whites dominated the local and supported Pittman inside the UPWA. Thomas's assiduous cultivation of black leadership paid off. At meetings of several locals in December 1953, one Pittman supporter complained that "the Negro members turned out a very high percentage attendance, which was unusual, and therefore outnumbered the white members by 4 and 5 to 1." Not long after these meetings, newly active black members swept the incumbent white officials out of office. Between the 1952 and 1954 UPWA conventions there was a complete change in the delegations of the four largest sugar locals.[69]

Racial tensions in the UPWA peaked just before the 1954 convention. In April, racist white union members disrupted a leadership training school in Moultrie, Georgia. John Henry Hall, a veteran black field representative, was called abusive racist names and forced to leave the premises at knife point.[70]

The Moultrie incident facilitated the defeat of the white opposition at the 1954 convention by identifying racism, rather than communism, as the major problem faced by the union. "I know there are those who feel so strongly on this question that they call our program against discrimination communism," said Helstein in his opening address. "Those within or without our ranks who make this charge do so, I am certain, because they believe in the discriminatory practices of segregation." The incident also made it impossible for northern dissidents to side with their former southern allies, because to do so would open them to charges that they did not support the union's anti-discrimination program. The convention overwhelmingly condemned the Moultrie incident, and delegates from the southern districts removed both McKinney and Pittman. This eliminated the last overt challenge to the anti-discrimination program.[71]

The UPWA paid a price for its decision to side with black workers. White workers initiated disaffiliation efforts in southern packing unions, sugar processing units in the New Orleans area, and all-white stockyards locals. Black workers and UPWA officials tried to retain white support by pointing to the enormous economic gains that a national labor organization had achieved. "We been helped, we've made some real gains by sticking with this union, this international union," L. C. Williams explained to whites in Fort Worth. These were "gains that we could never expect to make if we go independent or decert [decertify]." Such arguments kept losses to a minimum. After a year of conflict, the UPWA lost four all-white stockyards locals, two southern Swift unions, and five small sugar units. Total southern membership fell between two and three thousand. Despite these losses, the UPWA retained its national bargaining power by holding onto four large sugar locals that were part of national firms and most of its southern packing locals.[72]

Defeat of the racist opposition may have been a victory for social unionism, but it also threatened to alter the balance of power in the UPWA between the central administration and the local unions. Centralizing tendencies in the UPWA always had been balanced by the power of local unions and the relatively small size of the union staff. Locals rarely had more than one full-time union official, and the international staff numbered fewer than one hundred. Pressure emanating from the national office for local unions to implement the anti-discrimination program, however, contained the potential for the international union apparatus to achieve sufficient autonomy to force unpleasant decisions on recalcitrant local unions—and on issues other than anti-discrimination policy.

Tony Stephens, who replaced Frank Ellis as organization department head and international union vice president in 1950, tried to take advantage of the controversies over race to precisely this end. The struggle between Stephens and education department director Myles Horton, which peaked in the midst of the Fort Worth controversy, illustrates how anti-discrimination activities could be manipulated to serve as a foil for expanding the power of the union's bureaucracy.

A long-time practitioner of adult education at the Highlander Folk School, Horton was fond of calling his approach to education in the UPWA the "percolator system. Ideas will come from the workers up, and not as in the drip system, from the top down." These views placed Horton in direct conflict with Stephens, who did not share Horton's educational philosophy and instead wanted the union staff to be a vehicle for implementing policies already established at national gatherings. Moreover, Stephens felt he should have control over the activities of the five field representatives assigned to Horton's department. The most frequent clashes occurred when Stephens sought to assign members of the education staff to important organizing drives. Horton consistently objected to these assignments on the basis that his department's educational programs would be harmed.[73]

Horton's laudable but formalistic stance rapidly lost credibility in the furious battle over the UPWA's anti-discrimination program. In late October 1952 Stephens blamed Horton's policies for the reluctance of union staff members to push "the programs and policies of our union" and demagogically asserted that as a result, "work in the anti-discrimination field . . . fell off." Despite the dubious validity of these accusations, circulated in a letter to the UPWA's top leadership, they were hard to ignore a few weeks later when white workers in Fort Worth rebelled against the anti-discrimination program. Desperately in need of a union staff that would resolutely push the UPWA's "programs and policies," and not having the liberty to wait for Horton's percolator approach to show results, Helstein sided with Stephens against Horton. The education program was restructured in January 1953, and Horton bitterly resigned two months later. Following his departure, educational activities were merged into a program department whose responsibilities were more narrowly defined as implementation of union programs, and whose staff reported to Stephens as well as department head Richard Durham.[74]

With the victories over Horton and the racist opposition behind him, Stephens began to use his power in the union to replace Ralph Helstein as union president. To this end he formed a pragmatic alliance with a loose caucus of black staff members and local union leaders led by program department head Durham, who felt that the international union should make even greater use of its apparatus to oppose racial discrimination. Although these black officials represented, in essence, the optimism of blacks that the union could become a vehicle for a civil rights movement, Stephens's plans indicate how use of the international union structure to advance black rights also could accelerate formation of a union bureaucracy.

The blacks who supported Durham reflected an incipient "black power" movement inside the UPWA; Sam Parks effectively articulated their critique of the leadership. The union's "primary objective was winning collective bargaining rights," Parks later reflected. "Black advancement, black equality, black liberation was secondary." Parks and his circle, in essence, wanted to reverse these priorities. Because Chicago locals were overwhelmingly black in the mid-1950s, Parks's complaint probably was shared by other young black workers who saw the UPWA as a predominantly black organization still headed by white leaders. Replacement of liberal white unionist Harold Nielsen as District 1 director by the black Wilson leader Charles Hayes in 1954 reflected the assertiveness of Chicago's black rank and file.[75]

The dramatic shift in racial composition in Chicago, however, was unusual. In most meatpacking plants whites remained either a majority or a large minority of the workforce. In these areas there seems to have been little support for Durham among active black union members. Kansas City blacks generally remained aloof from the black caucus and were wary of the centralizing tendencies in the international. William Raspberry objected to the very notion of a black caucus because it dealt with the same issues "that they could talk about in regular meetings." In his estimation a black caucus was pointless because it did not have the power to implement its plans without securing support from the entire union, including its white members. Black workers disagreed, in effect, how important it was to confine union objectives to areas that could retain white support.[76]

The biggest obstacles to the aspirations of the black power group were the predominantly white unions in Iowa and Nebraska. Moreover, the entry of many younger white rural workers into these plants had already resulted in internal union conflict in places such as Ottumwa, Iowa, between older militants schooled in UPWA traditions and those whose employment postdated the 1948 strike. Although locals in Sioux City and Omaha may have lagged on the union's anti-discrimination policy, there was no way the UPWA could have forced greater compliance without exacerbating existing tensions inside local unions, seriously abrogating local union autonomy, and placing new strains on the national inter-racial coalition that had taken form in the 1940s.[77]

Stephens and Durham were willing to take this risk; President Helstein evidently was not. With reverberations of the struggle that occurred between 1953 and 1955 barely resolved, Helstein moved swiftly to terminate another potential disturbance to national unity. In March 1957 Durham resigned under pressure, and his main allies in the program department, Marian Simmons and District 1 representative Oscar Brown, were dismissed. While there were a few protests over the removal of Simmons, it is significant that none of the black leaders of Kansas City locals objected. Sam Parks was fired at the same time for accepting kickbacks from union members, a charge he later admitted; no doubt the cloud surrounding his departure inhibited any protests. Soon thereafter, Helstein recruited Austin Local 9 president Frank Schultz to replace Stephens as international union vice president at the 1958 convention.[78]

The selection of Schultz was a defeat for bureaucratic forces within the international as well as the black militant current. Because Schultz remained president of Local 9 and continued to reside in Austin, his election reassured local union leaders that pressures to limit their autonomy would abate. At the same time, the elevation of the president of an all-white local union sent a clear message that there would be no further escalation of the anti-discrimination program. The preservation of union democracy came at a price: The use of the UPWA's national structure to initiate an aggressive civil rights program, if that entailed overriding majority sentiment in local unions, would not occur.

The events of the late 1950s established distinct limits to the union's anti-discrimination program but did not roll back existing accomplishments or ongoing activities. The alliance between the UPWA and Martin Luther King, Jr., continued until his death. In 1966 the UPWA was one of the few unions to back King's campaign for open housing in Chicago, and it remained a staunch ally after he publicly spoke out against the war in Vietnam. The international union also continued its support for the national civil rights movement; unionists participated in the protests against Woolworth stores during the 1960 lunch-counter sit-ins, the 1963 March on Washington, and several southern voting rights protests. In places where local unions remained supportive of black activists, such as in Chicago, Waterloo, Cedar Rapids, and Kansas City, anti-discrimination activity remained an important part of union activity. But the transformation of the UPWA contemplated by Parks, Simmons, and Durham did not occur, precisely because of the constraints on union policy imposed by a majority white national membership.[79]

The tensions between social unionism and union democracy emerged most forcefully in the early 1960s when women began to press for changes in union policy toward the sexual division of labor. Technological change in the late 1950s and 1960s precipitated the controversy by reducing the need for female labor more rapidly than for men. "Oh yes, they were getting rid of the women," Velma Otterman Schrader observed when she described the changes in production techniques. Circular electric "wizard" knives in the offal and trim departments reduced the workforce by doubling productivity. In the bacon department, new slicing and weighing machines reduced labor needs by 40 to 60 percent. Especially massive job loss occurred in the sausage department, where machinery replaced labor at every step of the process. In the Waterloo, Iowa, Rath plant, employment fell from three hundred to twelve in the sausage department without any loss in the volume of production. Because of separate male-female jobs and seniority lists, it was routine for women to be laid off while men who had considerably less seniority continued to work.[80]

The experiences of women had a profound effect on their attitudes toward the traditional sexual division of labor in meatpacking. Resentment simmered after 1955, finding expression in the form of attacks on the system of separate female jobs and seniority lists. "The union is forced to look at automation; it is forced to look at the number of women unemployed, it is forced to look at the seniority structure," declared a leaflet, "To Their Union Brothers," that women distributed at a 1955 conference. The initial challenges were spearheaded by black women who had been able to move into jobs previously denied them because of race. Why, they reasoned, were they still barred from jobs by virtue of their sex? By the early 1960s, as the effects of technological change on women's employment became increasingly apparent, many white women joined the clamor for an end to the contractual sexual division of labor.[81]

Despite considerable pressure on local unions and the international, however, women were unable to persuade the UPWA to respond to this issue effectively. The national organization authorized combining male-female seniority lists on the local level, but there is no evidence that local unions did so. Airing of complaints and passage of resolutions at national gatherings could not overcome widespread local inertia.[82]

The main barrier to changes in women's work opportunities was their union brothers. The deeply entrenched sexual division of labor in meatpacking, and the absence of a union challenge to the notion of such a division, reinforced conservative male assumptions concerning gender roles. Male resistance to correcting the disproportionate layoff of women took the form of defending the right of men to have first claim on employment. "You heard all this stuff about the man's the breadwinner and therefore you shouldn't force him off his job or lay him off and let the women work," recalled the male chief steward in the Waterloo, Iowa, Rath plant. These attitudes were strong among young men hired in the late 1950s who were most vulnerable to layoffs and thus had the most to gain from the discriminatory treatment of women. Many white older union leaders in Iowa also shared this belief, although out of traditional attitudes toward the family rather than immediate self-interest. The former president of the Ottumwa, Iowa, local admitted that in the early 1960s he believed "that if the man's the head of the house he should have the job."[83]

The demographic composition of meatpacking in the early 1960s further inhibited women's capacity to seek changes in union policy. Although black workers were able to influence the international union because of their role on the killing floor and numerical majority in key plants, women had much less workplace power and tended to be a small minority in local unions. They also were a declining force in the plants experiencing technological change, composing less than 10 percent of the large local unions in Iowa and Nebraska affected by substantial female layoffs. Unlike black workers, women did not have the equivalent of a "Chicago" inside the union. Because of their ancillary role in the meatpacking work process and declining aggregate numbers, there was no set of local unions that they could use as a fulcrum to increase their leverage throughout the UPWA.[84]

Divisions among women further weakened their capacity to exert influence inside the UPWA. Black women, and most younger white women, generally favored eliminating separate male-female jobs and seniority. Merging seniority lists would have ended the problem of women experiencing layoffs while men with less seniority continued to work and would have facilitated transfers into departments with more stable employment. Older women, especially whites, were more likely to oppose merging the seniority lists because they were afraid that high-seniority men would take well-paid female jobs in departments such as sliced bacon, and force the older women into work that would be too physically taxing. Women who opposed merging the seniority lists also were more likely to believe that men had more need for employment. "I will not do a man's job. A man is supposed to be the breadwinner," Waterloo, Iowa, steward Goldie Lamb recalled telling her union. "He deserves that job." The job losses heightened complex divisions among female packinghouse workers and exposed a deep strategic disagreement over whether union policy should treat women the same as men or place women into a separate, protected category.[85]

The 1964 Civil Rights Act changed the rules of the debate by allowing women to draw the federal government into the controversy. Title VII's prohibition of employment discrimination by race and sex implicitly challenged a system of job classification that clearly was having discriminatory consequences. It is a measure of the discontent among female packinghouse workers, and the presence of strong female union leaders, that UPWA members were among the first women workers to take advantage of the act. In 1965 women in Waterloo and Ottumwa brought complaints against the UPWA and their companies to the Equal Employment Opportunities Commission, and filed lawsuits when their local unions resisted implementation of corrective measures. The involvement of the federal government gave the international union the impetus, and the power, to develop a solution to female job losses that it could impose on recalcitrant local unions. In 1965 the UPWA established a national commission of female union leaders charged with developing proposals to correct the situation. The committee proposed a system that became, at least formally, a compromise that all parties accepted: alteration of job classifications into an "ABC system" consisting of A jobs open to men; B jobs open to women; and C jobs open to both.[86]

Establishment of the ABC system did not end resistance among men to alteration of the traditional sexual division of labor. Women in the Ottumwa plant found that the men schemed to control the C jobs and made life miserable for women who transferred into previously male domains. A lawsuit filed by female union members in 1966 produced more forcible intervention from the federal government and the national union, and eventually extracted reluctant compliance from the local. By 1967 male resistance in Ottumwa and other locals had collapsed, and women were slowly breaking down the traditional sexual division of labor in meatpacking.[87]

"We got a lot of the things that were needed, but I'm not saying that it was enough," Mary Salinas judged in retrospect. Salinas's criticism reflected how the organization of women within the UPWA had raised consciousness and expectations. By holding women's-only meetings, demanding child care, paid maternity leave, representation in leadership bodies, and equal pay, female UPWA members anticipated many of the demands of women workers in the 1970s and 1980s. Despite the constraints on women's influence due the UPWA's masculinist bias, vital local union structures and internal democracy allowed female members to use the UPWA, in Nancy Gabin's words, as "a resource for female collective action."[88]

Female union members, because of their experience, began to move in a direction parallel to women in the UAW and to question the benefits of legislation and practices that supposedly "protected" women. In its meeting with the International Executive Board, the 1965 Women's Committee "observed that some legislation originally designed to 'protect' women workers may have become outdated and actually interfere with female employment under modern conditions." Only a year later, Addie Wyatt showed her commitment to women's issues by participating in the founding of the National Organization for Women. As in the UAW, the struggle over the boundary between men's and women's work had unleashed a "working-class feminism" among packinghouse workers that contributed to the contemporary women's movement.[89]

* * *

The UPWA's social unionism in postwar America grew out of shared mores and customs forged through common struggles against employers and tempered by interaction between male and female workers of different races inside union structures. The retention of a strong shop-floor apparatus allowed the UPWA to contest the ideological pressures of the 1950s, especially among active union stewards and officers. As blacks assumed greater responsibility for union activities that benefited all races, a majority of white packinghouse workers learned to at least tolerate efforts to use the union to end racial discrimination. Women appropriated the union's principles of equal treatment at work to secure male support for ending the wage differential. In this manner the UPWA produced a new cohort of working-class militants committed to the "community of our union" and its practice of social unionism.

Union initiatives around racial and sexual discrimination were not primarily the result of administrative fiat, but instead reflected the capacity of groups of workers to use union structures as conduits for their concerns and aspirations. Although the union bureaucracy grew in power in the 1950s, the very shortcomings of the UPWA indicate the extent to which it was rank-and-file pressure which shaped its social unionism. As such, the "community of our union" could act as a brake on, as well as a springboard for, the demands of particular groups of workers.

The contrast between union initiatives against racial discrimination and its actions on behalf of female members illuminates this tension. Although the union attacked, and to some extent dismantled, patterns of racial discrimination at work and in the union, it defended the rigid sexual division of labor and made little effort to alter the male culture that inhibited women's participation. Securing equality for women at work and in the UPWA remained constrained by traditional notions of women's place in a manner dissimilar from the union's more fundamental challenge to many racist norms of American society.

Specific historical developments partly explain the divergence between union actions against racism and sexism. Black male workers constituted a powerful group in the industry, and their support was critical for union formation and the exercise of union power. Their role on the killing floors, and substantial numbers in major metropolitan plants, gave black men both power within the union and the opportunity to persuade many white workers of the legitimacy of their particular concerns. Women workers, in contrast, were less powerful and remained relatively isolated from men because they generally worked in subsidiary departments that processed meat. Women also rarely were more than 20 percent of a plant's workforce. Consequently, they had far less leverage inside the union and fewer occasions to persuade male workers that their concerns deserved the full attention of the UPWA. Workplace composition, and the pattern of union formation, gave black men more power at work and within union structures than women of any race.

Structural considerations provide only part of the explanation. Equally important were the "mores and customs" that comprised union traditions. The union emerged from the 1930s with a challenge to racial discrimination that was far more profound than to the subordination of women. While workers built a labor organization that challenged racial and ethnic divisions, the UPWA also clearly espoused using its strength to create stable families supported by a male breadwinner. This deep commitment to a family wage inhibited objections to widely held male notions that women were temporary or secondary wage-earners who did not deserve access to male job preserves. Within the "community of our union," efforts to end racism could draw on a far stronger tradition to secure majority support than women's demands for complete equality.

The shortcomings of the UPWA's social unionism do not invalidate the powerful example it represented to Martin Luther King, Jr. As he explained to the union's 1957 Anti-Discrimination Conference, King's experiences with the UPWA led him to hope that "with the coming together of the powerful influence of labor and all people of good will in the struggle for freedom and human dignity, I can assure you that we have a powerful instrument." UPWA actions against discrimination did indeed provide a concrete link between the labor upsurge of the 1930s and 1940s and the civil rights movement of the 1950s and 1960s. Similarly, women's activities in the UPWA were part of a working-class women's movement that contributed to the development of the second wave of feminism in the 1960s and 1970s. Despite limits on what a union of a hundred thousand members could accomplish, the UPWA provides an example of how American unions could contribute to progressive postwar social movements.

PART 3

The Return to the "Jungle"

10

"My Scars Are Many": The Decline of Industrial Unionism in Meatpacking, 1955–90

Whether you're going to survive and prosper or whether you're going to fall by the wayside and close your door is dependent upon what you pay and what you get back. It's not a complicated business from that standpoint.

—Arden Walker, Iowa Beef Processors

You don't get anywhere with the packer by trying to be their friend and representing their employees at the same time. My scars are many: on my hands, arms, heart, mind and soul. I have learned that I am nothing to any packer but a fucking piece of dirt. I have made a promise to myself that as long as I have any involvement with these bastards, I will fight them with my last breath. . . . What troubles me most tonight is that I fear I don't know the difference between these pricks and my own union leaders.

—William Buckholtz, Morrell worker,
to United Food and Commercial Workers
President William Wynn, January 1989

Born in the South Bottoms, Sioux City's old packinghouse neighborhood, Lewie Anderson was pleased when a friend helped him get into the UPWA-organized Armour plant in the mid-1960s. He had heard from packinghouse workers that the UPWA was a strong union that had obtained good wages and benefits and looked out for its members. Once hired, he was quickly impressed with the strength of the organization. "The steward, I sensed, had as much authority as the foreman did," he later recalled. "The steward was always fighting . . . whenever there was a problem I didn't go to the foreman, I went to the steward." To Anderson, the union's power was apparent over the intensity of work. "The union had a fairly firm handle on chain speeds and proper crewing," he observed. As a result, the labor was at "a pace that you could handle. You could do the work and get it done without killing yourself."

It was Anderson's misfortune to enter the meatpacking industry at a moment when the conditions he encountered at Armour were unraveling. Dozens of UPWA-organized packinghouses had been closed in the preceding ten years, including Armour's original facility in Sioux City. He had found employment at a new plant built by Armour in an effort to modernize its operations. Anderson had less seniority than UPWA members from other cities who exercised their contractual right to transfer to Sioux City when their plants closed; consequently, he experienced repeated layoffs. Recently married, he wanted more stable employment. Anderson decided to apply for work at one of the new meat companies, Iowa Beef Processors (IBP), whose plant across the Missouri River in Dakota City, Nebraska, always was hiring.

He found IBP a very different place to work. The pace of production in the beef kill was more than twice as fast than at Armour, and there was constant turnover. The independent union that nominally represented workers had little influence over working conditions. "I don't remember anybody being steward, department steward on the kill floor," Anderson reflected. "Clearly, with management, whatever they said, went." While Armour's one foreman in the beef kill had cooperated with the UPWA steward, IBP had seven or eight supervisors who "were really brutal in their approach." Anderson remembered the "tremendous intimidation" by foremen who would scream at workers, "Keep up, or your ass is going out the door!" Unlike Armour, the supervisors were "right in there on top of the people. Not instructing them, but screaming at them and pushing them, literally pushing them, to go faster and faster."[1]

Anderson had seen the past and the future of labor-management relations in the meatpacking industry. Ironically, he was to play a role in the 1970s and 1980s trying to preserve, but ultimately presiding over, the decline of the brand of unionism the UPWA practiced in Sioux City's Armour plant. The expansion, and ultimate dominance, of IBP's approach to labor relations would result in a dramatic decline in the working conditions and living standards of packinghouse workers by 1990.

Plant closings in the late 1950s initially plunged industrial unionism into crisis. A merger in 1968 between the UPWA and its old rival, the Amalgamated Meat Cutters and Butcher Workmen, preserved the organizational expression of industrial unionism: chains of packinghouse local unions in the plants of the same national firm and national master agreements. Once the Amalgamated merged in 1979 with the Retail Clerks International Union to form the United Food and Commercial Workers (UFCW), however, the decline was rapid. By the end of the 1980s master agreements and the chains virtually had ceased to exist; wages and benefits fell precipitously as the UFCW granted repeated concessions, and the dominant firms in the meatpacking became predominantly non-union operations.

After 1990 unionism as such retained a foothold in meatpacking, but it was a very different type of unionism than had existed under the UPWA. Unions that had once set wage levels and regulated working conditions were largely ineffective as instruments of workers' power. Within the UFCW, packinghouse workers were a dwindling minority in large, multiunit locals covering entire states and headed by local union leaders who came from completely different trades. Coordinated national bargaining had disappeared. Regional directors controlled negotiations with packing firms, and only for the plants in their district. Contacts among unionized workers in different plants of the same firm were irregular and minimal. The industrial unionism established by the UPWA in the 1940s was no more.

The decline of industrial unionism in meatpacking reflected the convergence of several inter-related developments. First, a revolution swept the red meat industry. Changing economics of plant location, production methods, and meat distribution demolished the hold of the old Big Four packing companies and led to the consolidation of a new oligopoly of three firms. Second, the shifts in location and structure of meat production evaporated the historic base of the UPWA, as dozens of metropolitan midwestern plants closed and new packinghouses opened in far-flung rural areas. Finally, the same processes reconstituted the packinghouse workforce by eliminating the settled communities that had supported unionism since the 1930s and introducing new groups of workers, migrants from rural areas in America and immigrants from Asia and Latin America, to the packinghouses. These processes shattered industrial unionism by eliminating the firms in which it had been strong, the workers who were its base, and the labor organization that was its instrument.

The Transformation of the Meatpacking Industry

By 1960 the hold of the old Big Four firms over the meat industry had seriously eroded. In 1937 these companies accounted for 78 percent of the meat products sold in the United States; by 1962 the Big Four's total fell to 38.1 percent. Hundreds of new firms sprang up in the 1950s and 1960s and took large chunks of the market away from the old dominant companies. Profit rates are telling. The Big Four firms averaged a 4.9 percent return on net worth between 1948 and 1956, whereas all other packing companies received 9.4 percent. In the same period several rapidly expanding companies based in the pork sector of the industry—Hormel, Hygrade, Oscar Mayer, and Morrell—averaged a 12.1 percent return on their capital. The advantage clearly had shifted to upstart firms who were challenging the old metropolitan-based packers.[2]

The unsettled state of the industry did not last; by 1990 a new dominant set of firms had emerged. The new "Big Three" of IBP, Excell (a subsidiary of Cargill), and ConAgra quickly became almost as powerful as Armour, Cudahy, Swift, and Wilson in their heyday. By 1989 the Big Three slaughtered almost 70 percent of the nation's steers and heifers and 35 percent of its hogs. These impressive figures understate their power over the distribution of meat in the United States. By 1990 these three firms produced more than 75 percent of the nation's boxed beef, the form in which most supermarkets receive meat.[3]

The driving force behind the transformation of the meat industry was a fundamental alteration in the relationship between labor and capital. Successful firms increased control over the work process and reduced expenditures for labor through a variety of mechanisms, including reorganization of meat production and distribution, technological innovation, and plant relocation. New machinery curtailed the power of individual skilled workers and disturbed traditional relationships within work gangs. Changes in the organization and structure of production disrupted established methods of shop-floor bargaining, especially on the killing floor. Efforts to reduce shipping expenses and production costs for items like water no doubt also influenced the strategies of packinghouse companies. But the decisive factor behind the revolution in the meat industry was the drive by management to decrease the share of the industry's wealth that went to production workers.[4]

The collapse of the branch house distribution system was the first casualty of the reorganization of the meat industry. Large supermarket chains bypassed branch houses after World War II by purchasing meat in large amounts to process in central warehouses for distribution to affiliated stores. This reduced labor costs by replacing highly skilled retail butchers who prepared meat to order with meat cutters who could use machinery to refine large quantities to standard specifications. Between 1948 and 1963, as supermarkets' share of retail grocery sales grew from 28 to 69 percent, the number of branch houses fell by more than 50 percent. Ending the Big Four's stranglehold over meat distribution in turn created openings for new firms. As the expansion of the highway network after 1945 allowed more rural facilities away from rail lines to begin operations, they found supermarkets were enthusiastic clients. The Big Four found their world turned upside down; in a quarter of a century they had traded the role of dictators of the meat supply for that of suppliants of the supermarket chains.[5]

Concomitant with the decline of the branch houses was an enormous increase in meat jobbers, known as "breakers" and "boners." Used primarily by the new independent beef packers, jobbers took beef quarters from slaughterhouses and further processed the meat in preparation for resale to retail outlets. As their names imply, these wholesalers "broke" the meat down from quarters into basic sub-primal cuts such as ribs, loins, and rounds, "boned" them, and then shipped them to supermarket distribution centers. Retailers used the wholesalers because they provided more flexibility in the choice of cuts offered to consumers; independent packers used wholesalers because these new companies needed to do no more than simply kill and minimally process their product, reducing initial capital investment and labor costs.[6]

The decline of the Big Four's distribution system, however, only provided opportunity. It was the reduction of labor costs in the making of meat, achieved through changes in the organization and techniques of production, which allowed the "new breed" packers to surge into the industry.

Introduction of new production technologies by management marked the first stage of efforts to reduce labor costs and shake up the industry. The significance of these new techniques can be overstated. Meatpacking remained a labor-intensive, relatively unskilled industry in which the bulk of workers labored with their hands and used simple knives. But technological change affected workers in two critical ways: It eliminated key skilled jobs in the initial slaughtering process and significantly reduced the need for labor in the processing of meat.

In the pork sector of the industry, most changes resulted from the use of machinery and power tools to perform tasks previously dependent on skill and strength. In the hog-killing operation, for example, Best and Donovan's scissor-shaped Hog Head Dropper replaced the skilled header's long blade, and the circular "splitter" saw supplanted the cleaver previously used to sunder the pig's backbone. No longer did the company have to satisfy skilled butchers who took years to learn how to adroitly cut through the joint that connected the neck to the body or the splitter who combined brawn and a deft touch to sever the carcass into halves. New machinery in the preparation of processed meat often doubled productivity and reduced the total number of employers in affected departments. Changes of this sort were incremental, eliminating "skill" bottlenecks and increasing productivity but not transforming production methods.[7]

The cattle-killing process experienced a more substantial change—the development of "on the rail" dressing. Rather than lower the animal to the floor to remove its hide, new production methods allowed the carcass to remain on the continuous chain. In place of the dexterous floorsman, machines such as the Anco Can Pak Puller stripped the skin off the animal after several workers using power tools performed initial cutting operations. Workers equipped with power saws cut the carcass in half, eliminating the cleaver-wielding splitters. In addition to increased speed, these changes drastically reduced labor costs by eliminating floorsmen and cattle splitters, who were at the top of the plant's pay structure and earned more than the machinists in the maintenance department. In 1964 a food trade association estimated that on the rail dressing reduced labor costs by almost $2 per head. The emergence of hundreds of new firms in the beef industry after World War II reflected the enormous advantages of these new production methods over the ones that had predominated in the Big Four plants.[8]

Successful efforts by a few powerful firms to control the industry by further reducing labor costs mark the second stage of meatpacking's transformation. Astute packers such as IBP founder Currier Holman saw an opportunity to dominate the beef trade by attaching breaking and boning operations to their slaughterhouses and bypassing both the wholesaler and the supermarket warehouse. This innovation quickly became known as "boxed beef" because of the manner in which the meat was shipped.

Economies of scale and rigid control of the labor process were critical to the profitability of boxed beef. In one typical operation, several hundred semiskilled workers labored feverishly along a continuous conveyer belt, each performing a few simple operations as animal parts sped by. To one observer, workers' arms moved so fast "that someone looking down the long tables where they were lined up on either side could not distinguish one from another." A precise description of one job conveys the fragmentation of work. When ten-pound pieces of meat traveling on a conveyer belt reached one worker, "He used the meathook which was in his left hand to fling the meat to the workboard in front of him and then, with the knife in his right hand, he made two swift cuts on either side of the bone, placed his meat hook on the bone and then, with two short strokes, cut the bone out of the piece of meat . . . the piece of meat was flipped over with the hook, the fat on the edge was trimmed, and then the meat was shoved onto yet another conveyor belt. . . . It took him a few seconds." Packaged in vacuum-sealed bags, the boned beef was shipped directly to supermarkets. There, employees simply sliced the meat as if they were cutting bread and place the cuts in trays for consumer display. Boxed beef's high-volume production and fast "throughput" depended on rigid managerial control of the shop floor.[9]

Boxed beef reduced costs in two ways. Meat producers and retailers saved money because boxed beef eliminated the skilled meat cutters who had previously broken down carcasses into consumer cuts. Indeed, according to a 1987 survey, boxed beef's primary attraction to retailers was its reduced labor requirements. Moreover, because meatpacking companies no longer paid to ship unusable bones and meat scraps, savings in transportation expenses allowed them to undercut prices of firms that shipped beef in carcass form.[10]

With its cost advantage, boxed beef became the new method for controlling the distribution of beef, much as the branch houses had served the Big Four at the turn of the century. Its rapid growth was phenomenal. In less than two decades boxed beef grew from a supplementary source of supply to the preeminent method for marketing beef. Sales more than tripled between 1971 and 1979 to 4.8 million pounds, half of all federally inspected beef slaughtered. Boxed beef made up only 20 percent of the retail market in 1972; by 1989 boxed beef's national market share exceeded 80 percent. A survey of leading supermarkets revealed that beef shipped in the form of cattle quarters—the old method of transporting beef—accounted for only 4 percent of their receipts in 1986. Moreover, supermarkets became dependent on boxed beef after they eliminated the butchers who had fabricated carcass beef. Once retailers adapted to boxed beef, they were permanently addicted.[11]

Boxed beef was a particularly important source of dominance for a few large firms that mastered this technique of production and distribution. The smaller independent concerns of the 1950s and 1960s rapidly lost ground to the new industry giants as boxed beef flooded the market. The leading four firms accounted for 60 percent of boxed beef sales in 1979 and 82 percent in 1987. IBP alone produced 40 percent of the nation's boxed beef in the late 1970s. Small packinghouses went out of business, sold their plants to larger companies, or became "captive" suppliers, selling their entire product of slaughtered cattle to boxed beef producers such as IBP. The number of meatpacking plants with more than twenty employees fell from 955 in 1967 to 668 in 1982 and then to 503 in 1987—a decline of almost 50 percent in twenty years. Forward integration into boxed beef emulated the techniques of the old Big Four at the turn of the century, and it was equally effective as a method of controlling the industry, albeit under altered circumstances.[12]

Dominance in beef allowed the Big Three to move into hog slaughtering in the 1980s. Pork is sold in processed form far more than beef, and consumer preference for "brand" products initially insulated Oscar Mayer,

Hormel, and other pig-slaughtering firms from new competition. Nonetheless, aggressive entry into pork by the Big Three prompted the older pork-based firms to concentrate on processed meat and abandon killing operations. "Our ultimate objective is to sell nothing in a commodity form," Hormel president Richard Knowlton declared in 1985. By 1990 the pork industry had bifurcated into a slaughtering and processing sector, each dominated by a handful of firms.[13]

Transformation of the structure of meat production accompanied the corporate revolution. Dozens of old, multistory packinghouses in metropolitan centers closed and were replaced by single-story facilities located in the countryside near the source of livestock. The number of packinghouse workers in urban areas fell by more than fifty thousand between 1963 and 1984, and the proportion of workers in rural plants increased from 25 percent to 50 percent of the national workforce. The new plants generally employed fewer workers, only slaughtered one type of animal, and either killed or processed—not both. In the 1980s a spatial separation emerged between the pork industry, based in Iowa and neighboring states, and beef, overwhelmingly located on the high plains of Kansas, Texas, and adjacent areas (Table 12).[14]

Although relocating plants from city to countryside cut shipping and utility expenditures, the most significant contribution to company profits came from reduced labor costs. In addition to reorganizing production methods, locating the new plants in rural areas altered the wage structure within which the industry operated. New workers came not from the industrial labor market but from farms or, especially after the 1970s, from rural areas in Latin America and Asia. Long distances between packing plants further fragmented the packinghouse labor force and hindered the exercise of union power or the unionization of unorganized plants.

Table 12. Leading Beef Slaughter States, 1929 versus 1989

	Rank	Percent of National Kill		Rank	Percent of National Kill
1929			1989		
Illinois	1	19.0	Kansas[a]	1	17.0
Minnesota	2	8.3	Texas	2	16.6
Kansas[a]	3	8.2	Colorado	3	6.0
New York	4	7.8	Iowa	4	5.0

a. The 1989 Kansas plants were located in the western part of the state; the 1929 plants were in Kansas City and Wichita.

Sources: U.S. Department of Commerce, *Fifteenth Census of the United States, Manufactures: 1929* (Washington, 1933), 2:181; American Meat Institute, *Meat Facts, 1990* (Washington, 1990), 19.

The contrast between meatpacking in 1955 and 1990 is striking. In the old stockyard districts of Chicago, Kansas City, and Sioux City, several adjacent plants with thousands of employees slaughtered a variety of livestock. By the mid-1980s most meat production was from dispersed plants specializing in either beef, pork, or lamb, usually employing fewer than a thousand workers and widely scattered through the midwestern countryside. Impressive gains in productivity indicate the revolutionary nature of the industry's transformation. In 1952 one man-hour of labor produced 51.4 pounds of dressed meat. By 1977 output had tripled to 154.6 pounds.[15]

The strategy of lowering labor costs by reorganizing work had its limits. Intense competition tended to cancel the benefits of advances briefly achieved by individual firms as strong companies emulated each other's innovations. To compete with the aggressive new packers, Armour, Swift, and Wilson followed a reinvestment strategy of shutting their old packing-houses and opening modern, technologically advanced facilities. Even boxed beef, the key to the rise of a new Big Three, was initially copied by other packers. The Big Four's efforts even were partly successful. Swift remained the leading meatpacking company until passed by IBP in the 1970s, and Armour and Wilson remained powerful firms into the 1980s.

To gain a decisive advantage, firms needed to put wages back into competition by lowering the rates paid their workers below those of other firms that employed the same production methods. This could only be accomplished by ending pattern bargaining and weakening industrial unionism's capacity to standardize wages and labor costs. Ultimately, it was the collapse of the industry's wage standards in the 1980s that allowed a new Big Three to rise, like a phoenix, from the ashes of the Big Four.

The UPWA and the New Meatpacking Industry

The transformation of the industry challenged the UPWA in a far more profound manner than the 1948 strike or the shop-floor guerrilla warfare of the 1950s. The union's strength was its genuine rank-and-file base in the metropolitan plants of the Big Four; and it was precisely those plants, and the workers who labored in them, that took the brunt of the changes in the industry. In particular, the closing of Chicago plants hurt the UPWA far more than the considerable loss of members would indicate; gone as well was the dynamic influence of that city's workers on the national organization. Black workers, a particularly strong source of union strength, suffered disproportionately when the central stockyard districts declined and production shifted to predominantly white rural areas. Technological innovation also disrupted well-established boundaries between male and female jobs, inciting intense gender conflicts in many local unions.

The numbers are stark. Between 1956 and 1965 Armour closed twenty-one major plants employing more than fourteen thousand workers, including its facilities in Chicago, Kansas City, and Sioux City. In the mid-1960s the company replaced those packinghouses with a dozen modern plants that emulated the specialized single-story operations and advanced technology of its upstart rivals. Because the new packinghouses employed a total of no more than two thousand workers, job losses were enormous. UPWA membership in the Armour chain, always its strongest base, fell from 21,410 to 9,300 in this nine-year period. Taken as a whole, UPWA membership in the Big Four packers declined more than 50 percent in a decade; U.S. membership fell to 73,300 in 1960 from a high of 103,600 in 1954 (Table 13). Qualitatively, as packinghouse workers became more white and more rural they grew more distant from the episodes that had transmitted UPWA traditions to a new generation in the 1940s and 1950s.[16]

The changes in workforce composition had profound effects on the UPWA. The base of the left, and for aggressive social unionism, dwindled at the same time as the centrist "broad middle" grew significantly. In effect, the social base for the center-left coalition dissolved, leaving the center, especially President Ralph Helstein and his Iowa supporters, in uncontested control of the organization. Preoccupied with plant closings, technological change, and the erosion of its activist base, the UPWA was placed on the defensive. Although retaining its unusually progressive stands, aggressive outreach programs collapsed in the 1960s "because there was no one to carry them on."[17]

In its rear-guard battle, the union's strategic response to plant closings would have a positive long-term effect on the living standards of packinghouse workers and the retention of unionism in the industry. The UPWA's

Table 13. UPWA Membership, Big Four Firms, 1953–64

	Armour	Cudahy	Swift	Wilson	Total
1953	24,650	7,525	18,680	8,375	59,550
1964	9,300	3,500	9,300[a]	4,500	26,600

a. 1967 membership; that year the Amalgamated had 3,500 members at Swift and the NBPW 5,400, leaving the UPWA still the largest union in that company.

Sources: UPWA membership figures for 1953, UPWA Papers, box 497, folder 7. For 1964, see U.S. Department of Labor, Current Wage Developments 200 (Aug. 1964): 25–26. The 1967 figures are from UPWA International Executive Board Minutes, July 17, 1967, 4, Ralph Helstein Papers.

reaction was guided by a belief that plant closings were only one aspect of a larger scheme by firms to reduce labor costs through plant relocation, changes in production methods, and pressure for wage concessions. Although not opposing technological change as such, the UPWA insisted that "progress should not mean enrichment of a few and misery for many." The union repeatedly rejected company pressures for concessions that allegedly would have kept a plant open and contended that "the true test was the profitability of the company" not an individual facility.[18]

The UPWA's resistance to wage reductions differed considerably from the stance of the other two unions in the meatpacking industry, the Amalgamated Meat Cutters and the NBPW. Under threats of plant closings, both agreed to concessions in the early 1960s, generally in southern plants. The Amalgamated justified its action on the basis that southern wages in meatpacking were higher than prevailing wages in the immediate labor market. In contrast, the UPWA doubted that concessions could save plants and feared that weakening national wage standards would make it far more difficult for unions to retain their hold in the meatpacking industry and organize new plants.[19]

Unable to win commitments from packing firms to halt plant closings, the union tried to make them more costly and provide options for employees who lost their jobs. As early as 1949, the union had secured separation pay for workers affected by departmental closures, and between 1959 and 1962 it significantly expanded contractual defenses against technological displacement and plant closings. The union obtained ninety-day advance notice for termination of a plant or department, severance and technological displacement pay, early retirement at age fifty-five with pension rights, and companywide seniority to permit inter-plant transfers, with moving expenses borne by the companies. With Armour, the union secured company funding of a joint labor-management Automation Committee to monitor transfer and retraining programs.[20]

These measures gave the UPWA the opportunity to help its members through a painful process that was beyond the union's control. Its efforts were substantial. Stewards and union leaders from affected plants met individually with all workers and guided them through the choices at their disposal: separation pay, transfer, or retirement. Retraining classes organized by the Automation Committee provided options for workers unable to move. When black workers took advantage of the transfer program to relocate to a new Armour facility in the all-white town of Worthington, Minnesota, their way was smoothed by a team of union staffers who successfully arranged housing and prepared the community for racial integration. Costs to the packing firms were considerable. Separation pay to workers at just four of Armour's shuttered plants—Fort Worth, Sioux City, Kansas City, and Omaha—amounted to $8.7 million.[21]

Union vigilance was necessary to avert company sabotage of the transfer program. Armour tried to discourage transfers by laying off workers who moved to new plants and contending that newly constructed facilities—some within fifty miles of old plants—did not fall under the agreement. Activists at the local level found themselves arguing with company representatives who actively deterred workers from using their companywide seniority. As a result, few workers initially took advantage of the transfer program.[22]

The UPWA fought Armour's sabotage. It withdrew from the Automation Committee in 1963, charging that "our continued silence on the failure of the Committee would only result in maintaining a facade of humaneness and decency that would conceal a ruthless program of mass termination of employees of long service and cynical manipulation of the natural fears of its employees to accomplish drastic cuts in wages and working conditions." Using its right to strike while the contract was in effect (under clause 95E), the UPWA shut down Armour on October 3, 1963, and demanded that the company accept transfers at six new plants. The union also wanted workers to have "flowback" rights to return home and receive severance pay up to six months after accepting a transfer. After two weeks the company gave in and agreed that up to 80 percent of the jobs in new plants could be filled by transfers.[23]

Making new plants available for transfers was an important victory that benefited packinghouse workers for the next two decades. The most important aspect of the program was that it allowed the UPWA to seed new plants with pro-union workers. In Sioux City, Kansas City, and Omaha, 765 Armour employees exercised their transfer rights, and only 86 used the flowback provision to return home and accept severance pay. It is unclear how many workers from Chicago, Oklahoma City, St. Joseph, and other affected plants also transferred, but an estimate of five hundred is conservative. The transfers allowed experienced union members now in the new plants to recruit recently hired workers to the UPWA, secure union certification, and bring these facilities under the master agreements. Hence, deunionization of the old-line packers did not accompany plant closings and relocations. Despite the industry's upheaval, the UPWA was able to sustain its strength in the Big Four and preserve pattern bargaining.[24]

The retraining and reemployment programs were far less successful. "What you were doing was training people so that they could be unemployed at a higher level of skill," Helstein later reflected, "because they couldn't get jobs." Displaced packinghouse workers rarely had more than an eighth-grade education and tended to be in their forties and fifties. Black and female workers, who had benefited from the superior job opportunities in meatpacking, had to reenter a segmented labor market where discrimination severely constrained their options. Almost a third of 1,900 workers laid off by Armour in Kansas City exhausted their unemployment benefits. A minimum of 210 still had no jobs a year after the 1965 plant closing, and the Automation Committee could not locate another 300. In Sioux City, at least 100 of Armour's 1,150 workers were unemployed two years after the plant closed in 1963. Perhaps an even more telling statistic is that 54 percent of the men and 100 percent of the women who obtained new employment made less than half as much as they had earned at Armour. "It was one of the worst things that could ever happen," recalled Sioux City worker Sam Davis. "It was just like the bottom dropped out." For packinghouse workers without enough seniority to receive pensions or unable to transfer, plant closings were a personal tragedy that the union could do little to ease. The collective impact ravaged midwestern black communities in places such as Chicago and Kansas City, where packinghouse work had been a major source of employment and upward mobility for decades.[25]

UPWA leaders realized that the plant closings imperiled the very existence of their organization, because the union's base was in a shrinking sector of the industry. The union tried to escape its cul-de-sac by launching additional organizing initiatives in meatpacking and other food industries. In the packing industry, the UPWA targeted new firms, such as IBP, and second-tier pork companies that were expanding their operations. In addition, the union initiated organizing drives among workers in diverse food-related products, from fisherman to poultry workers to shellfish packers. The union even changed its name in 1960 to the United Packinghouse, Food and Allied Workers to reflect its broader orientation.[26]

The union's efforts halted its decline, with U.S. membership stabilizing at seventy thousand in the 1960s. The union secured contracts at three IBP plants and penetrated other new packing firms. Unionization of several additional Morrell and Hormel plants allowed the UPWA to establish several new chains. In the early 1960s the union won 60 percent of the 241 NLRB elections it contested in the meat industry (including sixty-one victories in the South), securing representation for ten thousand workers at twenty-nine packinghouses. Not reflected in those figures are union successes among grist mill, grain elevator, and other non-meat-product food workers. The union even tried to develop a national presence among fisherman by organizing in Florida, Alaska, and Gulf of Mexico ports.[27]

The moment for the UPWA, however, was almost over. The unrelenting drumbeat of plant closings placed a financial squeeze on the organization that made its rebuilding strategy impossible to sustain. The UPWA's membership in the old Big Four simply declined more quickly than the union was able to gain through new organizing. It almost ran a deficit in 1966, and only a significant dues increase averted a loss the following year. When Armour announced it would close five additional plants, the union projected a deficit of $85,000 in 1968 and laid off eight staff members (including five organizers) to compensate. The International Executive Board minutes plaintively note, "There was general discussion on how do you carry on organizing when you have fewer people?"[28]

The UPWA's leaders reluctantly accepted that their organization had reached the end of its road. Financial problems meant that an aggressive organizing program could not be sustained. Without organizing, the organization would implode financially. In October 1967, UPWA leaders Helstein and Prosten approached the Amalgamated Meat Cutters to reopen merger discussions. Similar talks had stalled in 1956 after lengthy negotiations, and again in 1965 after a brief exchange, but the UPWA now was desperate and in a weak position to impose conditions on the much larger Amalgamated. Union leaders hoped that the larger size of the combined organization would provide enough time for unions to follow the shift of capital in the meatpacking industry.[29]

UPWA members were far from enthusiastic about a merger. They feared the strong industrial unionism of the UPWA would be submerged within the Amalgamated. "For years, all our people from the top level on down had always told us that the Amalgamated top leadership were too easy on these companies," recalled Fort Worth leader Frank Wallace, "so I was against the merger." When Helstein went to Kansas City to defend the impending merger, union founder Thomas Krasick berated him, calling the Amalgamated "nothing but second-hand sell-out artists. No one could prove to me that they had gone out and fought sincerely for labor, organized labor or anything." Yet as the UPWA's central cadre grappled with their organization's dilemma, the merger garnered reluctant support. Helstein reminded Krasick of the plant closings, including the one in Kansas City, and argued that only a merger could preserve unionism in meatpacking. "And he was right," Krasick later recalled. "I knew he was right." Frank Wallace also came around. "If it would do the job that needed to be done for our members," he grudgingly admitted, "then merging was a worthwhile thing and a much needed thing."[30]

Industrial Unionism under the
Amalgamated, 1968–79

Viewed with the benefit of hindsight, the merger did stabilize industrial unionism for a decade. But the decentralized character of the Amalgamated, derived from its craft union roots, ultimately inhibited industrial unionism from expanding into the dynamic sector of the meatpacking industry. The slow erosion of industrial unionism in the 1970s thus paved the way for the crisis of the 1980s.

When the two unions merged in June 1968, the constitution and structure of the merged organization showed little sign of the UPWA. The Amalgamated expanded its International Executive Board to include four American UPWA leaders and the director of its Canadian district, but they were a tiny minority of the board's twenty-eight members. Ralph Helstein became a titular vice president but without any responsibilities in the merged organization. Two offices that had been important assets to UPWA chains and local unions, the grievance and wage-rate departments, went out of existence. Packinghouse workers would find that within the new organization they did not receive the services or attention they once had.[31]

The merger, however, did not eliminate the basic structures of industrial unionism in meatpacking. Long-time UPWA leader Jesse Prosten became director of a packinghouse department inside the Amalgamated that had authority over the chains and master agreements. The Amalgamated hired all former UPWA staff members, and a National Packing Committee of local union leaders provided general oversight of contract negotiations. These structures gave unionists from the UPWA's old midwestern strongholds considerable latitude in which to operate. "Without having any big-to-dos about it," recalled Minnesota field organizer Henry Giannini, "we just went about our work like we did in the UPWA."[32]

Throughout the 1970s Prosten worked diligently to maintain the chains and master agreements. He successfully brought locals from Amalgamated-organized plants into chains with former UPWA locals, shoring up the union at Armour and Swift and creating far stronger chains in companies like Morrell and Hormel. With his encouragement, Amalgamated members in IBP plants created a chain in the mid-1970s and established common expiration dates for their contracts. In 1976 the Amalgamated negotiated master agreements covering fifty thousand workers.[33]

There were critical differences, though, between industrial unionism under the UPWA and the Amalgamated's packinghouse department. Prosten had neither the resources nor the authority to initiate organizing campaigns against the non-union sector of the industry. In the Amalgamated, local unions and regional directors controlled organizing, not departments of the international union. In some cases union officials who nominally represented packinghouse workers refused to cooperate with Prosten and the National Packing Committee. By the late 1970s many new packinghouses had not been organized, and wages at some newly unionized plants were far below the master agreement rates. In Texas, for example, two MBPXL (later Excell) plants represented by the UFCW paid a base wage of $6.87 at the end of 1979—25 percent less than the master agreement level of $8.66 at the Texas plants of master agreement packers Armour and Swift. In time these problems would vitiate Prosten's efforts.[34]

The pressure of the Amalgamated also started to alter the character of the chains. In a gradual process that is difficult to chart, the chains began to change from instruments that created bonds among workers in different plants to mechanisms that controlled the often cantankerous packinghouse workers. Under the UPWA, the authority of the chains rested on solid traditions stretching back into the late 1930s, even though they never received recognition in the union's constitution. In the Amalgamated, the chains did not have this informal tradition on which to base their authority and had no formal standing in the union's structure. Hence, they were increasingly circumscribed by the Amalgamated's officers and regional directors. "Once it became the Amalgamated, they controlled you," recalled Loren Callender, a representative of the Sioux City local in the Swift chain for many years. Rather than institutions of union democracy, the chains gradually were reduced to critical support for Prosten's struggles within the Amalgamated's bureaucracy. The slow atrophy of ties among packinghouse workers would have serious consequences in the 1980s.[35]

The critical struggle for industrial unionism in meatpacking under the Amalgamated concerned the union's effort to bring wages at IBP into parity with the master agreement packers. IBP had quickly forged ahead of a number of new-breed companies to become an industry giant in the 1970s. At the time of the 1968 merger, Armour, Swift, and Wilson still were industry pacesetters in the beef sector. By 1978, with 16 percent of the national beef slaughter, IBP led all packers and killed more cattle than these three companies combined. Stabilization of the master agreements in the old firms was not enough in the 1970s; the new industry leader needed to be brought to the same wage and benefit levels to preserve pattern bargaining and union power.[36]

The Amalgamated had a foothold at IBP because of prior organizing successes by the UPWA at three plants. Immediately after the merger, former UPWA organizers played a central role securing a contract at IBP's new plant in Dakota City, Nebraska. With two thousand employees and a substantial boxed beef operation—IBP's first—the Dakota City plant was critically important to the company's expansion plans. Located across the Missouri River from Sioux City and in the heart of the UPWA's old Iowa-Nebraska district, the Dakota City plant was an obvious target for UPWA members now in the Amalgamated. The central figures in the organizing drive were former UPWA officials Dave Hart and Les Bishop, assisted by John Davidchick, a Russian whose family helped unionize Swift and Armour in the 1930s. "The UPWA organizers looked like packinghouse workers, talked like packinghouse workers, they related to packinghouse workers," recalled Lewie Anderson, an IBP worker active in the campaign. "They knew the issues to zero in on." Amalgamated organizers left a very different impression. "The Amalgamated would come out in suits and ties . . . had diamond rings, bracelets," he recalled. "They came across as slick-talking people who were not really . . . concerned about you and what you were doing."[37]

The Amalgamated won a certification election in 1969 against an independent union, but contract negotiations stalled over union demands to increase wages to the master agreement level. Both sides recognized that the disagreement reflected a fundamental clash over the future of unions in the meat industry. "If we paid the base rate the union wants, our whole program would fail," admitted Arden Walker, IBP's vice president of industrial relations. From its standpoint, the union realized that victory over IBP was necessary to maintain its strength in the 1970 master agreement negotiations, the first since the merger. "The other packers won't even talk to us about new contracts," the Dakota City union president told reporters. "They say, 'You get Iowa Beef up even with the rest of us, and then we'll talk.'"[38]

The strike that began on August 24, 1969, was probably the most violent in meatpacking since 1948. IBP imported strikebreakers and built a heavily fortified fence around the plant. Company efforts were aided by Nebraska labor laws which, among other restrictions, prohibited mass picket lines. Conflict between union and company supporters quickly degenerated into a guerrilla war of fistfights, bombings, and assaults in the Dakota City-Sioux City environs, which killed at least one person. Hundreds of union members were charged with violations of state laws; in the latter stages of the strike, a federal grand jury began hearing evidence for possible criminal indictments of union leaders.[39]

Despite the immense legal obstacles to a successful strike, the union almost brought IBP to its knees. Roving pickets closed three other unionized

IBP plants, and union butchers refused to handle IBP boxed beef shipped to New York City. With losses of $9 million in the first three months of 1970, IBP's bankers became nervous. On April 10, 1970, Chemical Bank summoned IBP President Currier Holman and other company executives to its New York City headquarters and demanded that the company immediately reduce its outstanding debt by $15 million. IBP was in no position to respond to the demand. "With the strike we're right in now," Holman told the bankers, "that's impossible."[40]

The confrontation in Dakota City sufficiently impressed other packing companies. The Amalgamated moved to take advantage of the strike's tenacity by opening negotiations with the master agreement packers nine months before the contracts expired, and it pressed for an early settlement. In early April, not long before Chemical Bank met with Holman, the Big Four packing companies reached an agreement with the Amalgamated that preserved the master agreements and included wage and benefit increases.[41]

With national negotiations successfully concluded, the Amalgamated decided to terminate the Dakota City strike. The violence of the struggle, and the threat of federal prosecution of union leaders, horrified national Amalgamated officials. Dakota City local union leaders were firmly instructed to settle with IBP on any terms possible.[42]

An added, sordid development contributed to the termination of the IBP strike. Immediately after his meeting with Chemical Bank, Holman used organized crime connections to arrange the payment of bribes to leaders of the Amalgamated's New York butcher locals. Following these payoffs the locals ended their opposition to the shipment of boxed beef into the critical New York City market. It remains unclear how much the bribery of union officials added to the pressure on Dakota City unionists to settle the strike, but it certainly undercut the bargaining power of the packinghouse workers at an important stage in their struggle.[43]

On balance, the 1969 Dakota City strike had a positive effect on the Amalgamated's position in meatpacking even though it failed to accomplish the union's immediate objectives. The strike secured the first contract with IBP at the critical Dakota City plant and helped the Amalgamated maintain strong master agreements with major meatpacking companies. The settlement allowed IBP to keep its pay rates far beneath the master agreement levels, however; by 1972 the gap ranged from 91 cents to $1.52 below the master agreement base rate of $4.71. The battle between the union and IBP had been joined, and both sides knew the stakes involved.[44]

Packinghouse workers made steady advances at IBP over the next five years. In 1972 workers established common expiration dates at all four unionized IBP facilities. In 1974 an arbitrator endorsed the union's contention that there should be a convergence between IBP wages and the master agreement rates. The resulting contract narrowed the differential by almost 50 percent and brought IBP wages to between 60 and 90 cents below the master agreement base rate of $6.47 by January 1977. The union slowly was closing the wage gap separating IBP and the old-line firms in the industry.[45]

IBP bitterly resented the union's presence because it threatened the company's control over the pace of work and its competitive wage advantage over the other packers. The company deliberately set out to turn back the Amalgamated's slow advance.[46]

IBP's strategy was simple: to close unionized plants and reduce its dependence on boxed beef from Dakota City. It built huge slaughtering and processing facilities in Amarillo, Texas, and Emporia, Kansas, to supplement Dakota City's capacity and closed or sold three unionized Iowa plants. Hughes Bagley, an IBP vice president between 1971 and 1975, told a congressional investigation that the expansion strategy reflected management's anticipation that "two out of three would carry the company" because "one of our plants [would] be down at all times with a labor situation." IBP also adopted a large-volume rebate program (of questionable legality) for selected large supermarket chains in order to undercut other packers and force small firms to sell their slaughtered animals to IBP for fabrication into boxed beef. In this manner IBP expanded its processing capacity and non-union sources of dressed beef.[47]

The company's aggressive strategy exploited the Achilles heel of the Amalgamated's packinghouse department: Authority and resources for organizing were in the hands of local unions and regions, not departments. IBP's new plants were in districts of the union controlled by Amalgamated officials who would not cooperate with Prosten or the packinghouse department. The aggressive posture of IBP discouraged organizing efforts by regional union leaders who saw no particular reason to target the meatpacking industry, especially its most notoriously anti-union firm. Packinghouse workers could only watch in frustration as the Amalgamated allowed the foundations of industrial unionism in meatpacking to erode slowly.[48]

The expiration of the Dakota City contract in 1977 thus occurred under unfavorable conditions because the strength of the union had declined precipitously. Dakota City no longed supplied all of IBP's boxed beef, and it was the only IBP packinghouse represented by the Amalgamated. After a brutal fourteen-month strike, the union accepted a contract that actually increased IBP's wage advantage over other meatpacking companies. By October 1978 the wage gap had doubled between IBP and the master agreement firms, and it grew steadily wider each year thereafter (Table 14). The defeat at IBP would have profound consequences on the union.

IBP's victory was a blow, not only to the packinghouse workers in the Amalgamated but also to the organization's retail butchers. With the surge of boxed beef into the market in the 1970s, the butcher locals were sapped by layoffs as supermarkets and meat markets dispensed with the services of skilled Amalgamated members. National union membership stagnated at five hundred thousand, the same as in 1969. The retirement of long-time leader Patrick Gorman in 1977 added to the Amalgamated's troubles. The national organization threatened to disintegrate as warring factions of regional directors struggled for control. To escape their dilemma, Amalgamated leaders began looking for another union with which to merge—and they found an eager suitor in the Retail Clerks International Union (RCIU). In 1979 the two organizations formed the United Food and Commercial Workers (UFCW).[49]

Almost from the beginning, long-time packinghouse unionists harbored grave doubts about the UFCW. To Frank Wallace, "It seemed we had moved from being a labor organization to becoming a small corporation of some type ourselves." Wallace particularly objected to the bureaucratic features of the UFCW, especially extensive paperwork and a dress code requiring organizers to wear suits. "If I'm servicing a poultry plant, I look like a fool going in there with a tie on and a pair of fifty dollar shoes," he pointed out a year after retiring. Omaha unionist Max Graham, while working for the UFCW, used the analogy of "a shot of whiskey" to compare the organizations. "When we was the UPWA, we was little but powerful. Then we joined the Amalgamated and we got like a mixed drink. Now it looks to me like we're a shot in a quart of Squirt."[50]

Table 14. Master Agreement and IBP Base Wages, 1970–81

Date	Master	IBP Slaughter/Processing	Difference
April 1970	$ 3.94	$3.34/2.74	$0.60/1.20
October 1973	4.71	3.80/3.19	0.91/1.52
February 1977	6.47	5.87/5.57	0.60/0.90
October 1978	7.56	6.22/5.92	1.34/1.64
October 1980	9.64	8.20/7.90	1.44/1.74
October 1981	10.69	9.14/8.84	1.55/1.85
December 1981[a]			

a. Master agreement companies demand concessions.

Sources: All figures drawn from U.S. Department of Labor, *Wage Chronology, Swift and Company, January 1942–September 1973*, Bureau of Labor Statistics Bulletin 1771 (Washington, 1973), and *Current Wage Developments*, 1970–82.

The concerns of former UPWA members had more than a visceral basis. Packinghouse workers represented less than 10 percent of the UFCW's membership, and the Retail Clerks who dominated the organization had even less experience with industrial unionism than the Amalgamated. "After all," Jesse Prosten pointed out in 1986, "this union was originally called the Retail Clerks International Protective Association and was a big, fat company union." To Prosten it was "classic, culturally, of the craft unions." Founded in 1890, the RCIU was a small, tightly controlled AFL union that grew rapidly after World War II by increasing its membership in the growing supermarket chains. Operating in local labor markets, RCIU local unions were used to relying on their own staff and business agents to service members and negotiate contracts with many firms in unrelated businesses. Departments in the international union merely assisted the locals and the regions and did not centralize union operations as in an industrial union. At both the local and international levels the RCIU was a hierarchical organization entirely unused to the free-wheeling membership participation accepted by the UPWA. "The one thing which the member does not receive from the union is a means of really active participation in the decisions affecting him," noted Michael Harrington in an otherwise positive 1962 study of the RCIU.[51]

The clash between craft and industrial unionism assumed a clear organizational form inside the UFCW. Throughout the 1980s former RCIU officials in the UFCW firmly resisted the efforts of packinghouse workers to control relations with their industry through a National Packing Committee. Instead, regional union leaders, and officials in large mixed locals, claimed primary authority over negotiations with packing companies in their geographic jurisdiction. At issue were two different traditions of unionism, and the packinghouse workers were at a distinct disadvantage in the struggle.

It had been Jesse Prosten's last triumph to retain, inside the Amalgamated, the structures of industrial unionism in meatpacking. Not surprisingly, his retirement in 1980 only added to the uneasiness among packinghouse workers. Omaha union founder George Fletemeyer credited Prosten with maintaining UPWA-style unionism under the Amalgamated. "But if you changed from him to somebody else," he prophetically warned, "I'm sure it would have been different." Fletemeyer's fears proved all too accurate. Prosten's young successor, former IBP worker Lewie Anderson, had neither Prosten's reputation nor experience in navigating packinghouse workers through a far more hostile corporate and union environment. As packinghouse workers contemplated the significance of Ronald Reagan's election victory in 1980, they no doubt looked at the coming decade with considerable concern. The

government, the companies, and their own union failed to promise conti-
nuity with the postwar pattern of industrial relations in meatpacking.[52]

Industrial Unionism in Decline, 1980–84

The UFCW was ill-prepared, structurally and culturally, to resist the
challenge to union strength in the 1980s. Although packinghouse workers
were not the only unionists to suffer in this decade, the decline of union
power in meatpacking was especially dramatic. Beginning with the concessions granted by the United Auto Workers to Chrysler, concessions and plant
closings ravaged American unions. President Ronald Reagan's peremptory
dismissal of striking air traffic controllers in 1982 encouraged employers to
resist the demands of labor organizations, and his appointments to the federal judiciary and the NLRB helped swing the legal system against unions.
In meatpacking, the consolidation of a new oligopoly of three firms in tandem with steadily declining union strength would end in a catastrophe for
America's packinghouse workers.[53]

Just before retiring, Jesse Prosten predicted that the "employers will do
anything to get rid of the master agreements." His prophecy would prove
eerily accurate in the 1980s. Concessions, and pressure on the master agreements, accelerated almost as soon as the UFCW formed. In 1980 and 1981 at
least two dozen companies asked for concessions while contracts were in
effect. Many threatened to close their plants if the union did not comply.
Despite opposition from the packinghouse division, at least a half-dozen
firms secured concessions by making agreements with local unions. In these
instances, the contracts were approved by UFCW President William Wynn
over the objections of Anderson.[54]

Inexorably, the pressure for concessions spread to the master agreement
packers. In December 1981, with one year left under the national contracts,
threats of plant closings persuaded the UFCW and the packinghouse division to grant concessions at five major packing companies with thirty thousand workers. Wages were frozen at $10.69, and future cost-of-living provi-
sions were to be paid in a lump sum that would not increase the base wage.
New employees were not eligible for the cost-of-living payments and received less than other workers during their first four months.[55]

Anderson tried to put a brave face on the UFCW's policy of "controlled
retreat." Publicly he asserted that the union would hold the "top" wages
steady while it worked to "move the bottom up" in order to reestablish "a
pure national wage structure." Inside the union, Anderson claimed that two
provisions of the new master agreements would help turn matters around

in the near future: The companies promised to not close any plants for eighteen months and to provide the union with their capital investment plans. He assured union members that these clauses would ensure that meatpacking firms reinvested the money saved through the wage freeze "into operating plants and the construction of new plants." This hope proved short-lived.[56]

The controlled retreat quickly disintegrated into a rout that not only lowered wage rates further but also shredded the master agreements and de-unionized the core firms of the industry. Their appetites whetted by the UFCW's concession, the master agreement packers used a variety of legal stratagems to remove themselves from the master agreements entirely. Esmark, the owner of Swift, sold all but five plants to an new company called Swift Independent (SIPCO). Three plants closed by Swift before the sale were reopened by SIPCO on a non-union basis with wages $3 an hour below the master agreement rate. SIPCO then closed six formerly unionized plants and acquired three Armour facilities, which it operated on a non-union basis. By 1982 the Swift master agreement had been reduced to coverage at three plants. Morrell sold its Arkansas City, Kansas, plant to Rodeo Meats, a firm that sold all its product to Morrell but whose workers were non-union and made only $5 an hour. Soon thereafter Morrell's corporate parent, United Brands, closed ten plants, leaving Morrell with just one facility under the old "master agreement." By the summer of 1983 the number of workers under the master agreements had fallen to thirty thousand, only a third of the packinghouse workers represented by the UFCW.[57]

In May 1983 came another major blow to the UFCW's controlled retreat: Wilson declared bankruptcy, abrogated the union contract, and unilaterally cut hourly pay to $6.50. After a strike, the union restored wages to $8 but accepted massive concessions, including a two-tier wage system and reductions in medical care. This left the Wilson "master agreement" covering only two plants. Within two years after the UFCW began its controlled retreat, national contracts had virtually disappeared at Swift, Morrell, and Wilson.[58]

Corporate manipulation of packing plants owned by Armour was the final blow to the master agreements. In 1983, Greyhound, which had bought Armour in the 1970s, closed thirteen plants and sold them to the food giant ConAgra. The new owners reopened the packinghouses on a non-union basis, with wages ranging from $5.50 to $6.50 an hour. ConAgra also was selective in its employment of former Armour workers; many active in the union were not rehired. Several years later the UFCW won a $6.6 million settlement against ConAgra for hiring discrimination, but the court upheld the company's refusal to recognize the union or the master agreement. Forty-five years of unionism at Armour, the first major packer organized by the UPWA, was over.[59]

The shakeout of 1982 through 1984 eliminated master agreements as an influence over industry wage patterns and allowed the new meatpacking oligopoly to take final form. In 1983 alone, twenty-three unionized plants employing nine thousand workers closed. Cargill and ConAgra used the turmoil to acquire production facilities of other firms and ensure that their new consortiums would be predominantly non-union. With wages and benefits in the dominant meatpacking companies no longer governed by master agreements, the whole tone of labor-management relations had changed fundamentally. All that remained of forty years of industrial unionism was pattern bargaining at the pork processing firms such as Hormel and Oscar Mayer, where there were no master agreements but the union was able to negotiate similar plant-level contracts. The UFCW retained the form of industrial unionism between 1984 and 1989, but with little of the content or power that had made it effective under the UPWA.[60]

Moreover, the defeats hurt Anderson's struggle inside the UFCW by weakening both the chains and the National Packinghouse Committee. As the number of representatives from packinghouse-based locals steadily declined, large diversified local unions that contained packinghouse workers either ignored the National Packinghouse Committee or sent officials hostile to the Anderson's efforts. The inability of the packinghouse division to stem the union's retreat also reduced Anderson's credibility inside the dues-conscious UFCW. Concerned that the packinghouse division would engage in unprofitable strikes, the UFCW closely monitored its meetings and activities. "It got to be that there were more international representatives at chain meetings than packinghouse workers," Anderson tellingly observed. The industrial unionism inherited from the UPWA was beginning to crack.[61]

Local P-9 and the Battle for Industrial Unionism, 1985–89

The collapse of the master agreements was a historic setback for unionism in the industry, but it did not occur without sustained resistance by packinghouse workers. Dozens of local strikes erupted in the early 1980s against the initial wave of concessionary pressures but were universally defeated. A second round of strikes that began in 1985 was far less isolated. Although usually based at one plant, these struggles attracted support from other packinghouse workers who saw their future tied to the success of efforts to preserve wage standards. It was the outcome of strikes between

1985 and 1988 that finally determined the fate of industrial unionism in meatpacking.

The conflict that attracted the most public attention was the highly visible clash between Hormel and UFCW Local P-9 in the company's flagship Austin, Minnesota, plant. In a strike that lasted from August 1985 to June 1986, Local P-9 transfixed the labor movement—and occasionally the nation—with its dramatic struggle against contract concessions. The strike also divided packinghouse workers inside the UFCW, because P-9 refused to accept the decisions of the packinghouse division and the Hormel chain, which disagreed with P-9's strategy. Consequently, the P-9 strike is instructive both of the rank-and-file anger among packinghouse workers at the historic decline in their wages and working conditions, and the atrophy of industrial unionism under the UFCW.

Superficially, there were many parallels between the 1985 strike and the Austin-based IUAW of the 1930s that had launched industrial unionism in meatpacking. The Hormel workers of the 1980s trod paths first blazed by their IUAW predecessors when they traveled to Ottumwa, Albert Lea, Chicago, and other industrial centers to seek support and encourage other workers to struggle against their employers. Pickets emulated the tactics of 1933 by blockading the plant to prevent strikebreakers from entering. And P-9 members received accolades from other workers for fighting corporate power, just as men like Charles R. Fischer had taken heart from the success of Austin workers in 1933.

Much had changed, however, in fifty years. Hormel was a one-plant company in the 1930s, highly vulnerable to even a brief stoppage and led by a creative owner who learned to live with, and profit from, unionization. In 1985 the company owned half a dozen facilities and was able to maintain its market share and sales volume in the event of a strike at its largest plant. Following World War II, Hormel was one of the small packers that expanded rapidly because of the increase in meat consumption and changes in the structure of the industry. A new corporate leadership also took over operation of the firm after Jay Hormel died in 1956. Dubbed the "Nebraska mafia" by Austin workers, the new officials were hard-nosed managers from new plants and determined to end the special relationship between the company and its Austin workers.[62]

Hormel's management especially wanted to terminate the 1940 guaranteed annual wage agreement that had made their Austin employees the highest-paid workers in the meatpacking industry. For almost four decades Austin packinghouse workers received a guaranteed wage calculated on a thirty-eight-hour week regardless of hours actually worked. In addition, they collected incentive earnings that grew from 41 percent of the base wage in 1947 to 68 percent in 1956. As a result, Austin workers earned on average $120 for thirty-five hours of work in 1956, compared to $87 for a forty-hour week in Iowa packinghouses. "People had a decent standard of living and they didn't have any financial troubles," recalled Bob Johnson, the son of a Hormel worker. One measure of this prosperity is that the union could not obtain a quorum for summer meetings in the early 1960s because so many workers departed on weekends for their vacation homes.[63]

The special relationship with Hormel precluded Austin workers from becoming integrated into the UPWA's chains. The hourly wage was pegged to the rates in the Big Four master agreements, but it was incentive pay that made Hormel's Austin employees the wealthiest packinghouse workers in the country. Because local agreements, rather than a national contract, governed industrial relations at Hormel, the formation of a Hormel chain in the 1960s had little effect on the earnings of Austin workers.[64]

The changes in the Hormel Company, however, rapidly undermined the "harmonious relationship" between labor and management. Under company pressure, the Austin local started granting concessions in 1963 in the form of higher production schedules that reduced incentive earnings. This erosion in earning levels continued throughout the 1960s and 1970s. In 1978, in order to exact a commitment from Hormel to build a new plant in Austin, the local union agreed to abandon the incentive system and not strike for three years after the completion of the new facility. The effect on wages was devastating. One hog-kill worker told a 1985 union meeting that he earned $637 weekly in the old plant; now he was taking home $312 and "working twice as hard."[65]

As that comment attests, the new plant (which opened in 1982) also disrupted long-established work habits and rhythms. The massive retirement of experienced workers and the hiring of new employees added to the disruption on the shop floor and created distinct generational cohorts within the workforce. Injury rates soared, especially among the thousand new employees hired after 1982. Three hundred older workers hired between 1945 and 1952, and another three hundred who started their employment between 1965 and 1970, chafed under the new shop-floor regime and the decline in earnings.[66]

The Hormel workers who led P-9's struggle in the 1980s generally were hired in the late 1960s, and their particular experiences colored the form and direction of the local union's strategy. They had grown up in Austin under conditions of steadily rising income and stable employment for parents who generally worked at Hormel. Like many of their supporters, P-9 president

James V. Guyette and business agent Pete Winkels were second-generation Hormel workers who had started their employment in the late 1960s. This cohort experienced declining real income almost from the moment they were hired, however, and in an environment where pattern bargaining seemingly provided little assistance. When Guyette and his supporters took control of the local in the 1980s, the master agreements were disappearing from the industry, and the UFCW was negotiating concessionary contracts. In fact, their main experience with pattern bargaining hurt Austin workers. As a result of concessions to the master agreement packers in 1982, an arbitrator held that Hormel could unilaterally cut hourly pay by $1.69 in accordance with a contract provision that tied P-9 wages to master agreement rates.[67]

For P-9's leaders, neither the traditions of the Austin local nor their recent experiences with the UFCW impressed them with the capacity of the chains to prevent concessions and represent packinghouse workers. As a result, it is not surprising that P-9 was unwilling to go along with the Hormel chain when it reached an agreement in September 1984 to lower wages to $9 an hour from $10.69. P-9 leaders maintained that the need to resist concessions and regain the $10.69 level outweighed participation in the chain. They argued that because their plant was one of the most modern in the industry, they should try for a high wage and act as an upward force on national pay levels. "If concessions are going to stop," Guyette observed at the time, "they are going to have to stop at the most profitable company with the newest plant." At a Hormel chain meeting in December 1984, other union leaders were appalled when P-9 leaders made this argument. Anderson angrily shouted that Austin's stance was "symptomatic of Reagan's philosophy, 'I'll get mine, and the hell with everyone else.'"[68]

Later these events would be critically reexamined to assign blame on who broke the solidarity of packinghouse workers. UFCW supporters claimed that P-9 was undermining industrial unionism, while P-9 partisans contended that they had tried to make every effort to maintain the solidarity of the Hormel chain against concessions. What had occurred, however, was not simply a conflict between a stubborn local and an intransigent international union. Fundamental strategic differences on the way to reinvigorate packinghouse unionism were involved.[69]

P-9's decision was based on the apparent collapse of pattern bargaining as a means of increasing—or even maintaining—the living standards of packinghouse workers. Never inculcated with the benefits of the chains, it was easier for Austin workers to make this historic break than other packinghouse workers. P-9 members felt they were simply recognizing that the chains were no longer effective. The majority of local union leaders in meatpacking, however, felt that P-9 was undermining what precious unity still existed. Anderson, who still had hopes of rebuilding the packinghouse division out of the chaos of the early 1980s, saw P-9's action as yet another blow to his efforts.

Although the P-9 strike reflected resistance to concessionary pressures typical in meatpacking, particular local concerns significantly fueled the militancy and direction of its struggle. Hormel's final proposal eliminated major contractual provisions the union had secured in the 1930s: a guaranteed annual wage, a year's notice before layoffs, and job placement in accordance with seniority. The contract also provided for a two-tier wage system, a 30 percent reduction in pensions, a common labor wage of $9.25 with no increases over three years, and eliminated maternity leave. To P-9 members descended from packinghouse workers, Hormel was trying to reassert the level of control that had existed before their parents and grandparents built a union. "They'd be worse off than they were before they organized in 1933 if they took the last contract they offered them," IUAW founder Casper Winkels cogently observed not long after strike began.[70]

The great tragedy of the P-9 strike was that the UFCW, the sole national union of packinghouse workers, could no longer accommodate and focus working-class militancy in the industry. This certainly was not the first time that a militant meatpacking local had clashed with the international—or even jumped the gun on a strike. But the UPWA never turned on one of its local unions like the UFCW did with P-9. In its heyday, the UPWA relied on, and tried to give direction to, the power and militancy of packinghouse workers rather than suppress those impulses. The UFCW, in contrast, tried to repress the combative spirit displayed by P-9 members. There simply was no precedent in meatpacking for the UFCW's attack on P-9.

Opposition from the UFCW, high unemployment in the Midwest, and the hostile political climate for labor doomed P-9's resistance. In January 1986 Hormel reopened the plant with new employees and, with the aid of the Minnesota National Guard, stymied P-9's efforts to block entrances to the facility. The UFCW refused to sanction P-9's request to use roving pickets to halt production at other Hormel plants. Nonetheless, more than five hundred workers respected P-9 pickets at Ottumwa and were promptly suspended. Without support from the international, however, this tactic was doomed. In Fremont, Nebraska, local UFCW officials instructed union members to cross P-9's picket lines; only a handful of workers stayed out. By February, the strike was no longer effective. Slowly, P-9 union members started to trickle back in Austin, even though the local remained on strike, until almost four hundred had joined a thousand new employees in the plant. As the strike unraveled, public recriminations between P-9 and the UFCW reached a crescendo, including a vitriolic clash between Anderson and Guyette on "Nightline," the ABC television show.[71]

In April UFCW President Wynn decided that the international union would settle the dispute on its own. The UFCW removed P-9's officers, terminated strike benefits, and signed a contract with Hormel (based on a settlement reached in the Oscar Mayer plants) for a $10 an hour base wage with increase to $10.70 in three years. Aside from wages, the Austin agreement was very close to the terms Hormel demanded when P-9 struck in August 1985. It eliminated two key contractual provisions that had been in the Austin agreements since 1940: a guaranteed annual wage and a fifty-two-week notice before any layoffs. The four-year contract also terminated the common expiration dates achieved under the Amalgamated and contained no language requiring the Hormel company to rehire 850 P-9 members still out of work. Fewer than a hundred of the P-9 members who refused to cross union picket lines ever regained their jobs.[72]

The failure of the P-9 strike was an enormous setback, not only to Austin workers but also to packinghouse unionism. The bitter split over strategy left rancor and division at a time when the union could ill-afford either. The Hormel locals were weakened: The Austin union was cowed from the strike's defeat, and Ottumwa was divided between those who respected the P-9 picket lines and those who went to work. Moreover, by settling the dispute directly, the UFCW had used the strike to intrude into turf previously conceded to the packinghouse division.

The November 1986 UFCW National Packinghouse Strategy and Policy Conference tried to put a positive light on the outcome of the P-9 strike. Scheduled speakers defended the UFCW's role by claiming that "P-9 used tactics that fit into Corporate America's program of breaking up Master Agreements, of splintering chainwide bargaining, and spreading poison about organized labor." In defense of the international, Anderson told the delegates that in 1985 "the union had stopped mid-term contract concessions." The recent agreements at Oscar Mayer and Hormel demonstrated that "the process of recovering some of those wages that were lost is firmly in place." He admitted, though, that the union no longer had master agreements, and when the report was mailed to the membership in April 1987 Anderson noted in a cover letter that more than five thousand workers were on strike against a new round of concessionary pressures. Despite the lofty rhetoric, the corporate assault on industrial unionism had not abated.[73]

The new round of strikes were centered around Sioux City. On December 13, 1986, IBP locked out its Dakota City workers after they rejected further pay cuts and other concessions. Soon thereafter, Morrell workers in Sioux Falls, South Dakota (sixty miles north) walked off their jobs when the company demanded concessions. With the UFCW's consent, the Sioux Falls Morrell workers set up picket lines at the company's Sioux City plant, prompting a sympathy walkout.[74]

Although these struggles received the full support of the packinghouse division, they fared no better than P-9's had. In July 1987 IBP forced the union to accept a permanent two-tier wage scale. New employees started at $6 an hour and could rise to no more than $7.60 after thirty months, 60 cents less than older workers. With IBP's notoriously high turnover, this was a substantial wage reduction for the leading firm in the industry. At Morrell, where replacement workers kept the two plants in operation, the UFCW called off the strike in October without obtaining a contract. Fewer than 20 percent of the strikers were able to return to work immediately, and subsequent events made it another crushing defeat. The Eighth Circuit Court of Appeals upheld a $24 million Morrell lawsuit against the UFCW on the basis that the sympathy strike was illegal.[75]

At some point in this seemingly endless and unsuccessful battle against concessions, UFCW leaders decided that Anderson's strategy was proving too costly. The strikes by IBP and Morrell workers had cost the union millions of dollars. Yet the efforts had been in vain; the concessions had gone through. Gradually, Anderson found himself excluded from negotiations with meatpacking companies, his advice and opinions ignored.[76]

Ironically, it was renewed pressures for concessions at the Austin Hormel plant that brought the simmering differences in the UFCW to a boil. In January 1988 Hormel closed the hog kill in its Austin plant. Using the stratagem of leasing it to an unknown firm, Quality Pork, Hormel threatened to keep the hog kill closed unless the union agreed to cut slaughtering wages to $7 an hour. The weakened Austin local complied on November 22, 1988— prompting a struggle inside the UFCW over whether President William Wynn should approve the concessions. Lewie Anderson fought desperately to block acceptance of the agreement. Wynn not only rejected Anderson's arguments and approved the contract but also fired Anderson as head of the packinghouse division in January 1989.[77]

The Austin agreement, combined with the dismissal of Anderson, brought a storm of protest from packinghouse workers. Thirteen presidents of locals representing fifteen thousand workers publicly attacked Wynn's actions. Harry Acker, the conservative head of the Madison, Wisconsin, Oscar Mayer local criticized the UFCW as a union "where the captains of the ships are fools." Jim Coleman, president of the Cedar Rapids, Iowa, union bitterly attacked UFCW leaders as "beancounters. All they're interested in is maintaining good relations with employers and collecting their per capita." Coleman had good reason to complain. The slaughterhouse represented by his local closed soon thereafter because the owner could not compete with the new low wage rates in Austin, less than a hundred miles north.[78]

Packinghouse unionists also were rankled at the UFCW's conduct in a contemporaneous organizing drive against IBP. Especially galling was the international union's tight control of the campaign and its resistance to local organizing initiatives that did not correspond to its central plan. Launched with great fanfare in 1986, the drive suddenly folded in 1988 after IBP agreed not to contest union recognition at a new plant in Joslin, Illinois. The willingness of IBP to "voluntarily let the union in is inherently suspicious," noted an unidentified labor lawyer at the time. Packinghouse workers were less restrained. "UFCW sold its soul to the devil and got a bad deal in the bargain," charged UFCW Local 179 in Cherokee, Iowa. Local 179 alleged that recognition at the Joslin plant was part of deal that included acceptance of the two-tier wage system in Dakota City by the UFCW and termination of the organizing drive at other IBP plants. Rather than a "new era of labor/management cooperation" at IBP, Local 179 charged that the UFCW had damaged opportunities to organize IBP workers. "The workers at IBP and the locals who assisted in the organizing drive feel betrayed," the local concluded.[79]

The dismissal of Anderson removed packinghouse workers' last foothold in the UFCW bureaucracy. With Anderson gone, the packinghouse division would no longer function as a center for industrial unionism. Local unions of packinghouse workers went into opposition and formed a dissident faction in the UFCW called REAP (Research, Education, Advocacy, People), which Anderson headed. With the end of the packinghouse division as a vehicle for pattern bargaining, chain negotiations, and master agreements, industrial unionism no longer functioned in the meatpacking industry.[80]

The Return of the Drive System in Meatpacking

By 1990 the unionism that existed in meatpacking corresponded to Kim Moody's notion of "general unionism." Packinghouse workers in the UFCW generally are members of large local unions with thousands of members in unrelated occupations. There are neither master agreements nor common expiration dates for workers in different plants of the same national company. Relatively strong plant-based local unions, with the best contracts, are limited to pork processing firms such as Oscar Mayer and Hormel, and pattern bargaining retains some influence at these companies. These "strongholds" of unionism, however, remain vulnerable because of growing nonunion operations in each firm. Elsewhere in the meatpacking industry, packinghouse workers have little connection with each other. Wage rates are set in local negotiations conducted by local union leaders and regional officials rather than through national bargaining. Because fewer than 50 percent of the workers in the new Big Three of IBP, ConAgra, and Cargill are organized, unions no longer exercise pressure on the overall level of wages in meatpacking or the conditions under which packinghouse workers labor. The result has been a return to the drive system that characterized meatpacking in the non-union era.[81]

The effect of industrial unionism's collapse and the return of the drive system can be measured painfully in declining wages, increasing labor turnover, and deteriorating shop-floor conditions. The relative and absolute drop in earnings is stunning. After World War II, the UPWA was able to transform meatpacking from a low-wage occupation to one that paid better than many other industrial jobs. By the 1960s, hourly pay in meatpacking exceeded the average for all American manufacturing by about 15 percent. The Amalgamated Meat Cutters packinghouse department was able to maintain this level in the 1970s. But by 1990 union concessions in meatpacking brought wages 20 percent below the average for manufacturing (Table 15). Real wages (adjusted for inflation) plummeted 30 percent between 1979 and 1990.[82]

Low pay stokes a system of labor turnover that packing firms count on to keep wage and benefit costs low. "There are some economies," admitted IBP labor relations head Arden Walker, "that result from hiring new employ-

Table 15. Wages for Meatpacking versus U.S. Manufacturing, 1950–90

Year	Meatpacking	Manufacturing	Percent Difference
1950	$1.40	$ 1.44	-2.8
1960	2.60	2.26	15.0
1965	2.99	2.61	14.7
1975	5.67	4.83	14.8
1979	7.73	6.70	13.3
1985	8.10	9.54	-16.6
1990	8.73	10.84	-20.1

Sources: Charles R. Perry and Delwyn H. Kegley, *Disintegration and Change: Labor Relations in the Meat Packing Industry* (Philadelphia, 1989), 21; American Meat Institute, *Meat Facts, 1991* (Washington, 1992), 34; REAP, *News and Views,* Nov.–Dec. 1991.

ees." Permanent two-tier wage systems proliferated in the late 1980s, with new employees starting around $6 an hour. Turnover usually ranges between 60 and 100 percent a year at slaughtering plants. At IBP's unionized Dakota City plant, a third of the workers had fewer than two years' seniority in 1986, and annual turnover averaged 70 percent. Although meatpacking always has had a high layoff and rehire rate, a government study pinpointed 1979 through 1982 as the period when voluntary quits soared to levels well over the average in manufacturing.[83]

As in the non-union era, the flow of casual labor in and out of packing-houses draws on workers who have the most limited job options. Packing-house workers travel in a cyclical pattern from plant to plant in the Midwest, seeking new employment after layoffs or trying to find slightly better wages and conditions. Packinghouse companies aggressively recruit Mexicans and Southeast Asians and are able to use federal job training programs to subsidize transportation and training costs. Supplementing the new immigrants are growing numbers of young single mothers from rural areas, women who need the income to support their children. This fundamental recomposition of the meatpacking labor force has impeded unionization. "A union organizer at a plant gate is like a straw in a tornado," noted attorney Peggy Hillman in a speech to a UFCW conference. She astutely asked the delegates how workers can "identify with traditional union concerns such as pensions, medical care, and wage increases when they have no expectations of continued employment?"[84]

Inside the plants, the decline of unionism has been accompanied by a ferocious increase in the pace of work. As with turnover, unionization of slaughtering plants does not seem to be a moderating factor. The Sioux Falls Morrell plant increased the speed of the hog-killing line from 640 an hour in the late 1960s to 1,065 in 1986, without an increase in the number of workers. IBP's Dakota City plant cattle kill went from 225 an hour in 1981 to 275 at the end of the decade, a 20 percent increase. Personal testimonies convey the speed of work in fabricating departments. In Sioux City, for example, Annie Becker and one other person trimmed 540 hog tongues an hour in the 1960s; in 1988 she handled 785 each hour by herself.[85]

Injury rates have risen along with the speed of the disassembly line. As the tempo of work has increased, human bodies have been unable to sustain the pace that the companies demand. Although meatpacking has always been a dangerous job, the increase in the repetitive motion disorder known as carpal tunnel syndrome is a human measure of the "authority relations" that now prevail in meatpacking. The incidence of occupational illness—primarily carpal tunnel syndrome—grew 264 percent between 1980 and

1988; days lost due to this "illness" more than tripled between 1984 and 1989 (Tables 16 and 17). Considering widespread documentation that official reports understate the extent of the disorder, these figures are conservative. Union representatives at IBP's Dakota City plant estimate that 70 percent of the workers suffer from symptoms of carpal tunnel syndrome. Overall, the number of job-related injuries and illnesses in meatpacking increased 24 percent in seven years, to 33.4 per hundred workers in 1986—three times the average injury rate in all manufacturing industries. The unionized Dakota City plant had an injury rate of forty-two per hundred workers in 1985. These numbers provide graphic documentation of increasing work speeds—and the evaporation of shop-floor union power.[86]

These raw numbers conceal the marked change in packinghouse workers from members of the blue-collar middle class in the 1950s to part of the working poor in the 1990s. Workers crowd into shabby trailer courts built by packing companies, while others sleep in their cars in parks and along riverbeds, cooking their food on open fires. Workers without vehicles pitch

Table 16. Illness Rate for Meatpacking, per One Hundred Workers

		Percent Increase	
Year	Rate	From 1980	From Previous Year
1980	2.5	0	0
1982	3.0	20	20
1984	4.4	76	47
1986	6.4	156	45
1988	9.1	264	42

Sources: American Meat Institute, *Meat Facts, 1990* (Washington, 1990), 25; American Meat Institute, *Meat Facts, 1991* (Washington, 1992), 35.

Table 17. Lost Workdays Due to Illness and Injury, per One Hundred Workers

Year	Illness	Injuries and Illness
1984	42.1	232.3
1986	48.1	238.4
1988	118.7	357.0
1989	136.0	358.7

Sources: American Meat Institute, *Meat Facts, 1990* (Washington, 1990), 25; American Meat Institute, *Meat Facts, 1991* (Washington, 1992), 35.

tents in local campgrounds or seek out bridges, overpasses, or run-down boardinghouses for shelter. Austin, Minnesota's downtown is now a strip of closed department stores, a far cry from the bustling commercial town in the days of the Hormel's guaranteed annual wage. Towns that lured packinghouses in hope of prosperity have found that the low wage levels have failed to provide a spur to the local economy; instead, the poorly paid workers bring crime and increased demands on local social services.[87]

Deteriorating conditions for packinghouse workers were a direct consequence, and not merely a by-product, of the transformation of the industry between 1955 and 1990. The development of new forms of meat production and distribution, and ascendance of a new oligopoly of three firms, rested on the virtual elimination of union power. The decline of industrial unionism reflected incessant pressures by capital for lower labor costs and more control over the work process. Companies that emerged victorious from the competitive scramble were those that most successfully increased the rate of exploitation of today's makers of meat. Almost a century after Upton Sinclair's pioneering expose of meatpacking, packinghouse workers in the United States have tragically returned to the jungle.

"For Your Future and Mine": Workers, Unions, and the Meatpacking Industry of the Twenty-first Century

For Your Future and Mine, Support Local P-9
—Slogan of UFCW Local P-9, 1985

On the high arid plains of western Kansas is a small town that represents, in microcosm, the future of America's meatpacking industry. Garden City is one of many rural communities turned into burgeoning meat-producing centers by the transformation of the contemporary packinghouse industry. In the 1980s IBP and ConAgra established two plants in Garden City employing more than four thousand workers. The companies were attracted by nearby feed lots, generous tax breaks, and Kansas's right-to-work laws, which inhibit unionism. Garden City, and other towns situated in similar rural areas, are the new meatpacking centers of the twenty-first century.[1]

If Garden City is the modern equivalent of the old Chicago stockyards, the workers who labor in its plants also resemble the packinghouse workers of the early twentieth century. They are, once again, immigrants, the rural poor, the most disadvantaged of the American labor force. The places once filled by East European immigrants have been assumed by Southeast Asians and transient illegal migrants from Mexico. Displaced farmers, single mothers, and hard-pressed midwestern workers make up the native-born white population in the plants.[2]

Like their early-twentieth-century counterparts, Garden City's packinghouse workers inhabit a different world than middle-class town residents. Initial housing shortages, which forced workers to live in tents and cars, were partly relieved through the construction of cheap mobile home parks on the outskirts of town. In East Garden Village, Asians, Latinos, and white packinghouse workers crowd into dilapidated homes along streets populated by others of similar ethnic backgrounds. Virtually untouched by city services, the neighborhood has been racked by destructive fires, burglaries, and automobile accidents. Another trailer court populated by packinghouse workers, the Wagon Wheel, has no paved streets and relies on an inadequate cesspool for disposing household waste. When it rains, children play in the foul "muddy quagmire" of dirt streets and sidewalks because open spaces available for playgrounds are choked with weeds and trash.[3]

The working conditions in Garden City's packinghouses also bear stark similarities with the early twentieth century. Workers risk dismissal if they buck their supervisors: "You just do what they tell you to do," recalled one IBP worker. With the killing lines slaughtering four hundred cattle an hour, "I don't have time to sweep my sweat from my face," complained one Garden City production worker. Workers routinely perform unpaid labor after working hours, the modern equivalent of "working for the church." The low starting pay of $6 an hour forces entire families to work in order to survive, and constant turnover prevents many workers from receiving fringe benefits tied to length of service. Six-day weeks and mandatory overtime alternate with sudden layoffs as the packers adjust to fluctuations in meat supply and demand. A steady stream of job applicants reminds current employees that there are plenty waiting to take their place. Inside the plants, ethnic divisions inhibit shop-floor cooperation and mute workers' resistance to company policies. Appearances may have changed, but Upton Sinclair's Jurgis Rudkus would immediately recognize the rules of the game for workers in Garden City's packinghouses.[4]

The lives of today's meatpacking workers impels us to appreciate the impact of twentieth-century industrial unionism on the American working class. Looked at over a long cycle of union advance and decline, the formation of the CIO and the UPWA certainly was "Labor's Giant Step" for packinghouse workers, although perhaps not as leftist Art Preis intended the phrase. Reflections of packinghouse workers themselves speak sensitively to what the UPWA attained. Chicago unionist Todd Tate linked the union's material accomplishments with increased community respect for packinghouse workers. "People used to have run-down shoes and old beat-up jalopies," he recalled. "Within a short period of time you're driving a Cadillac, wearing a suit and tie. These things have elevated the quality of life for a lot of people." Sam Davis, a Sioux City steward, emphasized that the UPWA gave a worker "some kind of rights without being afraid he's gonna get fired. They took that hammer from over his head." And many former UPWA activists echoed Nels Peterson's blunt assertion that "there's no management going to give you anything. You've got to be strong enough to take it away from them." Industrial unionism, by facilitating cooperation among male and female workers from different racial and ethnic groups, transformed the living standards, working conditions, and social status of America's packinghouse workers.[5]

Industrial unionism, as an organizational vehicle for working-class cooperation, functioned especially well in meatpacking. As in other industries, it satisfied two basic prerequisites for working-class power. First, workers of completely different backgrounds with little in common except their occupation were able to cooperate for objectives of mutual interest. Second, workers in different plants of the same national firm were able to coordinate their activities to force powerful corporations to negotiate with labor organizations. In meatpacking, however, the pattern of union formation added an egalitarian and democratic ethos to the UPWA's culture, imparted by a dynamic synthesis between the structural need for inter-racial cooperation and the concerted initiatives of union militants who created and sustained the UPWA. The result was an unusual labor organization in postwar America that successfully resisted anticommunism, retained internal diversity, and provided an important spur to the emerging social movements of the 1950s and 1960s.

The UPWA's legacy was such that the industrial union structures it established persisted for two decades inside organizations rooted in craft unionism. Indeed, its influence on the living standards of packinghouse workers extended outside of its nominal members to those whose wage levels were influenced by pattern bargaining. "Even though they're not union," Nels Peterson reflected on the packinghouse workers of the late 1980s, "they're still getting benefits from what we got." As Peterson's comment attests, the UPWA's influence continues to linger in the meatpacking industry.[6]

Conditions in Garden City today, a manifestation of industrial unionism's collapse, also forcefully pose the question of the UPWA's limitations and the appropriate strategies for labor in the meat industry of the next century. The UPWA simply did not have the resources to respond adequately to the shift of capital in the industry, and to extend unionism with sufficient speed and scope to new firms and a workforce undergoing profound recomposition. This limitation should not be overstated. The capacity of industrial unionism to challenge IBP in the 1970s was a direct result of the UPWA's organizing accomplishments in the 1960s. In contrast, the Amalgamated Meat Cutters and the UFCW may have had the resources to maintain industrial unionism but did not have the will. The persistence of a weakened "general unionism" in meatpacking under the UFCW, for all its problems, indicates how a labor organization not based in particular sectors of capital can endure even as its base in one industry fades. Yet the UFCW's evident shortcomings also demonstrate that general unionism is not an adequate vehicle for workers' power in meatpacking.

The dilemma for packinghouse workers in the twenty-first century will be how to rebuild strong ties among themselves and at the same time retain essential links with the labor movement. Recreating a union limited to meatpacking would encounter the same problems as the UPWA faced in the 1960s, because the industry remains turbulent. Yet simple perpetuation of the UFCW clearly is inadequate, as conditions in Garden City's packinghouses and working class neighborhoods attest.

Like their 1930s predecessors, contemporary pro-union packinghouse workers face the predicament of how to assemble sufficient resources to organize a national industry. Indeed, the emergence of industrial unionism at mid-century contains insights pertinent to today's challenges. Although initiatives from below, especially in Austin and Chicago, provided the initial spur to union formation during the New Deal, it took an alliance with other sectors of the working class through the CIO to secure sufficient resources for industrial unionism to triumph in meatpacking. This suggests that reorganizing the American meatpacking industry will once again entail a rank-and-file initiative combined with support from established labor organizations and a broader workers' movement.

One set of examples how the industrial unionism of the mid-twentieth century might be fruitfully adapted to the twenty-first century can be drawn from the P-9 strike of 1985–86. It was unfortunate that in the war of words between P-9 and the UFCW, few noticed that P-9's methods resurrected much of the content of working-class solidarity that had characterized the UPWA but declined in the Amalgamated and the UFCW. P-9 dispatched informational pickets to other packinghouses, distributing information on their strike and establishing personal relationships among rank-and-file packinghouse workers. Union members handed out thousands of leaflets about their struggle to working-class residents in towns throughout the Midwest. An Educational Committee trained more than a hundred P-9 members in public speaking and dispatched them to speak at union meetings throughout the United States and Canada. The level of membership participation in P-9's campaign recalled the halcyon days of the IUAW.[7]

P-9 also devoted considerable energy to involving the families of Hormel workers. The local kept its large hall open twenty-four hours a day, seven days a week, serving basic meals in the basement and distributing free food weekly to the families of union members. A "Santa's Workshop" organized before Christmas in 1985 made hundreds of toys for strikers' children. A "Tool Box Committee" run by workers and workers' spouses handled the financial, legal, and emotional problems of union members. Although Ray Rogers, a hired consultant from Corporate Campaign Inc., coordinated the union's strike activities, much of the initiative, energy, and resources came from the Austin United Support Group, an organization established in 1984 and made up of P-9 spouses.[8]

P-9's efforts, which tapped the creative energies of rank-and-file pack-inghouse workers, contain three important messages for future union efforts in the meatpacking industry. First, Austin workers tried to reestablish bonds of solidarity among midwestern packinghouse workers, especially other Hormel employees, in order to rebuild the chains that had been the center-pieces of the UPWA's power. That they had to oppose the formal chain struc-ture of the UFCW is a measure of how far industrial unionism had atrophied by 1985. Second, Local P-9 mobilized a working-class community dependent on the Hormel plant, not merely those who actually worked for wages. As in other moments of working-class insurgency, spouses, retired workers, and other community members became players in the strike and influenced union strategy. Third, P-9 aggressively reached out to workers in other, un-related trades to ask for their moral and material support. In so doing, Aus-tin Hormel workers tapped a "solidarity consciousness" of many thousands of workers who felt, as one supporter of the 1934 Toledo Auto-Lite strike related, that "we were fighting for a cause, which was the working man's cause. And we figured it was about time that the working man had some-thing going his way." What P-9 tried to put together was, in sum, a move-ment that combined broad participation of working-class people with a co-herent strategy for subduing a multiplant national corporation.[9]

The form in which a revival of unionism might occur has been heatedly discussed among today's union advocates in meatpacking. Certain desired features clearly reflect UPWA traditions: master agreements, democratical-ly functioning chains, plant-based local unions, and commitment to equal treatment of men and women from all ethnic and racial backgrounds. Some ideas draw on the structure of contemporary unionism, such as establish-ing a packinghouse department inside the UFCW that is democratically governed by packinghouse workers. Other suggestions reintroduce tech-niques employed by Chicago activists in the 1930s: for the union to raise community issues that affect workers, such as housing and child care, as the first "steps on a road to convince these employees that they, collectively, have power." Together, these ideas show how today's packinghouse workers are creatively combining the strategies of the past with their contemporary experiences to chart a new course for unionism in meatpacking.[10]

These discussions among union advocates also indicate how we can move past the debate among academics over the merits of "community unionism" versus "job-centered unionism." It is hard to imagine a powerful union movement succeeding in the contemporary meatpacking industry without developing a community unionism that can draw on the resources of a working-class community and develop ties with workers who live in the same area but labor in different trades. It is equally difficult to conceive of reestablishing union power in firms such as IBP, Excell, and ConAgra without a job-centered unionism that can contest shop-floor issues and institutionalize solidarity among workers in different plants of the same national firm. The form in which this synthesis could occur is impossible to predict, however.[11]

Particular strategies aside, the fundamental challenge for meatpacking's new "militant minority" will be to persuade workers that cooperation with other racial and ethnic groups in a labor organization can lead to a better life. This will not be an easy task. It was only at a very special moment that an earlier generation of packinghouse workers overcame their internal divisions and acted collectively to change the conditions under which they labored. As in the 1930s, the creation of a new spirit of collective action among packinghouse workers will have to emerge from an understanding that they share "basic conditions of existence" that only can be improved through collective action on the job. Cooperation based on common grievances and concerns as workers, as a class, moderating without necessarily eliminating differences of race, ethnicity, religion, and sex, will offer the best hope for packinghouse workers to unite and improve their lot in the twenty-first century.[12]

Notes

Introduction

1. Art Preis, *Labor's Giant Step* (New York, 1963), xix.

2. Jimmy Porter interview, United Packinghouse Workers of America Oral History Project [hereafter cited as UPWAOHP].

3. Wilson J. Warren, in "The Limits of New Deal Social Democracy: Working-Class Structural Pluralism in Midwestern Meatpacking, 1900–1955," Ph.D. diss., University of Pittsburgh, 1992, takes issue with my positive assessment of the UPWA. Despite the quality of some of his case studies, Warren's study remains imbalanced because it ignores key packing centers such as Chicago and Kansas City, where blacks represented a majority or substantial minority within local unions.

4. Throughout this study I attempt to balance the relative influence of structure and agency on the evolution of industrial unionism in meatpacking. The debate over this issue is extensive. A good summary can be found in Philip Scranton, "The Workplace, Technology, and Theory in American Labor History," *International Labor and Working-Class History* 35 (Spring 1989): 3–22, and Douglas V. Porpora, "The Role of Agency in History: The Althusser-Thompson-Anderson Debate," *Current Perspectives in Social Theory* 6 (1985): 219–41.

5. "Authority relations" is from Anthony Giddens, *The Class Structure of the Advanced Societies* (London, 1973), 10; see also Sanford Jacoby, *Employing Bureaucracy: Managers, Unions, and the Transformation of Work in American Industry, 1900–1945* (New York, 1985), esp. 20–23, and Sumner H. Slichter, *The Turnover of Factory Labor* (New York, 1921).

6. David Montgomery, *The Fall of the House of Labor: The Workplace, the State, and American Labor Activism, 1865–1925* (Cambridge, 1987), 2.

7. Perry Anderson, *Arguments within English Marxism* (London, 1980), 20; Giddens, *The Class Structure of Advanced Societies*, 113.

8. Words in quotation marks are from Joan Scott, "Reply to Criticism," *International Labor and Working Class History* 32 (Fall 1987): 41.

9. Jeremy Brecher, *Strike* (Boston, 1972); Staughton Lynd, "'We Are All Leaders': The Alternative Unionism of the Early 1930s," paper delivered at the North American Labor History Conference, Wayne State University, 1992.

10. Melvyn Dubofsky, *The State and Labor in Modern America* (Chapel Hill, 1994); David Brody, "The Enduring Labor Movement: A Job-Conscious Perspective," occasional paper of the Harry Bridges Center, University of Washington, 1991.

11. For example, in their debate at the 1992 North American Labor History Conference, both David Brody and Staughton Lynd used the case of the Independent Union of All Workers in Austin, Minnesota, to support contrary arguments.

Chapter 1: Purveyors to a Nation

1. Upton Sinclair, *The Jungle* (1906, repr. Urbana, 1988), 44–45.

2. U.S. Department of Labor, *Injuries and Accident Causes in the Slaughtering and Meat-Packing Industry, 1943*, Bulletin 855 (Washington, 1943), 3–4, 21–22, 35–41.

3. Figures on the average size of packinghouses from U.S. Department of Commerce, Bureau of the Census, *Census of Manufactures, Slaughtering and Meatpacking, 1925* (Washington, 1926), 62.

4. U.S. Bureau of Corporations, *Report on the Beef Industry* (Washington, 1905), 1–8; Federal Trade Commission, *Report of the Federal Trade Commission on the Meat-Packing Industry* [hereafter cited as FTC] (Washington, 1919), summary and pt. 1, 127, 1, map and table opposite 394, map and table opposite 397; see also Margaret Walsh, *The Rise of the Midwestern Meat Industry* (Lexington, Ky., 1982); Temporary National Economic Committee, *Large-Scale Organization in the Food Industries*, Monograph 35, 76th Cong., 3d sess. (Washington, 1940), 17.

5. For the development of refrigeration in meatpacking, see "The 'Significant Sixty': A Historical Report on the Progress and Development of the Meat Packing Industry, 1891–1951," *National Provisioner*, Jan. 26, 1952, 197–216, 360, and Alfred D. Chandler, Jr., *The Visible Hand: The Managerial Revolution in American Business* (Cambridge, 1977), 299–301.

6. Chandler, *The Visible Hand*, 391–402; "The 'Significant Sixty,'" 69–86; Mary Yeager, *Competition and Regulation: The Development of Oligopoly in the Meat Packing Industry* (Greenwich, 1981).

7. Branch houses and company railroad cars sold prime cuts of meat to local butchers, restaurants, and food stores. By 1916 the Big Four and Morris owned 91 percent of the nation's refrigerated railroad cars and operated 1,120 branch houses and an additional 1,297 car routes. During the teens and 1920s, Armour acquired many small refrigerated auto trucks to perform a similar function. FTC, summary, pt. 1, 40–42, 142–44. There were 1,157 branch houses in operation in

1929. Willard F. Williams, "Structural Changes in the Meat Wholesaling Industry," *Journal of Farm Economics* 40 (May 1958): 323.

8. These firms generally specialized in pork because more of the hog could be sold canned or smoked than beef, reducing the need for an extensive network to deliver fresh meat. Temporary National Economic Committee, *Large-Scale Organization in the Food Industries*, 16. On Hormel's growth in the 1920s, see Richard Dougherty, *In Quest of Quality: Hormel's First Seventy-five Years* (Austin, Minn., 1966), 115–21.

9. FTC, pt. 1, 37, 107, 200, 212, 216. Only 55 percent of a cow's liveweight and 75 percent of the hog can be used for fresh meat; an additional 15 to 20 percent of each animal can be used for a variety of by-products (the rest is lost in shrinkage). See C. V. Whalin, "By-Products of the Slaughtering and Meat Packing Industry," Exhibit 17, FTC, pt. 1, 545–74; "The Five Larger Packers in Produce and Grocery Foods," FTC, pt. 4, 14–19, 140, 274.

10. "Report of the Select Committee on the Transportation and Sale of Meat Products," Senate Report 829, 51st Cong., 1st sess. (Washington, 1890); FTC, pt. 1, 46–48; "Evidence of Combination among Packers," FTC, pt. 2, 13; Stanley L. Piott, *The Anti-Monopoly Persuasion: Popular Resistance to the Rise of Big Business in the Midwest* (Westport, 1985), 75.

11. On this case, see David Gordon, "*Swift & Co. v. United States:* The Beef Trust and the Stream of Commerce Doctrine," *American Journal of Legal History* 28 (July 1984): 244–79. See also Piott, *The Anti-Monopoly Persuasion*, 72–104.

12. FTC, pt. 1, 48–50, pt. 2, 18–98.

13. The Temporary National Economic Committee argued, probably correctly, that the consent decree inadvertently encouraged the growth of national supermarket chains whose roots lay outside of the meat industry; see *Large-Scale Organization in the Meat Industry*, 22; FTC, pt. 1, 25–26, 76–77; "The 'Significant Sixty,'" 109–12; Lewis Corey, *Meat and Man: A Study of Monopoly, Unionism, and Food Policy* (New York, 1950), 85–87; Robert M. Aduddell and Louis P. Cain, "Public Policy Toward 'The Greatest Trust in the World,'" *Business History Review* 55 (Summer 1981): 217–42.

14. Quotation from "Meat for the Multitudes," *National Provisioner,* July 4, 1981, 1:226. The only code affecting meatpacking reached under the NRA was a "President's Reemployment Agreement" establishing a maximum forty-hour week and minimum pay of 40 cents in northern plants and 30 cents in the South. See "Temporary Code of the Meat Packing Industry Respecting Hours of Employment, Salaries and Wages," Aug. 5, 1933 (Appendix B to "History—Negotiations with Reference to a Code of Fair Competitions for Meat Packing Industry"), copy in United Packinghouse Workers of America Papers, box 492, folder 11 [hereafter cited as UPWA Papers]; see also "The 'Significant Sixty,'" 158–60.

15. Alma Herbst, "The Negro in the Slaughtering and Meat Packing Industry in Chicago," Ph.D. diss., University of Chicago, 1930, 305.

16. Henry Ford, *My Life and Work* (1923, repr. New York, 1973), 80–81; James R. Barrett, *Work and Community in the Jungle* (Urbana, 1987), 23–26.

17. For the packinghouse study, see Barrett, *Work and Community in the Jungle*, 22; John R. Commons, "Labor Conditions in Meat Packing and the Recent Strike," *Quarterly Journal of Economics* 19 (Nov. 1904): 4.

18. Nels Peterson interview, Earl Carr interview, and Don Blumenshine interview, UPWAOHP.

19. Quotation from article on Armour and Company in *Fortune*, June 1934, 60.

20. The description draws on the following sources: Commons, "Labor Conditions in Meat Packing," 6; article on Armour and Company in *Fortune*, June 1934, 58–62; U.S. Bureau of Corporations, *Report on the Beef Industry*, 17–19; Kenneth Neidholt interview, March 20, 1986, and Lloyd Achenbach interview, UPWAOHP.

21. Quotation from Louis Tickal, Frank Hlavacek, Lester Rohlena, and Ray Lange interview, UPWAOHP. A similar division of labor characterized the hog kill, although the smaller size of the animal and removal of its hide later in the production process allowed the carcass to remain on the overhead chain and accelerated the entire dressing procedure. For the work process in the hog kill, see article on Swift in *Fortune*, Feb. 1930, 54–58; Alma Herbst, *The Negro in the Slaughtering and Meat-Packing Industry* (1932, repr. New York, 1971), 167–71; "The 'Significant Sixty,'" 247–48; Robert Burt interview, May 7, 1986, and Philip Weightman interview, UPWAOHP.

22. Quotation from Kenneth Neidholdt interview, March 20, 1986, UPWAOHP. Herb March recalled that "anytime it got to be over 90 in Chicago on those killing floors. I figured those stoppages are coming." Herbert March interview, July 15, 1985, UPWAOHP; Commons, "Labor Conditions in Meat Packing," 5.

23. Quotations from, respectively, Walter Bailey interview, UPWAOHP; Verne (Jack) Sechrest interview by author; and Frank Wallace interview, UPWAOHP.

24. Herbst, *The Negro in the Slaughtering and Meat-Packing Industry*, 170–71; Mary Elizabeth Pigeon, *The Employment of Women in Slaughtering and Meat Packing*, Women's Bureau Bulletin 88 (Washington, 1932), 21–22; Whalin, "By-Products of the Slaughtering and Meat Packing Industry," 547–57; Tillie Olsen, *Yonnondio: From the Thirties* (1924, repr. New York, 1975), 135; Virginia Houston interview, UPWAOHP.

25. "The 'Significant Sixty,'" 246; Herbst, *The Negro*, 167–71; Jesse Vaughn interview, Oct. 23, 1986, UPWAOHP.

26. Quotation from Don Winter in Henry Giannini, William Nolan, Chris Wicke, and Don Winter interview, UPWAOHP; "ice hell" is from Olsen, *Yonnondio*, 134; Pigeon, *Employment of Women in Slaughtering and Meat Packing*, 36–37, 42–45; Herbst, *The Negro*, 171; Hattie Jones interview and Jeanette Haymond and Louise Townshend interview, UPWAOHP.

27. Whalin "By-Products of the Slaughtering and Meat Packing Industry," 550–73; "The 'Significant Sixty,'" 252–59; Rudolf A. Clemen, *By-Products in the Packing Industry* (Chicago, 1927); Lloyd Achenbach interview, UPWAOHP; Chris Wicke quotation from Henry Giannini, William Nolan, Chris Wicke, and Don Winters interview, UPWAOHP.

28. Pigeon, *Employment of Women in Slaughtering and Meat Packing*, 64–72; Philip Weightman interview, UPWAOHP.

29. Eric Brian Halpern, "'Black and White, Unite and Fight': Race and Labor in Meatpacking, 1904–1948," Ph.D. diss., University of Pennsylvania, 1989, 90; his rich discussion of meatpacking's complex segmented labor markets is on 84–106. Between 1922 and 1926 in a Chicago packinghouse, the annual maximum employment averaged 2,630 and the annual minimum was 1,580, 60 percent of the top figure. Herbst, *The Negro*, 99, 125, 129.

30. Quotation from Olsen, *Yonnondio*, 134; Pigeon, *Employment of Women in Slaughtering and Meat Packing*, 17, 37–41. On sliced bacon's exclusion of black women, see Herbst, *The Negro*, 76, and Mary Salinas interview, UPWAOHP. The gendering of work in meatpacking is discussed more extensively in Roger Horowitz, "'Where Men Will Not Work': Gender, Power, Space and the Sexual Division of Labor in America's Meatpacking Industry, 1890–1990," *Technology and Culture* 38 (Jan. 1997): 92–118.

31. The particular ethnic and racial division of labor is explored in each of the next four chapters for the relevant city.

32. Quotation from Barrett, *Work and Community in the Jungle*, 20.

33. Sumner Slichter quoted in Sanford M. Jacoby, *Employing Bureaucracy: Managers, Unions, and the Transformation of Work in American Industry, 1900–1945* (New York, 1985), 20. When unemployment swelled in the early 1930s, contemporaries recalled that hundreds waited outside the employment offices of packinghouses looking for a chance to work. "If you were a young man, you could stand in front of those packinghouses for weeks at a time and never get employed," recalled George Fletemeyer. George and Francis Fletemeyer interview, UPWAOHP.

34. Mary Edwards interview by author. For comments on the differing treatment by foremen, see Pigeon, *Employment of Women in Slaughtering and Meat Packing*, 102.

35. Commons, "Labor Conditions in Meat Packing," 7–32 (quotation on 7); Barrett, *Work and Community in the Jungle*, 155–82, 197–201; David Brody, *The Butcher Workmen* (Cambridge, 1964), 45, 48, 79–84; Halpern, "'Black and White, Unite and Fight,'" 66–70, 168–72.

36. Quotation from *Chicago Tribune*, Aug. 1, 1904, in Barrett, *Work and Community in the Jungle*, 165, see also 179–81, 257–63; Brody, *The Butcher Workmen*, 99–105; Halpern, "'Black and White, Unite and Fight,'" 77–84, 199–202.

37. For company literature on welfare capitalism, see Arthur H. Carver, *Personnel and Labor Problems in the Packing Industry* (Chicago, 1928); John Calder, *Capital's Duty to the Wage-Earner* (New York, 1923); and Kate J. Adams, *Humanizing a Great Industry* (Chicago, 1919). The most extensive study of these programs is in Lizabeth Ann Cohen, "Learning to Live in the Welfare State: Industrial Workers in Chicago between the Wars, 1919–1939," Ph.D. diss., University of California-Berkeley, 1986, which provides the basis for her book, *Making a New*

Deal: Industrial Workers in Chicago, 1919–1939 (New York, 1990). Surveying five Chicago industries (including meatpacking) of the 1920s, she concluded that the practice of welfare capitalism diverged widely from its theoretical objectives of curtailing the "foremen's empire" and encouraging employment security. Although employers might have developed sophisticated labor management plans, "if the old 'drive' strategies led to profits, they closed their eyes" (263). Her assertion that "welfare capitalism, while falling short of its goals in the 1920's, set an agenda that workers carried into the 1930's" (295), however, implies that the companies determined the agenda that workers followed. I argue that welfare capitalism was itself an effort by companies to respond to the aspirations of workers, expressed so strongly in the union organizing efforts from 1900 to 1904 and during World War I. The same desires for better working conditions, more secure employment, and control over the labor process would again provoke a renewed surge of union organizing efforts in the 1930s. See also Rick Halpern, "The Iron Fist and the Velvet Glove: Welfare Capitalism in Chicago's Packinghouses, 1921–1933," *Journal of American Studies* 26 (1992): 159–83.

38. Quotations from, respectively, L. C. Williams and William Raspberry interviews, UPWAOHP.

Introduction to Part 1

1. Epigraph from Len De Caux, *Labor Radical: From the Wobblies to CIO* (Boston, 1970), 226; "Decision Order and Direction of Election," Cases C-1116 and C-1125, 21 NLRB 1181; "Decision and Certification of Representative," Case R-658, 7 NLRB 710; "Decision Order and Direction of Election," Cases C-901 and R-1134, 15 NLRB 676; Herbert March interview, July 15, 1985, UPWAOHP.

2. Herbert March interview, Oct. 21, 1986, UPWAOHP.

3. Sophie Kosciowlowski interview by Les Orear, 8–9, Chicago Stockyards interview series, 1971; Fred Blum, *Toward a Democratic Work Press: The Hormel Packing House Workers Experiment* (New York, 1953), 133; William Raspberry interview, UPWAOHP.

Chapter 2: "We Worked for Everything We Got"

1. Svend Godfredson interview, UPWAOHP; Henry Oots interview by author; John Winkels interview, UPWAOHP; *Austin Daily Herald*, Nov. 11, 13, Dec. 30, 1933; Frank Schultz, "A History of Our Union from 1933–1949," *The Unionist*, 1949, repr. May 21, 1971; Frank Ellis "Bits of Labor History," *The Unionist*, Jan. 29, 1960.

2. Quotations from "The Name Is HOR-mel," *Fortune*, Oct. 1937, 141; edited selections from Jay Hormel's speech were also published in the *Austin Daily Herald*, April 12, 1937. According to *Fortune*, the *Herald* cut the more "inflammatory" passages at the request of local businessmen who were outraged by Hormel's stated willingness to work with unions.

3. Dougherty, *In Quest of Quality*, 38–87, 169; U.S. Department of Commerce,

Sixteenth Census of the United States, Population (Washington, 1943), vol. 2, pt. 4, 162; "The Name Is HOR-mel," 130; *Austin Daily Herald,* March 27, Nov. 20, 1935, March 2, Nov. 18, Dec. 12, 1936.

4. Franklyn Curtiss-Wedge, *The History of Mower County, Minnesota* (Chicago, 1911), 155–83, 256–94; John G. Rice, "The Old-Stock Americans," in *They Chose Minnesota,* ed. June Drenning Holmquist (St. Paul, 1981), 59–65.

5. "The 'Significant Sixty,'" 309, 312; Dougherty, *In Quest of Quality,* 27–37, 115–20, 127–32, 156–60.

6. Casper Winkels interview and John Winkels interview, UPWAOHP; Henry Oots interview by author.

7. Employment levels remained above two thousand throughout the early 1930s. *Austin Daily Herald,* July 12, Aug. 17, Nov. 17, 20, 22, 1933, Nov. 22, 1935; O. J. Fosso to Industrial Commission, Nov. 17, 1933, reprinted in *Austin Daily Herald,* Nov. 19, 1933; Marie Casey interview, UPWAOHP; Larry Engelmann, "'We Were the Poor People'—The Hormel Strike of 1933," *Labor History* 15 (Fall 1974): 487–89; Blum, *Toward a Democratic Work Process,* 5.

8. John Winkels interview, UPWAOHP; Mike Holm, *Legislative Manual for the State of Minnesota, 1933* (Minneapolis, 1933), 296, 375.

9. Casper Winkels interview, UPWAOHP.

10. Quotations from Frank Schultz, "A History of Our Union from 1933–1949," *The Unionist,* 1949, repr. May 7, 1971; John Winkels interview, UPWAOHP.

11. Svend Godfredson interview and John Winkels interview, UPWAOHP; *Austin Daily Herald,* July 31, 1979; Roy Franklin to J. C. Lewis May 18, 1942, UPWA Papers, box 4, folder 7; Dave Neiswanger and Rollo Sissel interview by author, July 8, 1987; "Articles of Incorporation," Independent Union of All Workers, and Joe Ollman to Les Orear, June 7, 1958, both UPWAOHP additions to UPWA Papers.

12. Frank Ellis interview, July 2, 1972, Minnesota Historical Society; Frank Ellis, "Bits of Labor History," *The Unionist,* Jan. 22, 1960; Henry Oots, Dave Neiswanger, and Rollo Sissel interviews by author; Engelmann, "'We Were the Poor People,'" 491.

13. Other leftists in the plant included Carl Nilson, first editor of *The Unionist,* the IUAW's paper, and Ted Dombroff, another Socialist. After the Trotskyists joined the Socialist Party in 1937, the two groups caucused and worked together in the Hormel plant. Frank Schultz, "A History of Our Union from 1933–1949," *The Unionist,* 1949, repr. June 4, 1971; Svend Godfredson interview, UPWAOHP; Svend Godfredson to Comrades Heisler, Traeger, and Rasmussen June 5, 1937, Svend Godfredson Papers; Svend Godfredson to author, Aug. 7, 1989, copy in possession of author; Paul Rasmussen interview, UPWAOHP; *Austin City and Mower County, Minnesota Directory, 1933–1934* (Detroit, 1933).

14. Henry Oots interview by author; *Austin Daily Herald,* Nov. 6, 1935; Lyman Halligan interview and Svend Godfredson interview, UPWAOHP; R. L. Polk & Co., *Austin City Directory, 1928* (Detroit, 1928).

15. Dougherty, *In Quest of Quality*, 101, 251, 288; John Winkels interview, UPWAOHP.

16. Marie Casey interview and Svend Godfredson interview, UPWAOHP; quotation from John Winkels interview, UPWAOHP; Frank Schultz, "A History of Our Union from 1933–1949," *The Unionist*, 1949, repr. May 21, June 11, 1971.

17. *Austin Daily Herald* July 11, Nov. 4, Nov. 20, 1933; Schultz quoted in Irene French Clepper, "Minnesota's Definition of the Sit-Down Strike," Ph.D. diss., University of Minnesota, 1979, 43; Engelmann, "'We Were the Poor People,'" 483, 487–89; Lyman Halligan interview, UPWAOHP.

18. Frank Schultz, "A History of Our Union from 1933–1949," *The Unionist*, 1949, repr. May 7, 1971; John Winkels interview and Lyman Halligan interview, UPWAOHP; *Austin Daily Herald*, July 17, 20, 22, 27, 1933. Despite the similarities between the IUAW and the IWW, Ellis later explained, "I was afraid to put them in the Wobblies because we'd been wrecked so many times." Frank Ellis interview July 2, 1972, Minnesota Historical Society. The IUAW formed locals in each city it had members, and those locals were subdivided into units reflecting craft or industrial divisions. A central executive board coordinated the activities of each local. Thus the Hormel union was the packinghouse unit of Local No. 1. "The Independent Union of All Workers," Articles of Incorporation, UPWAOHP Papers.

19. *Austin Daily Herald*, July 27, 28, 31, Sept. 1, 4, 1933. Later that fall, IUAW members assisted FHA pickets around Austin. John Winkels interview, UPWAOHP; *Austin Daily Herald*, Nov. 7, 9, 1933.

20. *Austin Daily Herald*, Aug. 15, Sept. 1, 1933; Arthur Kampfert, "History of Unionism in Meat Packing," State Historical Society of Wisconsin. For use of the IUAW symbol and the Blue Eagle, see, for example, IUAW, "Victory for the Workers," Svend Godfredson Papers.

21. *Austin Daily Herald*, Sept. 1, 4, 1933.

22. *Austin Daily Herald*, Sept. 5, 1933.

23. *Austin Daily Herald*, Sept. 23, 1933.

24. IUAW, "Victory for the Workers"; *Austin Daily Herald*, Sept. 23, 1933.

25. Frank Ellis, "Bits of Labor History," *The Unionist*, Jan. 22, 1960; Frank Schultz, "A History of Our Union from 1933–1949," *The Unionist*, 1949, repr. May 14, 1971; John Winkels interview, UPWAOHP; all quotations from IUAW, "Victory for the Workers"; *Austin Daily Herald*, Sept. 23, 1933; *Austin City and Mower County, Minnesota Directory, 1933–1934*.

26. Frank Ellis, "Bits of Labor History," Jan. 22, 1960; John Winkels interview, UPWAOHP; *Austin Daily Herald*, Nov. 11, 1933.

27. *Austin Daily Herald*, Nov. 13, 1933; Frank Schultz, "A History of Our Union from 1933–1949," *The Unionist*, 1949, repr. May 21, 28, 1971; Henry Oots interview by author; Frank Ellis, "Bits of Labor History," *The Unionist*, Jan. 29, 1960.

28. Farrell Dobbs, *Teamster Power* (New York, 1973) and *Teamster Politics* (New York, 1975); Philip A. Korth and Margaret R. Beegle, *I Remember Like Today: The*

Auto-Lite Strike of 1934 (East Lansing, 1988); Gary Gerstle, *Working-Class Americanism: The Politics of Labor in a Textile City, 1914–1960* (Cambridge, 1989), 127–95.

29. First quotation from Svend A. Godfredson, "From My Yesterdays," Feb. 28, 1983, unpublished manuscript in possession of author; "The Name Is HORmel," 130; second quotation from *Austin Daily Herald*, April 14, 1938.

30. Frank Schultz, "A History of Our Union from 1933–1949," *The Unionist*, 1949, repr. June 11, May 14, 1971; *Austin Daily Herald*, Oct. 20, 21, 27, 28, 30, 1933, May 8, 9, 12, 16, 17, July 31, 1934; "Decision and Order—In the Matter of Wilson & Co., Inc. and Independent Union of All Workers or Its Successor United Packing House Workers," Case C-483, 7 NLRB 990–94; John Winkels interview and Robert H. Schultz interviews, UPWAOHP; Dougherty, *In Quest of Quality*, 136–37.

31. *Austin Daily Herald*, Oct. 9, Nov. 27, 1933, July 30, 31, Aug. 1, 7, 11, 13, 21, 1934, Feb. 5–12, 1935; "Decision and Order," Case C-483, 7 NLRB 990.

32. *Austin Daily Herald*, March 30, 1935.

33. *Austin Daily Herald*, April 2, 5, 17, 24, May 11, 15, June 27, July 2, 29, 1935. At the time of the 1933 Hormel strike, O. J. Fosso was a special agent for the Prudential Insurance Company. *Austin City and Mower County, Minnesota Directory, 1933–1934.*

34. The term *straight trade unionist* was applied to this group by Svend Godfredson. Svend Godfredson interview, UPWAOHP; Paul Rasmussen interview, UPWAOHP; *Austin Daily Herald*, Oct. 28, 1936. Frank Ellis assumed the presidency of the IUAW in 1936 in an uncontested election, and Voorhees was elected the business agent of the Austin IUAW local. Frank Schultz, "A History of Our Union from 1933–1949," *The Unionist*, 1949, repr. June 11, 18, 1971.

35. On the decline of unions in 1934 and 1935, see, for example, David Brody, "The Origins of Modern Steel Unionism: The SWOC Era," in *Forging a Union of Steel: Philip Murray, SWOC and the United Steelworkers*, ed. Paul F. Clark, Peter Gottlieb, and Donald Kennedy (Ithaca, 1987), 15–16; Roger Keeran, *The Communist Party and the Auto Workers Unions* (New York, 1980), 121–42; and Ronald Schatz, *The Electrical Workers: A History of Labor at General Electric and Westinghouse* (Urbana, 1983), 63–71.

36. Quotations from Frank Schultz, "A History of Our Union from 1933–1949," *The Unionist*, 1949, repr. June 11, 1971; Marie Casey interview and Svend Godfredson interview, UPWAOHP.

37. Frank Schultz, "A History of Our Union from 1933–1949," *The Unionist*, 1949, repr. May 28, 1971; *The Unionist*, July 30, 1937.

38. John Winkels interview and Svend Godfredson interview, UPWAOHP; Frank Schultz, "A History of Our Union from 1933–1949," *The Unionist*, 1949, repr. June 4 (source of quotation) and June 11, 1971.

39. Percy Stem, a Southern Tenant Farmers Union organizer, addressed the rally in 1935, and Vincent R. Dunne, a Minneapolis Teamster leader, spoke at the 1936 Labor Day rally. *Austin Daily Herald*, Aug. 31, Sept. 2, 3, 1935, Sept. 8,

1936. For IUAW dances, see *Austin Daily Herald*, calendar for 1936 and 1937. On the Women's Auxiliary, see *Austin Daily Herald*, Oct. 9, 1934, March 20, Dec. 6, 20, 21, 1935; Frank Schultz, "A History of Our Union from 1933–1949," *The Unionist*, 1949, repr. May 28, June 11, 1971.

40. Henry Oots interview by author; John Winkels interview, UPWAOHP; quotation from Svend Godfredson interview, UPWAOHP; *Austin Daily Herald*, June 30, Aug. 14, 15, Oct. 1, 1934, May 8, 1935, Sept. 12, 15, Nov. 13, 1936, June 8, July 27, 1937; Frank Schultz, "A History of Our Union from 1933–1949," *The Unionist*, 1949, repr. June 11, 18, 1971.

41. Joe Ollman to Les Orear, March 5, 1957, from Ollman's personal papers in the possession of Bruce Ollman. My thanks to Peter Rachleff for bringing this material to my attention. "History of Local No. 32 of Ottumwa, Iowa," in State Historical Society of Iowa, *CIO-First Iowa Convention, April 1938* (Iowa City, 1938); Wilson J. Warren, "Promotions Were Tough to Win: The Morrell Story," *Ottumwa Courier*, April 6, 1986; Sander Genis to Frank Rosenblum, May 11, 1937, "The CIO Files of John L. Lewis," microfilm edition, reel 11, frame 0786, University Publications of America, Frederick, Md.

42. *Des Moines Register*, Nov. 15, 1937; *Cedar Rapids Gazette*, Nov. 14, 1937; Robert H. Schultz interviews, UPWAOHP. Still active in the Madison labor movement in the 1980s, Schultz repeatedly referred to the assistance he received from the IUAW in the mid-1930s as the reason for his active support of the 1985–86 strike by UFCW Local P-9 at the Austin Hormel plant.

43. The Cedar Rapids, Iowa, union in the Wilson & Co. plant left the Amalgamated Meat Cutters in January 1935. Brody, *The Butcher Workmen*, 161; Kampfert, "History of Unionism in Meat Packing"; *Austin Daily Herald*, March 3, April 27, Nov. 20, 1935, Jan. 15, March 11, 1936; Joe Voorhees to John L. Lewis, Nov. 29, 1935, "Minutes of Meeting of Provisional Committee for a Mid-West Conference of Packinghouse Workers," Dec. 8, 1935, Patrick Gorman to John Brophy, Jan. 28, 1936, Joe Voorhees to Sam Twedell, Feb. 22, 1936, Dennis Lane to John L. Lewis, March 3, 1936, John Brophy to Patrick Gorman, March 6, 1936, Dennis Lane to John Brophy, March 18, 1936 (quotation), and Lewis J. Clark to John Brophy, Sept. 18, 1936, all in CIO Secretary-Treasurer Papers, box 65, Archives of Urban and Labor Affairs [hereafter cited as CIO ST].

44. Quotations from John Winkels interview, UPWAOHP; Frank Schultz, "A History of Our Union from 1933–1949," *The Unionist*, June 11, 1971; *Austin Daily Herald*, March 4, 19, 20, 25, 26, 29, April 1, 2, 3, 1937.

45. John Winkels interview, UPWAOHP; *Austin Daily Herald*, April 3, 8, 9, 10, 1937; Clepper, "Minnesota's Definition of a Sit-Down Strike," 191–217.

46. Lewis J. Clark to John L. Lewis, Nov. 3, 1936, Lewis J. Clark to John Brophy, Nov. 30, 1936, and Lewis J. Clark to John Brophy, June 1, 1937, all in CIO ST, box 65; *The Unionist*, Jan. 27, April 30, 1937; Brody, *The Butcher Workmen*, 161–66.

47. Peter Rachleff, *Hard-Pressed in the Heartland: The Hormel Strike and the Future of the Labor Movement* (Boston, 1993), 27–42.

48. Godfredson's editorial went on to say, "No matter how far away, how small a nook a place may be on the map, the C.I.O. is on the lips of every worker." *The Unionist*, May 21, 1937. An article by Ernie Jacobs with similar arguments is in *The Unionist*, May 7, 1937. Nilson, "Will We Join the CIO?" from personal papers of Marion Nilson, copy in possession of author. My thanks to Peter Rachleff for bringing this document to my attention. *Austin Daily Herald*, April 19, 21, May 28, 1937; Frank Schultz, "A History of Our Union from 1933–1949," *The Unionist*, 1949, repr. June 18, 1971.

49. Viola Jones to Rick Halpern, May 28, 1986, copy in possession of author; *CIO News—Packinghouse Workers Edition*, April 29, May 27, July 8, 22, Oct. 28, 1940, Feb. 3, 17, 1941; *Packinghouse Worker*, March 13, Sept. 25, 1942; Svend Godfredson interview, UPWAOHP; quotation from Ralph Helstein interview, Roosevelt University Oral History Project in Labor and Immigration History; Maurice Casey interview by author, May 9, 1986; "District Convention of District No. 3, PWOC, November 8, 1942" and "Conference of District No. 3, PWOC, February 6 and 7, 1943," both in UPWA Papers, box 5, folder 1; "Minutes of District No. 2 Conference, Jan. 12, 1941," UPWA Papers, box 3, folder 3; "Audit of PWOC Local No. 9," Feb. 24, 1942, UPWA Papers, box 1, folder 7; Frank Ellis to Sam Sponseller, Sept. 21, 1942, UPWA Papers, box 4, folder 10.

50. Frank Schultz, "A History of Our Union from 1933–1949," *The Unionist*, 1949, repr. July 2, 16, 23, 1971.

51. City Recorder John Wetland reported, "If interest in elections is the test of good citizenship, Austin's best citizens live in the third ward." *Austin Daily Herald*, May 26, 1936.

52. Fosso served as secretary-treasurer of the Mower County Farmer-Labor Association from 1933 to 1934. Other IUAW leaders who held various local FLP positions were T. B. Rockne, Mary O'Shaughnessy, Ray Hubbard, Claude Moore, and Ardell Nemitz. *Austin Daily Herald*, Nov. 27, Dec. 15, 1933, March 12, Sept. 6, Oct. 31, 1934, Aug. 2, 5, 1935, March 9, 1936, March 22, 1937; Robert Zieger, *American Workers, American Unions* (Baltimore, 1986), 70.

53. *Austin Daily Herald*, March 10, April 4, 1934, Jan. 9, Feb. 8, March 4, April 3, 1936, March 8, 9, 10, 11, 18, April 6, 1938; Frank Schultz, "A History of Our Union from 1933–1949," *The Unionist*, 1949, repr. May 28, July 9, July 16, 1971; *CIO News—Packinghouse Workers Edition*, May 27, 1940; *Packinghouse Worker*, April 17, 1942; *Austin City and Mower County, Minnesota Directory*, 1933–1934.

54. Frank Schultz, "A History of Our Union from 1933–1949," *The Unionist*, 1949, repr. July 2, 9, 16, 23, July 30, 1971; Svend Godfredson interview, UPWAOHP.

55. Frank Schultz, "A History of Our Union from 1933–1949," *The Unionist*, 1949, repr. July 9, 1971; "The Name Is HOR-mel," 138; "The 'Significant Sixty,'" 313; Jay C. Hormel, "The Hormel Annual Wage, Wage Incentive and Joint Earnings Plan," copy in possession of author; Dougherty, *In Quest of Quality*, 147–53.

56. First quotation from Dougherty, *In Quest of Quality*, 147; "The Name Is

HOR-mel," 138; Hormel, "The Hormel Annual Wage, Wage Incentive and Joint Earnings Plan," 2–4; Frank Schultz, "A History of Our Union from 1933–1949," *The Unionist,* 1949, repr. May 21, 28, 1971; *Austin Daily Herald,* Nov. 17, Nov. 20, 1933 (Ellis quotation), Nov. 21, 1934, April 6, 1935, Dec. 3, 1937, March 3, 7, 1938.

57. *Austin Daily Herald,* Nov. 20, 1935, Nov. 17, 1936, Nov. 17, 1937; "The Name Is HOR-mel," 138.

58. *Austin Daily Herald,* March 3, 7, 1938; *CIO News—Packinghouse Workers Edition* Jan. 9, 1939; *Packinghouse Worker* Nov. 24, 1944; Frank Schultz, "A History of Our Union from 1933–1949," *The Unionist,* 1949, repr. June 25, July 2, 9, 23, 1971; quotation from Jim McAnally interview, UPWAOHP.

59. Marie Casey interview and Casper Winkels interview, UPWAOHP.

Chapter 3: "They Just Had to Deal with the Union"

1. *Chicago Tribune,* July 16 and 17, 1939; *Chicago Daily Times,* July 17, 1939; Vicky Starr interview and Jesse Prosten interview, UPWAOHP; Herbert March interview by Elizabeth Balanoff, Nov. 16, 1970, Roosevelt University Oral History Project in Labor and Immigration History; Halpern, "'Black and White, Unite and Fight,'" 396–97; Barbara Warne Newell, *Chicago and the Labor Movement: Metropolitan Unionism in the 1930s* (Urbana, 1961), 168.

2. For the Armour advertisement, see the *Chicago Defender,* July 22, 1939.

3. H. H. McCarty and C. W. Thompson, "Meat Packing in Iowa," *Iowa Studies in Business* 12 (June 1933): 122; U.S. Department of Commerce, *Sixteenth Census of the United States, Manufactures: 1939* (Washington, 1942), 3:266.

4. First quotation from Philip Weightman interview, UPWAOHP; second quotation from Vicky Starr interview, UPWAOHP.

5. Ercell Allen and Rosalie Taylor interview, Sept. 18, 1985, UPWAOHP. The term *culture of unity* is from Cohen, *Making a New Deal,* 324. I disagree with Cohen's assertion that it was the reduction of ethnic and racial barriers due to mass culture that allowed labor unions to form in Chicago's packinghouses. Her study understates the continued salience of ethnic identity in Chicago in the 1930s, as well as the divisions between white and black. The children of the foreign-born remained tied to their particular community by a myriad of familial, religious, and cultural ties, and the growth of mass culture did not expand the range of shared experiences between blacks and whites in Chicago's segregated society. For a similar criticism, see Rudolph J. Vecoli, "Industrial Workers as 'Moral Capitalists,'" *Reviews in American History* 20 (1992): 529–35.

6. James R. Barrett has rightly criticized the tendency of Upton Sinclair's *The Jungle* and other contemporary works for depicting Chicago's packinghouse workers as "beaten, degraded men and women." See his *Work and Community in the Jungle,* 2.

7. Robert A. Slayton, *Back of the Yards: The Making of a Local Democracy* (Chicago, 1986), 211; Thomas J. Jablonsky, *Pride in the Jungle: Community and Everyday Life in Back of the Yards Chicago* (Baltimore, 1993), 17–24, 53–55.

8. Slayton, *Back of the Yards*, 67–70; John M. Bukowiczyk, *And My Children Did Not Know Me: A History of Polish-Americans* (Bloomington, Ind., 1987), 24–25.

9. Joseph Parot, "Ethnic versus Black Metropolis: The Origins of Polish-Black Housing Tensions in Chicago," *Polish-American Studies* 29 (1972): 18; Slayton, *Back of the Yards*, 26, 96; Jablonsky, *Pride in the Jungle*, 34–40, 97–98; Mark Reisler, "The Mexican Immigrant in the Chicago Area during the 1920s," *Journal of the Illinois State Historical Society* 66 (Summer 1978): 145–58. There was no survey of work force composition in the 1930s, so figures are estimates derived from census analysis in Estell Hill Scott, *Occupational Changes among Negroes in Chicago* (Chicago, 1939), 197, 239.

10. Lizabeth Cohen, "The Class Experience of Mass Consumption: Workers as Consumer in Interwar America," in *The Power of Culture: Critical Essays in American History*, ed. Richard Wrightman Fox and T. J. Jackson Lears (Chicago, 1993), 150; Slayton, *Back of the Yards*, 60–62, 73, 76–77, 96, 105; Jablonsky, *Pride in the Jungle*, 67, 70, 77–78; Cohen, *Making a New Deal* 175, 179, 193–95; Edward R. Kantowicz, *Polish-American Politics in Chicago 1888–1940* (Chicago, 1975), 168.

11. Quotation from William I. Thomas and Florian Znanieki, *The Polish Peasant in Europe and America* (Urbana, 1984, abridged ed.), 247; Dominic Anthony Pacyga, "Villages of Packinghouses and Steel Mills: The Polish Worker on Chicago's Southside, 1880 to 1921," Ph.D. diss., University of Illinois at Chicago, 1981, 182–84, 188; Cohen, *Making a New Deal*, 64, 71, 98, 422; Kantowicz, *Polish-American Politics*, 170; Slayton, *Back of the Yards*, 23, 45, 48, 50, 79–81, 97–99; Jablonsky, *Pride in the Jungle*, 104–5; David Hogan, "Education and the Making of the Chicago Working Class, 1880–1930," *History of Education Quarterly* 18 (Fall 1978): 250.

12. First quotation from Halpern, "'Black and White, Unite and Fight,'" 199, see also 179–81; second quotation from Ann Banks, *First-Person America* (New York, 1980), 68; Herbst, *The Negro*, 30–66.

13. The Kamarczyk quotation and term *social and cultural apartheid* are from Halpern, "'Black and White, Unite and Fight,'" 113; Chicago Commission on Race Relations, *The Negro in Chicago: A Study of Race Relations and a Race Riot* (Chicago, 1922), 139–40 [hereafter cited as CCRR].

14. Washington quotation from Halpern, "'Black and White, Unite and Fight,'" 210–11; CCRR, 163–65, 171–74, 361; Herbst, *The Negro*, 87; U.S. Department of Commerce, *Fifteenth Census of the United States, Population* (Washington, 1933), 4:447; Scott, *Occupational Changes among Negroes*, 233, 237, 239, 242, 236, 244.

15. Mary Elaine Ogden, *The Chicago Negro Community: A Statistical Description* (Chicago, 1939), 224; Scott, *Occupational Changes among Negroes*, 13–14, 17, 236, 241, 249.

16. Ogden, *The Chicago Negro*, 193; St. Clair Drake and Horace Cayton, *Black Metropolis* (1945, repr. New York, 1970), 379–80, 412–24, 632–35, quotation from 380; CCRR, 143.

17. Allan H. Spear, *Black Chicago: The Making of a Negro Ghetto* (Chicago, 1967), 15, 150; Ogden, *The Chicago Negro Community*, 6–7, 20–22, 48–60, 82; CCRR, 115, 122–23, 171, 186–92.

18. Drake and Cayton, *Black Metropolis*, 379–80; CCRR, 114–15, 232, 310–22; Spear, *Black Chicago* 42; Cohen, *Making a New Deal*, 156.

19. James R. Grossman, *Land of Hope: Chicago, Black Southerners, and the Great Migration* (Chicago, 1989), 97–100, 142, 200–202, 228, 239; William M. Tuttle, *Race Riot: Chicago in the Red Summer of 1919* (New York, 1977), 57, 101, 151; CCRR, 146–48.

20. First quotation from Herbst, *The Negro*, 77; Jesse Vaughn interview, Oct. 23, 1986, UPWAOHP; Scott, *Occupational Changes among Negroes*, 194, 197, 237, 239. Although total employment in the stockyards fell from forty-six thousand in 1920 to twenty-six thousand in 1925, the proportion of black workers remained steady at 30 to 31 percent. Alma Herbst, "The Negro in the Slaughtering and Meat Packing Industry in Chicago," Ph.D. diss., University of Chicago, 1930, 301.

21. Halpern, "The Iron Fist," esp. 171–82; Barrett, *Work and Community in the Jungle*, 251, 283–84. Descriptions of Armour's Employee Representation Plan can be found in NLRB Cases R-584 and C-695, Decided Sept. 16, 1938, 8 NLRB 1105. For Wilson's plan, know as the Joint Representation Committee, see NLRB Case C-1763, Decided April 29, 1941, 31 NLRB 444–47.

22. First quotation from "What It Means to Be an Employe Representative," in John Calder, *Capital's Duty to the Wage-Earner* (New York, 1923), 308, see also 116, 295–307. Second, third, and fifth quotations from Milton Norman in Milton Norman, Richard Saunders, Todd Tate, and James Samuel interview, UPWAOHP; fourth quotation from Anna Novak interview in Banks, *First-Person America*, 63; "working for the church" is from Herbert March interview, July 15, 1985, UPWAOHP, and Elmer Thomas interview in Banks, *First-Person America*, 70.

23. Quotation from Jane and Herbert March interview by Rick Halpern; Slayton, *Back of the Yards*, 190–91; Drake and Cayton, *Black Metropolis*, 462–67; Cohen, *Making a New Deal*, 307–38.

24. Herbert March interview, July 15, 1985, UPWAOHP; "Conference Held September 25, 1934 with Representatives of the Stock Yards Labor Council Regarding Drawing Up of a Code for the Meat Packing Industry," Labor Advisory Board of the National Recovery Administration, Region Nine, file 354, National Archives.

25. First two quotations from Drake and Cayton, *Black Metropolis*, 603; other quotations from Tate in Milton Norman, Richard Saunders, Todd Tate, and James Samuel interview, UPWAOHP; Herbert March interview, Oct. 21, 1986, and Svend Godfredson interview, UPWAOHP; Jane and Herbert March interview by Rick Halpern; Paul Rasmussen interview, UPWAOHP; Halpern, "'Black and White, Unite and Fight,'" 266–69; Frances Fox Piven and Richard Cloward, *Poor People's Movements* (New York, 1977), 43–55; Roy Rosenzweig, "Organizing the Unemployed: The Early Years of the Great Depression, 1929–1933," *Radical America* 10 (1976): 37–61.

26. Milton Norman, Richard Saunders, Todd Tate, and James Samuel interview,

Oct. 1, 1985, Todd Tate interview, Annie Jackson Collins, Richard Saunders, and Todd Tate interview, UPWAOHP; Halpern, "'Black and White, Unite and Fight,'" 268–71; Slayton, *Back of the Yards*, 185–87; Vicky Starr interview, UPWAOHP; Stella Nowicki [Vicky Starr] interview in *Rank and File: Personal Histories by Working-Class Organizers*, ed. Alice Lynd and Staughton Lynd (Princeton, 1973), esp. 69–77.

27. Herbert March interviews, UPWAOHP; see chapter 4 for March's activities in Kansas City.

28. Quotations from Jesse Prosten interview, UPWAOHP; Herbert March interview, Oct. 21, 1986, UPWAOHP.

29. Herbert March interview, July 15, 1985, UPWAOHP; Halpern, "'Black and White, Unite and Fight,'" 295.

30. Report by Thomas Powers, May 17, 1934, Report by Heitman, March 27, 1934, and March 28, 1934, all in Mary McDowell Papers, folder 15; H. A. Millis, "A Study of New Unions Organized in Chicago May, 1933 to June, 1934," John Fitzpatrick Papers, box 18, folder 131; Herbert March interview, Oct. 21, 1986, UPWAOHP; Jane and Herbert March interview by Rick Halpern; *Austin Daily Herald*, Nov. 28, 29, 1933.

31. Leon Beverly interview by Elizabeth Butters, 6, Roosevelt University Oral History Project in Labor and Immigration History; final quotation from Halpern, "'Black and White, Unite and Fight,'" 292.

32. Halpern, "'Black and White, Unite and Fight,'" 296–301; Brody, *The Butcher Workmen*, 155–60. For workers dismissed in the 1933–37 period, see Frank McCarty to J. C. Lewis, June 24, 1941, UPWA Papers, box 4, folder 5.

33. First quotation from Patrick Gorman to John Fitzpatrick, July 31, 1935, Fitzpatrick Papers, box 19, folder 134; Ed Nockels to William Green, March 7, 1935, Green to Nockels, March 9, 1935, and "Proposal for Action to the Executive Committee of the Chicago Federation of Labor from District Committee, Communist Party," all in Fitzpatrick Papers, box 18, folder 12; Tate quotation from *Unionist and Public Forum*, Aug. 15, 1935; Jane and Herbert March interview by Rick Halpern; Herbert March interview, July 15, 1985, UPWAOHP; Halpern, "'Black and White, Unite and Fight,'" 305–12.

34. Quotation from Jesse Vaughn interview, Oct. 23, 1986, UPWAOHP; Kampfert, "History of Unionism in Meat Packing," 3:18; Jesse Vaughn interview, Oct. 4, 1985, Vicky Starr interview, and Herbert March interviews, UPWAOHP; Frank McCarty to John Brophy, March 16, 1937, and "Meat Packing Locals Chartered by the CIO," Aug. 16, 1937, both in CIO ST, box 65; Halpern, "'Black and White, Unite and Fight,'" 313–17. See chapter 2 for the pressure exerted by Austin and Cedar Rapids on the CIO.

35. Quotation from Jim Cole interview in Banks, *First-Person America*, 67. On the participation of blacks in SWOC, see George S. Schuyler, "Negro Workers Lead in Great Lakes Steel Drive," *Pittsburgh Courier*, July 31, 1937, reprinted in *Black Workers: A Documentary History from Colonial Times to the Present*, ed. Philip S. Foner and Ronald L. Lewis (Philadelphia, 1989), 469–79.

36. On Johnson, see Stephen Brier, "Labor, Politics, and Race: A Black Workers' Life," *Labor History* 23 (Summer 1982): 416–21. Quotations from Jesse Prosten interview, UPWAOHP. For Communist activity at City College in the early 1930s, see Harvey Klehr, *The Heyday of American Communism: The Depression Decade* (New York, 1984), 309–16. On the IWO see Roger Keeran, "The International Workers Order and the Origins of the CIO," *Labor History* 30 (Summer 1989): 385–408.

37. Quotations from Jesse Vaughn interview, Oct. 4, 1985 and Oct. 23, 1986, UPWAOHP; "Meat Packing Groups Chartered by the CIO, Aug. 16, 1937," CIO ST, box 65; *CIO News—Packinghouse Workers' Edition*, Dec. 19, 1938, May 22, July 10, Sept. 4, 1939; *Midwest Daily Record*, May 16, 18, June 30, 1938; Kampfert, "History of Unionism in Meat Packing," 4:48; Halpern, "'Black and White, Unite and Fight," 343–49.

38. First quotation from Pat Balskus in Halpern, "'Black and White, Unite and Fight,'" 349; Jesse Vaughn interview, UPWAOHP. For community reaction, see Harold Preece, "What Goes on in Packingtown?" *Chicago Defender*, Sept. 23, 1939.

39. Kampfert, "History of Unionism in Meat Packing," 4:26.

40. Cases R-584 and C-695, 8 NLRB 1108, 1110, 1115–16; Frank McCarty to J. C. Lewis, June 24, 1941, UPWA Papers, box 5, folder 5; testimony by Arthur Kampfert in "Special Meeting of Packinghouse Workers Delegates," April 15, 1941, 5:44, CIO ST, box 65; *Packinghouse Worker*, March 22, 1942; Jesse Perez interview in Banks, *First-Person America*, 66; Jack Sechrest interview by author, July 7, 1987; Leon Beverly interview by Elizabeth Butters; Leon Beverly from interview of Chicago stockyards workers by Herbert Hill, April 1, 1967, copy in possession of author; Herbert March interview by Elizabeth Balanoff; Halpern, "'Black and White, Unite and Fight,'" 357.

41. Kampfert, "History of Unionism in Meat Packing," 4:20–24, 28, 46; Halpern, "'Black and White, Unite and Fight,'" 316–17; NLRB Cases R-584 and C-695, Decided Sept. 15, 1938, 8 NLRB 1108–9; Slayton, *Back of the Yards*, 195; Vicky Starr interview, Milton Norman, Richard Saunders, Todd Tate, and James Samuel interview, Annie Jackson Collins, Richard Saunders, and Todd Tate interview, UPWAOHP; Leon Beverly interview by Elizabeth Butters.

42. Cases R-584 and C-695, 8 NLRB 1110; Frank McCarty to J. C. Lewis, June 24, 1941, UPWA Papers, box 4, folder 5; Master Agreement between Armour and Co. and the PWOC, Sept. 6, 1941, UPWA Papers, box 1, folder 5; Milton Norman, Richard Saunders, Todd Tate, and James Samuel interview, UPWAOHP; Jane and Herbert March interview by Rick Halpern; Herbert March interview, July 15, 1985, UPWAOHP.

43. Sophie Kosciowlowski interview by Les Orear, Chicago Stock Yards Interview Series, 1971, quotation from 5; Sophie Kosciowlowski interview by Elizabeth Butters, Jan. 15, 1971, Roosevelt University Oral History Project in Labor and Immigration History; Anna Novack interview in Banks, *First-Person America*, 62–65; Cases R-584 and C-695, 8 NLRB 1108.

44. Cases R-584 and C-695, 8 NLRB 1105–10. The acknowledged leader of the EMA was C. H. Tally, an employee representative since 1923 and president of Armour's "Efficiency Club" at the Wabash YMCA. *Chicago Defender* July 15, 1939.

45. Cases R-584 and C-695, 8 NLRB 1110–15; Frank McCarty to J. C. Lewis, June 24, 1941, UPWA Papers, box 4, folder 5.

46. Herbert March interview, July 15, 1985, UPWAOHP.

47. Quotation from Herbert March interview by Elizabeth Balanoff, 62–63. On the Armour steward system, see Kampfert, "History of Unionism in Meat Packing," 4:29–35; Newell, *Chicago and the Labor Movement*, 167; *Midwest Daily Record*, July 2, 16, 1938; Halpern, "'Black and White, Unite and Fight,'" 356–65.

48. Herbert March interview by Elizabeth Balanoff, 60–63; *Midwest Daily Record*, June 11, 1938.

49. Leon Beverly quotation from interview of Chicago stockyards workers by Herbert Hill, April 1, 1967, 74; Herbert March interview, July 15, 1985, UPWAOHP; *CIO News—Packinghouse Workers Edition*, Jan. 2, 1939; *Chicago Defender*, Sept. 23, 1939.

50. Cases R-584 and C-695, 8 NLRB 1100; PWOC to Carl R. Schodler, May 16, 1939, UPWA Papers, box 1, folder 5; Herbert March interview by Elizabeth Balanoff; Herbert March interview, July 15, 1985, UPWAOHP.

51. Herbert March interview by Elizabeth Balanoff; "Statement of Herbert March," Nov. 14, 1938, and Citizen's Emergency Committee on Industrial Relations to Police Commissioner James P. Allen, Nov. 17, 1938, both in Mary McDowell Papers, folder 15; *Midwest Daily Record*, Sept. 21, 1938, April 15, 1939; *CIO News—Packinghouse Workers Edition*, Nov. 21, Dec. 12, 1938.

52. First quotation from Herbert March interview by Elizabeth Balanoff, 80–81; *CIO News—Packinghouse Workers Edition*, Oct. 14, Dec. 5, 1938, Aug. 14, Sept. 4, 1939; *Midwest Daily Record*, Oct. 16, 18, 20, Nov. 1, 26, 1938; Milton Norman, Richard Saunders, Todd Tate, and James Samuel interview and Todd Tate interview, UPWAOHP; Sophie Kosciowlowski quotation from interview by Elizabeth Butters, 8–9; Sophie Kosciowlowski interview by Les Orear.

53. Quotation from *St. Louis Dispatch Sunday Magazine*, April 20, 1947, copy in Herbert March Papers. Ondrek worked as an unskilled packinghouse laborer in the early 1920s. Slayton, *Back of the Yards*, 183–207; Vicky Starr interview, Herbert March interviews, Charles Hayes interview, and Svend Godfredson interview, UPWAOHP; Sanford D. Horwitt, *Let Them Call Me Rebel: Saul Alinsky, His Life and Legacy* (New York, 1989), 58–76.

54. NLRB Case R-1561, 16 NLRB 345 and 18 NLRB 255; *CIO News—Packinghouse Workers Edition*, Feb. 19, April 1, July 8, 1940, March 3, 17, July 7, 1941; Tate quotation from Milton Norman, Richard Saunders, Todd Tate, and James Samuel interview, UPWAOHP; Herbert March interview, July 15, 1985, UPWAOHP.

55. Philip Weightman interview, UPWAOHP; Kampfert, "History of Unionism in Meat Packing," 3:34; Stella Nowicki (Vicky Starr) interview in Lynd and Lynd, *Rank and File*, 80.

56. Copies of *Swift Flash* in "Special Meeting of Packinghouse Workers Delegates," CIO ST, box 66; *Swift Flash*, Feb. 25, 1941, UPWA Papers, box 9, folder 4; Philip Weightman interview and Vicky Starr interview, UPWAOHP; Vicky Starr interview in Lynd and Lynd, *Rank and File*, 181; Theodore V. Purcell, *The Worker Speaks His Mind on Company and Union* (Cambridge, 1954), 53–60.

57. Kampfert, "History of Unionism in Meat Packing," 3:30–32; Philip Weightman interview and Vicky Starr interview, UPWAOHP.

58. Philip Weightman interview, UPWAOHP; *CIO News—Packinghouse Workers' Edition*, June 26, 1939, March 4, April 29, Aug. 19, 1940, June 9, Aug. 4, 1941, Jan. 16, 1942; organizing material in UPWA Papers, box 11, folder 3; Paul Street, "The Swift Difference: Workers, Managers, Militants, and Welfare Capitalism in Chicago's Stockyards, 1921–1942," in *Unionizing the Jungle: Essays on Labor and Community in the Twentieth-Century Meatpacking Industry*, ed. Marvin Bergman and Shelton Stromquist (Iowa City, 1997).

59. Kampfert, "History of Unionism in Meat Packing," 4:1B–5B, 5:11B–17B; NLRB Case C-1763, Decided April 29, 1941, 31 NLRB 440.

60. *CIO News—Packinghouse Workers Edition*, Jan. 22, Feb. 5, March 4, Sept. 30, Dec. 23, 1940, Feb. 17, May 12, Aug. 18, Sept. 29, 1941, Feb. 13, 27, March 6, April 10, May 22, Sept. 11, Dec. 25, 1942; NLRB Case C-1763, Decided April 29, 1941, 31 NLRB 440; Walter Piotrowski to William Mooney, Sept. 5, 1942, William Mooney to Sam Sponseller, Sept. 11, 1942, and Sam Sponseller to William Mooney, Sept. 14, 1942, all UPWA Papers, box 4, folder 6; Slayton, *Back of the Yards*, 162; Kampfert, "History of Unionism in Meat Packing," 5:11B–24B; Halpern, "'Black and White, Unite and Fight,'" 377–78, 427–43; Charles Hayes interview and Sam Parks interview, UPWAOHP.

61. Dock Williams et al. to Allan Haywood, Oct. 29, 1943, Dock Williams to Lewis J. Clark, Feb. 24, 1944, Dock Williams and Mary Smith to Allan Haywood, April 27, 1944, Dock Williams and Mary Smith to Lewis J. Clark, April 27, 1944, and Dock Williams et al. to Frank Bender, May 4, 1944, all in CIO ST, box 67; Sam Parks interview and Charles Hayes interview, UPWAOHP.

62. Charles Hayes interview by Dan Collison, copy in possession of author; Sam Parks interview, UPWAOHP. Although worried over the growing influence of the left in Chicago meatpacking unions, Philip Weightman nonetheless supported Williams's ouster because of his public attacks on the CIO's political action program. Philip Weightman to Philip Murray, Sept. 13, 1944, CIO ST, box 57.

63. For details on Communist organization among packinghouse workers, see Herbert March, "Building a Mass Party in the Packing Industry," *Daily Worker*, March 25, 1946, and J. Kellor, "How the Party Was Built in Chicago Packinghouses," *Daily Worker*, April 5, 1946; Herbert March interviews, UPWAOHP, quotation from July 15, 1985, interview; Vicky Starr interview, UPWAOHP. It is notable that the majority of Armour workers voted for the PWOC just days after the House Un-American Activities Committee summoned March, Johnson, and oth-

er union leaders to hearings in Chicago and charged that Communists dominated the CIO. House of Representatives, *Hearings Before a Special Committee on Un-American Activities,* 76th Cong., 3d sess. (Washington, 1952), esp. 215–341.

Chapter 4: "Without a Union, We're All Lost"

1. *Kansas City Star,* Sept. 9 (quotation) and 10, 1938; Charles R. Fischer interview, UPWAOHP.

2. *Midwest Daily Record,* Sept. 14, 1938; Urban League of Kansas City, *The Negro Worker of Kansas City* (Kansas City, Mo., 1940), 17; Charles R. Fischer interview, UPWAOHP.

3. Charles R. Fischer interview, UPWAOHP.

4. Charles Glaab, "Meat Packing—Working Paper," unpublished manuscript, n.d., A. Theodore Brown Papers, folder 11; Eva Lash Atkinson, "Kansas City's Livestock Trade and Packing Industry, 1870–1914: A Study in Regional Growth," Ph.D. diss., University of Kansas, 1971; U.S. Immigration Commission, *Immigrants in Industry,* part 11: *Slaughtering and Meatpacking* (Washington, 1922), 273, 285; Susan Greenbaum, "The Historical, Institutional Parameters of Social Cohesiveness in Four Urban Neighborhoods," Ph.D. diss., University of Kansas, 1980, 127; R. L. Polk & Co., *Kansas City Directory, 1938* (Detroit, 1938), 17–18; U.S. Department of Commerce, *Sixteenth Census of the United States, Manufactures: 1939* (Washington, 1942), vol. 2, pt. 1, 62.

5. Ann and Thomas Krasick interview, UPWAOHP; Susan Greenbaum, *Strawberry Hill: A Neighborhood Study* (Kansas City, Kans., 1978), 4–6; "Overview of the East Europeans in Kansas City," unpublished manuscript, Kansas City Museum, 1976, 12; Greenbaum, "Social Cohesiveness in Four Urban Neighborhoods," 128; *Kansas City Times,* March 5, 1899, Patricia Wagner Papers, folder 10.

6. In 1909 male Croatians and blacks each earned around $500 annually, whereas Irish and native-born employees received more than $700 a year. U.S. Immigration Commission, *Immigrants in Industry,* pt. 11, 268, 271, 291–92; U.S. Department of Commerce, *Fifteenth Census of the United States, Population,* 4:569.

7. Nell Irvin Painter, *Exodusters: Black Migration to Kansas after Reconstruction* (New York, 1977); Urban League of Kansas City, *The Negro Worker of Kansas City,* 13, 22–24; Clifford Naismith, "History of the Negro Population of Kansas City, Missouri 1870–1930," unpublished manuscript, n.d., 221–23, A. Theodore Brown Papers, folder 5; *Kansas City Star,* May 2, 3, 4, 1899, Patricia Wagner Papers, folder 10; National Urban League, *A Study of the Social and Economic Conditions of the Negro Population of Kansas City, Missouri* (Kansas City, Mo., 1946), 38; T. Arnold Hill to Thomas A. Webster, Nov. 25, 1935, National Urban League Papers, series 4, box 30.

8. William Raspberry interview and Finis Block interview, UPWAOHP; quotation from *Kansas City Star,* Oct. 19, 1913, copy in clipping file of Kansas City, Missouri Public Library; U.S. Immigration Commission, *Immigrants in Industry,* pt. 11, 273–74, 285; U.S. Department of Commerce, *Fourteenth Census of the Unit-*

ed States, Population (Washington, 1923), 4:1123, 1125; Naismith, "History of the Negro Population," 202–38; Asa Martin, *Our Negro Population* (Kansas City, Mo., 1913), 50–51, 56–57.

9. Quotation from Martin, *Our Negro Population*, 51–52; "Guide to Black History in Kansas City," unpublished manuscript, Kansas City Museum, n.d.; Urban League of Kansas City, *The Negro Worker of Kansas City* 12–14, 23–25; Hill to Webster, Nov. 25, 1935; U.S. Immigration Commission, *Immigrants in Industry*, pt. 11, 273.

10. William Raspberry interview, UPWAOHP.

11. Naismith, "History of the Negro Population," 240; Urban League of Kansas City, *Housing Negro Families in Kansas City* (Kansas City, Mo., 1941), 5–11, 28, FEPC Records, RG 225, box 449; William Raspberry interview, UPWAOHP; League of Women Voters, *The Negro in Kansas City* (Kansas City, Mo., 1944), 10.

12. "Committee Report on Community Resources for Race Relations Survey, 1945," National Urban League Papers, series 6, box 52; Nathan W. Pearson, *Goin' to Kansas City* (Urbana, 1987), 19–21; Susan Greenbaum, *The Afro-American Community in Kansas City, Kansas* (Kansas City, Kans., 1982), 68–70; Janet Bruce, *The Kansas City Monarchs: Champions of Black Baseball* (Lawrence, 1985), 45, 52, 74, 93, 101; League of Women Voters, *The Negro in Kansas City*, 12–19; William Raspberry interview, UPWAOHP and interview by author, Dec. 10, 1987; Virginia Houston interview, UPWAOHP; Barbara Gorman, "Overview of the Black Community in Kansas City," unpublished manuscript, Kansas City Museum, n.d.; A. Theodore Brown and Lyle Dorset, *K.C.: A History of Kansas City, Missouri* (Boulder, 1978), 97.

13. Martin, *Our Negro Population*, 141–44; Greenbaum, "Social Cohesiveness in Four Urban Neighborhoods," 121–27; Greenbaum, *The Afro-American Community in Kansas City, Kansas*, 27–29; William Raspberry interviews; Noel Avon Wilson, "The Kansas City Call: An Inside View of the Negro Market," Ph.D. diss., University of Illinois, 1968, 30–43; National Urban League, *A Study of the Social and Economic Conditions of the Negro Population of Kansas City, Missouri*, S-10.

14. Ann and Thomas Krasick interview and Charles R. Fischer interview, UPWAOHP. In 1909 Croatians made up 54.3 percent of the foreign-born in Kansas City, Kansas. U.S. Immigration Commission, *Immigrants in Industry*, pt. 11, 268, 271, 291–92; U.S. Department of Commerce, *Fifteenth Census of the United States, Population*, vol. 3, pt. 1, 860–61, vol. 4, 569, 571.

15. Kate Duffy, "Polish Hill," *Kansas City*, June 1984; Ann and Thomas Krasick interview, UPWAOHP; Greenbaum, *Strawberry Hill*, 5–10, 12; "Overview of the Irish Community," unpublished manuscript, Kansas City Museum, 1976; Katherine Sherman, "The Response of the Leavenworth Archdiocese to Slavic Catholic Immigration, 1880–1893," master's thesis, University of Missouri-Kansas City, 1983, 68, passim; U.S. Department of Commerce, *Fourteenth Census of the United States, Population*, 2:1018, 3:360; Carroll D. Clark and Roy L. Roberts, *People of Kansas: A Demographic and Sociological Study* (Topeka, 1936).

16. U.S. Immigration Commission, *Immigrants in Industry*, pt. 11, 295–97, 282, 304, 318, and 323; U.S. Department of Commerce, *Fifteenth Census of the United States, Population*, 4:474–75. In the late 1920s the Women's Bureau also found high levels of home ownership. Out of 192 families with at least one women packinghouse worker, 64 percent owned their home. Pidgeon, *Employment of Women in Slaughtering and Meatpacking*, 189.

17. *Zajednicar*, Feb. 22, March 8, 15, 1933, Feb. 2, 26, 1936, Feb. 24, 1937, April 6, 1938, March 15, 1939, March 13, 1940; Clark and Roberts, *People of Kansas*, 56; Ann and Thomas Krasick interview, UPWAOHP.

18. First quotation from Peter Rachleff, "Class, Ethnicity and the New Deal: The Croatian Fraternal Union in the 1930s," in *The Ethnic Enigma: The Salience of Ethnicity for European Origin Groups*, ed. Peter Kristivo (Philadelphia, 1989), 94–95; second quotation from *Zajednicar*, Sept. 8, 1937.

19. The only lodge with weak packinghouse identification was 112, the all-women's lodge. Its main leaders were a restaurant owner and a seamstress. Identity of lodge officers drawn from numerous issues of *Zajednicar*, 1933–40; employment from R. L. Polk & Co., *Kansas City Directory, 1938*.

20. Ann and Thomas Krasick interview, UPWAOHP; George R. Prpic, *The Croatian Immigrants in America* (New York, 1971), 262–64; *Zajednicar*, June 9, 1937, June 28, Nov. 1, 1939. Information on social events and sports activities drawn from numerous issues of *Zajednicar*, 1933–40.

21. *Kansas City Star*, Dec. 5, 1915, copy in clipping file of Kansas City, Missouri, Public Library; Manuel C. Elmer, "Armourdale: A City within a City," *Bulletin of the University of Kansas*, June 15, 1919, 46; "In the Matter of Cudahy Packing Company and the United Packinghouse Workers Local Industrial Union No. 194," Cases C-650 and R-208, 17 NLRB 311–47; *New York Times*, Dec. 6, 8, 28, 1921; *Kansas City Labor Herald*, May 3, Nov. 17, 1922; quotation from Chamber of Commerce of Kansas City, *Book of Kansas City Facts* (Kansas City, Mo., 1925), 12.

22. R. L. Polk & Co., *Kansas City Directory, 1938*, 17–18; Philip Neff and Robert M. Williams, *The Industrial Development of Kansas City* (Kansas City, Mo., 1954), 131–34; Ann and Thomas Krasick interview and Charles R. Fischer interview, UPWAOHP.

23. Herbert March interview, Oct. 21, 1986, UPWAOHP; *Kansas City Star*, Feb. 10, 1931. My thanks to Neal Basen for bringing the latter citation to my attention.

24. Ronald Schatz, "Union Pioneers: The Founders of Local Unions at General Electric and Westinghouse, 1933–1937," *Journal of American History* 66 (Dec. 1979): 586–602; Charles R. Fischer interview, UPWAOHP and interview by author, Dec. 8, 1987; Paul Rasmussen to National Labor Secretary, Socialist Party, June 8, 1937, Svend Godfredson Papers; *CIO News — Packinghouse Workers Edition*, Dec. 5, 1938, April 17, 1939; *Thirtieth Biennial Report of the Secretary of State* (Topeka, 1936), 183.

25. The family left Pennsylvania in 1910 after Fischer's father was blacklisted for his union activities. Charles R. Fischer interviews.

26. Charles R. Fischer interview by author.

27. Charles R. Fischer interview and Finis Block interview, UPWAOHP.

28. Grisnik was one of the union representatives in negotiations with the company during the 1938 plant occupation. *Kansas City Kansan,* Sept. 10, 1938. On Grisnik and his family's CFU activities, see *Zajednicar,* May 2, 1933, Dec. 19, 1934, March 4, Dec. 18, 1935, Aug. 19, 1936, June 28, 1939; Charles R. Fischer interviews.

29. Hill to Webster, Nov. 25, 1935. The number of blacks grew to nine hundred on the eve of World War II. Urban League of Kansas City, *The Negro Worker of Kansas City,* 58.

30. Quotation from Finis Block interview, UPWAOHP; Neal Weaver to Edward F. Roche, Nov. 10, 1943, CIO ST, box 67.

31. Finis Block interview, UPWAOHP.

32. Charles R. Fischer interviews, quotation from UPWAOHP interview; Finis Block interview, UPWAOHP; Neal Weaver to Edward F. Roche, Nov. 10, 1943, CIO ST, box 67; *CIO News—Packinghouse Workers Edition,* Jan. 19, 1939.

33. Charles R. Fischer interviews; Minutes of Conference of Packinghouse Workers in Des Moines, Aug. 29, 1937, *Appeal* Mailing List, and Paul Rasmussen to National Labor Secretary, Socialist Party, June 8, 1937, all in Svend Godfredson Papers. Fischer's membership in the Socialist Party made it easy for Socialists in the IUAW, such as Svend Godfredson, to locate him through the *Socialist Appeal's* mailing list.

34. William Raspberry interview, Ann and Thomas Krasick interview, and Charles R. Fischer interview, UPWAOHP.

35. *Kansas City Labor Herald,* March 30, Aug. 3, 1934; Charles R. Fischer interview and Finis Block interview, UPWAOHP; *Unionist and Public Forum,* April 8, 1937; Paul Rasmussen to National Labor Secretary, June 8, 1937, Svend Godfredson Papers.

36. Quotation from Charles R. Fischer interview, UPWAOHP; "In the Matter of Armour and Company and Local Union No. 15, United Packinghouse Workers of America, Packinghouse Workers Organizing Committee, Affiliated with the Congress of Industrial Organizations," Case C-1741, 32 NLRB 539–44.

37. Charles R. Fischer interviews, quotation from UPWAOHP interview; Finis Block interview, UPWAOHP.

38. Case C-1741, 32 NLRB 539–42.

39. *The Unionist,* Aug. 13, 1937; Charles R. Fischer interview, UPWAOHP; Neal Weaver to Edward F. Roche, Nov. 10, 1943, CIO ST, box 67; Case C-1741, 32 NLRB 539–42.

40. Case C-1741, 32 NLRB 541–52; Charles Fischer interview, UPWAOHP.

41. The NLRB later held that Lambie was unfairly laid off by the company, but its June 10, 1941, ruling only ordered back pay dating from January 1939. Case C-1741, 32 NLRB 541–49.

42. *Kansas City Star,* Sept. 9 (quotation), 10, 1938; *Kansas City Kansan,* Sept. 9, 1938; Urban League of Kansas City, *The Negro Worker of Kansas City,* 17; *Kansas*

City Star, Sept. 11, 1938; *Midwest Daily Record,* Sept. 10, 14, 1938; Finis Block interview, UPWAOHP.

43. PWOC National Director Don Harris supported Local 15 by threatening to shut down the entire Armour chain. *Kansas City Star,* Sept. 9, 10, 11, 1938; *Kansas City Kansan,* Sept. 10, 1938; *Midwest Daily Record,* Sept. 14, 1938; Charles R. Fischer interviews.

44. Charles R. Fischer interview, UPWAOHP; *Kansas City Star,* Sept. 10, 1938; *CIO News—Packinghouse Workers Edition,* April 17, 1939.

45. *Midwest Daily Record,* Sept. 14, 1938; *Kansas City Star,* Sept. 12, 1938; *Kansas City Kansan,* Sept. 9, 12, 1938; Charles R. Fischer interview by author.

46. *Kansas City Star,* Sept. 12, 14, 1938; Urban League of Kansas City, *The Negro Worker of Kansas City,* 18; *Midwest Daily Record,* Sept. 14, 1938.

47. Charles R. Fischer interview by author; *Kansas City Star,* Sept. 14, 1938; *CIO News—Packinghouse Workers Edition,* Dec. 5, 1938, Jan. 16, April 17, May 1, 15, June 23, Aug. 7, Dec. 15, 1939, Jan. 8, 1940, Aug. 4, 1941.

48. Urban League of Kansas City, *The Negro Worker of Kansas City,* 45; Charles R. Fischer interviews; Ann and Thomas Krasick interview and Finis Block interview, UPWAOHP.

49. *CIO News—Packinghouse Workers Edition,* Dec. 5, 1938, April 17, 1939; Charles R. Fischer interviews; *Thirty First Biennial Report of the Secretary of State* (Topeka, 1938), 140–41. On Local 15's classes see *CIO News—Packinghouse Workers Edition,* Dec. 5, 1938, Jan. 16, April 17, May 1, 15, June 23, 26, Aug. 7, Dec. 15, 1939, Jan. 8, 1940, Aug. 4, 1941.

50. *Kansas City Kansan,* Sept. 10, 1938.

51. *CIO News—Packinghouse Workers Edition,* Nov. 28, 1938, Jan. 2, 9, 23, March 3, June 12, 26, Oct. 2, 16, 1939, June 10, 1940, Aug. 4, Sept. 21, Dec. 18, 1941; "Meat Packing Groups Chartered by the CIO," Aug. 16, 1937, CIO ST, box 65; Walter Bailey interview, UPWAOHP; Urban League of Kansas City, *The Negro Worker of Kansas City,* 17.

52. Theodore V. Purcell, *Blue Collar Man: Patterns of Dual Allegiance in Industry* (Cambridge, 1960), 20; *Packinghouse Worker,* Jan. 1, June 25, 1943, April 28, 1944.

53. Ann and Thomas Krasick interview, UPWAOHP; quotation from Purcell, *Blue Collar Man,* 196. For examples of pro-company attitudes among white Swift workers, see also 68, 87, 88, 127, 188–90.

54. Quotations from ibid., 198 and 189; for similar comments, see 20, 21, 27, 28, 76, 128, 139, 202, 203, and 208.

55. Quotation from ibid., 132; for similar comments see 50, 127, 197, and 269. Mexican workers made similar criticisms of their treatment by Swift; ibid., 66, 67, 72, and 135.

56. Ann and Thomas Krasick interview and Finis Block interview, UPWAOHP; *Packinghouse Worker,* Jan. 1, June 25, 1943, April 28, 1944; Purcell, *Blue Collar Man,* 21, 28, 76.

57. *Packinghouse Worker,* June 25, 1943.

58. Charles R. Fischer interview, UPWAOHP. On Fischer's reputation see Marian Simmons interview, Virginia Houston interview, and Ann and Thomas Krasick interview, UPWAOHP.

Chapter 5: "We Had to Have Somebody Behind Us"

1. H. R. Ballard, "Cops Picket Organizer," *Solidarity: A Yearbook of the Iowa-Nebraska States Industrial Union Council* (Sioux City, 1939), 48, 58.

2. *Unionist and Public Forum*, July 1, 1937; Clyde Wensel interview, UPWAOHP; "Intermediate Report by Trial Examiner W. P. Webb in the Matter of Swift and Company and the United Packing House Workers Local Industrial Union 874 Through the Packing house Workers Organizing Committee (C.I.O.)," 5, NLRB Case Files, Case C-1116, RG 25; "Meat Packing Groups Charted by the CIO Aug. 16, 1937," CIO ST, box 65.

3. R. L. Polk & Co., *Polk's City Directory—Sioux City, Iowa, 1931* (Detroit, 1930), 17–18; Iowa Writers Project, *Woodbury County History* (Sioux City, 1942), 14–15; U.S. Department of Commerce, *Fifteenth Census of the United States, Population,* vol. 3, pt. 1, 755, 796.

4. Iowa Writers Project, *Woodbury County History;* U.S. Department of Commerce and Labor, *Twelfth Census of the United States, Population* (Washington, 1901), pt. 1, 800–803, 868–69, 953–61; U.S. Department of Commerce, *Fifteenth Census of the United States, Population* (Washington, 1932), vol. 2, pt. 1, 787–88, and (Washington, 1933), 4:534–36.

5. U.S. Department of Commerce and Labor, *Twelfth Census of the United States, Population,* pt. 1, 800–803; U.S. Department of Commerce, *Fourteenth Census of the United States, Population* 3:317; Mabel F. Hoyt, "History of Community House Sioux City, Iowa," *Annals of Iowa* 21 (Jan. 1938): 191–92; Jennie Shuck interview by author, Nov. 3, 1987; Mary Edwards interview by author, Nov. 3, 1987.

6. Suzanne Dores O'Dea Schenken, "Mary J. Treglia: A Community Leader," master's thesis, Iowa State University, 1987, 25; "Catholic Churches of Sioux City and Estimate of Number of Families and of Individual Members, 1931. Furnished at request of Sioux City Public Library," Sioux City Public Library Clipping File, "Sioux City—Churches and Clergymen (Catholic)" folder; Thomas P. Christensen, "An Industrial History of Woodbury County," *Unionist and Public Forum,* Sept. 5, 1940.

7. U.S. Department of Commerce, *Fourteenth Census of the United States, Population,* 2:317, 793, 1030–31; U.S. Department of Commerce, *Fifteenth Census of the United States, Population,* vol. 3, pt. 1, 787–88; Jennie Shuck and Mary Edwards interviews by author. On Jews in Sioux City, see Bernard Shuman, *A History of the Sioux City Jewish Community 1869–1969* (Sioux City, 1969), and Bernard Marinback, *Galveston: Ellis Island of the West* (Albany, 1983).

8. Jennie Shuck commented, "There was constant bickering [among the Russians] . . . . Everybody thought they ought to be the boss. The poor priest that they would have over there really were not treated very well." Jennie Shuck interview

by author; Hoyt, "History of Community House, Sioux City, Iowa," 193; R. L. Polk & Co., *Polk's City Directory—Sioux City Iowa* (Detroit, 1918–40). For the impact of the Russian revolution on the American wing of the Russian Orthodox Church, see Jerome Davis, *The Russian Immigrant* (New York, 1922), 91–101, 118, and Stanford Gerber, "Russkoya Celo: The Ethnography of a Russian-American Community," Ph.D. diss., University of Missouri—Kansas City, 1966, 100–106.

9. *Sioux City Journal,* May 1 (quotation), Nov. 9, 1919; Mrs. Wallace M. Short, *Just One American* (Sioux City, 1943), 130; Jennie Shuck and Mary Edwards interviews by author.

10. The family lived on a farm at the edge of town, and Davidchick's mother was well known among Russians for her Russian-style cheese and bread sold at local groceries. Clyde Wensel interview, UPWAOHP; Jennie Shuck and Mary Edwards interviews by author; *Sioux City Journal,* Jan. 22, 1966.

11. Jennie Shuck interviews. Zenkovich's date of emigration was early for the Russian Orthodox immigrants and coincides with the reaction to the 1905 revolution in Russia. Along with his unusual education and religious views, this suggests he might have been a political activist in Russia. Unfortunately, Zenkovich never discussed this subject with his daughter. City directories for 1915–35 confirm his occupation and common residence with Jennie.

12. Jennie Shuck interviews.

13. A WPA-sponsored survey in the mid-1930s showed that 129 blacks held packinghouse jobs, four times the number in any other category. "Tabulation as to Economic Status as to Type of Work and the Number," Works Progress Administration Papers, series A, box 142; Iowa Writers Project, *Woodbury County History,* 145; Department of Commerce and Labor, *Thirteenth Census of the United States, Statistics for Iowa* (Washington, 1913), 624; U.S. Department of Commerce, *Fourteenth Census of the United States, Population,* 3:329; William L. Hewitt, "So Few Undesirables: Race, Residence, and Occupation in Sioux City, 1890–1925," *Annals of Iowa* 50 (Fall–Winter 1989–90): 169–76; Leola Nelson Bergmann, *The Negro in Iowa* (1948, repr. Iowa City, 1969), 40; quotation from Clyde Wensel interview, UPWAOHP; see also Sam Davis interview, UPWAOHP.

14. Iowa Writers Project, *Woodbury County History,* 148; Johnny Shores interview by author, Nov. 3, 1987; Sam Davis interview, UPWAOHP. Jennie Shuck recalled attending school and playing with black children; one of their mothers would watch her after school until her father finished work. Jennie Shuck interview by author.

15. "Blacks in Packinghouses," Works Progress Administration Papers, series A, box 142; Clyde Wensel interview and Sam Davis interview, UPWAOHP; Johnny Shores interview by author; Grant Holbrook interview by author; Bruce Nolan and Grant Holbrook interview, UPWAOHP. There are some reports of blacks being brought in as strikebreakers in 1921, but the number of blacks in Sioux City fell from 1,139 in 1920 to 871 in 1930, with a decline in the male population whereas the number of women grew slightly. This indicates that use of

black strikebreakers was minimal and had only a marginal impact on the black packinghouse work force.

16. Sam Davis interview (quotation) and Jesse Vaughn interview, Oct. 4, 1985, UPWAOHP; R. L. Polk & Co., *Polk's Sioux City Directory, 1930* (Detroit, 1930). On Shelton's links with the Communist Party, see the affidavits in the Ralph Helstein Papers, box 3, "Iowa Affidavits" file.

17. Bruce Nolan interview by author.

18. These unionists closely followed organizing drives in meatpacking, especially the progress of the IUAW in Austin, Minnesota. Bruce Nolan and Grant Holbrook interviews by author; Bruce Nolan and Grant Holbrook interview, UPWAOHP.

19. The Iowa Communist Party only had 157 members in June 1937. Harvey Klehr, *The Heyday of American Communism* (New York, 1984), 138–40; John Stover, *Cornbelt Rebellion: The Farmers Union Alliance* (Urbana, 1965), 83; *Union Advocate*, Aug. 11, 1932; *Unionist and Public Forum*, Aug. 23, 1934, April 18, 1935, May 27, 1937, Feb. 19, 1938. Iowa-Nebraska PWOC regional director Don Harris and organizer James Porter were Communist Party members but played no role in Sioux City until the 1938 Swift strike. See the statement from Archie Helm, n.d., Affidavits by Ben Henry, July 18, 1940, H. R. Ballard to J. C. Lewis, Aug. 1, 1940, and Affidavit by James P. Dean, Dec. 22, 1939, all in Ralph Helstein Papers, box 3. On Socialists see Ames Local, Socialist Party, "Analysis of the Iowa Farmer-Labor Party," March 17, 1936, Roland White Papers, box 10, folder 4; A. M. Prescott to Roland White, July 29, 1936, Roland White to Prescott, July 22, 1936, and Sioux City Socialist Party to Mary Elva Sather, April 9, 1936, all in Roland White Papers, box 10, folder 6; Bruce Nolan interview by author.

20. Bruce Nolan and Grant Holbrook interview, UPWAOHP; Bruce Nolan interview by author.

21. Sophie Ferdig's husband was very active in the union. See her testimony in "Transcript of Proceedings before the NLRB In the Matter of Swift and Company and United Packing House Workers Local industrial Union No. 874 Through the Packing House Workers Organizing Committee (C.I.O.)," Cases C-1116 and R-1125, "Transcripts and Exhibits," boxes 1531–33, 1670–701, NLRB Records, RG 25 [transcript hereafter cited as "Transcripts and Exhibits," Cases C-1116 and R-1125]; Jennie Shuck interview, UPWAOHP.

22. Peter Ecker, "Labor and Social Disorders in Sioux City," n.d., 10–16, Works Progress Administration Papers, series A, box 142; Iowa Writers Project, *Woodbury County History*, 146–48; Thomas P. Christensen, "An industrial History of Woodbury County," *Unionist and Public Forum*, Aug. 22, Sept. 22, 1940; William H. Cumberland, *Wallace M. Short: Iowa Rebel* (Ames, 1983), 64–67; Jennie Shuck interview, UPWAOHP; *Sioux City Journal*, Feb. 2, 1922.

23. Ecker, "Labor and Social Disorders," 16; Iowa Writers Project, *Woodbury County History*, 148; Thomas P. Christensen, "An Industrial History of Woodbury County," *Unionist and Public Forum*, Sept. 22, 1940.

24. "Memorandum of Company Policies," reproduced in "Intermediate Report," Case C-1116; Peter Ecker, "Sioux City Baseball 1924," Works Progress Administration Papers, series A, box 142.

25. "Decision Order and Direction of Election—In the Matter of Swift and Company and United Packing House Workers Local Industrial Union No. 874 Through the Packing House Workers Organizing Committee (C.I.O.)," Cases C-1116 and R-1125, 21 NLRB 1069; "Transcripts and Exhibits" Cases C-1116 and R-1125, 2793–897; Bruce Nolan and Grant Holbrook interview and Clyde Wensel interview, UPWAOHP; "Decision Order and Direction of Election—In the Matter of the Cudahy Packing Company and United Packinghouse Workers Local Industrial Union No. 873, Affiliated with the PWOC and CIO," Cases C-901 and R-1134, 15 NLRB 681.

26. Bruce Nolan and Grant Holbrook interview, UPWAOHP; Jennie Shuck interview.

27. Jennie Shuck interview by author; Schenken, "Mary J. Treglia: A Community Leader," 58. Home construction fell from 154 houses in 1929 to only 46 in 1933. In 1925, 609 new homes were built. R. L. Polk & Co., *Polk's City Directory—Sioux City, Iowa, 1931*, 17; Iowa Writers Project, *Woodbury County History*, 161; *Unionist and Public Forum*, Aug. 31, 1940, Jan. 25, Oct. 25, 1934, March 28, May 2, June 13, 1935, July 1, 1937; *Sioux City Journal*, April 30, May 5, 1934. On the Farm Holiday Association protests in Sioux City, see Iowa Writers Project, *Woodbury County History*, 157, and Short, *Just One American*, 153. The standard work on the Farm Holiday Association is Stover, *Cornbelt Rebellion*.

28. *Unionist and Public Forum*, Dec. 14, 1933, Feb. 1, March 3, May 17, 24, 1934, May 2, 1935.

29. Alvin Edwards recalled that because Swift foremen often belonged to the Masons, many workers joined the Masons in order to receive preferential treatment. Mary and Alvin Edwards interview and Bruce Nolan and Grant Holbrook interview, UPWAOHP. On the practices of company unions, see "Decision Order and Direction of Election," Cases C-1116 and R-1125, 1075; "Decision Order and Direction of Election," Cases C-901 and R-1134, 681–92.

30. Clyde Wensel interview, UPWAOHP; Jennie Shuck and Grant Holbrook interviews by author; Bruce Nolan and Grant Holbrook interview, UPWAOHP.

31. In its investigation, the NLRB obtained the membership cards of the union and used this information to produce a list of CIO members at Swift, along with the date they signed their membership card. Combined with a department-by-department breakdown of the workforce obtained from Swift by NLRB investigators, I was able to determined the dates that individuals joined the union in each department. "Intermediate Report," Case C-1116, Exhibits 2 and 4.

32. "Transcripts and Exhibits," Cases C-1116 and R-1125, 296–496, 670–99; Jennie Shuck interview by author; "Decision Order and Direction of Election," Cases C-1116 and R-1125, 1178; Mary and Alvin Edwards interview, UPWAOHP.

33. After the Supreme Court found the National Labor Relations Act constitutional in 1937, former representatives to Swift's Assembly reconstituted themselves as the ESL. "Decision Order and Direction of Election," Cases C-1116 and R-1125, 1179–81; "Intermediate Report," Case C-1116, 4–18.

34. "Decision Order and Direction of Election," Cases C-1116 and R-1125, 1181–82.

35. "Intermediate Report," Case C-1116, 4–14, and Exhibits 2 and 4; "Decision Order and Direction of Election," Cases C-1116 and R-1125, 1178.

36. "Decision Order and Direction of Election—In the Matter of Armour and Company and United Packing House Workers Industrial Local Union No. 389 Affiliated with CIO," Case R-658 7 NLRB 710; *Packinghouse News*, mimeographed by L.I.U. 389, May 27, June 24, July 22, 1938, in "Rejected Exhibits," NLRB Case C-901, Administrative Division, box 635, RG 25; *Unionist and Public Forum*, June 30, 1938.

37. "Intermediate Report," Case C-1116, Exhibits 2 and 4.

38. Ibid., "Transcripts and Exhibits," Cases C-1116 and R-1125, 338.

39. "Intermediate Report," Case C-1116, 27–30; "Decision Order and Direction of Election," Cases C-1116 and R-1125, 1184–85.

40. "Intermediate Report," Case C-1116, 30–34; "Decision Order and Direction of Election," Cases C-1116 and R-1125, 1185–86; "Transcript and Exhibits," Cases C-1116 and R-1125, 338.

41. By "union leaders," I am referring to stewards, officers, and members of the executive board and bargaining committee. "Intermediate Report," Case C-1116, Exhibits 2 and 4.

42. Scott Alan Sorenson, "Law Enforcement during the 1930's in Sioux City, Iowa," master's thesis, University of South Dakota, 1976, 44–46; *CIO News— Packinghouse Workers Edition*, Nov. 14, Dec. 12, 19, 1938.

43. "Transcripts and Exhibits," Cases C-1116 and R-1125, 2573–74; Sorenson, "Law Enforcement during the 1930's," 48, 52–54; Don Pinkston, "Men against Money: An Epic That Needs the Writing—The Story of the Sioux City Swift Strike," *Solidarity: A Yearbook of the Iowa-Nebraska States Industrial Union Council* (Sioux City, 1939), 19–22.

44. *Packinghouse Worker*, Dec. 12, 19, 1938, Jan. 2, 1939; Attorneys Gillespie, Burke, and Gillespie to the Packinghouse Workers Organizing Committee, April 10, 1939, UPWA Papers, box 8, folder 11.

45. "Intermediate Report," Case C-1116, passim; Lee Loevinger to Charles Fahy, Jan. 21, 1939, NLRB Case Files, Case C-1116.

46. *Packinghouse Worker*, March 6, 1939; "Informal Report, 18th Region, Week Ending April 1, 1939," and Robert J. Wiener to Gerhard P. Van Arkel, July 14, 1939, both in NLRB Case Files, Case C-1116; Mary and Alvin Edwards interview, UPWAOHP; "Decision Order and Direction of Election," Cases C-1116 and R-1125, 1188, 1192–94.

47. Grant Holbrook interview by author. For membership figures, see "Finan-

cial Report, PWOC" for Aug. 1942–Aug. 1943, CIO ST, box 66; *Packinghouse Worker*, May 1, 1942; Tony Stephens to Sam Sponseller, Dec. 6, 1941, UPWA Papers, box 5, folder 3.

48. Attorneys Gillespie, Burke, and Gillespie to the Packinghouse Workers Organizing Committee, April 10, 1939; *Midwest Daily Record*, Dec. 20, 1938; *CIO News—Packinghouse Workers Edition*, Jan. 9, 1939; Bruce Nolan and Grant Holbrook interview, UPWAOHP; Mary and Alvin Edwards interview, UPWAOHP.

49. Clyde Wensel interview, UPWAOHP; Bruce Nolan interview, UPWAOHP. For examples of community support for the union, see for example the affidavits by Father E. J. Smith and George M. Cesna, in "In the Matter of The Cudahy Company and United Packinghouse Workers Local Industrial Union No. 873, Affiliated with P. W. O. C. and C. I. O. Report of Objections," NLRB Case Files, Cases C-901 and R-1134, RG 25. Cesna was the priest at St. Casimir Catholic Church, the Lithuanian church in the Bottoms neighborhoods.

50. Jennie Shuck interview, UPWAOHP.

51. Quotation from "Decision Order and Direction of Election," Cases C-1116 and R-1125, 1181; Bruce Nolan and Grant Holbrook interview, UPWAOHP.

52. Sioux City FLP activists were drawn from skilled workers in AFL unions and white-collar employees, Short's old base of support. Jess Pauley, a staunch union activist who worked closely with Arthell Shelton in Swift, was a delegate to the 1938 Woodbury Country FLP convention. There is no other evidence of participation in the FLP by packinghouse workers. Cumberland, *Wallace M. Short*, 137; *Unionist and Public Forum*, March 31, July 7, Nov. 17, 1938; Sorenson, "Law Enforcement during the 1930's," 5–15; R. L. Polk & Co., *Sioux City Directory, 1938* (Detroit, 1938).

53. *Unionist and Public Forum*, Oct. 25, Nov. 1, 1934, emphasis in original. For the internal divisions in the Iowa FLP, see Cumberland, *Wallace M. Short*, 112–38. On the Union Party, see Alan Brinkley, *Voices of Protest: Huey Long, Father Coughlin and the Great Depression* (New York, 1982), 226–37, 252–61.

54. *Unionist and Public Forum*, March 31, 1938; Erling Sannes, "'Make Sioux City a Good Place to Live': Organizing Teamsters in Sioux City, 1933–1938," *Annals of Iowa* 50 (Fall–Winter 1989–90): 230–31. Loepp went to the plant on the day of the strike to help end the dispute and offered several proposals for arbitration that the company rejected. Sturgeon kept the Sioux City police from interfering with the PWOC's picket lines—it was the county sheriff's deputies who fought with union pickets on October 18, 1938. On the political action program of Sioux City unions, see Loren Callender interview, UPWAOHP, and Grant Holbrook interview by author.

55. *Sioux City Journal*, Sept. 8, 1942.

Chapter 6: "So That Your Children Will Not Have to Slave as We Have"

1. *Proceedings, First Constitutional Convention of the United Packinghouse Workers of America*, 243.

2. Jesse Vaughn interview, Oct. 23, 1986, UPWAOHP; Kampfert, "History of Unionism in Meat Packing," 3:35–36, 41; Robert H. Schultz interview, Sept. 23, 1985, UPWAOHP; Mason City members quoted in J. C. Lewis to Van A. Bittner, Feb. 23, 1940, UPWA Papers, box 306, folder 12.

3. Certification of Armour locals from National Labor Relations Board published decisions; Van A. Bittner to Carl Schedler, May 16, 1939, UPWA Papers, box 1, folder 5; Van A. Bittner to Alan Haywood, Feb. 15, 1940, CIO ST, box 65; *CIO News—Packinghouse Worker Edition*, Feb. 5, April 15, 1940; Kampfert, "History of Unionism in Meat Packing," 3:41; Newell, *Chicago and the Labor Movement*, 169–70; Brody, *The Butcher Workmen*, 179.

4. Alan Haywood to Van A. Bittner, April 22, 1940, and enclosed statements by Kansas City PWOC leaders (all quotations), CIO ST, box 65.

5. Lawrence J. Minor to John L. Lewis, April 24, 1940, Alan Haywood to Minor, April 29, 1940, and "Special Meeting [in Mason City] of Executive Committee and Stewards Committee with Delegation from St. Paul and Kansas City," April 10, 1941 [hereafter cited as "Special Meeting [in Mason City]," both in CIO ST, box 65; Glenn Wiedenhamer to James Cunningham, Dec. 5, 1939, UPWA Papers, box 306, folder 11; "Minutes of District No. 2 conference, PWOC," Jan. 12, 1941, UPWA Papers, box 3, folder 3; Herbert March interview, Oct. 21, 1986, and Charlie McCafferty interview, UPWAOHP; quotation from J. C. Lewis to Allan Haywood, March 7, 1940, CIO ST, box 65. Lewis had just completed similar duties in the Washington State Industrial Union Council. Van A. Bittner to J. C. Lewis, Nov. 30, 1939, UPWA Papers, box 306, folder 12; Jerry Lembke and William M. Tattan, *One Union in Wood: A Political History of the International Woodworkers of America* (New York, 1984), 90–91.

6. "Special Meeting of Packinghouse Workers Delegates," April 14, 1941, 5:107 (quotation), 168–72, 6:2–13, CIO ST, box 65; Resolution Adopted May 26, 1940 by Eleven PWOC Locals, attached to J. C. Lewis to Arthur Kampfert, "History of Unionism in Meat Packing," June 5, 1940, UPWA Papers, box 9, folder 4; Memoirs of Ben Henry, Ben Henry Papers. Extensive material pertaining to Communist Party activity is in Ralph Helstein Papers, box 3, "Iowa Affidavits" file; Herbert March interview, Oct. 21, 1986, A. J. Pittman interview, and Nels Peterson interview, UPWAOHP; J. C. Lewis to Allan Haywood, March 7, 1940, CIO ST, box 65.

7. Weidenhammer to Cunningham, Dec. 5, 1939, UPWA Papers, box 306, folder 11; C. E. Winterringer in "Special Meeting [in Mason City]," CIO ST, box 65, Statements by Laurence Gebhardt, May 26, 1940, Herbert Lockardt, May 26, 1940, and Nels Peterson, May 26, 1940, all in Ralph Helstein Papers, box 3, "Iowa Affidavits" file.

8. Certification victories from National Labor Relations Board published decisions, 1939–40, and Bittner to Schedler, May 16, 1939, in UPWA Papers, box 1, folder 5.

9. Johnson to Packing Locals, attached to Nels Peterson to Arthur Kampfert,

Nov. 6, 1940, and Arthur Kampfert to All Local Unions, PWOC, Nov. 8, 1940, both in UPWA Papers, box 9, folder 4; Arthur Kampfert to Meyer Stern, March 3, 1941, UPWA Papers, box 9, folder 5. For Alsup's meandering career, see his testimony in "Transcripts and Exhibits," Case C-1116, 3866–75.

10. Quotation from "Special Meeting of Packinghouse Workers Delegates," 2:54.

11. Van A. Bittner to Jesse Vaughn, Nov. 29, 1940, UPWA Papers, box 9, folder 4; Roy Franklin to John Doherty, Jan. 7, 1941, UPWA Papers, box 306, folder 4; quotation from Statement of Locals 27, 29, 100, and 347 to Philip Murray et al., n.d., CIO ST, box 65; "Minutes of Meeting of Local 42," June 6, 1941, UPWA Papers, box 9, folder 10; Hank Johnson to Earl Young, Feb. 25, 1941, UPWA Papers, box 9, folder 5; Walter Strabawa to J. C. Lewis, June 26, 1941, UPWA Papers, box 9, folder 10; Jesse Vaughn interview and Annie Jackson Collins, Richard Saunders, and Todd Tate interview, UPWAOHP.

12. First quotation from Resolution of District 2 Conference, Jan. 12, 1941, CIO ST, box 65; Resolutions of District 2, and Locals 74, 53, 37, and 4, Representatives of Locals 27, 29, 100, and 347 to Philip Murray, Alan Haywood, and John L. Lewis, n.d., all in CIO ST, box 65; Boyd Collins statement on 14–15 of "Minutes of District 2 Conference," Jan. 12, 1941, UPWA Papers, box 3, folder 3; Kampfert, "History of Unionism in Meat Packing," 3:35–36; Henry Giannini interview, UPWAOHP.

13. "Special Meeting [in Mason City]," with quotation from "Special Meeting of Packinghouse Workers Delegates," 5:159, both in CIO ST, box 65; Charles R. Fisher interview and Jake Cooper interview, UPWAOHP.

14. For District 3 statements on Johnson, see Resolutions Adopted by District 3, ca. Dec. 1940, UPWA Papers, box 306, folder 11. For conflict over integrated social events in Omaha, see statement of Lewis J. Clark, "Special Meeting of Packinghouse Workers Delegates," 5:36–38, CIO ST, box 65. On contacts between Cedar Rapids, Sioux City, and Omaha, see George and Francis Fletemeyer interview, Walt Mason and Darryl Poe interview, Fred Romano interview, and Nels Peterson interview, UPWAOHP.

15. Arthur Kampfert to Meyer Stern, March 3, 1941, UPWA Papers, box 9, folder 5; Pete Brown testimony in "Special Meeting of Packinghouse Workers Delegates," 5:199–207, CIO ST, box 65.

16. Herbert March interview, Oct. 21, 1986, UPWAOHP. For Johnson's relationship to the Communist Party, see material in "US Military Intelligence Reports: Surveillance of Radicals in the United States, 1917–1941," microfilm ed., University Publications of America, 1984, reels 10 and 11.

17. Allan Haywood meeting, Feb. 8, 1941, with representatives of packinghouse locals, David MacKenzie to Allan Haywood, Feb. 26, 1941, and John Doherty to Allan Haywood, Feb. 27, 1941, all in CIO ST, box 65. District 50 fired March for his action, but he was once again placed on the PWOC staff as Chicago district director. Arthur Kampfert to Nicholas Fontecchio, Feb. 2, 1941, UPWA Pa-

pers, box 9, folder 5; Harry Cyril Reed to Tom Doherty, CIO ST, box 65; Herbert March interview, Oct. 21, 1986, UPWAOHP.

18. Executive Board of Local 9 to Philip Murray, April 2, 1941, and quotations from "Special Meeting [in Mason City]," both in CIO ST, box 65.

19. "Minutes of Seventh Conference of District No. 2," PWOC, Jan. 12, 1941, 7, 17, UPWA Papers, box 3, folder 3. Ollman may have left the Trotskyist Socialist Workers Party (SWP) over this controversy while retaining his left-wing politics. Roy Franklin to J. C. Lewis, May 18, 1942, UPWA Papers, box 4, folder 7; Farrell Dobbs, *Teamster Power* (New York, 1973), 51; Jake Cooper interview, UPWAOHP.

20. "Minutes of Seventh Conference of District No. 2," Jan. 12, 1941, UPWA Papers, box 3, folder 3; "Local 9 Offers Proposals for PWOC Reorganization," *CIO News—Packinghouse Workers Edition*, May 12, 1941; "Plan for Setting Up National Union," adopted June 22, 1941 by delegates of Locals 1, 9, and 31, UPWA Papers, box 4, folder 10.

21. "Minutes of Seventh Conference of District No. 2," Jan. 12, 1941, UPWA Papers, box 3, folder 3; Jesse Vaughn interview, Oct. 4, 1985, UPWAOHP; "Forward to a Packinghouse Workers CIO International Union!" and attachments, CIO ST, box 65. The SWOC struggle at Bethlehem Steel reached its climax in March and April 1941. Van Bittner, as Chicago SWOC director, spent most of his time on the steel organizing drive. See Preis, *Labor's Giant Step*, 107–11.

22. A complete transcript of the hearings, "Special Meeting of Packinghouse Workers Delegates," is in CIO ST, box 65. Composition and positions of the two factions can be found in 1:1–3, 2:1, 3:1–19, 4:1–3, and 7:1–3. Carey's statement from vol. 3. Arthur Kampfert to Meyer Stern, April 25, 1941, UPWA Papers, box 9, folder 5; *CIO News—Packinghouse Workers Edition*, April 28, 1941.

23. Statements by Carey in vol. 3, and Haywood, vol. 6, "Special Meeting of Packinghouse Workers Delegates" and "Local Unions Withholding Tax for April, 1941," both CIO ST, box 65.

24. Philip Murray to PWOC-CIO, May 7, 1941, CIO ST, box 65; *CIO News—Packinghouse Workers Edition*, May 12, 1941; *Packinghouse Worker*, May 22, 1942; J. C. Lewis to All Local Unions, July 7, 1941, UPWA Papers, box 9, folder 5; John Doherty to Roy Franklin, May 6, 1941, UPWA Papers, box 306, folder 4; Herbert March interview, Oct. 23, 1986, UPWAOHP; Sophie Kosciowlowski to Allan Haywood, April 30, 1941, CIO ST, box 65.

25. Joseph Showalter to Eddie Folan, May 23, 1941, UPWA Papers, box 4, folder 11; Roy Franklin to J. C. Lewis, June 19, 1941, UPWA Papers, box 4, folder 8; Sam Sponseller to J. C. Lewis, June 19, 1941, UPWA Papers, box 5, folder 2; Ramsey Wilson to J. C. Lewis, June 21, 1941, UPWA Papers, box 5, folder 7; Arthur Kampfert to J. C. Lewis, July 22, 1941, UPWA Papers, box 9, folder 7; J. C. Lewis to A. J. Shippey, June 23, 1941, CIO ST, box 65; Roy Franklin to J. C. Lewis, Sept. 4, 1941, UPWA Papers, box 4, folder 8; Roy Franklin to J. C. Lewis, Feb. 11, 1942 and March 3, 1942, UPWA Papers, box 4, folder 9; A. J. Pittman to J. C. Lewis, June 19, 1942,

and Lewis to Pittman, June 20, 1942, both in UPWA Papers, box 5, folder 7; Frank Ellis to Sam Sponseller, Aug. 6, 1942, UPWA Papers, box 4, folder 10; Arthur Parenteau to Roy Franklin, March 20, 1943, and Franklin to Parenteau, March 25, 1943, both in UPWA Papers, box 4, folder 11; Floyd Broulliard to Sam Sponseller, March 20, 1943, UPWA Papers, box 2, folder 3; Annie Jackson Collins, Richard Saunders, and Todd Tate interview, Sept. 13, 1985, UPWAOHP.

26. Death certificate, County Clerk of Cook County, Dec. 13, 1944, Chicago Municipal Records Office; *Chicago Daily News*, Oct. 25, 1944. My thanks to Sanford Horwitt, who provided these documents to Rick Halpern. Horwitt, *Let Them Call Me Rebel*, 124–25; Herbert March interview, Oct. 21, 1986, and Jesse Vaughn interview, UPWAOHP.

27. *CIO News—Packinghouse Worker Edition*, July 21, 1941; J. C. Lewis to Francis Perkins, July 11, 1941, and Ralph T. Seward to J. C. Lewis, July 26, 1941, both in UPWA Papers, box 1, folder 5; J. C. Lewis to Francis Perkins, July 24, 1941, Lewis to All District Directors and Local Unions, PWOC, and Ralph Seward to J. C. Lewis, July 29, 1941, all in UPWA Papers, box 2, folder 9.

28. Maintenance of membership prevented workers from leaving a union after an initial fifteen-day escape period. *CIO News—Packinghouse Workers Edition*, Aug. 18, Sept. 15, 29, Oct. 10, Dec. 22, 1941; Master Agreement between Armour and the PWOC, UPWA Papers, box 1, folder 5; Svend Godfredson to Allan Haywood, Oct. 31, 1941, CIO ST, box 65; J. C. Lewis to All Local Unions, Jan. 20, 1942, UPWA Papers, box 2, folder 9.

29. "Plan for Setting Up National Union" by Austin, Fort Dodge, and Ottumwa locals, June 22, 1941, UPWA Papers, box 4, folder 10; "Joint Conference of Districts Two and Three," June 19, 1941, UPWA Papers, box 4, folder 8; Resolution Adopted by Local 58, Aug. 16, 1941, UPWA Papers, box 5, folder 5; Roy Franklin to J. C. Lewis, Oct. 28, 1941, UPWA Papers, box 4, folder 8; Sam Sponseller to J. C. Lewis, Nov. 17, 1941, UPWA Papers, box 7, folder 1; Roy Franklin to J. C. Lewis, Feb. 11, Feb. 16, 1942, UPWA Papers, box 4, folder 9; L. McDonald to J. C. Lewis, March 12, 1942, UPWA Papers, box 7, folder 1; *Packinghouse Worker*, May 8, 1942; "Delegates Attending Chicago Conference," May 3, 1942, and "Policy Committee and Alternates," both in UPWA Papers, box 11, folder 4.

30. Robert H. Zieger, *The CIO: 1935–1955* (Chapel Hill, 1995), 133–39; Svend Godfredson to Joe Ollman, July 30, 1942, Svend Godfredson Papers; Daniel T. Smyth to Philip Murray, June 23, 1942, CIO ST, box 65; Allan Haywood to J. C. Lewis, July 16, 1942, UPWA Papers, box 8, folder 11; Sam Sponseller to All Local Unions, July 23, 1942, UPWA Papers, box 2, folder 9; "Policy Adopted in Policy Committee with International Chairman Sam Sponseller and Assistant Chairman Roy Franklin," Aug. 14, 1942, UPWA Papers, box 2, folder 10; quotations from "Policy for Packinghouse Workers Organizing Committee," CIO ST, box 66; *Packinghouse Worker*, July 24, 1942.

31. Jesse Prosten interview, UPWAOHP; Resolution Adopted July 19, 1942, at Joint Executive Board Meeting of Omaha Locals, Resolution Adopted July 21,

1942, by Local 3, Executive Board, Local 347 to Allan Haywood, July 15, 1942, Local 84 Executive Board to Philip Murray, July 16, 1942, Joseph Karceski to Philip Murray, July 15, 1942, Henry Schoenstein to Philip Murray, July 17, 1942, and Leondies McDonald to Philip Murray, July 15, 1942, all in CIO ST, box 66; Motion Adopted by Joint Meeting of Sioux City Executive Boards, July 30, 1942, UPWA Papers, box 4, folder 2; Joe Ollman to Svend Godfredson, July 29, 1942, and Godfredson to Ollman, July 30, 1942, both in Svend Godfredson Papers; Joe Ollman to Sam Sponseller, June 24, 1943, UPWA Papers, box 7, folder 6; final quotation from Philip Weightman interview, UPWAOHP.

32. Quotation from Resolution Adopted by Joint Executive Board, Sioux City Locals, July 30, 1942, UPWA Papers, box 4, folder 2; "District Conference of District No. 3," Aug. 2, 1942, UPWA Papers, box 5, folder 1; Harvey C. Fremming to Sam Sponseller, July 25, 1942, UPWA Papers, box 5, folder 4; Resolution of PWOC Policy Committee, Aug. 20, 1942, UPWA Papers, box 12, folder 5; Sam Sponseller to Chester Qualley, Sept. 2, 1942, UPWA Papers, box 2, folder 10; Allan Haywood to Sam Sponseller, Sept. 8, 1942, UPWA Papers, box 5, folder 1; Nels Peterson to Philip Murray, Sept. 22, 1942, "Motion Passed at Conference of District 3 and 16," Sept. 13, 1942, and Sam Sponseller to Nels Peterson, Oct. 12, 1942, all in UPWA Papers, box 5, folder 1; *Packinghouse Worker*, Sept. 18, 1942; Minutes, PWOC Meeting, Nov. 12, 1942, UPWA Papers, box 8, folder 5; Philip Murray to Sam Sponseller, Dec. 7, 1942, UPWA Papers, box 12, folder 5; Sam Sponseller to All Local Unions, Dec. 28, 1942, UPWA Papers, box 2, folder 10; Nels Peterson interview, UPWAOHP.

33. Herbert March interview, July 15, 1985, UPWAOHP. On the formation of the USWA, see Brody, "The Origins of Modern Steel Unionism," in *Forging a Union of Steel*, ed. Clark, Gottlieb, and Kennedy, 13–29; PWOC Wage and Policy Conference, Feb. 19 to 21, 1943, 571 (quotations), UPWA Papers, box 524; Philip Weightman interview, UPWAOHP.

34. The resolution was jointly submitted by Fort Dodge and Omaha Swift Local 47, opponents in District 3 debates barely two years before. Sponseller ruled the resolution failed—although no vote was recorded. In its place, the conference passed a shorter motion offered by Herb March urging the CIO to convene a constitutional convention of packinghouse workers in 1943. PWOC Wage and Policy Conference, Feb. 19 to 21, 1943, 540–90, UPWA Papers, box 524; Minutes of Second Meeting of Constitutional Convention Committee, July 12, 1943, UPWA Papers box 3, folder 4. The transcript of the July 8–10, 1943, wage and policy conference can be found in the UPWAOHP additions to the UPWA Papers.

35. Ted Covey to Sam Sponseller, June 23, 1943, and Sponseller to Covey, June 25, 1943, both in UPWA Papers, box 5, folder 6; Minutes of Second Meeting of Constitutional Convention Committee, July 12, 1943, UPWA Papers, box 3, folder 4.

36. Although the CIO favored Sponseller, widespread opposition blocked any serious effort to advance his candidacy. Wilson from Local 347 and Franklin from

Local 9 did not have the support of their unions. Before the convention Austin publicly endorsed Stern for UPWA secretary-treasurer. See Frank Schultz, "A History of Our Union from 1933–1949," *The Unionist*, 1949, repr. July 23, 1971; *Proceedings, First Constitutional Convention of the United Packinghouse Workers of America*, 223–53; Philip Weightman interview, A. J. Pittman interview, Svend Godfredson interview, and Jesse Prosten interview, UPWAOHP.

37. *Proceedings, First Constitutional Convention of the United Packinghouse Workers of America*, 257–69.

Introduction to Part 2

1. Quotation from De Caux, *Labor Radical*, 244; Mike Davis, *Prisoners of the American Dream* (New York, 1986); Howell John Harris, *The Right to Manage* (Madison, 1982).

2. See material in UPWA Papers, boxes 118, 127, and 128, and Ralph Helstein's report to the *Second Special Convention of UPWA*, May 1956, 10–13; Brody, *The Butcher Workman*, 262–72; Joel Seidman, "Unity in Meatpacking: Problems and Prospects," in *New Dimensions in Collective Bargaining*, ed. Harold W. Davey et al. (New York, 1959), 29–43.

Chapter 7: "We Are Not Asking for Favors"

1. George and Francis Fletemeyer interview, UPWAOHP.

2. *Proceedings, Second Constitutional Convention of the United Packinghouse Workers of America* (1944), 148–57; Philip Weightman interview, UPWAOHP.

3. The national officers of the United Rubber Workers experienced a similar crisis of authority because of the power of its Akron locals during World War II. See Nelson Lichtenstein, *Labor's War at Home: The CIO in World War II* (Cambridge, 1982), 197–201.

4. Lichtenstein, *Labor's War at Home*, 110–35, 178–202; Christopher L. Tomlins, *The State and the Unions: Labor Relations, Law, and the Organized Labor Movement in America, 1880–1960* (Cambridge, 1985), 247–81; Joshua Freeman, "Delivering the Goods: Industrial Unionism during World War II," *Labor History* 19 (Fall 1978): 570–93.

5. First quotations from Herbert March interview, July 15, 1985, UPWAOHP; last quotation from Lichtenstein, *Labor's War at Home*, 1126–27.

6. Sam Sponseller to All Swift Locals, April 1, 1943, UPWA Papers, box 2, folder 10; table, "Working Conditions and Safety," UPWA Papers, box 9, folder 4; Bureau of Labor Statistics table, Oct. 27, 1945, UPWA Papers, box 196, folder 7; Clark Kerr, "The Meat Packing Commission," NWLB Papers, RG 202, series 370, box 2641.

7. Fred Whitney, *Wartime Experiences of the National Labor Relations Board, 1941–1945* (Urbana, 1949), 119–20.

8. "Bi-Monthly Labor Market Report for: Kansas City," May 1, 1944, War Manpower Commission, and "Office for Emergency Management of War Man-

power Commission, Aug. 5, 1944, for Wilson & Co.," both Region IX, series 283, National Archives—Kansas City Center; "[Austin] Employees on Plant Payroll," UPWA Papers, box 493, folder 2; Halpern, "'Black and White, Unite and Fight," 435, 458; Ralph Helstein to Local Unions, Feb. 4, 1944, UPWA Papers, box 195, folder 1.

9. Bureau of Labor Statistics table, Oct. 27, 1945, UPWA Papers, box 196, folder 7; Russell Bull to Lewis J. Clark, Nov. 16, 1944, UPWA Papers, box 306, folder 15.

10. The PWOC asked the NWLB for union security provisions because the no-strike pledge had "placed strains" on the union and prevented it from engaging in "trade unionism as usual." "Supplemental Brief of PWOC," UPWA Papers, box 190, folder 1; quotation from NWLB ruling, 6 War Labor Reports 395; Kerr, "The Meat Packing Commission," 9; PWOC Officer's Report to Wage and Policy Conference, Feb. 19, 1943, UPWA Papers, box 2, folder 10; Eugene Cotton interview, UPWAOHP.

11. Kerr, "The Meat Packing Commission," passim; Lichtenstein, *Labor's War at Home,* 120; Lewis J. Clark and Philip Weightman to William H. Davis, July 15, 1944, UPWA Papers, box 188, folder 12; quotation from N. I. Callowick to William F. Rasky, March 3, 1944, UPWA Papers, box 189, folder 6.

12. Clyde Wensel interview, UPWAOHP. For extensive documentation of unsanctioned job action, see letters from Ralph Helstein to sixteen Armour locals, seven Swift locals, and all Wilson locals, UPWA Papers, box 1, folder 6, box 11, folder 10, box 12, folder 8, and box 196, folder 1. Subsequent responses and descriptions of job actions, often accompanied by information supplied by the company, provides a rich picture of these incidents. William Nolan interview, Philip Weightman interview, Walter Bailey interview, Helen Zrudsky interview, Walt Mason and Darrel Poe interview, Bruce Nolan and Grant Holbrook interview, and Henry Giannini interview, UPWAOHP.

13. Jerome Scaglione to Ralph Helstein, Sept. 11, 1946, and "Slowdowns, Work Stoppages and Strikes since Aug. 11, 1944" for East St. Louis, both in UPWA Papers, box 196, folder 1; *Proceedings, Second Constitutional Convention of the United Packinghouse Workers of America,* 82–87.

14. Ralph Helstein to Douglas McMannes, Nov. 23, 1943, McMannes to Helstein, Nov. 24, 1943, McMannes to Helstein, Dec. 6, 1942, and McMannes to Virginia Spence, March 20, 1944, all UPWA Papers, box 1, folder 6.

15. *Proceedings, First Constitutional Convention of the United Packinghouse Workers of America,* 169–70; *Proceedings, Second Constitutional Convention of the United Packinghouse Workers of America,* 70–75; Charles Ingersoll to Ralph Helstein, Nov. 29, 1943, UPWA Papers, box 1, folder 5; Ralph Helstein to James Quigley, Nov. 23, 1943, and attached documents, UPWA Papers, box 1, folder 6; table, "Slowdowns, Work Stoppages, and Strikes since August 11, 1944" for Local 58, UPWA Papers, box 196, folder 1; *Packinghouse Worker,* May 1, 8, June 5, July 3, Aug. 27, 1942, Jan. 8, 22, Feb. 19, June 11, Sept. 24, Oct. 8, 1943; Frank Schultz, "A History of Our Union from 1933–1949," *The Unionist,* 1949, repr. July 16, 1971.

16. Ralph Helstein to James Quigley, Nov. 23, 1943, and attached documents, UPWA Papers, box 1, folder 6; table, "Slow-downs, Work Stoppages, and Strikes since August 11, 1944" for Local 58, UPWA Papers, box 196, folder 1; Martin Glaberman, *Wartime Strikes* (Detroit, 1980), 120.

17. Herbert March interview, July 15, 1985, UPWAOHP; *Proceedings, Second Constitutional Convention of the United Packinghouse Workers of America*, 85. There were many job actions at Chicago Armour during World War II. Frank Green to William H. Davis, July 8, 1944, and Lewis J. Clark to William H. Davis, July 15, 1944 and attachments, both in UPWA Papers, box 188, folder 12; table, "Slow-downs, Work Stoppages and Strikes since August 11, 1944" for Local 58, UPWA Papers, box 196, folder 1. For a similar gap between Communist rhetoric and practice on the no-strike pledge, see Howard Kimmeldorf, "World War II and the Deradicalization of American Labor: The ILWU as a Deviant Case," *Labor History* 33 (Spring 1992): 248–78.

18. Frank Green to Milton Handler, May 6, 1944, Jesse Prosten, "Re Armour Stoppage," and Ralph Helstein to Milton Handler, June 10, 1944, all in UPWA Papers, box 189, folder 6.

19. Herbert March interview, July 15, 1985, Vicky Starr interview, and Todd Tate interview, UPWAOHP.

20. Mary Salinas interview, Frank Wallace interview, Walt Mason and Darrel Poe interview, and Herbert March interviews, UPWAOHP. Armour inadvertently accepted the distinction drawn by many workers. The tables it produced listing unsanctioned job actions were titled "Slow-Downs, Work Stoppages, and Strikes." For a discussion of the issue of "sacrifice," see Mark H. Leff, "The Politics of Sacrifice on the American Home Front in World War II," *Journal of American History* 77 (March 1991): 1296–316.

21. See letters to local unions from Ralph Helstein, UPWA Papers box 1, folder 6, box 11, folder 10, box 12, folder 8, and box 196, folder 1; Saunders in Annie Jackson Collins, Richard Saunders, and Todd Tate interview, UPWAOHP.

22. Lewis J. Clark to James O'Connor, Feb. 8, 1944, Resolution of Local 214, Adopted Feb. 13, 1944, Lewis J. Clark to Sam Finch, Feb. 4, 1944, Lewis J. Clark to Sam Finch, Feb. 18, 1944, Local 43 to Lewis J. Clark, n.d., Resolution of Local 43, Adopted March 7, 1944, all in UPWA Papers, box 1, folder 6; *Proceedings, Second Constitutional Convention of the United Packinghouse Workers of America*, 81–88; quotation from "Officers Report," *Proceedings, Third Constitutional Convention of the United Packinghouse Workers of America* (1946), 28.

23. Lichtenstein, *Labor's War at Home*, 180–93.

24. Frank Ingersoll to UPWA National Office, Jan. 1944, UPWA Papers, box 1, folder 6.

25. Svend Godfredson to James Carey, Feb. 20, 1943, CIO ST, box 57; Joseph Keenan to William H. Davis, June 13, 1944, UPWA Papers, box 189, folder 6; *Proceedings, Second Constitutional Convention of the United Packinghouse Workers of America*, 62–70, 81–89; Lewis J. Clark, "Recommendations to the UPWA Executive Board Meeting, Feb. 2, 1945," UPWA Papers, box 26, folder 1; quotations from

transcript, International Executive Board meeting, March 30, 1945, 199–230, UPWA Papers, box 27, folder 2.

26. Throughout the NWLB hearings, local union representatives were part of the UPWA delegations. Contract Committee to All Armour Locals, March 24, 1944, UPWA Papers, box 188, folder 12; Ralph Helstein to All Armour Locals, Oct. 13, 1944, UPWA Papers, box 188, folder 12; all quotations from Officers Report, *Proceedings, Third Constitutional Convention of the United Packinghouse Workers of America*, 30–31; UPWA, *The Union Makes Us Strong: Thirty Years of Progress* (Chicago, 1955), 3–5, copy in Herbert March Papers; *Chicago Daily News*, Feb. 9, 1945, and UPWA press release, Feb. 19, 1945, both UPWA Papers, box 189, folder 6; *Packinghouse Worker*, Feb. 16, 1945.

27. 21 War Labor Reports 652; Officer's Report to 1946 Convention, 31–32; quotations from UPWA, *The Union Makes Us Strong*, 5–6; *Packinghouse Worker*, March 2, 1945.

28. The Kansas City stoppage was a typical example of wartime strike dynamics. When Martin Mayta, a motive plant worker, was discharged over a job load dispute, a walkout of his department sparked the plantwide strike. "Slowdowns, Work Stoppages, and Strikes since August 11, 1944," for Kansas City Armour, and Henry Craddock and C. H. Boyd to Ralph Helstein, Sept. 19, 1945, both in UPWA Papers, box 196, folder 1; Officer's Report to 1946 Convention, 31; Transcript, UPWA International Executive Board meeting, May 28, 1945 and May 31, 1945, UPWA Papers, box 27, folder 2; Lewis J. Clark to All Local Unions, June 4, 1945, UPWA Papers, box 188, folder 11.

29. U.S. Department of Labor, *Wage Chronology, Armour and Co., 1941–63*, Bulletin 187 (Washington, 1964), 5; Officer's Report to 1946 Convention, 32; UPWA, *The Union Makes Us Strong*, 6; *Packinghouse Worker*, May 25, June 8, 1945.

30. NWLB, "Directive Order Establishing the Meat Packing Commission," March 30, 1945, UPWA Papers, box 189, folder 6; Kerr, "The Meat Packing Commission," 1–3; Officer's Report to 1946 Convention, 32, 37–38; Charles R. Fischer interview, UPWAOHP.

31. Kerr, "The Meat Packing Commission," 1–3 and Appendix A; Officer's Report to 1946 Convention, 32, 39.

32. PWOC Officers Report to Wage and Policy Conference, Feb. 19, 1943, UPWA Papers, box 2, folder 10; PWOC Wage and Policy Conference, Feb. 19 to 21, 1943, 407, UPWA Papers, box 524; *Proceedings, First Constitutional Convention of the United Packinghouse Workers of America*, 160; "1943 Report of the Wage Rate Department," CIO ST, box 4; Officer's Report to 1946 Convention, 38; Rollo Sissel interview and Marie Casey interview, UPWAOHP.

33. Quotation from Clyde Wensel interview, UPWAOHP; R. C. Winkler to George K. Batt, July 7, 1943, and R. C. Winkler, "Petition for Modification of Cancellation of Union Maintenance and Check-off Provisions," both in UPWA Papers, box 12, folder 8.

34. Ann and Thomas Krasick interview, UPWAOHP; Richard R. Jefferson,

"Report of the Field Services Specialist in Employment and Industrial Relations," in National Urban League, *A Study of the Social and Economic Conditions of the Negro Population of Kansas City, Missouri,* 19–20; Tilford Dudley testimony in U.S. House of Representatives, *Hearings Before a Subcommittee of the Committee on Education and Labor on S.101 and S.459,* 79th Cong., 1st sess., March 12–14, 1945 (Washington, 1945); Halpern, "'Black and White, Unite and Fight,'" 332–420; Sam Parks interview, Walt Mason and Darryl Poe interview, George and Francis Fletemeyer interview, James C. Harris interview, Charles Pearson interview, and Robert Burt interviews, UPWAOHP.

35. Charles R. Fischer interview, UPWAOHP. Despite protests from the Kansas City, Kansas black community, North American Aviation operated a lily-white training program for machinists on the grounds of the city's premier black high school. *Kansas City Kansan,* March 31, 1941, and *Kansas City Times,* March 31, 1941, both in NAACP Papers, series C, box 99; Report by John R. Davis, Aug. 16, 1944, *Kansas City Call,* June 30, 1944, and Ray A. Hoglund to Clarence Mitchell, July 13, 1944, FEPC Records, RG 228, box 449; "Minutes, Citizens Interracial Committee," July 10, 1944, National Urban League Papers, series 6, box 51. For the racial practices of the IAM and UAW during World War II, see Herbert Hill, *Black Labor and the American Legal System* (Madison, 1977), 206–17, 260–70.

36. Leona Tarnowski interview, Jeanette Hammond, and Louis Townsend interview, and Mary and Alvin Edwards interview, UPWAOHP; "Employment of Women in Wartime," *Monthly Labor Review* 55 (Sept. 1942): 419–45.

37. "Bi-Monthly Labor Market Report for: Kansas City," May 1, 1944, War Manpower Commission, Region IX, National Archives—Kansas City; Charles R. Fischer interview, UPWAOHP; Clyde Schockey et al. to Allan Haywood, Nov. 2, 1942, and J. L. Lumpkins et al. to Sam Sponseller and Harvey Fremming, Oct. 30, 1942, both in CIO ST, box 66.

38. A. T. Stephens to Sam Sponseller, May 12, 1942, UPWA Papers, box 5, folder 2; N. I. Callowick to William F. Rasky, March 4, 1944, UPWA Papers, box 189, folder 6. There is considerable material on equal pay for equal work grievances in UPWA Papers box 193, folder 7. On this issue see especially Ruth Milkman, *Gender at Work: The Dynamics of Job Segregation by Sex during World War II* (Urbana, 1987).

39. Eunetta Pierce interview, Addie Wyatt interview, Virginia Houston interview, Nels Peterson interview, James C. Harris interview, George and Francis Fletemeyer interview, and Rowena Moore interview, UPWAOHP.

40. Addie Wyatt interview, UPWAOHP. Similar life stories can be found in Eunetta Pierce interview and Ercell Allen and Rosalie Taylor interview, UPWAOHP.

41. U.S. Department of Commerce, *Statistical Abstract of the United States: 1944–45* (Washington, 1945), 159; Lewis Corey, *Meat and Man* (New York, 1950), 253; Ann and Thomas Krasick interview, UPWAOHP; "UPWA Veterans Program," in transcript of International Executive Board meeting, Sept. 21 and 22, 1945, UPWA Papers, box 26, folder 1; Virginia Houston interview, UPWAOHP.

42. *Packinghouse Worker,* Oct. 4, 1946; Jeanette Haymond and Louise Townsend interview, UPWAOHP; Mary Edwards in Mary and Alvin Edwards interview, Jeanette and Emerson Dappen interview, Walt Mason and Darrel Poe interview, Frank Wallace interview, and Charles R. Fischer interview, UPWAOHP.

43. Hattie Jones interview, UPWAOHP; Nancy Gabin, "'They Have Placed a Penalty on Womanhood': The Protest Actions of Women Auto Workers in Detroit-Area UAW Locals, 1945–1947," *Feminist Studies* 8 (Summer 1982): 373–98.

44. Eunetta Pierce interview, Saunders in Milton Norman, Richard Saunders, Todd Tate, and James Samuel interview, and Eddie Humphrey interview, UPWAOHP. For other comments by black veterans, see Earl Carr interview, Charles Pearson interview, L. C. Williams interview, and Frank Wallace interview, UPWAOHP; U.S. Department of Commerce, *Census of Population: 1950* (Washington, 1952), vol. 2, pt. 15, 62, 216, pt. 23, 101.

45. Officer's Report to 1946 Convention, 39; membership data from UPWA Papers, box 99, folder 4, based on per capita tax.

46. Ellis quotation from transcript, International Executive Board Meeting May 28 and 31, 1945, UPWA Papers, box 27, folder 2; other quotations from "An Open Letter to the Farmers," UPWA Papers, box 198, folder 5; "Suggested Program for General Wage Increase Demand," adopted Aug. 17, 1945 by International Executive Board, UPWA Papers, box 26, folder 10.

47. First quotation from "To the People of Omaha," UPWA Papers, box 198, folder 5; table, "Real Weekly Earnings in Meat Packing," UPWA Papers, box 196, folder 3; other quotations from *Unionist and Public Forum,* Jan. 24, 1946.

48. Table, "Slowdowns, Work Stoppages, and Strikes since Aug. 11, 1944," for Chicago and East St. Louis, UPWA Papers, box 196, folder 1; Lewis J. Clark to Lewis B. Schwellenbach, Oct. 29, 1945, UPWA Papers, box 193, folder 1; Clark to UPWA National Strike Strategy Committee, Jan. 3, 1946, UPWA Papers, box 198, folder 5; UPWA, *The Union Makes Us Strong,* 7; quotation from transcript, International Executive Board meeting, Dec. 13, 14 and 15, 1945, 33, UPWA Papers, box 26, folder 9.

49. Minutes, Strike Strategy Conference, Dec. 9, 1945, UPWA Papers, box 198, folder 5; *Proceedings, Third Constitutional Convention of the United Packinghouse Workers of America,* 14.

50. Herbert March, "Manual on Strike Organization," 6, passim, UPWA Papers, box 198, folder 5; National Strike Strategy Committee to All District Directors, Dec. 28, 1945, UPWA Papers, box 198, folder 5; Homer Early interview, UPWAOHP; Henry Giannini interview, UPWAOHP.

51. Brody, *The Butcher Workmen,* 229; U.S. Department of Labor order, Jan. 17, 1946, UPWA Papers, box 198, folder 10. On the 1945–46 strike wave see Lichtenstein, *Labor's War at Home,* 225–30. The "seizure" was a cosmetic measure designed to suspend the dispute until a presidential commission issued a nonbinding decision. Although the secretary of agriculture nominally directed meatpacking operations, the seizure order appointed existing packing officials "Com-

pany Manager for the Government of the United States" and provided that "the management of the plants, facilities and property taken under this order to continue its managerial functions." Executive Order 9685, Jan. 24, 1946, UPWA Papers, box 198, folder 10. Quotations from "Memorandum of Agreement Between Government and Packing Companies, Pursuant to Executive Order 9695," Jan. 24, 1946, UPWA Papers, box 198, folder 5.

52. Quotation from UPWA, *The Union Makes Us Strong,* 8; Martin Halpern, *UAW Politics in the Cold War Era* (Albany, 1988), 67–69.

53. Quotations from, respectively, Philip Weightman interview, UPWAOHP, and UPWA, *The Union Makes Us Strong,* 8; UPWA statement Jan. 25, 1946, UPWA Papers, box 502, folder 15; UPWA statement Jan. 26, 1946, UPWA Papers, box 198, folder 5; Ralph Helstein interview by Rick Halpern and author, Jan. 14, 1984; "National Wage Stabilization Board, General Pattern Approval No. 1, Meat Packing Industry," Feb. 21, 1946, and Grace Ault to Lewis J. Clark, Feb. 27, 1946, both in UPWA Papers, box 198, folder 10; Office of Economic Stabilization statement, Feb. 26, 1946, UPWA Papers, box 198, folder 10. For local union responses, see UPWA Papers, box 198, folder 9.

54. First quotation from Svend Godfredson interview, UPWAOHP; Norman Dolnick interview, Oct. 1, 1985, Jennie Shuck interview, Clyde Wensel interview, Philip Weightman interview, Charles R. Fischer interview, William Nolan interview, and Henry Giannini interview, all UPWAOHP. The comments by Fischer, Nolan, and Giannini are particularly significant as these men were often in conflict with Lewis's successor, Ralph Helstein, between 1948 and 1954.

55. Ed Roche to Herbert March, Sept. 11, 1945, Lewis J. Clark to Herbert March, Nov. 7, 1945, Philip Weightman to Herbert March, April 10, 1946, Herbert March to Philip Weightman, April 18, 1946, Lewis J. Clark to Herbert March, April 29, 1946, and Herbert March to Lewis J. Clark, May 8, 1946, all in UPWA Papers, box 308, folder 1; Transcript, International Executive Board meeting, May 28, 1946, 68–71, UPWA Papers, box 27, folder 4.

56. Biography of Ralph Helstein, Feb. 1950, UPWA Papers, box 69, folder 1; Eugene Cotton interview and John Winkels interview, UPWAOHP; Ralph Helstein interviews by Elizabeth Balanoff, Roosevelt University Oral History Project in Labor and Immigration History.

57. Quotations from Address by Ralph Helstein, Dec. 1953, UPWA Papers, box 99, folder 6. At the time of his death, Helstein was a member of the Democratic Socialists of America.

58. *Proceedings, Third Constitutional Convention of the United Packinghouse Workers of America,* 157–58; Jesse Prosten interview, UPWAOHP; Ralph Helstein interview Jan. 14, 1984; Herbert March interview, Oct. 21, 1986, UPWAOHP; Irving Martin Abella, *Nationalism, Communism, and Canadian Labour: The CIO, the Communist Party, and the Canadian Congress of Labour, 1935–1956* (Toronto, 1973), 65.

59. *Proceedings, Third Constitutional Convention of the United Packinghouse Workers of America,* 12, 153–59.

60. My calculations are based on statements of support for Helstein and Clark by local unions. March was reelected director of District 1 by a 124–81 vote, and I assume that the anti-March vote would have gone to Clark. *Chicago Sun Times,* June 7, 1946; *Proceedings, Third Constitutional Convention of the United Packinghouse Workers of America,* 73–82, 152–61; Herbert March interview, Oct. 21, 1986, UPWAOHP.

61. *Proceedings, Third Constitutional Convention of the United Packinghouse Workers of America,* 171–78.

62. Herbert March interview, Oct. 21, 1986, UPWAOHP; Reuther quoted in Halpern, *UAW Politics in the Cold War Era,* 112; Nelson Lichtenstein, *The Most Dangerous Man in Detroit: Walter Reuther and the Fate of American Labor* (New York, 1995), 252–53; Ronald W. Schatz, *The Electrical Workers: A History of Labor at General Electric and Westinghouse, 1923–1960* (Urbana, 1983); Robert Korstad, "Daybreak of Freedom: Tobacco Workers and the CIO, Winston-Salem North Carolina, 1943–1960," Ph.D. diss., University of South Carolina, 1987; Michael Honey, *Southern Labor and Black Civil Rights: Organizing Memphis Workers* (Urbana, 1993); Toni Gilpin, "Left by Themselves: A History of the United Farm Equipment and Metal Workers Union, 1938–1955," Ph.D. diss., Yale University, 1992.

Chapter 8: "Something New Is Added"

1. Cooney quotation from Subcommittee of the Committee on Expenditures in the Executive Departments, Hearings on "Investigation as to the Administration of the Law Affecting Labor Disputes, Interstate and Foreign Commerce and the Anti-racketeering Statute, the Interstate Transportation of Pickets, and the Activities of the Department of Justice, in Connection with Strikes in the Meat-Packing Industry in Twenty States," May 20–21, 80th Cong., 2d sess. [hereafter cited as "Investigation"], 109–10. The investigation into the 1948 UPWA strike was only one of many fishing expenditures for the Subcommittee of the Committee on Expenditures in the Executive Departments. The committee used the far-fetched notion that federal regulation of labor relations entitled them to investigate the UPWA's strike (and any other labor dispute). Charles Alexander Byler, "Trial by Congress: The Controversy over the Powers and Procedures of Congressional Investigations, 1945–1952," Ph.D. diss., Yale University, 1990.

2. *Proceedings, Fifth Constitutional Convention of the United Packinghouse Workers of America* (1948), 72.

3. Leading executives of packing companies participated regularly in NAM's semiannual institutes on industrial relations in the late 1940s. NAM Papers, box 89. Leading packing executives also were active on NAM's Industrial Relations Committee between 1945 and 1950. NAM Papers, boxes 15, 281, 282.

4. The UPWA's unique status as a left-influenced union that remained in the CIO is reflected in two works. The UPWA was not considered within the parameters of Steve Rosswurm, ed., *The CIO's Left-Led Unions* (New Brunswick, 1992) because it was not expelled from the CIO. Michael Goldfield, in "Race and the

CIO: The Possibilities for Racial Egalitarianism during the 1930s and 1940s," *International Labor and Working Class History* 44 (Fall 1993): 1–32, places the UPWA in the category of "Left-led Unions" because of its practice on racial issues.

5. Transcript, UPWA International Executive Board meeting, Feb. 6, 1947, 2, UPWA Papers, box 28, folder 2; Edwin E. Witte, "Industrial Relations in Meat Packing," in *Labor in Postwar America*, ed. Colston Warne et al. (New York, 1949), 489–508.

6. Harris, *The Right to Manage*, 135. Other quotations from Clyde Wensel interview, Robert Burt interview, July 30, 1986, and Viola Jones interview, all UPWAOHP; table, "Slow-Downs, Work Stoppages, and Strikes since August 11, 1944," UPWA Papers, box 196, folder 1.

7. Harvey Mader to Ralph Helstein, "Analysis of Armour Proposed Responsibility Clause," Aug. 3, 1946, UPWA Papers, box 196, folder 3.

8. *Proceedings, Fourth Constitutional Convention of the United Packinghouse Workers of America* (1947), 17–19; Nelson Lichtenstein, "From Corporatism to Collective Bargaining: Organized Labor and the Eclipse of Social Democracy in the Postwar Era," in *The Rise and Fall of the New Deal Order, 1930–1980*, ed. Steve Fraser and Gary Gerstle (Princeton, 1989), 122–52.

9. Ralph Helstein to All Local Unions, Sept. 11, 1946, UPWA Papers, box 198, folder 6; UPWA statements Nov. 12, 27, 1946, UPWA Papers, box 198, folder 6.

10. Quotation from "Master Agreement Between Swift & Co. and the United Packinghouse Workers of America-CIO, 1946," UPWA Papers, box 290, folder 4; Armour contracts are in UPWA Papers, box 269, folder 2.

11. "Officers Report," 1946 convention, 29–30; *Proceedings, Second Constitutional Convention of the United Packinghouse Workers of America*, 159–60; "Master Agreement, Swift & Co. and United Packinghouse Workers," 1950, 52, UPWA Papers, box 290, folder 4.

12. Quotation from Halpern, *UAW Politics in the Cold War Era*, 76; see also Lichtenstein, *Labor's War at Home*, 221–243, and Bert Cochran, *Labor and Communism: The Conflict That Shaped American Unions* (Princeton, 1977), 329.

13. "Officers Report," in *Proceedings, Third Constitutional Convention of the United Packinghouse Workers of America*, 39–44; quotation from Lichtenstein, *Labor's War at Home*, 238; Joel Seidman, *American Labor from Defense to Reconversion* (1953, repr. Chicago, 1976), 262–69; Tomlins, *The State and the Unions*, 282–316.

14. UPWA International Executive Board meeting, Nov. 24, 1947, 98–100, 156–57.

15. Transcript, UPWA International Executive Board meeting, July 14, 1947, 1–4, and "Statement on Taft-Hartley" approved by that meeting, both in UPWA Papers, box 28, folder 5; Transcript of UPWA Policy Conference, July 15, 1947, UPWA Papers, box 524; "Memorandum—Strengthening the Steward System," UPWA Papers, box 436, folder 3; Frank Ellis to All Local Unions, Nov. 28, 1947, UPWA Papers, box 445, folder 15.

16. Preis, *Labor's Giant Step*, 315–20; Halpern, *UAW Politics in the Cold War Era*, 207–8.

17. "Memo on Organizational Developments since Taft-Hartley Act," n.d., UPWA Papers, box 436, folder 3; Transcript, UPWA International Executive Board meeting, Sept. 17, 1947, UPWA Papers, box 28, folder 8; Transcript, UPWA International Executive Board meeting, Nov. 24, 1947, esp. 115–18, UPWA Papers, box 28, folder 6. Coordination by the six right-wing UPWA International Executive Board members is apparent from the timing and similarities of their communications with Helstein. See letters to Helstein from A. J. Pittman, G. R. Hathaway, Wayne Thurmand, Ralph Baker, James Stanton, and Philip Weightman, all in UPWA Papers, box 27, folder 8.

18. Transcript, UPWA International Executive Board meeting, Nov. 24, 1947, esp. 98–105, UPWA Papers, box 28, folder 6; see also March comments at UPWA International Executive Board meeting, Jan. 30, 1948, 40–46, UPWA Papers, box 29, folder 2.

19. Transcript, UPWA International Executive Board meeting, Nov. 24, 1947, 144–66, UPWA Papers, box 28, folder 6.

20. Frank Ellis to All District Directors, International Representatives and Field Representatives, Nov. 26, 1947, UPWA Papers, box 445, folder 15, emphasis in the original; Transcript, UPWA International Executive Board meeting, Nov. 24, 1947, 170–80, UPWA Papers, box 28, folder 6; Transcript, UPWA International Executive Board meeting, Jan. 30, 1948, 35–70, UPWA Papers, box 29, folder 2; see also affidavits in UPWA Papers, box 44, folder 10.

21. Transcript, UPWA International Executive Board meeting, Nov. 24, 1947, 170–80, UPWA Papers, box 28, folder 6; Transcript, UPWA International Executive Board meeting, Jan. 30, 1948, 35–70, UPWA Papers, box 29, folder 2.

22. Quotation from Ralph Helstein, *Proceedings, Fifth Constitutional Convention of the United Packinghouse Workers of America*, 44. His speech on 42–51 contains a useful summary of the strike chronology. Notices sent to Armour, Cudahy, Swift, Wilson, Morrell, and Hygrade companies, Dec. 19, 1947, UPWA Papers, box 445, folder 17; Transcript, International Executive Board meeting, Jan. 30, 1948, UPWA Papers, box 29, folder 2; Ralph Helstein to all Local Unions, Jan. 30, 1948, UPWA Papers, box 445, folder 14; *Unionist and Public Forum*, March 25, 1948; UPWA Strike Bulletin, March 16, 1948, UPWA Papers, box 459, folder 2.

23. Helstein from Transcript, UPWA International Executive Board meeting, Jan. 30, 1948, 53, UPWA Papers, box 29, folder 2; Harry Truman to Ralph Helstein, March 15, 1948, UPWA Papers, box 502, folder 16; final quotation from *Strike Bulletin*, March 16, 1948, UPWA Papers, box 459, folder 2.

24. "Manual on Strike Organization—1948," UPWA Papers, box 452, folder 14; Material on strike vote in UPWA Papers, box 202, folder 3; National Strike Strategy Committee Minutes, UPWA Papers, box 201, folder 3, and box 524; strike bulletins, UPWA Papers, box 459, folder 2; Mary Salinas interview, Frank Wallace interview, Annie Jackson Collins, Richard Saunders, and Todd Tate interview, Henry Giannini interview, and Frank Wallace interview, all UPWAOHP.

25. Annie Jackson Collins, Richard Saunders, and Todd Tate interview,

UPWAOHP; Leon Beverly interview, Dec. 16, 1970, Roosevelt University Oral History Project in Labor and Immigration History; Helen Zrudsky interview, Frank Wallace interview, Mary Salinas interview, Vic Meyers interview, James C. Harris interview, Herb Cassano interview, George and Francis Fletemeyer interview, Eugene Crowley and Marjorie Carter interview, Jake Cooper interview, Bruce Nolan and Grant Holbrook interview, Clyde Wensel interview, and Mary and Alvin Edwards interview, UPWAOHP; E. Howard Hill to Ralph Helstein, April 19, 1948, Covington, Kentucky, *Enquirer*, April 30, 1948, Wisconsin Farm Bureau Federation to Armour, Swift, Cudahy and Wilson, May 4, 1948, and H. E. Slusher to Lyle Cooper, May 11, 1948, all in UPWA Papers, box 477, folder 6; *Unionist and Public Forum*, May 20, 1948.

26. Todd Tate interview, Helen Zrudsky interview, Vic Meyers interview, Fred Romano interview, Eugene Crowley and Marjorie Carter interview, Henry Giannini interview, Bruce Nolan and Grant Holbrook interview, Eddie Humphrey interview, Herb Cassano interview, and Rowena Moore interview, UPWAOHP; William C. Pratt, "Workers, Bosses, and Public Officials: Omaha's 1948 Packinghouse Strike," *Nebraska History* 66 (Fall 1985): 300.

27. *Packinghouse Worker*, June 25, July 15, 1948; Henry Giannini interview, Jim McAnally interview, and Casper Winkels interview, UPWAOHP; "Strike Receipts and Disbursements District One, UPWA-CIO," March–May 30, 1948, UPWA Papers, box 308, folder 2; Lewis J. Clark to James Carey, April 8, May 8, 1948, CIO ST, box 58.

28. Sam Curry to All Members of Local 347, March 31, 1948, Beverly Papers; *Unionist and Public Forum*, April 1, 1948; Homer Early interview and Helen Zrudsky interview, UPWAOHP; quotation from Norman in Milton Norman, Richard Saunders, Todd Tate, and James Samuel interview, UPWAOHP; Todd Tate interview, Annie Jackson Collins, Richard Saunders, and Todd Tate interview, Frank Wallace interview, Charles McCafferty interview, Walt Mason and Darryl Poe interview, and Max Graham interview, UPWAOHP.

29. Helen Zrudsky interview, Milton Norman, Richard Saunders, Todd Tate, and James Samuel interview, Henry Giannini interview, and Clyde Wensel interview, UPWAOHP; *Chicago Sun-Times,* April 29, 1948, copy in UPWA Papers, box 502, folder 16.

30. *Proceedings, Fifth Constitutional Convention of the United Packinghouse Workers of America*, 46; Mary Salinas interview, Howard Nielson interview, Annie Jackson Collins, Richard Saunders, and Todd Tate interview, Jeanette and Emerson Dappen interview, Jake Cooper interview, Sam Davis interview, William Nolan interview, and Ann and Thomas Krasick interview, UPWAOHP; Strike Bulletins, March 16, 20, 25, April 15, 23, 1948, UPWA Papers, box 459, folder 2; Selwyn Pepper, "Investigation Shows Police at Kansas City, Kansas, Beat Strikers, Smashed Hall, without Sanction," *St. Louis Post-Dispatch*, May 2, 1948, UPWA Papers, box 452, folder 14; "Investigation," 86, 122; *Chicago Sun-Times*, April 29, 1948, UPWA Papers, box 502, folder 16; Strike Bulletin April 21, 1948, UPWA Papers, box 459, folder 2.

31. Frank Wallace interview, L. C. Williams interview, Mary Salinas interview, Walter Bailey interview, James C. Harris interview, George and Francis Fletemeyer interview, Herb Cassano interview, and William Nolan interview, UPWAOHP.

32. "Comment on Charts Showing Changes in Federally Inspected Slaughter, April 1948" and attachments, UPWA Papers, box 502, folder 6. See district-by-district assessment of strike in Minutes of Strike Strategy Committee, May 2, 1948, UPWA Papers, box 524; Herbert March to All Members of the UPWA-CIO District One, May 12, 1948, Beverly Papers. Wilson J. Warren does not agree that Omaha was a strong center of the strike. His argument, however, ignores the evidence on the sharp decline in slaughtered cattle in April and instead relies on reports by the viciously anti-union *Omaha World-Herald*, which had an interest in minimizing the strike's effectiveness. See Warren, "The Limits of New Deal Social Democracy," 369–83.

33. As the union correctly pointed out at the time, the company could not legally terminate seniority and other contractual rights as the master agreements remained in effect until Aug. 11. Nonetheless, the threats doubtless frightened many workers. Sam Curry to Union Members, May 12, 1948, Beverly Papers.

34. Herbert March et al. to All Striking Packinghouse Workers, n.d., Beverly Papers; Pratt, "Workers, Bosses," 304–5. There is a graphic depiction of the St. Paul confrontations in *Life*, May 24, 1948, 30–31. "Investigation," 1–73, 131–33; Jake Cooper interview, Henry Giannini interview, and William Nolan interview, UPWAOHP; Paul C. Young, "UPWA Local 46 and the Shooting of Chuck Farrell: A Study in the Efficacy of an Anti-Discrimination Policy," unpublished manuscript, University of Iowa, 1990; *Chicago Defender*, May 22, 1948; Charles Pearson interview and Velma Otterman Schrader interview, UPWAOHP.

35. March from transcript, UPWA International Executive Board meeting, June 3, 1948, 173, UPWA Papers, box 29, folder 3; Minutes, National Strike Strategy meeting, May 2, 1948, UPWA Papers, box 524; Strike Bulletin May 11, 1948, UPWA Papers, box 459, folder 2; Hathaway and Stern comments in transcript, UPWA International Executive Board meeting, May 15, 1948, UPWA Papers, box 29, folder 1.

36. Charles Hayes interview, UPWAOHP; "Strike Receipts and Disbursements District One, UPWA-CIO," March–May 30, 1948, UPWA Papers, box 308, folder 2; Henry Giannini interview, UPWAOHP; National Strike Strategy Committee meeting, May 18 and 19, 1948, UPWA Papers, box 210, folder 1; UPWA Press Release No. 9, June 1948, UPWA Papers, box 502, folder 16; *Proceedings, Fifth Constitutional Convention of the United Packinghouse Workers of America*, 336–42.

37. In early June, the union had $16,886 in its treasury and debts of close to $200,000. Transcript, International Executive Board meeting, June 3, 4, 109–43, 218–26, UPWA Papers, box 29, folder 3; Lewis J. Clark to James Carey, June 1, 1948, CIO ST, box 58; Frank Ellis to All International Officers, District Directors, International Representatives and Field Representatives, May 25, 1948,

UPWA Papers, box 50, folder 3; membership information in UPWA Papers, box 99, folder 4.

38. Statement by UPWA International Executive Board, March 23, 1949, UPWA Papers, box 57, folder 9; A. T. Stephens to All Executive Officers, Aug. 11, 1949, UPWA Papers, box 56, folder 9; Organization Department Reports in UPWA Papers, box 50, folder 4, box 50, folder 3, box 56, folder 10, and box 56, folder 12; "List of Elections for All Plants in which the Amalgamated Meat Cutters Attempted Raids since January 1st, 1948," filed Jan. 25, 1949, UPWA Papers, box 70, folder 4; leaflets from UPWA Papers, box 423, folder 3, box 423, folder 4, and box 445, folder 3.

39. Emphasis in original. *Life*, May 24, 1948, 29–33. On the effect of these widely read articles on UPWA members, see William Nolan interview, UPWAOHP; leaflets quoted are in UPWA Papers, box 423, folder 2, and box 445, folder 3.

40. Charles Hayes interview, Sam Parks interview, and Tony Fetter interview, UPWAOHP; Cooney statement from "Hearings . . . into Strike in the Meat Packing Industry," 107; UPWA press release, June 5, 1948, UPWA Papers, box 452, folder 2; Transcript, UPWA International Executive Board meeting, June 3, 1948, UPWA Papers, box 29, folder 3; other quotations from *Sparks* [newsletter of UPWA Local 25], Dec. 14, 1948, UPWA Papers, box 423, folder 5.

41. Charles Hayes interview, Sam Parks interview, and Walter Bailey interview, UPWAOHP; *Sparks*, UPWA Papers, box 423, folder 5; UPWA, *The Union Makes Us Strong*, 11; "Facts about the Union-busting Actions of Wilson & Co.," n.d. UPWA Papers, box 345, folder 18.

42. UPWA, *The Union Makes Us Strong*, 11; leaflets and other materials in UPWA Papers, box 345, folder 18, and box 345, folder 19.

43. First quotation from Herbert March interview, July 15, 1985, UPWAOHP; Frank Wallace interview, Charles Mueller interview, May 10, 1986, Vic Meyers interview, Lyle Taylor interview, Virginia Houston interview, and Betty Watson interview, UPWAOHP.

44. First quotation from George and Francis Fletemeyer interview, UPWAOHP; Helen Zrudsky interview, and Henry Giannini, William Nolan, Chris Wicke, and Don Winters interview, UPWAOHP; membership figures from UPWA Papers, box 99, folder 4.

45. Ralph Helstein to All Armour Locals, July 12, 1948, UPWA Papers, box 477, folder 9; International Executive Board quotation from Report of Grievance Department, March 16, 1949, UPWA Papers, box 58, folder 8; *Packinghouse Worker*, June 11, Oct. 15, 1948, Jan. 14, Feb. 11, April 22, and May 6, 1949. A complete list of discharges can be found in UFCW Accession M80–118, box 35, folder, "Jesse Prosten—Personal" file; Tony Fetter interview, Charles Hayes interview, Jesse Prosten interview, Vic Meyers interview, Walt Mason and Darrel Poe interview, Jake Cooper interview, Eugene Cotton interview, William Nolan interview, and Todd Tate interview, UPWAOHP.

46. Alvin and Mary Edwards interview, George and Francis Fletemeyer inter-

view, Henry Giannini interview, Mary Salinas interview, and Jesse Prosten interview, UPWAOHP.

47. First quotation from Tony Stephens in Transcript, UPWA International Executive Board meeting, June 28, 1950, 136, UPWA Papers, box 32, folder 4; Frank Ellis to All Local Unions, May 26, 1949, UPWA Papers, box 50, folder 3; Max Graham interview, Charles Mueller interview, May 19, 1986, and Virginia Houston interview, UPWAOHP; final quotation from Betty Watson interview, UPWAOHP.

48. Eddie Humphrey interview, Charles Pearson interview, and L. C. Williams interview, UPWAOHP; "UPWA Self-Survey of Human Relations, 1948–49," UPWA Papers, box 345, folder 13.

49. Charles R. Fischer interview, UPWAOHP. Many packinghouse workers made similar observations in UPWAOHP interviews.

50. UPWA, *The Union Makes Us Strong*, 11; U.S. Department of Labor, *Wage Chronology, Armour and Co.*, 6; "1949 Contract between the UPWA and Armour & Co.," 42–50, UPWA Papers, box 269, folder 2.

51. Max Graham interview, UPWAOHP. As for the Amalgamated Meat Cutters, whose efforts to raid the UPWA failed so miserably, union leaders were able to call them "pariahs coming in to feed off what they thought was a corpse." Ralph Helstein interview, July 18, 1983.

52. Leaflets in UPWA Papers, box 423, folder 5 and box 50, folder 8; Eugene Cotton interview, UPWAOHP.

53. Jimmy Hilsinger interview and James C. Harris interview, UPWAOHP. Many packinghouse workers echoed Hilsinger's suspicions in their UPWAOHP interviews.

54. Norm Dolnick interview, Walt Mason and Darrel Poe interview, Jeanette Haymond and Louise Townsend interview, and Max Graham interview, UPWAOHP. Other UPWAOHP interviews with Cedar Rapids workers echo these themes.

55. *Packinghouse Worker*, June 11, 1948; Jesse Prosten interview, Saunders in Annie Jackson Collins, Richard Saunders, and Todd Tate interview, and Bill Webster interview, UPWAOHP.

56. Charles Hayes interview, Bill Webster interview, James Porter interview, Sam Parks interview, and Philip Weightman interview, UPWAOHP.

57. *Proceedings, Fifth Constitutional Convention of the United Packinghouse Workers of America*, 9.

58. Recommendations by the UPWA, CIO Executive Board to All Affiliated Local Unions, May 28, 1946, UPWA Papers, box 445, folder 13; Transcript, UPWA International Executive Board meeting, May 28, 1946, 15–26, UPWA Papers, box 27, folder 4; Transcript, UPWA International Executive Board meeting, Feb. 6–8, 1947, UPWA Papers, box 28, folder 2; Herbert March to Ralph Helstein, Aug. 28, 1947, UPWA Papers, box 27, folder 8.

59. The "statement of policy" was prepared by an International Executive

Board subcommittee that included March and Ollman as well as right-wing board members A. J. Pittman and Philip Weightman. Transcript, UPWA International Executive Board meeting, May 28, 1946, 15–26, UPWA Papers, box 27, folder 4; Transcript, UPWA International Executive Board meeting, Feb. 6–8, 1947, UPWA Papers, box 28, folder 2; "Memorandum re. Board Meeting held in Cleveland Prior to and during the Convention," UPWA Papers, box 28, folder 4; all quotations from *Proceedings, Fourth Constitutional Convention of the United Packinghouse Workers of America*, 143–44.

60. Jerome De Gulio to Ralph Helstein, June 21, 1948, Ralph Helstein Papers, general correspondence, 1948; *Proceedings, Third Constitutional Convention of the United Packinghouse Workers of America*, 125–27; *Proceedings, Fourth Constitutional Convention of the United Packinghouse Workers of America*, 126–41; Curtis D. MacDougall, *Gideon's Army* (New York, 1965), 42–47, 283, 672–75.

61. Transcript, UPWA International Executive Board meeting, Jan. 30, 1948, 101–10, UPWA Papers, box 29, folder 2; *Packinghouse Worker*, Feb. 20, 1948; Helstein speech in CIO ST, box 176; Herbert March interview, Oct. 21, 1986, UPWAOHP. There is evidence of support for Wallace by UPWA members in New York, New Jersey, Austin, Omaha, and St. Paul. Brief by Local 167, CIO ST, box 178; John Stover interview by William Cumberland, June 18, 1980; Bruce Nolan interview by author; Earl Carr interview, Henry Giannini interview, Rowena Moore interview, Walt Mason and Darrel Poe interview, and Charles Fischer interview, UPWAOHP.

62. MacDougall, *Gideon's Army*, 612; Henry Giannini interview, UPWAOHP; Transcript, UPWA International Executive Board meeting, Jan. 30, 1948, 110, UPWA Papers, box 29, folder 2.

63. *Proceedings, Fifth Constitutional Convention of the United Packinghouse Workers of America*, passim; Svend Godfredson interview, Philip Weightman interview, Charles R. Fischer interview, and Jesse Prosten interview, UPWAOHP.

64. *Proceedings, Fifth Constitutional Convention of the United Packinghouse Workers of America*, 224, quotation on 290–91. For the wide-ranging debate on the 1948 strike, see 43–79. For retrospective views of CIO Policy Caucus supporters, see UPWAOHP interviews of Charles R. Fischer, Virginia Houston, Nels Peterson, Herb Cassano, Henry Giannini, William Nolan, Philip Weightman, A. J. Pittman, and Svend Godfredson.

65. *Proceedings, Fifth Constitutional Convention of the United Packinghouse Workers of America*, 55, 57, 68, 76.

66. Henry Giannini interview, UPWAOHP; *Proceedings, Fifth Constitutional Convention of the United Packinghouse Workers of America*, 134–207; Brief by Local 167, CIO ST, box 176.

67. *Proceedings, Fifth Constitutional Convention of the United Packinghouse Workers of America*, 289–97. A brief by Local 167 in CIO ST, box 176 discusses this issue and reproduces the original resolution signed by Sioux City leader Bruce Nolan. Jesse Prosten interview, UPWAOHP; Bruce Nolan interview by author. Follow-

ing the convention, UPWA members from seven Chicago locals participated in "Packinghouse Workers for Wallace and Taylor." See leaflet in Beverly Papers.

68. "Minutes of National Conference of the UPWA-CIO Policy Caucus," UPWA District 8 Papers, box 29, folder 2; Ralph Gantt to Ralph Helstein, Aug. 16, 1948, UPWA Papers, box 50, folder 4; Ralph Helstein to Officers of Local Union No. 28, Sept. 21, 1948, UPWA Papers, box 50, folder 4; William Nolan to CIO Policy Caucus members, Sept. 28, 1948, UFCW Accession M80-118, box 35. Policy Caucus leaders later admitted that withholding dues cost them support. Leonard O. LaShomb to Robert Oliver, May 22, 1953, CIO ST, box 178; Charles R. Fischer interview, UPWAOHP.

69. A. T. Stephens to All District Directors, Aug. 18, 1948, and Harold E. Nielsen to Local 28 Members, "Warning! Your Union Is in Danger,'" UPWA District 8 Papers, box 29, folder 2; *National Provisioner*, Aug. 21, 1948; *Proceedings, Sixth Constitutional Convention of the United Packinghouse Workers of America* (1949), 56, 61–71, 107; Brief by Local 167, CIO ST, box 178; Andrew Pitts and Sylvester Pluzynski to Delegates, Sixth Constitutional Convention, May 31, 1949, and attachments, Unprocessed UFCW Accession M80-118, box 35; Purcell, *The Worker Speaks His Mind*, 66–68; "Short History of Factional Attacks, 1948–1953," UPWA Papers, box 50, folder 8.

70. A. J. Pittman to Philip Murray, Feb. 2, 1950, and Philip Murray to Pittman, March 9, 1950, CIO ST, box 113; Paul Elston to Philip Murray, Feb. 10, 1950, and William Nolan to Philip Murray, April 11, 1950, both in CIO ST, box 114; *Proceedings, Seventh Constitutional Convention of the United Packinghouse Workers of America* (1949), 97.

71. *Proceedings, Seventh Constitutional Convention of the United Packinghouse Workers of America*, 160; "Agreement-1950 Convention," CIO ST, box 178; Henry Gianinni interview, UPWAOHP; Brief by Local 167, CIO ST, box 178.

72. March quotations from interview Oct. 21, 1986, UPWAOHP; other quotations from Norm Dolnick interview, UPWAOHP; Herbert March to UPWA Executive Officers, Jan. 27, 1949, Tony Stephens to March, Feb. 2, 1949, and Ralph Helstein to March, Feb. 15, 1949, all in Herbert March Papers. At the December 1948 International Executive Board meeting, Helstein reported that the CIO was demanding the dismissal of March, Prosten, and Orear. Transcript, UPWA International Executive Board meeting, Dec. 20, 1948, UPWA Papers, box 30, folder 3.

73. *Proceedings, Fifth Constitutional Convention of the United Packinghouse Workers of America*, 89, 226–28; *Proceedings, Sixth Constitutional Convention of the United Packinghouse Workers of America*, 154; Jake Cooper interview and Harold Nielsen interviews, UPWAOHP.

74. Transcript, UPWA International Executive Board meeting, Dec. 19, 1949, 169–96, UPWA Papers, box 31, folder 4; Brief by Local 167, CIO ST, box 178; Charles Fischer interview, UPWAOHP (not to be confused with Charles R. Fischer); Eugene Cotton interview and Charles Pearson interview, UPWAOHP; U.S.

Congress, House Committee on Un-American Activities, 82d Cong., 2d sess., 1952, "Communist Activities in the Chicago Area," pt. 2, 3754–830; William D. Andrew, "Factionalism and Anti-Communism: Ford Local 600," *Labor History* 20 (Spring 1979): 227–55. The retention of leftist influence has some similarity to the ability of UAW Local 600 to shield Communists from the international. However, tolerance by the UPWA international union allowed leftists in Chicago far more national influence than the beleaguered UAW group. Nelson Lichtenstein, "Life at the Rouge: A Cycle of Workers' Control," in *Life and Labor: Dimensions of American Working-Class History,* ed. Charles Stephenson and Robert Asher (Albany, 1986), 237–59.

75. Leo Troy, *Trade Union Membership, 1897–1962* (New York, 1965), A20–A41; Steve Rosswurm, "An Overview and Preliminary Assessment of the CIO's Expelled Unions," in *The CIO's Left-Led Unions,* ed. Rosswurm, 1–17.

Chapter 9: "This Community of Our Union"

1. For King's speech, see "The Fourth Biannual Wage and Contract Conference, the Third National Anti-Discrimination Conference, and the Third National Conference on Women's Activities," Sept. 30–Oct. 4, 1957, 208–33, UPWA Papers, box 526.

2. Quotations from "Proceedings, the Montgomery, Ala. Bus Boycott Conference," Feb. 13, 1956, UPWA Papers, box 373, folder 6; "Montgomery Passive Resistance Movement," resolution adopted March 2, 1956 by UPWA District 3, UPWA Papers, box 379, folder 24; Martin Luther King, Jr., to John Franklin, June 6, 1956, and Martin Luther King, Jr., to Marian L. Davis, June 6, 1956, both in UPWA Papers, box 373, folder 6. See also Helstein correspondence in UPWA Papers, box 129, folder 6; Russell Lasley, Minutes of "Southern Negro Leaders' Conference," Feb. 14, 1957, UPWA Papers, box 140, folder 10; David J. Garrow, *Bearing the Cross: Martin Luther King, Jr., and the Southern Christian Leadership Conference* (New York, 1986), 90–97.

3. "Program Proposal . . . UPWA Fund for Democracy in the South," and "District Quotas for UPWA Fund for the South," both in the UPWA Papers, box 379, folder 1; "UPWA Fund for Democracy in the South—Progress Report," June 21, 1957, UPWA Papers, box 379, folder 2; Addie Wyatt interview, UPWAOHP.

4. Philip S. Foner, *Organized Labor and the Black Worker, 1619–1973* (New York, 1974), 316–17; Michael Goldfield, "Race and the CIO: The Possibilities for Racial Egalitarianism during the 1930s and 1940s," and responses, *International Labor and Working-Class History* 44 (Fall 1993): 1–63.

5. Herbert Hill, "The AFL-CIO and the Black Worker: Twenty-five Years after the Merger," *Journal of Intergroup Relations* 10 (Spring 1982): 5–78; Robert J. Norrell "Caste in Steel: Jim Crow Careers in Birmingham, Alabama," *Journal of American History* 73 (Dec. 1986): 669–94; Karl Korstad, "Black and White Together: Organizing in the South with the Food, Tobacco, Agricultural and Allied Workers Union (FTA-CIO)," in *The CIO's Left-Led Unions,* ed. Rosswurm, 69–94.

6. Speech by Ralph Helstein to Fisk University Race Relations Institute, June 28, 1949, UPWA Papers, box 57, folder 11.

7. Michael Mann, *Consciousness and Action among the Western Working Class* (London, 1973), 20.

8. Eddie Humphrey interview, UPWAOHP. I agree with Steven Jefferys in *Management and Managed: Fifty Years of Crisis at Chrysler* (New York, 1986) that scholars of the American labor movement have seriously underestimated the extent of shop-floor resistance by workers in the 1950s.

9. Norman Brommal quoted in *National Provisioner*, April 10, 1948, 53.

10. Herbert March interview, July 15, 1985, UPWAOHP; Armour Delegates to Robert H. Cabell, Sept. 25, 1938, and Minutes of National Armour Wage Conference, March 23, 1941, both in UPWA Papers, box 1, folder 5; Arthur Kampfert to All District Directors . . . , April 3, 1941, UPWA Papers, box 3, folder 6; Cudahy Local Union Representatives to Philip Murray, Oct. 28, 1941, CIO ST, box 65; Minutes, National Wilson Conference, Feb. 14, 1942, UPWA Papers, box 3, folder 4; J. C. Lewis to All District Directors . . . , Feb. 7, 1942, UPWA Papers, box 2, folder 9; *CIO News—Packinghouse Worker Edition*, Nov. 21, 1938, Aug. 5, 1940, Feb. 17, Sept. 1, 1941; *Packinghouse Worker*, March 20, 1942.

11. Louis Tickal, Frank Hlavacek, Lester Rohlena, and Ray Lange interview, William Nolan interview, and Jeanette and Emerson Dappen interview, UPWAOHP.

12. "Report of Panel on Union Participation and Representation of Women Workers," UPWA District 8 Papers, box 79, folder 1; Henry Giannini interview, UPWAOHP.

13. Jeanette and Emerson Dappen interview and Loren Callender interview, UPWAOHP.

14. L. C. Williams interview and Eugene Cotton interview, UPWAOHP; "Officers Report," *Proceedings, Fifth Constitutional Convention of the United Packinghouse Workers of America*, 316–18; U.S. Department of Labor, *Wage Chronology: Swift and Company January 1942–September 1973*, Bureau of Labor Statistics Bulletin 1771 (Washington, 1973).

15. Sam Davis interview and Todd Tate interview, UPWAOHP.

16. Loren Callender interview and Eddie Humphrey interview, UPWAOHP.

17. Rosalie Widman in District 4 Conference, Oct. 14, 1950, 11, UPWA Papers, box 345, folder 1; George and Francis Fletemeyer interview, UPWAOHP; "A Word to Stewards" and "Report on Publicity and Education, 1946," UPWA Papers, box 457, folder 4; *Proceedings, Third Constitutional Convention of the United Packinghouse Workers of America*, 48–50. For corroborating observations from an Armour plant superintendent, see Kenneth Neidholt interview, March 20, 1986, UPWAOHP.

18. The Highlander Folk School in Monteagle, Tennessee, was one of the most important centers of labor education in the United States in the mid-twentieth century. The UPWA frequently used the Highlander offices for staff training schools, as it was one of the few places in the South where the union could hold integrated gatherings. John M. Glenn, *Highlander: No Ordinary School, 1932–1962*

(Lexington: University Press of Kentucky, 1988). Svend Godfredson interview, UPWAOHP; "Officers Report," *Proceedings, Fifth Constitutional Convention of the United Packinghouse Workers of America*, 346–48; Education Department Reports, April 23, Sept. 28, 1951, UPWA Papers, box 342, folder 10; "Report of District No. 1 Education Committee for 1951–52," UPWA Papers, box 348, folder 14; Education Department Report, March 20, UPWA Papers, box 346, folder 24; Education Department Report, Sept. 1952, UPWA Papers, box 347, folder 12; Program Department Report for 1952–54, UPWA Papers, box 359, folder 7.

19. Nels Peterson interview, UPWAOHP. For discussion of how unions can use the grievance procedure to expand shop-floor control, see Stephen Meyer, *"Stalin over Wisconsin": The Making and Unmaking of Militant Unionism, 1900–1950* (New Brunswick, 1992), esp. 105–46.

20. George and Francis Fletemeyer interview, Loren Callender interview, and Jeanette and Emerson Dappen interview, UPWAOHP.

21. Sam Davis interview, Loren Callender interview, Emerson and Jeanette Dappen interview, and Ercell Allen and Rosalie Taylor interview, UPWAOHP.

22. Nevada Isom interview, Addie Wyatt interview, and Milton Norman, Richard Saunders, Todd Tate, and James Samuel interview, UPWAOHP.

23. Quotation from Addie Wyatt interview, UPWAOHP.

24. Milton Norman, Richard Saunders, Todd Tate, and James Samuel interview, Jake Cooper interview, Earl Carr interview, Louis Hlavacek, Louis Tickal, Lester Rohlena, and Ray Lange interview, and Sam Davis interview, UPWAOHP. See also comments by a beef-kill foreman on output restriction in Purcell, *The Worker Speaks His Mind*, 136.

25. George and Francis Fletemeyer interview, Walt Mason and Darrel Poe interview, and Lucille Bremer interview, UPWAOHP.

26. Staff Newsletter July 15, 1949, UPWA Papers, box 58, folder 14; *District Three Blade*, Oct. 1951, CIO ST, box 178.

27. *UPWA Stewards Bulletin*, June 1951, UPWA Papers, box 346, folder 13; Buford Thompson interview and Bill Webster interview, UPWAOHP. Morrell contracts contained a similar clause. U.S. Department of Labor, *Collective Bargaining in the Meat-Packing Industry*, Bulletin 1063 (Washington, 1952), 48.

28. Milton Norman, Richard Saunders, Todd Tate, and James Samuel interview, UPWAOHP.

29. First quotation from UPWA, *The Union Makes Us Strong*, 13, Herbert March Papers; Virginia Houston interview, Nels Peterson interview, and Jeanette and Emerson Dappen interview, UPWAOHP; *Chicago Daily News*, Jan. 3, 8, 11, 12, 15, 16, 18, 23, 24, 25, 28, 29, and Feb. 3, and 4, 1952, copies in Herbert March Papers; "Work Stoppages Knife into Meat Production; Weekly Total Off 8 Percent," *National Provisioner*, Jan. 26, 1952. The UPWA employed the "stop and go" strikes during contract negotiations as late as 1964. Charles R. Perry and Delwyn H. Kegley, *Disintegration and Change: Labor Relations in the Meat Packing Industry* (Philadelphia, 1989), 135.

30. First two quotations from "Full Report on Contract Negotiations to Date," Aug. 16, 1952, UPWA Papers, box 92, folder 7; other quotations from Organization Department Report, Oct. 15, 1952, UPWA Papers, box 92, folder 6; Charles Fischer to All District Directors, Sept. 4, 16, 1952, UPWA Papers, box 92, folder 6.

31. First quotation from Organization Department Report, Oct. 15, 1952; second quotation from Charles Fischer to All District Directors . . . , Oct. 6, 1952, and Ralph Helstein to International Executive Board, Oct. 14, 1952, all in UPWA Papers, box 92, folder 6. In the previous three years September per capita receipts had averaged 10 percent below August levels. Figures in UPWA Papers, box 99, folder 4.

32. Clause 95E was slightly modified to give the International Executive Board authority to approve local strikes over job loads. This made no difference in the exercise of 95E because the UPWA constitution already required local unions to secure strike permission from the international. "Summary of New Agreement Signed with Armour & Company," Oct. 27, 1952, and Charles Fischer to District Directors . . . , Nov. 3, 1952, both in UPWA Papers, box 92, folder 6; 1952 Armour contract, UPWA Papers, box 269, folder 2.

33. L. C. Williams interview, UPWAOHP; Report on District One Anti-Discrimination Conference, Report to District One Conference, April 1952, and "Anti-Discrimination Clause Enforcement," convention resolution submitted by District 1, all in UPWA Papers, box 348, folder 14; *Proceedings, Eighth UPWA Convention,* 110–13; "Major Contract Demands of UPWA-CIO," June 27, 1952, UPWA Papers, box 348, folder 8; Frank D. Green to Ralph Helstein, Oct. 29, 1952, and J. J. Feeney to Ralph Helstein, Nov. 3, 1952, both UPWA Papers, box 345, folder 21.

34. Bill Webster interview and Buford Thompson interview, UPWAOHP.

35. This generation of union militants contributed to other labor organizations as well. Joe Brown, an activist for Hospital Workers Local 1199 in the 1960s, had participated in the 1948 strike and served as UPWA shop steward in the early 1950s. Leon Fink and Brian Greenberg, *Upheaval in the Quiet Zone: A History of the Hospital Workers Union, Local 1199* (Urbana, 1989), 48–49, 65, 78.

36. First quotation from "Report of Vice-President Lasley to International Executive Board meeting, January 14, 1953," UPWA Papers, box 33, folder 7; Todd Tate interview and Jimmie Porter interview, UPWAOHP.

37. For examples of protests against racist incidents, see *Packinghouse Worker,* July 17, 1942, May 27, June 25, July 2, 1943, July 20, 1945, March 22, 1946.

38. Ralph Helstein interview July 18, 1983; John Hope II to Ralph Helstein, Russell Lasley, and Herman H. Long, n.d., UPWA Papers, box 52, folder 10; John Hope II, "United Packinghouse Workers of America, CIO, Self-Survey of Human Relations," Preliminary Report, May 1950, 10, 21–22; John Hope II, *Equality of Opportunity: A Union Approach to Fair Employment* (Washington, 1956).

39. International Executive Board transcript, Sept. 28, 1950, UPWA Papers, box 32, folder 5. The international refused to sign contracts negotiated by local unions

that did not include "applicant" in the anti-discrimination clause. "Report of the International Anti-Discrimination, Education, and Publicity Departments," Nov. 20, 1950, UPWA Papers, box 342, folder 10; Ralph Helstein to Kermit Fry, April 4, 1952, UPWA Papers, box 83, folder 10.

40. Anna Mae Weems interview, UPWAOHP; Summary of Conference on Kansas City Program, Feb. 7–8, 1950, UPWA Papers, box 342, folder 1; Report on District 4 Staff Conference, handwritten notes, Aug. 14–15, 1950, UPWA Papers, box 345, folder 1; Officers Report to District 4 Convention, March 20–22, 1953, UPWA Papers, box 350, folder 10; Earl Carr interview, UPWAOHP.

41. "Departments Practicing Discrimination," "Some of the Areas Where Discrimination Is at Its Worst," and "Progress Report on UPWA-CIO In-Plant Anti-Discrimination Campaign," all distributed at the UPWA Anti-Discrimination Conference, Oct. 30–31, Nov. 1, 1953, personal papers of Herbert Hill; Nevada Isom interview, Mary Salinas interview, Sam Parks interview, Walter Bailey interview, and Robert Burt interviews, UPWAOHP; John Hope II, "United Packinghouse Workers of America," 22; "Program Department Report for 1952–1954," Jan. 12, 1954, UPWA Papers, box 359, folder 7; "Convention Report of UPWA Anti-Discrimination Department and Program Department," June 18, 1956, UPWA Papers, box 347, folder 13.

42. Joan Kelley to Russell Lasley and Hazel Hayes, June 22, 1950, UPWA Papers, box 343, folder 7; *Swift Flash,* July 5, 1950, UPWA Papers, box 342, folder 7; *Action against Jim Crow,* UPWA District 8 Records, box 60, folder 8; "Officers Report—Anti-Discrimination Department," March 1952, UPWA Papers, box 346, folder 24; Report by Lewis Roach, June 20, 1953, UPWA Papers, box 347, folder 3; *Proceedings, Eighth UPWA Convention,* 107–21; *Packinghouse Worker,* Sept. 1952.

43. Weems and Moore were both active in the NAACP before their employment in meatpacking. Wyatt was primarily active in community affairs through her church. Addie Wyatt interview, Anna Mae Weems interview, and Rowena Moore interview, UPWAOHP.

44. UPWA press release, Nov. 30, 1949, UPWA Papers, box 58, folder 7; *Packinghouse Worker,* Nov. 18, 1949, July 1952; "Council against Discrimination of Greater Chicago Information Bulletin," July 3, 1952, UPWA Papers, box 347, folder 8; *Action against Discrimination,* Leon Beverly Papers; "Operation Elimination of Discrimination," UPWA District 8 Papers, box 60, folder 8; "Since Sioux City: A Summary of Programmatic Work in District One," UPWA Papers, box 359, folder 7; Sam Parks interview, Addie Wyatt interview, Charles Hayes interview, Annie Jackson Collins, Richard Saunders, and Todd Tate interview, and Herbert March interview, July 15, 1985, UPWAOHP. The organized movement supporting Trumball Park residents is not sufficiently appreciated by Arnold Hirsch in "Massive Resistance in the Urban North: Trumball Park, Chicago, 1953–1966," *Journal of American History* 82 (Sept. 1995): 522–50.

45. Charles Hayes interview and Sam Parks interview, UPWAOHP; "Operation Elimination of Discrimination," UPWA District 8 Papers, box 60, folder 8.

46. "Minnesota Avenue Project of the K.C. Area A-D Committee," Jan. 17, 1955, UPWA Papers, box 368, folder 5; William Raspberry interview, UPWAOHP; William Raspberry interview by author, Dec. 10, 1987; Minutes of District 4 Anti-Discrimination Conference, UPWA Papers, box 346, folder 18; Hazel Hayes to Russell Lasley, April 1, 1952, UPWA Papers, box 348, folder 1; *Kansas City Call,* Oct. 10, Nov. 14, Dec. 5, 1952, UPWA Papers, box 347, folder 21; Staff Report by Rosalie Widman, Nov. 16, 1953, UPWA Papers, box 347, folder 21; Staff Report by Rosalie Widman, n.d., and Rosalie Widman to Richard Durham, Dec. 17, 1953, both UPWA Papers, box 346, folder 18; Minutes of Executive Board, District 4, Dec. 7, 1952, UPWA Papers, box 84, folder 1; Nevada Isom interview, UPWAOHP.

47. Anti-Discrimination Committee Report, n.d., UPWA Papers, box 345, folder 12; Program Department Report, Jan. 12, 1954, UPWA Papers, box 359, folder 7; Anna Mae Weems interview, Charles Pearson interview, Jimmie Porter interview, and Ada Tredwell interview, UPWAOHP; Bruce Fehn, "'The Only Hope We Had': United Packinghouse Workers Local 46 and the Struggle for Racial Equality in Waterloo, Iowa, 1948–1960," *Annals of Iowa* 54 (Summer 1995): 185–216.

48. Herbert Hill to Walter White, April 12, 1949, NAACP Papers, series 3–A, box 582; Herbert Hill interview and Milton Norman, Richard Saunders, Todd Tate, and James Samuel interview, UPWAOHP. Donations to NAACP branches by UPWA locals can be found in NAACP Papers, series 2–A, box 346. UPWA Anti-Discrimination Department Report, 1952–54, UPWA Papers, box 342, folder 11; Sam Parks interview and Eddie Humphrey interview, UPWAOHP; "Outline of Program Activity in District 4 since Sioux City Convention—May 1954," UPWA Papers, box 359, folder 13; O. J. Johnson to All Members Local 60, July 20, 1955, NAACP Papers, series A, box 346; Anna Mae Weems interview, Homer Early interview, and J. C. Harris interview, UPWAOHP.

49. Grant Holbrook interview by author; Russell Lasley to Russ Bull, March 24, 26, 1952, UPWA Papers, box 350, folder 8; Bud Simonson to Richard Durham, March 30, 1953, UPWA Papers, box 350, folder 6; "Convention Report of UPWA Anti-Discrimination Department and Program Department," June 18, 1956, UPWA Papers, box 347, folder 13.

50. Charles Pearson interview, UPWAOHP.

51. Henry Giannini interview, Betty Watson interview, Marian Simmons interview, and Anna Mae Weems interview, UPWAOHP.

52. Quotation from *Discrimination: A $20 Billion Business* (1953), UPWA District 8 Papers, box 60, folder 8; Eugene Cotton interview, UPWAOHP; U.S. Department of Labor, *Wage Chronology, Armour and Co.,* 5–11.

53. Ralph Helstein interview, July 18, 1983.

54. My apologies to Robert Korstad and Nelson Lichtenstein for adapting the title of their article, "Opportunities Found and Lost: Labor, Radicals, and the Early Civil Rights Movement," *Journal of American History* 75 (Dec. 1988): 787–811.

55. "An Open Letter to the Farmers," UPWA Papers, box 198, folder 5; Ralph

Helstein speech in "Wage and Contract, Anti-Discrimination, and Women's Activities Conference," May 9–13, 1955, 32, UPWA Papers, box 525.

56. Betty Watson interview, UPWAOHP; *Proceedings, Seventh Constitutional Convention of the United Packinghouse Workers of America*, 173; *Proceedings, Eighth Constitutional Convention of the United Packinghouse Workers of America* (1952), 70.

57. Addie Wyatt interview, Eunetta Pierce interview, and Ercell Allen and Rosalie Taylor interview, UPWAOHP; *Packinghouse Worker*, Sept. 20, 1946.

58. Virginia Houston interview by author; Report by Rosalie Widman, Sept. 26, and 1953 Minutes of District 4 Conference, UPWA Papers, box 346, folder 18; "District 4 Program Status," and Report by Marian Simmons, May 16, 1954, UPWA Papers, box 360, folder 1; Marian Simmons interview, UPWAOHP.

59. Mary Salinas interview and Lucille Bremer interview, UPWAOHP; Mary Edwards interview by author; Marie Casey interview, Betty Watson interview, and Leona Tarnowski interview, UPWAOHP.

60. First quotation from Mary Salinas interview, UPWAOHP; Addie Wyatt interview, UPWAOHP; Helstein from "Fourth Biennial Wage and Contract Conference, the Third National Anti-Discrimination Conference, and the Third National Conference on Women's Activities," Oct. 2, 1957, 237, UPWA Papers, box 526.

61. First quotation from *District Three Blade*, Oct. 1952, CIO ST, box 178; other quotations from *Proceedings, Eighth Constitutional Convention of the United Packinghouse Workers of America*, 115–21; U.S. Department of Labor, *Wage Chronology, Armour and Co.*, 5–8; Exhibits 8 and 9 to Meat Packing Commission, UPWA Papers, box 196, folder 7. In *A Women's Wage* (Lexington, Ky., 1990), Alice Kessler-Harris understates the critical role that women workers played to secure equal pay for equal work.

62. Mary Salinas interview, Addie Wyatt interview, Velma Otterman Schrader interview, and Virginia Houston interview, UPWAOHP; 1949 Armour Contract, UPWA Papers, box 269, folder 2; *Proceedings, Ninth Constitutional Convention of the United Packinghouse Workers of America* (1954), 269.

63. "Report of Panel on Union Participation and Representation of Women Workers," 1955, 2–4, UPWA District 8 Papers, box 79, folder 1; *Proceedings, Tenth Constitutional Convention of the United Packinghouse Workers of America* (1956), 130.

64. Velma Otterman Schrader interview, UPWAOHP; "Report of Panel on Union Participation and Representation of Women Workers," 1955 Women's Activities Conference, UPWA District 8 Papers, box 79, folder 1. For description of a male-initiated rumor campaign against UPWA official Rosalie Widman, see Report by Marian Simmons, May 10, 1954, UPWA Papers, box 360, folder 1.

65. "Report of Vice-President Lasley to International Executive Board Meeting, Jan. 14, 1953," UPWA Papers, box 33, folder 7; L. C. Williams interview, Frank Wallace interview, and Mary Salinas interview, UPWAOHP; Ralph Helstein interview, July 13, 1983; Rick Halpern, "Interracial Unionism in the Southwest: Fort Worth's Packinghouse Workers, 1937–1954," in *Organized Labor in the Twentieth*

Century South, ed. Robert Zieger (Knoxville, 1991), 158–81; Barbara S. Griffith, *The Crisis of American Labor: Operation Dixie and the Defeat of the CIO* (Philadelphia, 1988), 83–87.

66. "This Is What Happened" and statements by James Reed and Robert McDowell, July 29, 1953, personal papers of Herbert Hill; Report of John H. Telfer, July 25, 1953, CIO ST, box 114. For charges against McKinney, see UPWA Papers, box 352, folder 2 and box 351, folder 15; Glenn Chinander, Kermit Fry, A. J. Pittman, and A. O. McKinney to Walter Reuther, Sept. 8, 1953, CIO ST, box 114; "Minutes of CIO Meeting Held at CIO Southern Drive Headquarters," Aug. 1, 1953, George L-P. Weaver to James B. Carey, Oct. 20, 23, 1953, and "Final Statement by David Burgess," all in CIO ST, box 114; "CIO Statement in the Matter of the United Packinghouse Workers of America, CIO," *Packinghouse Worker*, Nov. 1953; Ralph Helstein to A. O. McKinney, Oct. 17, 1953, UPWA Papers, box 352, folder 2. The participation of CIO officials in the campaign against UPWA policies contradicts Alan Draper's contention that top union officials in the South generally opposed Jim Crow policies. Draper, *Organized Labor and the Civil Rights Movement in the South, 1954–1968* (Ithaca, 1994).

67. Transcript of District Council 8 Meeting, July 17, 1953, personal papers of Herbert Hill; Russell Lasley to A. T. Stephens, Dec. 15, 1953, UPWA Papers, box 351, folder 1; G. R. Hathaway to Ralph Helstein and A. T. Stephens, Feb. 4, 1954, UPWA Papers, box 108, folder 3; *Proceedings, Ninth Constitutional Convention of the United Packinghouse Workers of America*, 212–13.

68. Russell Lasley to Bishop E. Jones, Sept. 2, 1954, UPWA District 8 Papers, box 78, folder 19; A. J. Pittman interview, Frank Wallace interview, Mary Salinas interview, L. C. Williams interview, and Eddie Humphrey interview, UPWAOHP.

69. Quotation from Antoine Songy to Walter Reuther, Jan. 4, 1954, CIO ST, box 178; Frank Wallace interview, UPWAOHP; *Proceedings, Eighth Constitutional Convention of the United Packinghouse Workers of America*, 39; *Proceedings, Ninth Constitutional Convention of the United Packinghouse Workers of America*, 47; Ralph Helstein interview, July 15, 1983.

70. John H. Telfer to Richard Durham, April 6, 1954, UPWA Papers, box 108, folder 3; *Proceedings, Ninth Constitutional Convention of the United Packinghouse Workers of America*, 212–13.

71. *Proceedings, Ninth Constitutional Convention of the United Packinghouse Workers of America*, 6. "I think we were always hurt by these anti-civil rights people because they were always pointed to as the ones which were running this [opposition]," recalled St. Paul dissident leader William Nolan. William Nolan interview, UPWAOHP.

72. L. C. Williams interview, UPWAOHP; "Report to the International Officers on District 9 Situation," Nov. 19, 1954, UPWA Papers, box 108, folder 3; table on sugar locals in UPWA Papers, box 356, folder 6; *Proceedings, Eighth Constitutional Convention of the United Packinghouse Workers of America*, 39; *Proceedings, Ninth Constitutional Convention of the United Packinghouse Workers of America*, 47;

Proceedings, Tenth Constitutional Convention of the United Packinghouse Workers of America, 57–58; Antoine Songy to Walter Reuther, Jan. 4, 1954, CIO ST, box 178; John Hope II, "Equality of Employment Opportunity: A Process Analysis of Union Initiative," *Phylon* 18 (Spring 1957): 144–51.

73. Myles Horton, Education Department Report, March 20, 1952, UPWA Papers, box 346, folder 24; Myles Horton to Ruth Haines, Oct. 13, 1952, UPWA Papers, box 94, folder 2.

74. Tony Stephens to Myles Horton, Oct. 21, 1952, UPWA Papers, box 347, folder 12; Myles Horton to UPWA Educational Staff, Jan. 29, 1953, UPWA Papers, box 353, folder 10; Myles Horton to Ralph Helstein, March 14, 1953, UPWA Papers, box 98, folder 4. In a careful study of this controversy, Jeff Zacharakis-Jutz considers the dismissal of Horton to mark the ascension of a bureaucratic rule inside the UPWA. Although he correctly identifies one factor behind Horton's dismissal, the bureaucratic aspirations of Stephens, Jutz ignores how the demands for implementation of anti-discrimination by black workers created the political context for Horton's dismissal. Jeff Zacharakis-Jutz, "Straight to the Heart of the Union, Straight to the Heart of a Movement: Workers' Education in the United Packinghouse Workers of America between 1951 and 1953," Ph.D. diss., Northern Illinois University, 1991, 246–68.

75. Sam Parks interview, Marian Simmons interview, Charles Hayes interview, and Harold Nielson interviews, UPWAOHP. Even the secretive Communist Party organization was affected by the black power mood among Chicago packinghouse workers. Herb March was summarily expelled from the party for "white chauvinism" for suggesting he run for a district office rather than a black woman. Ironically, it was this action by the Communists that finally forced March out of the UPWA in 1955. Herbert March interviews, UPWAOHP.

76. William Raspberry interview by author. For observations that echo Raspberry's, see Sam Davis interview, UPWAOHP.

77. Wilson J. Warren, "When 'Ottumwa Went to the Dogs': The Erosion of Morrell-Ottumwa's Militant Unionism, 1954–1973," *Annals of Iowa* 54 (Summer 1995): 217–43.

78. Charles Hayes to Ralph Helstein, March 1957, and Richard Durham to Ralph Helstein, March 11, 1957, both in UPWA Papers, box 380, folder 7; Marian Simmons to G. R. Hathaway, April 13, 1957, and related correspondence, UPWA Papers, box 141, folder 4; Sam Parks interview, Marian Simmons interview, and Jim McAnally interview, UPWAOHP; *Proceedings, Eleventh Constitutional Convention of the United Packinghouse Workers of America* (1958), 116–17.

79. For UPWA civil rights activity in the 1960s, see UPWA Papers, box 396, folder 15, box 402, folder 2, 458, and folder 12; Garrow, *Bearing the Cross*, 280, 465, 511; Alan B. Anderson and George W. Pickering, *Confronting the Color Line: The Broken Promise of the Civil Rights Movement in Chicago* (Athens, 1986), 174; James R. Ralph, Jr., *Northern Protest: Martin Luther King, Jr., Chicago, and the Civil Rights Movement* (Cambridge, 1993), 71, 118, 157; Charles Hayes interview and Addie

Wyatt interview, UPWAOHP; Philip S. Foner, *U.S. Labor and the Vietnam War* (New York, 1989), 55–56.

80. Velma Otterman Schrader interview, Lucille Bremer interview, Betty Watson interview, Mary and Alvin Edwards interview, and Max Graham interview, UPWAOHP; "How Mechanization and Plant Closings Are Holding Down Packinghouse Employment," 1957, UPWA Papers, box 382, folder 5; Robert Lubar, "Armour Sees Fat Years Ahead," *Fortune* Oct. 1959, 125.

81. "UPWA Women Speak Out—To Their Union Brothers," UPWA Papers, box 454, folder 8; Marion Simmons interview, Rowena Moore interview, and Addie Wyatt interview, UPWAOHP; Bruce Fehn, "Striking Women: Gender, Race and Class in the United Packinghouse Workers of America (UPWA), 1938–1968," Ph.D. diss., University of Wisconsin-Madison, 1991, 264–67.

82. Fehn, "Striking Women," 264–66; Lyle Taylor interview, UPWAOHP.

83. First quotation from Charles Mueller interview, July 30, 1986, UPWAOHP. For conservative male views see, for example, Casper Winkels interview, UPWAOHP, and Charles Oots interview by author, July 8, 1987; final quotation from Fehn, "Striking Women," 274.

84. "Women in the UPWA," Feb. 10, 1965, UPWA Papers, box 468, folder 1.

85. Rowena Moore interview, Betty Watson interview, Addie Wyatt interview, Lucille Bremer interview, Velma Otterman Schrader interview, and Goldie Lamb interview, UPWAOHP; see *Proceedings, Tenth UPWA Convention*, 119–39, for a debate on separate seniority lists.

86. *Packinghouse Worker*, March 1965; Fehn, "Striking Women," 272–76. The danger to the international was similar to the conflict over enforcement of the anti-discrimination program in the 1950s—alienation of important local unions. In the 1967 Morrell negotiations, the embittered Ottumwa local refused to cooperate with the international. UPWA International Executive Board Minutes, July 17, 1967, Ralph Helstein Papers, International Executive Board file.

87. This tawdry affair is best recounted in Bruce Fehn, "Chickens Come Home to Roost: Industrial Organization, Seniority, and Gender Conflict in the United Packinghouse Workers of America, 1955–1966," *Labor History* 34 (1993): 324–41; see also Dennis A. Deslippe, "'We Had an Awful Time with Our Women': Iowa's United Packinghouse Workers of America, 1945–75," *Journal of Women's History* 5 (Spring 1993): 10–32.

88. Mary Salinas interview, UPWAOHP; Nancy Gabin, *Feminism in the Labor Movement: Women and the United Auto Workers, 1935–1975* (Ithaca, 1990), 5.

89. *Packinghouse Worker*, March 1965; Addie Wyatt interview, UPWAOHP. On "working-class feminism," see Nancy Gabin, "Time Out of Mind: The UAW's Response to Female Labor Laws and Mandatory Overtime in the 1960s," in *Work Engendered: Toward a New History of American Labor*, ed. Ava Baron (Ithaca, 1991), 320–50; Carol Kates, "Working Class Feminism and Feminist Unions: Title VII, the UAW and NOW," *Labor Studies Journal* 14 (Summer 1989): 28–45; Dorothy Sue Cobble, *Dishing It Out: Waitresses and Their Unions in the Twentieth Century* (Urbana, 1991), 10–12; and Fehn, "Striking Women," 325–27.

Chapter 10: "My Scars Are Many"

1. Walker quoted in *Chicago Tribune*, Oct. 25, 1988; copy of Buckholtz letter in possession of author; Lewie Anderson interview by author, July 20, 1992.

2. Richard J. Arnould, "Changing Patterns of Concentration in American Meat Packing, 1880–1963," *Business History Review* 45 (Spring 1971): 33; James Franklin Crawford, "Wage Pattern Following in the Meat Packing Industry," Ph.D. diss., University of Wisconsin-Madison, 1957, 79; Marvin Hayenga et al., *The U.S. Pork Sector: Changing Structure and Organization* (Ames, 1985), 128.

3. American Meat Institute, *Meat Facts, 1991* (Chicago, 1992), 28–29; *Farm to Market Review*, Jan. 1992.

4. Recent accounts of the transformation of the meatpacking industry routinely contain errors about the history of unionism in the industry and understate the pivotal importance of reducing labor costs and union power in this process. For the most sophisticated account (which nonetheless still contains these weaknesses), see Brian Page, "Agro-Industrialization and Rural Transformation: The Restructuring of Midwestern Meat Production," Ph.D. diss., University of California-Berkeley, 1993.

5. James M. Mayo, *The American Grocery Store: The Business Evolution of an Architectural Space* (Westport, 1993), 189, 203; Robert M. Aduddell and Louis P. Cain, "The Consent Decree in the Meatpacking Industry, 1920–1956," *Business History Review* 55 (Autumn 1981): 363–66; Willard F. Williams, "Structural Changes in the Meat Wholesaling Industry," *Journal of Farm Economics* 41 (May 1958): 327.

6. Aduddell and Cain, "The Consent Decree," 368; Williams, "Structural Changes," 322 and 328; Lawrence A. Danton, "The Decline of an Oligopoly: Changes in the Meat Packing Industrial Structure," *Rocky Mountain Social Science Journal* 5 (1968): 40–42; Arnould, "Changing Patterns," 28–32; Dale E. Butz, and George L. Baker, Jr. *The Changing Structure of the Meat Economy* (Boston, 1960), 49–54.

7. Best and Donovan, *Catalogue No. 2857* (Cincinnati, 1987), 9–11; Philip Weightman interview, UPWAOHP. Single-floor plants also allowed firms to use conveyor belts to transport meat rather than rely on laborers. "How Mechanization and Plant Closings Are Holding Down Packinghouse Employment," 1957, UPWA Papers, box 382, folder 5.

8. U.S. Department of Agriculture, *Cattle Killing-Floor Systems and Layouts*, Marketing Research Report 657 (Washington, May 1964), 23, passim; U.S. Department of Labor, *Wage Chronology, Armour and Co.*, 11–12; Richard B. Carnes, "Meatpacking and Prepared Meats Industry: Above-Average Productivity Gains," *Monthly Labor Review* 107 (April 1984): 40; Arnould, "Changing Patterns," 28; "Beef Packer Eyes High Chain Rates," *National Provisioner*, July 27, 1968, 10–19, 34–36.

9. James H. Cothern, "Technological Change, Market Power and Beef Product Pricing Practices," in "Small Business Problems in the Marketing of Meat and

Other Commodities," *Hearings Before the Subcommittee on SBA and SBIC Authority and General Small Business Problems of the Committee on Small Business, House
of Representatives,* 96th Cong., 1st sess. (Washington, 1979), pt. 1, 47–49 [hereaf-
ter cited as "Small Business Problems"]. Quotation from testimony of Peggy
Hillman, in "Underreporting of Occupational Injuries and Its Impact on Workers' Safety," *Hearings Before a Subcommittee of the Committee on Government Operations, House of Representatives,* 100th Cong., 1st sess. (Washington, 1987), pt. 2,
147–48 [hereafter cited as "Underreporting of Occupational Injuries"].

10. William Burns, "Changing Corporate Structure and Technology in the
Retail Food Industry," in *Labor and Technology: Union Response to Changing Environments,* ed. Charles Craypo, Donald Kennedy, and Mary Lehman (College Park,
1982), 27–51; Cryovac Division, W. R. Grace & Co. *1986 Retail Beef Study* (Dun-
can, S.C., 1987), 10; A. V. Krebs, *Heading Toward the Last Roundup: The Big Three's
Prime Cut* (Des Moines, 1990), 23.

11. U.S. Department of Labor, *Technology and Labor in Four Industries,* Bureau
of Labor Statistics Bulletin 2104 (Washington, Jan. 1982), 1–4; *National Provisioner,* April 18, June 20, 1987.

12. Krebs, *Heading Toward the Last Roundup,* 23; Willard F. Williams, "The
Changing Structure of the Beef Packing Industry," in "Small Business Problems,"
pt. 4, 72, 194–95; *Wall Street Journal,* May 29, 1981, March 4, 1988; U.S. Department of Commerce, *1967 Census of Manufactures* (Washington, 1971), vol. 2, pt.
1, 20A-4; U.S. Department of Commerce, *1982 Census of Manufactures, Industry
Series: Meat Products* (Washington, 1985), 20A-5; U.S. Department of Commerce,
1987 Census of Manufactures, Industry Series: Meat Products (Washington, 1990), 2.

13. Quotation from *Wall Street Journal,* Dec. 2, 1985; Krebs, *Heading Toward the
Last Roundup,* 37–38.

14. U.S. Department of Labor, *Industry Wage Survey: Meat Products* (Washington, Nov. 1963), 12; U.S. Department of Labor, *Industry Wage Survey: Meat Products* (Washington, June 1984), 6; "Meat Packing Becomes Decentralized," *Business Conditions,* Nov. 1959, 4–10; Williams, "Changing Structure," 321; Arnould,
"Changing Patterns," 27.

15. "How Mechanization and Plant Closings Are Holding Down Packinghouse Employment," 1957, UPWA Papers, box 382, folder 5; Krebs, *Heading Toward the Last Roundup,* 27; U.S. Department of Labor, *Technology and Labor in Four
Industries,* 5–6; Richard B. Carnes, "Meatpacking and Prepared Meats Industry:
Above-average Productivity Gains," *Monthly Labor Review* 107 (April 1984): 37–
39.

16. George P. Schultz and Arnold R. Weber, *Strategies for the Displaced Worker* (New York, 1966), 6–7; "Summary Fact Sheets Documenting Job Crisis in
Meat Packing Industry," UPWA Papers, box 175, folder 5; "Trend of UPWA
Membership vs. Employment in Meat Packing Industry," UPWA Papers, box
497, folder 7.

17. Quotation from Todd Tate interview, UPWAOHP.

18. First quotation from *Proceedings, Twelfth Constitutional Convention of the United Packinghouse Workers of America* (1960), 32; second quotation from Ralph Helstein interview July 18, 1983, 5; "The UPWA Rejects the Armour Program for Employee Obsolescence," 1963, UPWA Papers, box 175, folder 5. For an article that validates the union's perspective on the packers' strategy, see Robert Lubar, "Armour Sees Fat Years Ahead," *Fortune,* Oct. 1959, 117–25, 208, 211–12, 216–18.

19. Hervey A. Juris, "Union Crisis Wage Decisions," *Industrial Relations* 8 (May 1969): 247–58; U.S. Department of Labor, *Wage Chronology, Swift & Company,* 4–5; U.S. Department of Labor, *Wage Chronology, Armour and Co.,* 4–5; David H. Greenberg, "Deviations from Wage-Fringe Standards," *Industrial and Labor Relations Review* 21 (Jan. 1968): 197–209.

20. U.S. Department of Labor, *Current Wage Developments* 11 (Oct. 1959); James L. Stern, "Evolution of Private Manpower Planning in Armour's Plant Closings," *Industrial Relations Research Institute,* Reprint 125 (Madison, 1970), originally published in *Monthly Labor Review,* Dec. 1969; U.S. Department of Labor, *Wage Chronology, Armour and Co.,* 3–4, 24–31.

21. Mary Salinas interview, Betty Watson interview, Charles R. Fischer interview, and Bill Webster interview, UPWAOHP; *Worthington Daily Globe,* July 19, 20, 1965; James L. Stern, "Adjustment to Plant Closing: Retraining, Relocation, and Re-employment Experience of Workers Displaced in the Shutdown of the Armour Plant in Kansas City," Nov. 1966, sec. 3, copy in possession of author; Henry Giannini interview and Nevada Isom interview, UPWAOHP. The UPWA's skillful efforts to smooth the entry of minority workers into Worthington contrasts favorably with the chaos occasioned by the arrival of Asian workers in the 1990s, when there was no longer a union in the ConAgra plant. *Wall Street Journal,* Oct. 31, 1995.

22. Rick Halpern, "Technological Change and Industrial Relations in Meat Packing: The Armour Automation Committee, 1959–1964," typescript, University of Wisconsin, 1983, 40–43; Milton Norman, Richard Saunders, Todd Tate, and James Samuel interview, UPWAOHP; Norman M. Bradburn, "Inter-Plant Transfer: The Sioux City Experience," National Opinion Research Center Report 98 (Chicago, May 1964), 17–21.

23. Quotation from "The UPWA Rejects the Armour Program for Employee Obsolescence," 2; UPWA Papers, box 175, folder 5; Halpern, "Technological Change," passim. Armour still tried to avoid the transfer program through deception. Following the strike, UPWA members in Fort Worth had to picket a new Armour warehouse which the company tried to operate under a different name. Eddie Humphrey interview, UPWAOHP; Ralph Helstein interview, July 18, 1983.

24. Stern, "Evolution of Private Manpower Planning in Armour's Plant Closings," 23; Stern, "Adjustment to Plant Closing," I-9; Bill Webster interview and Todd Tate interview, UPWAOHP.

25. Stern, "Adjustment to Plant Closing," ix, II-7; Stern, "Evolution of Private Manpower Planning in Armour's Plant Closings," 25; Eaton H. Conant, "Report

and Appraisal: The Armour Fund's Sioux City Project," *Monthly Labor Review* 88 (Nov. 1965): 1298–301; Eaton H. Conant, "Retraining and Placement Experience of Workers Displaced by Shutdown of the Armour Plant in Sioux City, Iowa" (Automation Fund Committee Report, n. d.), 26, 47; Sam Davis interview, UPWAOHP.

26. "Trend of UPWA Membership vs. Employment in Meat Packing Industry," UPWA Papers, box 497, folder 7; *Proceedings, Twelfth Constitutional Convention of the United Packinghouse Workers of America*, 126–27.

27. Bound membership tabulation in Ralph Helstein Papers; *Packinghouse Worker*, March 1965; Tony Fetter interview and Frank Wallace interview, UPWAOHP; "Organization Department Report," Sept. 30, 1957, UPWA Papers, box 458, folder 6; "Organization Department Report," May 23, 1960, UPWA Papers, box 458, folder 7. For information on organizing among fisherman, see material in UPWA Papers, box 140, folder 10, and Ben Green, "If We'd Stuck Together," *Southern Exposure* 10 (1982): 69–76; Hy Lefkowitz interview, UPWAOHP; Bruce Nolan interviews.

28. "United Packinghouse Food and Allied Workers, AFL-CIO: Report on Examination," Dec. 31, 1967, 7, UPWA International Executive Board Minutes Nov. 14–15, 1967, 2, quotation from UPWA International Executive Board Minutes, Feb. 8 and 9, 1968, 5–6, and UPWA International Executive Board Minutes April 26, 1968, all in Ralph Helstein Papers, International Executive Board file.

29. Thomas J. Lloyd and Patrick Gorman to International Executive Board Members, Sept. 2, 1965, UPWA International Executive Board Minutes, Nov. 14 and 15, 1967, 3–4, and Patrick Gorman to Jesse Prosten, Oct. 11, 1967, all in Ralph Helstein Papers; Amalgamated Meat Cutters International Executive Board Minutes June 4, 1964, and Amalgamated Meat Cutters International Executive Board Minutes, April 23, 1968, both in Amalgamated Meat Cutters Papers; Eugene Cotton interview, UPWAOHP.

30. Frank Wallace interview and Ann and Thomas Krasick interview, UPWAOHP.

31. Amalgamated Meat Cutters International Executive Board Minutes May 24, 1968, Amalgamated Meat Cutters Papers; UPWA International Executive Board Minutes April 26, 1968, Ralph Helstein Papers; "Merger Agreement Between the Amalgamated Meat Cutters and Butcher Workmen of North America and the United Packinghouse, Food, and Allied Workers," June 6, 1968, Ralph Helstein Papers; U.S. Department of Labor, *Collective Bargaining in the Meat-Packing Industry*, Bulletin 1063 (Washington, 1952), 43; Bill Webster interview, UPWAOHP.

32. "Merger Implementation Agreement," June 6, 1968, Ralph Helstein Papers; Henry Giannini interview, UPWAOHP.

33. Lewie Anderson interview; U.S. Department of Labor, *Current Wage Developments* 28 (Jan. 1976): 3–5; Williams, "Changing Structure," 70.

34. Jesse Prosten interview by James V. Cavanaugh, UFCW Leadership Oral

History Project; Lewie Anderson interview; Peter Capelli, "Plant-Level Concession Bargaining," *Industrial and Labor Relations Review* 39 (Oct. 1985): 94; Jesse Prosten, "Packinghouse Division Report," Feb. 27, 1980, 16–20.

35. Loren Callender interview, UPWAOHP. On the role of chains in internal Amalgamated politics, see Lewie Anderson interview and Jesse Prosten interview, UFCW Leadership Oral History Project.

36. Spencer and MBPXL ranked third and fourth in beef slaughter in the mid-1970s. MBPXL later became part of Excell, and Spencer was acquired by Con-Agra. Williams, "Changing Structure," 79 and 110; on IBP, see series of articles by Dale Kasler in the *Des Moines Register*, Sept. 18–25, 1988.

37. Donald Whistler, "The Involvement of Governor Harold E. Hughes in Three Labor Disputes," master's thesis, Iowa State University, 1967; Dale C. Tintsman and Robert L. Peterson, *Iowa Beef Processors, Inc.* (Princeton, 1981), 9; Jonathan Kwitney, *Vicious Circles: The Mafia in the Marketplace* (New York, 1979), 286–88; Lewie Anderson interview; Tony Fetter interview, UPWAOHP.

38. Quotations from the *New York Times*, Dec. 17, 1969; Lewie Anderson interview; Tony Fetter interview, UPWAOHP.

39. Kwitney, *Vicious Circles*, 292–95; Lewie Anderson interview; *New York Times*, April 12, 1970; "Amalgamated Meat Cutters & Butcher Workmen of North American, AFL-CIO, and Iowa Beef Packers, Inc." Case 17-CC-386, 182 NLRB 410.

40. Kwitney, *Vicious Circles*, 296.

41. U.S. Department of Labor, *Wage Chronology, Swift & Company*, 7–8.

42. Lewie Anderson interview.

43. Holman later was convicted of bribery, but his only punishment was a $7,000 fine. Kwitney, *Vicious Circles*, 296–358.

44. U.S. Department of Labor, *Wage Chronology, Swift & Company*, 7–8, 25–26; *New York Times*, April 12, 1970; wage data from U.S. Department of Labor, *Current Wage Developments*, vols. 25, 26; Lewie Anderson interview.

45. Perry and Kegley, *Disintegration and Change*, 138–43; wage levels from U.S. Department of Labor, *Current Wage Developments*, vols. 25–29; U.S. Department of Labor, *Wage Chronology, Swift & Company*, 25–26.

46. On managerial philosophy see Tintsman and Peterson, *Iowa Beef Processors*, 16.

47. Williams, "Changing Structure," 74–78, 196–97; Bagley quoted in "Small Business Problems," pt. 1, 23.

48. In addition, meatpacking contracts negotiated by regional Amalgamated officials in the Southwest were based on local wage levels rather than the national pattern, usually $1 to $2 below the master agreement standard. Jesse Prosten, "Packinghouse Department Report," 16–18; Lewie Anderson interview.

49. Mayo, *The American Grocery Store*, 224; Burns, "Changing Corporate Structures," 50–52; U.S. Department of Labor, *Technology and Labor in Four Industries*, 1–4; Bob Berglund, in "Small Business Problems," pt. 3, 9; Jesse Prosten interview, UPWAOHP; Lewie Anderson interview.

50. Frank Wallace interview and Max Graham interview, UPWAOHP.

51. Jesse Prosten interview, UPWAOHP; Mayo, *The American Grocery Store,* 184–89; Michael Harrington, *The Retail Clerks* (New York, 1962), 52; Marten S. Esey, "Patterns of Union Membership in the Retail Trades," *Industrial and Labor Relations Review* 8 (July 1955): 557–64.

52. George and Francis Fletemeyer interview, UPWAOHP.

53. Kim Moody, *An Injury to All: The Decline of American Unionism* (New York, 1988), esp. 165–220; Michael Goldfield, *The Decline of Organized Labor in the United States* (Chicago, 1987).

54. Jesse Prosten interview, UFCW Leadership Oral History Project; "Packinghouse Division Report," March 8, 1981; "UFCW Packinghouse Division Report," March 22, 1982; Peter Cappelli, "Plant-Level Concession Bargaining," *Industrial and Labor Relations Review* 39 (Oct. 1985): 95–97; Lewie Anderson interview.

55. U.S. Department of Labor, *Current Wage Developments* 34 (April 1982): 3, 34 (Oct. 1982): 4.

56. First quotation from *Wall Street Journal,* Dec. 24, 1981; "UFCW Packinghouse Division Report," March 22, 1982, 1–13, second quotation from 13.

57. *Business Week,* Aug. 16, 1982; *Chicago Tribune,* June 5, 6, 7, 1983; *Wall Street Journal,* Aug. 4, 6, 1982; *Dollars and Sense,* Feb. 1983; Charles Craypo, "Strikes and Relocation in Meatpacking," in *Grand Designs: The Impact of Corporate Strategies on Workers, Unions, and Communities,* ed. Charles Craypo and Bruce Nissen (Ithaca, 1993), 189; Kathleen Stanley, "The Role of Immigrant and Refugee Labor in the Restructuring of the Midwestern Meatpacking Industry," typescript, Oct. 1988, 16–17.

58. UFCW, "Report on the U.S. Meat Packing Industry and the Challenges Workers Face," 1986; *Wall Street Journal,* May 23, 1983; U.S. Department of Labor, *Current Wage Developments* 35 (Sept. 1983): 3.

59. *Wall Street Journal,* June 30, Dec. 7, 1983; Krebs, *Heading Toward the Last Roundup,* 52; *National Provisioner,* Sept. 12, 1987.

60. Craypo, "Strikes and Relocation," 189.

61. Quotation from fieldnotes, Lewie Anderson interview.

62. Dougherty, *In Quest of Quality,* 222–335; Casper Winkels interview, UPWAOHP.

63. "An Analysis of the Wages and Hours of Hormel Employees Compared to the Meat Packing Average of a Particular State," UPWA Papers, box 493, folder 2; quotation from Richard Shatek, Paul Losey, Bob Johnson, and Dave Taylor interview, UPWAOHP; Casper Winkels interview, UPWAOHP.

64. Affidavit of James V. Guyette, in *Local P-9 v. William H. Wynn et al.,* May 2, 1986, copy in possession of author; Jim McAnally interview, UPWAOHP.

65. First quotation from Johnson in Richard Shatek, Paul Losey, Bob Johnson, and Dave Taylor interview, UPWAOHP; Jim McAnally interview, UPWAOHP; "Cost Adjustment Local P9 Gave to the Hormel Company," n.d., from files of Local 9, copy in possession of author; final quotation from *American Dream,* a film directed by Barbara Kopple (1990).

66. Cohorts of union membership from "Local P-9 Seniority List," *The Unionist,* July 26, 1985; "Legacy of Pain: Hormel's Injured Workers in Austin," special edition of *The Unionist,* May 1985.

67. Pete Winkels was the son of union founder Casper Winkels and had been told stories of the old days by Uncle Johnny Winkels, one of the hog-kill gang who had started the IUAW during the 1930s. U.S. Department of Labor, *Current Wage Developments* 36 (March 1984).

68. Affidavit of James V. Guyette, 11–17; UFCW, "UFCW Local P-9 Strikes Hormel: The International Union's Perspective," *Leadership Update* 8 (Feb. 1986): 2; Guyette quotation from Nicholas Mills, "Why Local P-9 Is Going It Alone," *The Nation,* April 26, 1986; Anderson quotation from *American Dream.* Many retired UPWA members, interviewed during the height of the P-9 struggle in 1985 and 1986, simultaneously manifested sympathy with the local's struggle with concern that it had ignored the majority vote of the Hormel chain.

69. James V. Guyette and Ray Rogers, "The Controlled Retreat: The Crisis of Leadership at the United Food and Commercial Workers Union," n.d., Kim Moody, "Issues in the P-9 Strike: Taking Wages Out of Competition," n.d., and Lance Compa, "A Second Look at the Hormel Strike," all in possession of author.

70. P-9 Negotiating Committee, "Contract Summary," copy in possession of author. Curiously, and without any evidence, the UFCW charged that P-9 was responsible for management's contract proposal. In fact, the concessions in Hormel's proposal were consistent with its long-term strategy of reversing the union's accomplishments. "UFCW Local P-9 Strikes Hormel: The International Union's Perspective," 3.

71. *Chicago Tribune,* Jan. 21, 1985; *Minneapolis Star and Tribune,* Jan. 23, 1986; *The Unionist,* Feb. 28, 1986; *Des Moines Register,* March 16, 1986; *New York Times,* Jan. 28, April 21, 1986.

72. The contract also prohibited employees from distributing leaflets, displaying banners, or organizing boycotts against Hormel or "related" companies. *The Guardian,* Sept. 10, 1986; *Labor World,* Sept. 25, 1986; "Ending the Hormel Strike: The UFCW Acts to Save Jobs, Union," UFCW press release, n.d.

73. UFCW, "General Report, 1986 National Packinghouse Strategy and Policy Conference," quotations from 42 and 50.

74. *Omaha World Herald,* July 28, 1987; *The Guardian,* Sept. 16, 1987; Krebs, *Heading Toward the Last Roundup,* 57–58; Lewie Anderson to UFCW Local Unions, Nov. 4, 1987, copy in possession of author; "Notice to Public: Corporate Greed Again Attacks the Ark City (Morrell) Workers," leaflet in possession of author.

75. *National Provisioner,* May 16, Aug. 1, 1987; *New York Times,* Jan. 18, 1987; *Omaha World-Herald,* July 27, 1987; William Wynn to AFL-CIO State Federations and Central Labor Bodies, Dec. 4, 1987, copy in possession of author; Bureau of National Affairs, *Current Developments,* March 9, 1992.

76. For allegations that Anderson was excluded from negotiations, see "REAP Briefing Paper Number One," Feb. 14, 1989.

77. *National Provisioner,* March 12, 1988; *P-3 Pacer,* Sept. 1989; "REAP Briefing Paper Number Three," April 20, 1989; *Sioux Fall Argus Leader,* May 3, 1989.

78. It is notable that these local union leaders, especially Acker, had been bitter critics of the P-9 strike. *In These Times,* Feb. 8, 1989; *Sioux City Journal,* Jan. 15, May 6, 1989; *Los Angeles Times,* April 22, 1990.

79. Quotations from, respectively, *Chicago Tribune,* June 15, 1988, and "Business Union Organizing," *P-3 Pacer,* Sept. 1989, 1–3; see also *Chicago Tribune,* June 16, 1988.

80. REAP, "Its Time Has Come," report from founding convention, April 7, 8, 1990; *REAP News and Views,* May–June 1992, Nov.–Dec. 1991.

81. Moody, *An Injury to All,* 193–220; information on pork industry firms from interview of Janice R. Herritz, executive board member, Oscar Mayer Local 538, Oct. 13, 1992, and *Union Labor News* (Madison), Oct. 1992.

82. The Consumer Price Index for all items increased 61 percent between 1980 and 1990. U.S. Department of Commerce, *Statistical Abstract of the United States, 1991* (Washington, 1991), 474.

83. Arden Walker quoted in U.S. House of Representatives, Subcommittee of the Committee on Government Operations, *Here's the Beef: Underreporting of Injuries,* Report 100–542 (Washington, March 1988), 11; "Underreporting of Occupational Injuries," pt. 2, 40, 76; *Wall Street Journal,* April 3, 1990; Michael J. Broadway, "Settlement and Mobility among Newcomers to Garden City, Nebraska," *Journal of Cultural Geography* 10 (1989): 53; Martin E. Personik and Katherine Taylor-Shirley, "Profiles in Safety and Health: Occupational Hazards of Meatpacking," *Monthly Labor Review* 112 (Jan. 1989): 6–8; UFCW, "1986 Report on the U.S. Meat Packing Industry and the Challenges Workers Face," sec. 7, 1–2.

84. David Griffith, "The Impact of the Immigration Reform and Control Act's (IRCA) Employer Sanctions on the U.S. Meat and Poultry Processing Industries," unpublished manuscript, April 1990, 29, 50, 54–55; PrairieFire Rural Action, *Shattered Promises: The Plight of Non-English Speaking Workers in Iowa's Meatpacking Industry* (Des Moines, 1991), 1–6; Hillman quotation from UFCW, "General Report, 1986 National Packinghouse Strategy and Policy Conference," 25.

85. *New York Times,* June 14, 1987; U.S. House of Representatives, Subcommittee of the Committee on Government Operations, *Here's the Beef,* 14; *Chicago Tribune,* Oct. 23, 1988; *New York Times,* Aug. 21, 1988; "Underreporting of Occupational Injuries," pt. 1, 54.

86. Personik and Taylor-Shirley, "Profiles in Safety and Health," passim; U.S. Department of Labor, *Technology and Labor in Four Industries,* 9; "Underreporting of Occupational Injuries," pt. 2, 77; Donald D. Stull and Michael J. Broadway, "Killing Them Softly: Work in Meatpacking Plants and What It Does to Workers," in *Any Way You Cut It: Meat Processing and Small-Town America,* ed. Donald Stull, Michael Broadway, and David Griffith (Lawrence, 1995), 81.

87. Osha Gray Davidson, *Broken Heartland: The Rise of America's Rural Ghetto* (New York, 1991), 125–30; *Wall Street Journal,* April 3, 1990; Lewie Anderson in-

terview in *P-3 Pacer,* Sept. 1989; *Chicago Tribune,* June 6, 1983; Broadway, "Settle-ment and Mobility," 51–62; Donald D. Stull et al., "Changing Relations: Newcom-ers and Established Residents in Garden City, Kansas," Institute for Public Pol-icy and Business Research, *University of Kansas Report* 172 (1990): 55, 93.

Conclusion

1. Stull et al., "Changing Relations," 1–4; Michael Broadway, "Meatpacking and Its Social and Economic Consequences for Garden City, Kansas in the 1980s," *Urban Anthropology* 19 (Winter 1990): 324–26; Stull, Broadway, and Griffith, eds., *Any Way You Cut It.*

2. Donald Stull, "'I Come to the Garden': Changing Ethnic Relations in Gar-den City, Kansas," *Urban Anthropology* 19 (Winter 1990): 308–11; U.S. Department of Commerce, *1990 Census of Population and Housing, Summary of Population and Housing Characteristics: Kansas* (Washington, 1992), 52; Donald D. Stull, Michael J. Broadway, and Ken C. Erickson, "The Price of a Good Steak: Beef Packing and Its Consequences for Garden City, Kansas," in *Structuring Diversity: Ethnograph-ic Perspectives on the New Immigration,* ed. Louise Lamphere (Chicago, 1992), 51.

3. *Chicago Tribune,* June 8, 1983; Broadway, "Settlement and Mobility," 51–62; Ken C. Erickson, "Vietnamese Household Organization in Garden City, Kansas: Southeast Asians in a Packing House Town," *Plains Anthropologist* 33 (Feb. 1988): 32–33; Peggy Hillman, in UFCW, "General Report, 1986 National Packinghouse Strategy and Policy Conference," 18–28 [speech]; Janet E. Benson, "Good Neigh-bors: Ethnic Relations in Garden City Trailer Courts," *Urban Anthropology* 19 (Winter 1990): 361–86; quotations from Stull et al., "Changing Relations," 85, see also 83–93.

4. See Hillman, in "General Report, 1986 National Packinghouse Strategy and Policy Conference," 22, on daily occurrences of unpaid labor; quotations from Stull et al., "The Price of a Good Steak," 47, 50; Stull et al., "Changing Relations," 55–60; Donald D. Stull, "Knock 'Em Dead: Work on the Killfloor of a Modern Beefpacking Plant," in *Newcomers in the Workplace: Immigrants and the Restructur-ing of the U.S. Economy,* ed. Louise Lamphere, Alex Stepick, and Guillermo Gre-nier (Philadelphia, 1994), 44–77.

5. Todd Tate interview, Sam Davis interview, and Nels Peterson interview, UPWAOHP.

6. Nels Peterson interview, UPWAOHP.

7. Information from fieldnotes made in Austin, Minnesota, Dec. 1985; Rich-ard Shatek, Paul Losey, Bob Johnson, and Dave Taylor interview, UPWAOHP; Hardy Green, *On Strike at Hormel: The Struggle for a Democratic Labor Movement* (Philadelphia, 1990), 75–91; Roger Horowitz, "Behind the Hormel Strike: The Fifty Years of Local P-9," *Against the Current* 2 (March–April 1986): 13–18; Rach-leff, *Hard-Pressed in the Heartland.*

8. Information from fieldnotes made in Austin, Minnesota, Dec. 1985; Rich-ard Shatek, Paul Losey, Bob Johnson, and Dave Taylor interview, UPWAOHP;

Jan Butts interview by author, July 9, 1987; Horowitz, "Behind the Hormel Strike"; Green, *On Strike at Hormel*, 75–91. Dave Hage and Paul Klauda, *No Retreat, No Surrender: Labor's War at Hormel* (New York, 1989) virtually ignore the Support Group. A good corrective is Neala J. Schleuning, *Women, Community, and the Hormel Strike of 1985–86* (Westport, 1994).

9. The term *solidarity consciousness* is from Moody, *An Injury to All*, 309; quotation from Korth and Beegle, *I Remember Like Today*, 121.

10. "Rank and File Packinghouse Workers Bill of Rights," adopted at Mid-America Rank and File Packinghouse Workers Conference, Austin, Minnesota, May 1987, copy in possession of author; REAP, "Its Time Has Come"; *REAP News and Views*, Nov.–Dec. 1991, May–June 1992; quotation from Hillman, in UFCW, "General Report, 1986 National Packinghouse Strategy and Policy Conference," 26.

11. See, for example, David Brody, "The Breakdown of Labor's Social Contract," and Alice Kessler-Harris, "Beyond Industrial Unionism," both in *Dissent* 39 (Winter 1992): 32–41, 61–66.

12. Quotation from Benson, "Good Neighbors," 380.

Primary Sources Consulted

Manuscript Collections

Archives of Labor and Urban Affairs, Detroit:
    CIO Secretary-Treasurer Papers
    Katherine Pollack Ellickson Papers
    Mary Heaton Vorse Papers
Chicago Historical Society:
    John Fitzpatrick Papers
    Mary McDowell Papers
Hagley Museum and Library:
    National Association of Manufacturers Papers
Herbert Hill, personal papers
Kansas City, Missouri, Public Library Clipping File
Kansas City Museum Archives
Library of Congress Manuscript Division:
    NAACP Papers
    National Urban League Papers
    Works Progress Administration Papers
National Archives and Records Administration (NARA):
    Fair Employment Practices Commission Records, RG 228
    National War Labor Board Papers, RG 202
National Archives—Kansas City Center:
    War Manpower Commission, Region IX
National Archives—Washington National Record Center (WNRC):
    National Labor Relations Board Case Files

Sioux City Museum Archives
Sioux City Public Library Clipping File
State Historical Society of Wisconsin:
    Herbert March Papers
    Leon Beverly Papers
    Ralph Helstein Papers
    Roland White Papers
    Svend Godfredson Papers
    United Packinghouse Workers of America Papers
    Unprocessed United Food and Commercial Workers Accession M80-118
    UPWAOHP additions to the UPWA Papers
University of Texas at Austin:
    UPWA District Eight Papers
Western Historical Manuscripts Collection, University of Missouri–Kansas City:
    A. Theodore Brown Papers
    Patricia Wagner Papers

Newspapers

Austin Daily Herald	*Midwest Daily Record*
Cedar Rapids Gazette	*New Majority*
Chicago Defender	*New York Times*
CIO News-Packinghouse Workers Edition	*Packinghouse Worker*
	Sioux City Journal
Daily Worker	*The Unionist* (Austin,
Des Moines Register	Minnesota)
Kansas City Star	*Unionist and Public Forum*

Oral History Interviews

United Packinghouse Workers of America Oral History Project, 1985–86, State Historical Society of Wisconsin, principal interviewers Rick Halpern and Roger Horowitz:

Lloyd Achenbach	Eugene Cotton
Ercell Allen	Eugene Crowley
Steve Balters	Emerson Dappen
Finis Block	Jeanette Dappen
Don Blumenshine	William Davinroy
Robert Burt	Sam Davis
Loren Callender	Harry DeBoer
Earl Carr	Norman Dolnick
Marjorie Carter	Homer Early
Marie Casey	Alvin Edwards
Herb Cassano	Mary Edwards
Annie Jackson Collins	Tony Fetter

Magnolia Fields

Charles Fischer

Charles R. Fischer

Francis Fletemeyer

George Fletemeyer

Henry Giannini

Svend Godfredson

Max Graham

Douglas Hall

Lyman Halligan

James C. Harris

Charles Hayes

Jeanette Haymond

Herbert Hill

Jimmy Hilsinger

Frank Hlavacek

Grant Holbrook

Virginia Houston

Eddie Humphrey

Nevada Isom

Viola Jones

Ann Krasick

Thomas Krasick

Goldie Lamb

Ray Lange

Herbert March

Walt Mason

James McAnally

Charles McCafferty

Jack Melsha

Stella Melsha

Vic Meyers

Charles Mueller

Kenneth Niedholdt

Howard Nielson

Bruce Nolan

William Nolan

Rowena Moore

Milton Norman

Sam Parks

Charles Pearson

Clyde Peoples

Eunetta Pierce

A. J. Pittman

Darryl Poe

James Porter

Jesse Prosten

Paul Rasmussen

William Raspberry

Lester Rohlena

Fred Romano

Mary Salinas

James Samuel

Richard Saunders

Velma Otterman Schrader

Jennie Shuck

Robert Schultz

Marian Simmons

Vicky Starr

Leona Tarnowski

Todd Tate

Lyle Taylor

Rosalie Taylor

Buford Thompson

Louis Tickal

Ada Tredwell

Jesse Vaughn

Frank Wallace

Betty Watson

Bill Webster

Anna Mae Weems

Philip Weightman

Clyde Wensel

Chris Wicke

L. C. Williams

Casper Winkels

John Winkels

Don Winters

Addie Wyatt

Helen Zrudsky

Oral History Project in Labor and Immigration History, Roosevelt University, Chicago, 1971 and 1972:

Leon Beverly interview by Elizabeth Butters
Ralph Helstein interview by Elizabeth Balanoff
Sophie Kosciowloski interview by Elizabeth Butters
Herbert March interview by Elizabeth Balanoff
UFCW Leadership Oral History Project, State Historical Society of Wisconsin:
Jesse Prosten interview by James V. Cavanaugh
Interviews by author, deposited at the State Historical Society of Wisconsin:
Jan Butts, July 9, 1987
Mary Edwards, November 3, 1987
Charles R. Fischer, December 8, 1987
Ralph Helstein (with Rick Halpern), July 18, 1983, January 14, 1984
Grant Holbrook, November 2, 1987
Virginia Houston, December 8, 1987
Dave Neiswanger and Rollo Sissel, July 8, 1987
Henry Oots, July 8, 1987
William Raspberry, December 10, 1987
Verne Sechrest, July 7, 1987
Johny Shores, November 3, 1987
Jennie Shuck, November 3, 1987

Other Interviews

Leon Beverly. Interview by Herbert Hill, April 1, 1967, from personal papers of Herbert Hill.

Lawrence Denton. Interview by Kansas City Jazz Oral History Collection, Western Historical Manuscript Collection, University of Missouri–Kansas City.

Frank Ellis. Interview by Martin Duffy, July 2, 1972, Minnesota Historical Society.

Sophie Kosciowlowski. Interview by Les Orear, 1971, Chicago Stock Yards Interview Series.

Jane and Herbert March. Interview by Rick Halpern, November 23, 1988, copy in possession of author.

John Stover. Interview by William Cumberland, June 18, 1980.

Index

ROGER HOROWITZ is associate director of the Center for the History of Business, Technology, and Society at the Hagley Museum and Library in Wilmington, Delaware, and teaches history at the University of Delaware. He is the author of *Meatpackers: An Oral History of Black Packinghouse Workers and Their Struggle for Racial and Economic Equality* (1996). He also has published articles on World War II and on the southern poultry industry. Currently, he is examining the effects of military service on working-class Americans.

BOOKS IN THE SERIES
THE WORKING CLASS IN AMERICAN HISTORY